Comparative Philosophy without Borders

Also available from Bloomsbury

The Bloomsbury Research Handbook of Chinese Philosophy and Methodologies, edited by Sor-hoon Tan

The Bloomsbury Research Handbook of Chinese Philosophy and Gender, edited by Ann A. Pang-White

The Bloomsbury Research Handbook of Indian Aesthetics and the Philosophy of Art, edited by Arindam Chakrabarti

The Bloomsbury Research Handbook of Indian Epistemology and Metaphysics, edited by Joerg Tuske

The Bloomsbury Research Handbook to Indian Ethics, edited by Shyam Ranganathan

Doing Philosophy Comparatively, Tim Connolly

An Introduction to Indian Philosophy, second edition, Christopher Bartley

Landscape and Travelling East and West, edited by Hans-Georg Moeller and Andrew Whitehead

Understanding Asian Philosophy, Alexus McLeod

Comparative Philosophy without Borders

Edited by
Arindam Chakrabarti and Ralph Weber

Bloomsbury Academic
An imprint of Bloomsbury Publishing Plc

BLOOMSBURY
LONDON • OXFORD • NEW YORK • NEW DELHI • SYDNEY

Bloomsbury Academic
An imprint of Bloomsbury Publishing Plc

50 Bedford Square
London
WC1B 3DP
UK

1385 Broadway
New York
NY 10018
USA

www.bloomsbury.com

BLOOMSBURY and the Diana logo are trademarks of Bloomsbury Publishing Plc

First published 2016
Paperback edition first published 2017

British Library Cataloguing-in-Publication Data
A catalogue record for this book is available from the British Library.

ISBN: HB: 978-1-4725-7624-8
PB: 978-1-3500-3665-9
ePDF: 978-1-4725-7626-2
ePub: 978-1-4725-7625-5

Library of Congress Cataloging-in-Publication Data
Comparative philosophy without borders / edited by Arindam Chakrabarti and Ralph Weber. – 1 [edition].
pages cm
Includes bibliographical references and index.
ISBN 978-1-4725-7624-8 (hb : alk. paper) – ISBN 978-1-4725-7625-5 (epub : alk. paper) – ISBN 978-1-4725-7626-2 (epdf : alk. paper)
1. Philosophy, Comparative. I. Chakrabarti, Arindam, editor.
B799.C645 2015
109–dc23
2015019488

Typeset by Deanta Global Publishing Services, Chennai, India

Contents

Notes on Contributors

Arindam Chakrabarti earned his D.Phil from Oxford University in 1982, working under Peter Strawson and Michael Dummett. He has taught at Calcutta University, University College London, University of Washington, Seattle, and Delhi University, and for the last seventeen years, he has been teaching at the University of Hawaii, Manoa. After being trained as an analytic philosopher of language, he spent several years receiving traditional training in Indian logic (Navya Nyaya). Chakrabarti has edited or authored ten books in English, Sanskrit, and Bengali, including *Denying Existence*, *Knowing from Words* (with B. K. Matilal), *Universals, Concepts and Qualities* (with Peter Strawson), and *Thinking about Food and Clothing: Essays in Quotidian Philosophy* (in Bengali) and has published more than eighty papers and reviews. He is currently working on a book on moral psychology of the emotions and "*The Book of Questions: Introduction to Analytical Indian Philosophy.*" He directs the Eastern Philosophy of Consciousness and the Humanities (EPOCH) program at the University of Hawaii, Manoa.

Barry Hallen is professor of philosophy in the Department of Philosophy and Religion at Morehouse College, Atlanta, Georgia; associate at the W. E. B. Du Bois Institute for African and African-American Research, Harvard University, and director of Southern Crossroads. His areas of specialization are Theory of Knowledge, Africana Philosophy and Aesthetics, Philosophy and Anthropology, and Intercultural and Interdisciplinary Studies. His book publications include *African Philosophy: The Analytic Approach* (Trenton, NJ: Africa World Press, 2006); *A Short History of African Philosophy*, (Bloomington: Indiana University Press, 2002, revised edition 2009); *The Good, the Bad, and the Beautiful: Discourse about Values in Yoruba Culture* (Bloomington: Indiana University Press, 2000); and *Knowledge, Belief, and Witchcraft: Analytic Experiments in African Philosophy*, coauthored with J. Olubi Sodipo (Stanford University Press, 1995).

Chien-hsing Ho is associate professor in the Graduate Institute of Religious Studies at Nanhua University, Taiwan. He received his doctorate in philosophy from the University of Delhi, India, in 1999. He specializes in Indian and Chinese Madhyamaka, Buddhist epistemology, and Buddhist philosophy of language, with additional research interests in Chan Buddhism, Indian philosophy, and comparative philosophy. He has published articles in such international refereed journals as *Philosophy East and West*; *Dao: A Journal of Comparative Philosophy*; *Asian Philosophy*; the *Journal of Chinese Philosophy*; and the *Journal of Indian Philosophy*. He is currently planning a book in English on Chinese Madhyamaka.

Masato Ishida is associate professor of philosophy at the University of Hawaii at Manoa. His specializations are Japanese philosophy, classical American philosophy, and the history and philosophy of logic. His recent articles include "The Sense of Symmetry: Comparative Reflections on Whitehead, Nishida, and Dōgen" (*Process Studies*, 2014) and "A Peircean Reply to Quine's Two Problems" (*Transactions of the Charles S. Peirce Society*, 2013).

Sari Nusseibeh is professor of philosophy at al-Quds University, Palestine. He presently directs a graduate program "Philosophy in Islam," besides fulfilling other teaching duties in the department. He has written extensively on the Palestinian question, as well as on various topics in Islamic philosophy, the most recent being "The Possible Worlds of Avicenna and Leibniz," in *The Misty Land of Ideas and the Light of Dialogue: An Anthology of Comparative Philosophy: Western & Islamic*, ed. Ali Paya, ICAS Press, 2014. He is presently finalizing his latest book, *The Story of Reason in Islam*, due to be published by Stanford University Press. He has recently been selected as Senior Fellow of The School of Criticism and Theory, presently hosted by Cornell University.

Laurie L. Patton is the author or editor of nine books on early Indian religion, mythology, and ritual, and over fifty articles in these fields. She is also the translator of the Indian classical text, "The Bhagavad Gita," for Penguin Classics Series (2008), and the author of two books of poems, "Fire's Goal: Poems from a Hindu Year" (White Cloud Press, 2003) and "Angel's Task: Poems in Biblical Time" (Station Hill Press, 2011). She served as Charles Howard Candler Professor of Religion at Emory University until 2011, and as Durden Professor of Religion and Dean of Arts & Sciences at Duke University from 2011 to 2015. She assumed the role of president of Middlebury in 2015.

Sor-hoon Tan is associate professor of philosophy at the National University of Singapore. She is author of *Confucian Democracy: A Deweyan Reconstruction* and editor of *Challenging Citizenship: Group Membership and Cultural Identity in a Global Age*. Her recent works include "Materialistic Desires and the Ethical Life in the Analects and the Mencius," in *Moral Cultivation and Confucian Character: Engaging Joel J. Kupperman*, "Early Confucian Concept of Yi (议) and Deliberative Democracy," *Political Theory* 42.1, and "The Concept of Yi (义) in the Mencius and the Problems of Distributive Justice," *Australasian Journal of Philosophy* 92.3.

Tom J. F. Tillemans is Professor Emeritus of Buddhist Studies at the University of Lausanne, Switzerland. His published work has focused largely on comparative philosophy, Buddhist logic, epistemology, and philosophy of the middle (madhyamaka). His most recent book is *How do Mādhyamikas Think?*, appearing in the "Studies in Indian and Tibetan Buddhism," Boston: Wisdom Publications. Tillemans was editor of the *Journal of the International Association of Buddhist Studies* and is presently editor in chief of the 84000, a project to translate Buddhist canonical literature from Tibetan and Sanskrit (www.84000.co).

Ralph Weber is Tenure Track Assistant Professor at the Institute for European Global Studies of the University of Basel, Switzerland. He is the Book Review editor (Europe) of *Philosophy East and West*. His research specialization is in Confucianism, political philosophy, comparative philosophy, and the philosophy of comparison. His recent publications include "Comparative Philosophy and the tertium: Comparing What with What, and in What Respect?" (*Dao* 12.2) and "'Who Are We?'—An Essay on Richard Rorty, Rhetoric and Politics" (with Giorgio Baruchello, *The European Legacy* 19.2) as well as a coedited volume on *Modernities: Conceptual Challenges and Regional Responses* (Lanham: Lexington Books, 2015).

Introduction

Arindam Chakrabarti and Ralph Weber

Because the human being is the connecting being who must always separate and cannot connect without separating—that is why we must first conceive intellectually of the merely indifferent existence of two river-banks as something separated in order to connect them by means of a bridge. And the human being is likewise a bordering creature who has no border . . .

Georg Simmel (1909), "The Bridge and the Door"[1]

On borders

Three concepts need to be clarified before we can speak intelligibly about *Comparative Philosophy without Borders* avoiding calculated confusion or foreseeable misunderstanding: the concept of *philosophy*, the concept of *comparison* (from which the concept of "comparative" is derived), and the concept of *borders*. Everybody understands and agrees that "without" simply means *lacking*, which, in this context, must signify coming to lose or erase rather than never having had. Therefore, we need not dwell separately and tediously on the meaning of "without," although in some branches of classical and contemporary Indian metaphysics, the meaning of the particular sort of negation that expresses that peculiar "absence" whereby one thing lacks or sheds another thing or property is also a hot topic. Of the three crucial concepts, then, let us start with the concept of a border, since the concept of philosophy is inexhaustibly controversial (two sides across a border often do not mean the same by "philosophy") and paradox-generatingly self-inclusive and we shall have much more substantial and provocative things to say about *comparison*.

A border, literally, is a line, often conventional, seldom natural, that separates two regions of space. Borders connect what is separated and separate what is connected. In principle, borders can be crossed. Frequent unstoppable crossings often result in the borders being redrawn. They can be redrawn, undone or un-thought, as bridges can be traversed from one to the other side and doors can be opened. When borders are crossed, the separating connections may linger on as if untouched, or, indeed, come to be no more, having fallen into pieces. Were there borders that we could not cross at all, they would have to be the sort of borders that do not connect what is separated; they would have to be limits. If they were limits, then we would be unable to get to the other side, let alone separate or connect both sides. Hence, these boundaries are not limits.

They are borders. We put up such borders that can be crossed if needed. It might even be thought that the function of some borders is to make it appear to most people on both sides that they are insurmountable walls. Still, since we are such creatures who constantly erect frontiers and barriers that in principle can be transcended, Simmel is right to suggest that we have no borders (*Grenze*) that would really be, rather than appear to be, limits (*Grenze*). The mobility or openability of doors is the metaphor that Simmel uses to capture the very significance and value of such borders, that is, the possibility at each moment to step out, beyond the conditional confinement that borders might represent, into the open and into freedom, or perhaps into another confinement.

Borders—between philosophy and science and religion within the Western tradition, between epistemology, metaphysics, and ethics within Western philosophy as a whole, between continental and analytic philosophy, between rationalism and empiricism within epistemology or libertarianism and determinism within metaphysics; between Chinese philosophy and European philosophy and African philosophy, between African and Hawaiian philosophies, between Nyāya and Buddhist philosophy within Indian philosophy, between Mu'tazilites and Asharites within Islamic philosophy, between Chinese and Indian Buddhism, between Utilitarian and Kantian ethics within Western moral philosophy, between Daoists and Confucians within Chinese philosophy, between European, Russian, and Chinese Marxism within Marxism, and so on—have to be first drawn in order for us to open up possibilities of infiltrations if not mergers.

Comparative philosophy is all about the erecting, detecting, smudging, and tearing down of borders, borders between philosophical traditions coming from different parts of the world, different time periods, different disciplinary affiliations, and even within a single period and pedigree, between opposite or at least distinguishable persuasions. Philosophical comparisons, more often than not, separate and connect at the same time what are very likely or unlikely pairs of, or entire sets of, *comparanda* (that which we set out to compare). Aaron Stalnaker, in his book on Xunzi and Augustine (an unlikely, therefore interesting, pair), has observed that the challenge of comparative study is that "it must bring distant ethical statements into interrelation and conversation, and it must simultaneously preserve their distinctiveness within the interrelation."[2] This familiar dialogical view of comparative ethics may not turn out to be the magic formula to which all comparison can be reduced. How can one put one view or tradition next to another and conduct the comparison as if they have the *same* agenda, if it is clear from the beginning that the two traditions or views are *different*? This is the circle that comparison apparently squares. And the task is far from impossible if one is sufficiently careful about what precisely "same" and "different" mean. Take the concept of rationality. A good comparative philosopher, if she does not slide back to the nineteenth-century view that rationality is exclusively or originally a European concept simply missing outside of Europe, would say something inconsistent like "the Chinese concept of rationality is utterly distinct from the European concept of rationality, but they both are and are not versions of some more general concept of rationality." In other words, that comparison is all about this same-yet-not-the-same, if put too bluntly, becomes no more than a cliché.

On the inescapability of comparison

Let us pause here and think in deeper detail about the very concept of comparison. In a most intriguing passage of his voluminous eleventh-century Sanskrit work on literary aesthetics titled "Illuminating the Erotic,"[3] the poet-philosopher Bhoja tries to prove that not only is comparison a reliable means of knowledge, but also that all means of knowledge including direct sense perception are, indeed, at heart forms of comparison. One can imagine how all inferential reasoning would be reduced to analogical reasoning by similarity, but the hardest bit of this radical reductionist thesis is to show that even simple sense perception consists in seeing resemblances. Let us try to translate this bit of Bhoja's text:

> For a perception to be usable in practice (such as seeing water as water that a thirsty person could pour in a container and drink, or seeing a snake as a cobra and running away from it to be safe), it must be predicative or judgment-like (*savikalpaka*). For a perception to be predicative judgment-like, it must involve implicit employment of words (*śabda*) one understands (for there is no concept-application or categorization without some minimal semantic coding, in this very general sense or preparedness to use a word). For a word to be mastered, at the time of first grasping its meaning, a particular sample or set of the meant entity or process has to be presented. Every subsequent application of that word/phrase works (arouses the awareness of its meaning) by means of resemblance or similarity with the original instances perceived at the time of acquisition of the vocabulary. Thus, how can we deny that every perception is a case of comparison?[4]

What is the relevance of this strange insight, that comparison encompasses all the accredited sources of knowledge, in the present context? Suppose one is teaching or writing just about Sanskrit epistemology or aesthetics in English (as we did in the immediately preceding paragraph). On the surface, it is not a comparative exercise. It is simply and purely Indian philosophy. But one has to use words such as "perception," "word," "judgment," "categorization," each of which is saturated with thousands of years and pages of European theorizing. A parallel implicit switch of putatively equivalent terms would be inevitable when one spoke of Greek philosophy in English or Spanish or of Daoism in Sanskrit (e.g., using terms like "śūnyatā" or "mārga"). Thus, even pure classical Indian philosophy, done in the most expository, historical, "Orientalist" style, unless it is done in archaic Sanskrit (even the Sanskrit that one would write today would be imperceptibly influenced by translational, hence comparative, considerations!), would be inescapably, albeit unavowedly, comparative. That is the relevance. Even within one single culture and language-family, if one writes in a modern idiom about an ancient system of thought, one's observations are bound to be based on comparison.

The subject matter of comparative philosophy

As early as 1977, Archie Bahm confidently affirmed that "comparative philosophy has become a recognized philosophical discipline or field."[5] It is quite true that comparative philosophy has been increasingly institutionalized as a subdiscipline of philosophy throughout the twentieth century, most successfully in terms of professional associations,[6] conferences, monograph series,[7] and journals.[8] As is the case with most disciplines, however, there is no common definition of what comparative philosophy is about, but the subdiscipline assembles different, in parts even mutually contradictory, views. Two frequently cited definitions of comparative philosophy are taken from Internet encyclopedias. Ronnie Littlejohn writes in his entry on *IEP* (Internet Encyclopedia of Philosophy):

> Comparative philosophy—sometimes called "cross-cultural philosophy"—is a subfield of philosophy in which philosophers work on problems by intentionally setting into dialogue sources from across cultural, linguistic, and philosophical streams.[9]

While the metaphor of dialogue is often employed to characterize the nature, aim, and method of comparative philosophy,[10] the definition is conspicuously unclear as regards the entities that are put into dialogue: on the one hand, the dominant understanding of comparative philosophy as cross-cultural philosophy is mentioned, but the use of both the inverted commas and the phrase "cultural, linguistic, and philosophical streams" seems to leave open the possibility that comparative philosophy could simply be concerned with different languages or philosophical streams without a commitment to the notion of "cultures." The matter is not elucidated when Littlejohn thereafter demarcates comparative philosophy from "more traditional philosophy in which ideas are compared among thinkers within a particular tradition; comparative philosophy intentionally compares the ideas of thinkers of very different traditions, especially culturally distinct traditions."[11]

David Wong, the author of "Comparative Philosophy: Chinese and Western" in the Stanford Encyclopedia of Philosophy (*SEP*), begins his entry with the following sentence:

> Comparative philosophy brings together philosophical traditions that have developed in relative isolation from one another and that are defined quite broadly along cultural and regional lines—Chinese versus Western, for example.[12]

Here, besides the oddity of writing an entry on comparative philosophy with the restriction of "Chinese versus Western" and then mentioning as an example of two philosophical traditions "Chinese versus Western," the criterion of "relative isolation" is introduced. It remains, however, unclear whether, for instance, the development of Islamic philosophy would be considered "relatively isolated" (P. T. Raju, in his own map of comparative philosophy, apparently ignores Islamic philosophy for lack of such isolation[13]); or how the copresence of Buddhism in Indian, Chinese, and Japanese philosophy would be dealt with.

Yet another set of questions might be posed in view of Koji Tanaka's characterization:

> Comparative philosophy is a branch of philosophy which examines and contrasts different traditions of philosophy. For example, a comparative philosopher may

> examine African, Buddhist, Chinese, Indian, Muslim and Western traditions of philosophy in comparison with one another. Comparisons may also be made between sub-traditions within a tradition: one may compare Confucianism and Daoism within the tradition of Chinese philosophy, for example.[14]

Like Wong, and, indeed, like most commentators of comparative philosophy today, Tanaka sees the subdiscipline as inquiring into different philosophical traditions,[15] which are usually, but not always, presented in some combination with terms such as "cultures" (including "intercultural" and "cross-cultural"), "civilizations," and "worldviews." Tanaka, who seems to confine comparative philosophy to the comparison of philosophies ("examines and contrasts"), adds a rather peculiar (but by no means unusual) list of philosophical traditions, comprising religious and nonreligious traditions (mentioning Muslim, but not Christian or Shinto, and Indian, but not Hindu "philosophical tradition"). He also alludes to comparison between "sub-traditions *within* a tradition"; it is probably fair to assume that he would also be prepared to include comparisons between "sub-traditions" *across* different philosophical traditions (say, Indian Buddhism with Chinese Buddhism), even if his example of Confucianism and Daoism might suggest a more clear-cut picture of different traditions, each boasting a different set of sub-traditions. Tanaka is certainly aware of the problem of general talk about traditions, but he sees it less in the sort of entanglement, for instance, of Buddhism across traditions, and more in internal disagreement within any one tradition, which must—he writes—in any case still be based on some common ground, since otherwise communication would not be possible and development of any one tradition unlikely.[16]

Entanglement of (sub-)traditions is today often acknowledged, as with Edelglass and Garfield, the editors of the *Oxford Handbook of World Philosophy*, who stress "intercultural philosophical influence" and hold that "the notion of hermetically sealed traditions in parallel development is largely a historical fiction."[17] Tanaka would probably readily agree, but his—as well as Littlejohn's and Wong's—characterization of comparative philosophy showcases the difficulties involved in delineating a subject-matter that would form the subdiscipline's proper domain of research.

Whether or not comparative philosophy has an object and methods clearly its own has been disputed. Robert E. Allinson has insisted:

> All philosophy is comparative philosophy and in this sense the term is too wide to be very useful. In this regard, the notion of comparative philosophy, as a unique self-subsistent discipline in itself, is a myth. Philosophy always has been comparative philosophy. The phrase "comparative philosophy" is redundant. All philosophy must contain a comparative basis for its inspiration and as part of its data base.[18]

Hence, "in this sense," comparative philosophy is tantamount to philosophy. Yet, in another sense, Allinson comes to reserve an exclusive domain for comparative philosophy "in its more proper understanding" as "integrative philosophy," which he sees in "the service of intercultural dialogue."[19]

The need for a third in comparing two philosophies

When we compare two philosophies (in whatever way we might have drawn their borders), we need a *tertium* or third element in two senses. In the *first sense*, initially, the comparer who notices similarities and dissimilarities between the two, with or without the motive of evaluating which is more cogent, more acceptable, more philosophically fecund etc., needs to position himself or herself in a neutral third place or at least a third philosophical point of view. Frits Staal commented half a century back, "It passes our understanding how scholars have been able to compare two philosophies, without realizing that a standard of comparison is needed resulting from a third philosophy (which in special cases, may be the same as the first or the second)."[20]

The *second sense* of a *tertium* is this: When we compare A and B we always have to specify with respect to what. So "compare" is a three-place rather than a two-place verb/predicate. We compare A and B with respect to F, compare Plotinus and Samkara with respect to the concept of God or the concept of Oneness (as did Frits Staal himself). To be more precise, following this second sense of a required "third" for any comparison and combining it with the first sense, "compare" turns out to be a four-place predicate: "From his specific historical cultural context P compares A and B with respect to F."

Hence, in what follows, we want to present to the reader an account of comparison, first in its naked form as a mechanism from which some important insights that would be true for each and any comparison can be gleaned. We then complicate matters by introducing that mediating creature that would be the comparer who is at once border-circumscribed and borderless. Being such creatures, we all work in a time and place that has some historical coordinates. We should hence assume that there are contending narratives of the "history" of comparative philosophy, which inform the comparers' doings. Rather than attempting a comprehensive taxonomy of existing narratives and their predicaments, we should like to sketch the narrative that informs our advocacy of fusion philosophy. Needless to say, the urgency of theorizing on or problematizing comparativism is brought upon us by the political/cultural/economic phenomenon controversially called "globalization."

So, can there be a comparison without a *tertium comparationis*? Several notions of similarity are available in the literature ranging from Western to Eastern metaphysics. From Wittgenstein's family resemblances, through the debate between Prābhākara Mīmāmsā and Nyāya as to whether similarity is a separate sort of objectively real entity or not, all the way up to Foucault's *The Order of Things,* one needs to examine, then compare and contrast distinct notions of resemblance. In comparative philosophy, similarity stands as a notion seemingly in no need of further differentiation, which forms a marked contrast to the high level of discussions about similarity elsewhere in philosophy. A separate philosophy of comparison may draw profitably on work about comparison done in disciplines other than philosophy.

Naked comparison

A comparison always involves two or more *comparanda*, which are put next to each other in view of an aspect that is presumed to be common to both *comparanda*, the mentioned *tertium comparationis*. If, for example, early Chinese and Greek ethics are selected for comparison of their articulated views on honor, then early Chinese (A) and Greek (B) ethics each come to serve as a *comparandum* and some concept of honor as a *tertium comparationis* (F). Such a comparative framework presumes that there is a concept of honor to be compared here and there, which is in some sense the same concept. The framework also presumes other commonalities between the *comparanda*, which, clustered together, might be called the pre-comparative *tertium*, such as the common description or qualification of both Greece and China as being "early," and possibly some common background against which a distinction between Greece on the one side and China on the other is drawn (e.g., Greece and China as "cultural traditions," "civilizations," "empires," "antiquities," etc.). To be sure, the distinction between pre-comparative *tertium* and the *tertium comparationis* is mainly a matter of emphasis, as each refers to commonalities describing or qualifying the *comparanda*. But the former refers to commonalities that are not explicitly, or not primarily, put up for comparison, whereas the latter specifies the common aspects at the center of the comparative inquiry.[21]

A comparative inquiry does not necessarily—and certainly does not explicitly—proceed from a familiar *comparandum* to one or several other unfamiliar *comparanda*, say, by inference or analogy. Two unfamiliar *comparanda* may well come to serve as objects of inquiry, and there need not be more interest in one than in the other. Of course, when we speak of "familiar" or "unfamiliar," somewhat like "native" and "alien," we are speaking from the point of view of P, the comparer. A specialist of contemporary ethics might be comparing early Chinese and Greek ethics while being unfamiliar with both and claiming a roughly equal interest in their respective ethics and their notion of honor. But, of course, the comparer in this case is a specialist of contemporary (let us admit with self-critical candor, Western) ethics, or, if no specialist, is at least familiar with ethics to some degree. From this point of view, it might be fair to say that each comparer sets out to compare from the standpoint of a certain "cultural tradition." This can be phrased more hermeneutically or it can be fashioned as an implicit comparison,[22] so that our example would feature three rather than two *comparanda* at work (contemporary ethics, Chinese ethics, and Greek ethics), with the comparer being more familiar with one *comparandum* (contemporary ethics) than with the other *comparanda* (Chinese ethics and Greek ethics). In each way, the comparer emerges as a further variable to contend with, so that a fuller conceptualization of comparison would read as follows:

1. A comparison is always made by someone (person P);
2. At least two *relata* (*comparanda*) are compared (A and B);
3. The *comparanda* are compared in some respect (*tertium comparationis*) (F);
4. The result of a comparison is at least a four-term relation between the two *comparanda* on the basis of the chosen respect and the comparer.

In their book *Philosophical Questions: East and West*, Gupta and Mohanty list a series of earlier, rather simplistic and sweeping, comparisons.[23] Hegel, of course, "accepts" the Indian and Chinese philosophical temper as earlier and less mature "stages" of Reason's dialectical march toward progress, which would reach its pinnacle with Hegel's own thought. So his comparison is the most ridiculous of all. With Hegel as P and Western, Indian, and Chinese philosophies as A, B, and C, to be compared, the *tertium* F with respect to which he compares them would be "the central focus of philosophical attention," which, for the West is concepts, for the Indian is intuition, and for the Chinese is action. It is staggering to see how influential this uninformed, crude, and false stereotyping has been and still is. Radhakrishnan—the philosopher President of India in the 1960s—for example, would take philosophical temperament (F) as the basis of comparison and pass the verdict that the West is intellectual, India is intuitive, and China is active! It is outrageous that being steeped in Indian philosophy and Sanskrit learning he would buy Hegel's myth and manage to simply not notice two millennia of purely intellectual wrangling tradition in India, but would also be ready to classify a Zhuangzi or a Dogen as merely an action-oriented thinker! With respect to pure theory (F), Husserl (P) compares the West, India, and China (A, B, C) and comes up with the judgment that the West has pure theory but India does not because it is practical-spiritual and China also does not because it is practical-ethical. Albert Schweitzer (P) compares Western philosophy (A), Indian philosophy (B), and Chinese philosophy (C) with respect to attitude toward life/world (F) and comes up with the generalized answer that the West affirms it, India denies or negates it, and the Chinese affirm it. Charles Moore compares the same trio with respect to a determinate concept of reality, coming up with the comparative verdict that the West has such a determinate concept of objective reality, India does not have it because Indian philosophy is perspectivist and subject-dependent, while the Chinese have a hierarchical notion of reality. Obviously, much hinges on the time and the epistemic-political milieu in which the comparer comes to believe that (although everything is somehow comparable with everything else) the chosen *comparanda* are particularly worthy of being thrown together side by side (παραβάλλειν), that is, that they should be compared.

A fifth aspect, the mentioned pre-comparative *tertium*, is hence profitably distinguished:

5. The two (or more) *comparanda* share a pre-comparative *tertium*, constituted by at least one commonality (i.e., being chosen for comparison by the comparer) and likely by many more commonalities (*tertia*).

One advantage of separating out these terms of the complex relation of comparison is that once we lay out who is doing the comparison between what and what with respect to which concept, different comparisons can be compared with one another.

Crucially, most of these commonalities are already well established (pre-theoretically, if only vaguely, implicitly or unconsciously absorbed by the comparer like the popular Euro-American blatantly false background belief that Hindus do not eat the flesh of a cow because they fear that the cow could be their own dead ancestor reborn—that is assumed to be what it is to be a Hindu) before the comparer sets out to compare them. From this perspective, there are certainly no naked comparisons, let alone history-less perspective-less context-free comparers, but it is as Mark Twain has observed a long time ago: "Clothes make the man. Naked people have little or no influence on society."[24] The clothed comparer has a standpoint, which reflects a specific hermeneutical background, but at the same time a set of purposes which the comparison is designed to serve (ranging from the most innocent of "scholarly" interest to a straightforward political agenda). If naked comparison offers a limited perspective, then it seems that inquiries into the mechanisms of how comparison works have to take into account the comparer more fully. As we will see, some interesting insights about the mechanisms of comparison emerge, once we elaborate the point about familiarity touched upon above.

Clothed comparison

Familiarity, which is what *re-cognition* makes and finds, is always at work in comparison, because what we call seeing the "same" things, processes, or patterns of thinking consists in noticing more or less close resemblances between different occasions of encountering distinct things and distinct events. In what follows, we shall for the sake of simplicity restrict our reflections to the more blatant (but structurally similar) case of a comparer who is more "familiar" with one *comparandum* than with the other, which is often said to fundamentally distort the results of the comparison, as when, say, a specialist of Plato or John Rawls dares casting a comparative glance at the Confucian *Analects* or Kautilya's *Artha Śāstra*.

A rather crude version of the criticism holds that "one-sided" comparisons unduly take one *comparandum* as a *tertium comparationis* and thereby distort the results of the comparison with the other *comparandum*. The specialist of Plato cannot but come to completely Platonize the *Analects* or the *Artha Śāstra* with the disastrous but necessary consequence of presenting Confucius or Kautilya as a deficient version of Plato. A radical criticism along this line could be called to constitute the fallacy of mistaking A for F, in terms of our symbolic representation above. If this is meant to say that a domain like early Greek ethics could come to serve as both the *comparandum* and the *tertium comparationis*, then the criticism simply seems to misunderstand how comparison works. A domain such as Greek ethics can be understood as constituted by an empirical referent and statements about it. Now we should very much like to fancy the empirical referent as singular, even if our description of the domain (because of the impossibility of a private language, let alone the description of somebody else's private language) already takes away from the presupposed singularity. Singularity cannot be captured conceptually, which is why we help ourselves with the use of proper names. Saying that something is singular (or unique, peerless, incomparable, sui generis) like something else is singular undermines its singularity. Singularity, in the sense of uniqueness, hence, could not possibly serve as a *tertium comparationis*. If the *tertium comparationis* is adopted from some empirical referent, then it has to be an abstraction of the singularity of that referent, that is, an abstraction that, like a concept, can be predicated over the many, at least in the sort of relatability that is the minimal condition for a productive *tertium comparationis*. Perhaps it is useful to imagine the abstraction on a scale running from maximal particularity (bordering on singularity) to the highest universal generality, where both ends of the scale appear "singularly" unattractive for the purposes of comparison. Both maximal particularity and maximal generality would preempt the result of the comparison and thus undermine the openness of the inquiry, since with the former only differences and with the latter only commonalities could possibly be captured. In this respect, comparison comes down to choosing an appropriate level on the ladder of abstraction.

What exact level of abstraction is chosen in a case at hand has myriad implications. The level of abstraction chosen anticipates to no minor extent the results of the comparison and crucially qualifies how the results have to be understood. There seems to be a direct relation between the level of abstraction and the result of a comparison in terms of commonalities and differences (or similarities and dissimilarities). Any move on the scale of abstraction toward more generality should produce more commonality and less difference, and any move in the opposite direction, toward more particularity, should end up showing more difference and less commonality. The relations between the levels of abstraction chosen for a *tertium comparationis* and the outcome of a comparison deserve more attention and critical study. An important preliminary observation concerns the qualification of the results of a comparison as being necessarily contingent, insofar as any set of commonalities and differences that come out of the comparison are directly related to the chosen level of abstraction. Comparative inquiry is a powerful tool, but much of its power is lost when the resulting commonalities and differences are not understood as fundamentally relational notions, that is, as fundamentally related to the level of abstractness that the comparing person chooses to adopt. From this point of view, it seems, indeed, apposite to understand the results of comparison as necessarily relational relations, that is, the relation of A and B with respect to F, but also and constitutively in relation to the level of abstractness that is chosen by the comparer P.

Can comparative philosophy be hard-core philosophy?

Comparative religion cannot be and does not claim to be a religion. Comparative politics is not a politics. But comparative philosophy, as we conceive of it, has to be philosophy. Not just peripheral but absolutely central to the enterprise of philosophy done in the current politically and culturally interconnected world, though this remains a utopia.

In his Commentary on *De Anima,* 426b7, Thomas Aquinas remarks: "There is always more pleasure to be gained from combinations than from simplicity." Comparison is a special sort of combination or complexity, which is why asking "Did Plato mean by '*eidos*' what Nyāya means by '*sāmānya*'" gives more philosophical pleasure than simply asking what Plato meant by "forms" (which, by the way, is already comparative, for we are using an English translation of the Greek word). Unfortunately, in actual mainstream academia in Europe and America, comparative philosophy is not only treated as a marginal or fringe phenomenon, but also taken as a "soft option" meant for those who cannot handle hard-core analytic or genealogically rooted continental philosophy. This is most ironic since any comparative philosophy, like comparative literature, probably requires much harder work than a mono-cultural or monolingual philosophy or literature. In a review essay, Alisdair MacIntyre wrote in 1983:

> The Indian political theorist has a harder task than his Western counterpart. He first of all has to be a good deal more learned, for he is required to know the history of Western political thought as well as the history of Asian thought. . . . He has to possess an array of linguistic skills that are uncharacteristic nowadays of Western political theorists. Second, he has to sustain a relationship with his Western colleagues in which he takes their concerns with a seriousness that they rarely . . . reciprocate. Thus a genuine dialogue is for the most part lacking. It is we in the West who are impoverished by our failure to sustain our part in this dialogue.[25]

Thirty years after this, in spite of so much more lip service to intellectual cosmopolitanism, the Western political theorist has only chosen to be even more impoverished. What we shall idealize in this introduction as a "fusion" of traditions, concepts, and styles of thinking is dismissed as intercultural flotsam. It is almost taken for granted that one either gets into comparative philosophy with an adolescent zeal of radical counter-culturism or culture-tourism, or slows down into soft-core "New-Age" comparative philosophy at the senile end of one's (not-so-)successful career in one of the hard-core mainstream philosophical disciplines such as Epistemology or Metaphysics or Philosophy of Mind or Aesthetics or Philosophy of Language or Philosophy of Science or Ethics or Political Philosophy or Phenomenology or American Process Philosophy. Yet, for an entire generation of astute Asian, African, or Latin American (and perhaps fewer European) philosophers, comparative philosophy has been both the passion of their youth and the preoccupation of their top-of-the-career maturity. Some had to read both Plato and the *Upaniṣads*, both Aquinas and Udayana, both Confucius and Aristotle, both Kant and Dharmakīrti, both Wittgenstein and Nāgārjuna, both Kukai and Quine, as they were taught how to philosophize. Long before one was aware of the "dangerous liaisons" of international academic politics (where colonialism still rules under the garb of the postcolonial), not just one's thought and talk, but even one's everyday sensibilities had become incorrigibly "comparative." Now, when one painfully finds out that, in the insular power-enclaves of philosophy, even a mention of non-Western theories of mind, Indian theories of knowledge, Japanese theory of *amae*, or South African theory of *ubuntu* is punished by polite exclusion, well-preserved prestigious ignorance about other cultures, that mono-cultural hubris defines the mainstream of professional philosophy in Euro-America, that the discovery of exciting connections, sharp oppositions, or imaginable dialogues between some ancient or modern Eastern and ancient or contemporary Western ideas is going to be greeted with condescension or cold neglect, it is already too late. While we lament the misfortune of our purist (and power-blinkered) colleagues who are missing out on this fun, one of the best ways to deepen the collective celebration of culture-straddling contemplation is to reflect, critically and analytically, on the very concept of philosophical comparison. This is what we are doing and shall continue to do in the next two or three sections of this introduction.

Quoting Borges, in his preface to *The Order of Things*, Foucault wonders at "a certain Chinese encyclopedia's" division of animals into (a) belonging to the emperor, (b) suckling pigs, (c) stray dogs, (d) innumerable, (e) frenzied, (f) fabulous, etc. And he uses a deeply sarcastic phrase (see the emphasis below), even while deconstructing the sense of impossibility or absurdity of such an "alien" (Chinese) system of classification. "In the wonderment of this taxonomy, the thing we apprehend in one great leap, the thing that, by means of the fable, is demonstrated as *the exotic charm of another system of thought*, is the limitation of our own, the stark impossibility of thinking *that*. But what is it impossible to think, and what kind of impossibility are we faced with here?"[26] Yet, the standardized taxonomy of the types of philosophy courses that one can teach in contemporary American academia is no less "exotic," indeed, it is bizarre. Philosophy courses and philosophers are usually divided into (a) Analytic (b) Continental (c) Feminist and (d) Asian/Comparative. Sometimes the species "American philosophy" (which one might expect to be the overarching genus!) is added to this list with the good intention of recognizing Process Philosophy and Pragmatism. Yet, everybody knows that some feminist philosophers are formidably analytic, that some very good analytic philosophers are pragmatists, that wonderful work in analytic philosophy of mind, language, or mathematics is routinely produced on the European continent, and that some comparative philosophers are very continental in their phenomenological or deconstructive style of doing philosophy.

On the putative comparative-analytic rift

The only place where this category-mistaken cross-division is often thought to have a modicum of justification is the alleged rift between the analytic and the Asian/comparative. "I have done enough of left-brain exercise through analytic philosophy," one senior philosophy professor from a liberal arts college told the participants at the start of a Summer Institute on Indian philosophies and religions, "and now, I want to develop my right brain, the non-rational emotional side of my personality through learning about Indian thought." The rift between reason and intuition, between argumentation and direct experience, between conceptual clarification and supra-conceptual edification resurfaces regularly in the form of this conviction that the gulf between analytic philosophy and Asian-comparative philosophy could not and should not be bridged. Later in this Introduction, we will try to give one obvious example of the fruitful practice of comparative analytic philosophy, showing that the above mentioned rift is a figment of politically motivated or blinkered imagination. Of course, everyone knows that such great comparative philosophers as Bimal Matilal and Karl Potter have been uncompromisingly analytic in their methodology. But, to the extent that they did and do Indian philosophy at all, the academia refused to regard them as straightforward analytic philosophers. In spite of his path-breaking work on the logic, ontology, and epistemology of negation, Oxford University Sub-faculty of Philosophy hesitated a lot before listing Professor Matilal's classes on Indian Logic or Indian Epistemologies in the philosophy lecture list. Karl Potter's seminal work on free will and truth has never been anthologized in an analytic philosophy reader on those topics. This seems to be the price one pays for mastering and writing about hard-core Indian philosophy: notwithstanding one's perfect facility with and original contributions to analytic philosophy, one ceases to qualify for the narrow sense of an analytic philosopher simply because one has crossed the cultural/historical border of the Frege-to-Quine tradition. Ignorance of Indian philosophy, at least a decade or two back, was a necessary qualification for a hard-core analytic philosopher of good standing in the United Kingdom, Australia, and the United States. We know of at least one very established American analytic philosopher who has not only studied and taught but even published on technical classical Indian philosophical semantics in addition to pursuing his interest in Meinongian semantics and metaphysics of events. He reported in private conversation that when one of the topmost West coast philosophy departments was about to hire him, he told them of this newly acquired additional expertise and they pretended not to hear and thought that he was changing the subject. Needles to say, in this analytic philosophy department, he cannot teach Indian philosophy of language, which he has researched well.

That indeed is the fear: if we allow comparisons or fusions with a "foreign" (most often meaning non-Western, since philosophy is taken to be native to Europe only) tradition, then the purity of the Aristotle-Kant-Frege-Wittgenstein-Quine-Kripke tradition or the Plato-Plotinus-Spinoza-Hegel-Husserl-Heidegger tradition will somehow get tainted. The subject would change. It would no longer be philosophical analysis or existential phenomenology as we know it. The sheer fear of such comparisons degenerating into (comparative) religion or comparative history of cultures surely does not explain this Euro-American myth-preservation about the spiritual, therefore non-analytic, East! One never needed to be a radical atheist like Bertrand Russell in order to get a membership to the analytic or continental clubs. Some of the stalwarts of current Anglo-American analytic philosophy are frankly Christian and proudly practice analytic philosophy of religion. Indeed, anti-theistic Western philosophers can find fresh chewable meat in the Buddhist (e.g., Santaraksita) or Jaina (e.g., Haribhadrasuri) arguments against the existence of any sort of God. So the old uninformed argument about most Eastern philosophy being overly religious and hence unfit for secular rational analysis no longer holds any water.

Luckily, Indian philosophy as practiced for the last sixty years has not had the converse fears or insecurities. Much first-rate philosophy in India has been done in English in the twentieth century—and we are not talking about Sri Aurobindo or Tagore or Gandhi, or Radhakrishnan from the colonial period—using a mixed Western and Indian philosophical idiom, raising questions that revel in straddling traditions, such as: "What is the objectively graspable meaning of the first person pronoun 'I'?" "Is *prāmāṇya* truth or knowledgehood?" "Is *apoha* a negative nominal essence or a complement-set of particular images?" "Is the five-skandha self a Humean bundle?" "Is karma retributive causation?" "Is knowledge derived from verbal testimony reducible to inference?" Why have the Western philosophers of language, mind and knowledge not asked the converse type of trans-traditional questions? Why do we not hear the interrogatives: "Does Russell's theory of error and false belief count as an 'anyathākhyāti' (misallocated predication) theory?" "Is Armstrong a Carvaka-style 'dehatmavadin'?" Now, we have grown up believing that liberal, cosmopolitan, nonhierarchical rationality and multicultural openness are typically Western ideals, whereas provincial insularity, considerations regarding who has the right to which kind of knowledge, and privileged access to special disciplines were features of caste-dominated Hindu sort of thinking. Yet, Western analytic philosophy has, in general, shown little interest in opening up to the vigorous and rich traditions of epistemological, metaphysical, linguistic, and aesthetic analysis found in the—now-translated—major works of Nyāya, Vedanta, and grammarian and literary theoretic traditions in Sanskrit. Indeed, we have heard both Richard Rorty, whose "linguistic turn" ended in a neo-pragmatist relativistic/deconstructive cul-de-sac, and Timothy Williamson, whose Oxford-style philosophical analysis has led to staunch metaphysical realism, remark that Western analytic philosophy has nothing to learn from Asian thought.[27] Unfortunately, some very sincere and competent specialists of Asian, even Indian, thought agree with this precisely because they have a rather exotic soteriological (liberation-obsessed) image of "Indian ways of thinking" and a rather crude and narrow notion of what analytic philosophy is up to.[28]

Four major arguments are given in different contexts in support of this persistent image of Indian thought as typically nonanalytic: (1) Analytic philosophy is motivated by the Aristotelian search for pure theory whereas most Indian philosophies are motivated by the practical soteriological purpose of eradicating existential suffering. (2) Analytic philosophy is historically connected to the enlightenment project of individualistic antiauthoritarian free thinking, whereas all Indian thought is deeply rooted in unquestioning reverence to revealed tradition or prophetic authority. (3) Analytic philosophy reaches its conclusion on the basis of deductive, inductive, and abductive arguments whereas Indian philosophies routinely base themselves on alleged intuitive mystical experiential knowledge. And finally, (4) there is no clear conception of formal logic, deductively valid arguments, or a priori truth or analytic propositions in Indian thought, whereas analytic philosophy is crucially based on such notions. These allegations against the very idea of Indian analytic philosophy are very easy to answer.[29]

Sometimes a more serious worry is expressed, not from the analytic (Western) side but on behalf of the authentic traditional Indian philosophers (especially of the Yoga-Vedanta type) about doing Indian comparative philosophy in an analytic vein. The worry as expressed by Stephen Phillips[30] is that "success on the front of (analytic) legitimization may have come at the cost of distorting some of the history of Indian philosophies" and losing sight of the "mystic empiricism" that grounds much Vedantic thought. But we wish to point out that this is a baseless worry. The intellectual clarity achieved by well-defined conceptual distinctions, intricate rational argumentation, and skeptical flushing out of conflicting metaphysical beliefs is very much at the service of that spiritual experience of direct encounter with the Self or Emptiness that one hears about. A traditional Samkhya, Yogacara Buddhist, or Kashmir Shaiva philosopher would not have any anxiety that such logical noise would be distracting for a mystical poise. Indeed, as Abhinavagupta (early eleventh century), the greatest champion of direct mystical experience, has maintained in his magnum opus Tantraloka (pt IV), good logical reasoning is the surest means to Yogic perfection: "*tarko yogangam uttamam.*"

An example: On reflexivity of consciousness and concept-free perception

To illustrate comparative philosophy as hard-core philosophy most vividly, with a rather detailed example, let us look at the narrow but vibrant topic of the reflexivity of consciousness, which has most recently been discussed again by Paul Bernier in the latest (January 2015) issue of *Philosophy East and West*.[31] The following rehearsal of that debate (not based on Bernier's discussion) is offered here as an example of one of the ways one can do analytic comparative philosophy of mind. This is the topic of a research-program in what Mark Siderits has called "fusion philosophy" and that derives its inspiration from an in-depth study of Buddhist epistemology, contemporary cognitive science, and Abhinavagupta's epistemology of self-consciousness. Abhinavagupta (the dynamic non-dualist philosopher-aesthete from early-eleventh-century Kashmir) observes that even the nonverbal bodily perceptions of a running man are functions of a discursive spontaneity of self-consciousness (*vimarśa*), such that the implicit awareness "I am running" is pregnant with conceptual-linguistic capacities, which get triggered in imitating others' actions (an observation uncannily anticipating the mirror-neuron debates in the twenty-first century).[32] John McDowell, a contemporary philosopher who worked first at Oxford and then at Pittsburgh, also comes to a similar conclusion that even the rawest sense experience involves employment of concepts, using a similar argument:

> In the throes of an experience of the kind that putatively transcends one's conceptual powers . . . one can give linguistic expression to a concept that is exactly as fine-grained as the experience, by uttering a phrase like "that shade," in which the demonstrative exploits the presence of the sample.[33]

In the light of these two similar lines of thought from two very different times and climes, let us explore the links between two distinct issues of philosophy of consciousness and perception.

Whenever I perceive a brown cat, must I directly perceive that I am perceiving a brown cat? Those who answer "yes" to this question can be called "reflexivists." Reflexivists believe that a state's being a conscious mental state consists in its being transparent, that is, immediately and incorrigibly known to the subject. Those who answer "no" to our opening question would take a cognitive event to be as external to the subject's mind as any other event (such as a stimulation of the C-fibers in one's own brain) and therefore capable of happening without the subject's knowledge. We can call these philosophers "irreflexivists." They insist that the existence of the first perception is not dependent on or constituted by any synchronous and necessary recognition by the possessor of the cognitive state.

In classical Indian epistemology, reflexivism took the form of the Prābhākara Mīmāmsā theory of the self-illuminating nature of consciousness. It is true, the Prābhākara Mīmāmsā philosopher argues, that a knife does not cut itself and the eyes do not see themselves. But, unlike material or sensory tools, awareness is conscious and self-luminous. Its job is to reveal. How can an awareness reveal its external intentional object to the subject, if it itself remains unrevealed to herself? If I do not know *that* I have known, how would I know *what* I have known? All awarenesses arise in the form "I am aware of this," and not in the form "some awareness of this object has occurred" or "this is presented." When I disclose an object with the light of my awareness, both the object and the awareness get disclosed together. So, basically, the reflexivist is rejecting the externalist observational model for our knowledge of our own cognitions.

In the classical Indian scene, opponents of reflexivism came in two major teams. The first group insisted that while my eyes can see the brown cat, my seeing of it is an event or act that even I—the first person—cannot directly perceive. Actions in general, according to this school of Vedic hermeneutics, are imperceptible. They have to be inferred from their results. Even by the perceiver herself, the cognitive act, because it is an act, has to be inferred from its effect. In this case, the effect of the cognitive act is the peculiar feature of known-ness that is noticed in the cat besides its brownness and felinity. The perception of the cat has to be postulated as the only explanation of this occasion-specific feature of cognizedness. The other group rejected both the self-illumination theory and the opposite, extreme theory of holding that cognitions are imperceptible by the subject herself. They held that my own perception of the cat can be known and ascribed to myself by myself through a distinct but equally perceptual awareness episode operating through the inner sense. While the first cognition is verbalized as "That is a brown cat," the second apperceptive one is verbalized as "I see a brown cat." Thus, perceptions are neither self-intimating nor only inferable. They are accessible by a second "look within," or a kind of metacognitive glance.

Now, there is, on the face of it, a totally separate issue, which too has proved its vitality by showing up in both classical Indian epistemology and contemporary analytic philosophy of mind. This is the question of nonconceptual or pre-predicative perceptual content. Philosophers such as John McDowell and Bill Brewer (and, in the Indian tradition, Bhartṛhari and Vyāsatīrtha) have maintained that all perceptual cognitions have conceptual content, whereas philosophers such as Christopher Peacocke, José Bermudez, and Susan Hurley hold that there must be nonconceptual perception first if we are to ever have verbalizable concept-enriched experience. In Sanskrit philosophical traditions, the supporters of nonconceptual perception came in two varieties. The radical champions of non-conceptualism were the Yogācāra Buddhists, who held that all genuine perceptions are concept-free and untainted by language, which is the vehicle of imaginary conceptual generalities. When we make perceptual judgments, we have already slipped into inferential cognition and lost touch with the pure self-featured or featureless particulars that are given to the senses. Yogācāra Buddhists also argued that cognitions are reflexively self-aware. More moderate non-conceptualists were the Nyāya realists who felt compelled to postulate a pre-predicative, concept-free perception in order to explain the full-fledged predicative and concept-endowed perceptions that also directly reveal the world as it is. While the Buddhists were suspicious of concepts or generalities and therefore of language, the Nyāya direct realists considered publicly verbalizable determinate perceptual judgments to be their philosophical life-supports. So they held that perceptions can be nonconceptual or conceptual, and that only the latter can be correct or incorrect, whereas the former are only logical postulates that we can never apperceive, let alone put into words.

This last bit of the moderate non-conceptualist stance of Nyāya is crucially significant. If the complex Nyāya argumentation about this issue is correct, then the price at which nonconceptual perceptions are accommodated in the theory is the admission of a form of fully intentional perceptual cognition that is not only not self-intimating, but also incapable of being apperceived or directly intuited in any fashion. For deeply Kantian reasons, it seems inconceivable that a perceptual cognition would be such that one could not apperceptively or introspectively claim it to be one's own. This suggests that the idea of concept-free perception must be given up, unless we want to get committed either to reflexivism, which collapses perception with apperception and therefore puts no constraint on its content, or to the complete inaccessibility of one's own intentional cognitive state. Now, there could be dispositional properties of one's own knowledge, or sub-personal states that constitute one's broad perceptual field and enable one to have object-recognizing sensory cognitions. These could very well be un-apperceivable precisely because they are not episodes of one's own perceiving something as this-such. What is hard to stomach is the combination of the reflexive introspectibility theory of cognitive states with the celebration of nonconceptual cognitions as full-fledged perceptions.

In any case, it seems that the two issues—"Is awareness necessarily self-aware?" and "Are there non-conceptual perceptions?"—are closely linked. It may be wrong to assert the particular link that has been asserted here, but there exists some link between them. Only an uncompromisingly analytic and fusion style of thinking that does not primarily ask for historical or cultural causes of views, but judges them for cogency and truth as seriously offered philosophical options can do justice to the comparative insights that one can get by reconstructing the debates between Indian and contemporary Western reflexivists and nonreflexivists on the one hand, and those between conceptualists and non-conceptualists on the other.

Three grave objections threatening the possibility of comparative philosophy

Apart from the political resistance against comparative philosophy that we have hinted at above, there is one extremely frustrating charge against it that should worry all of us who have dedicated considerable parts of our intellectual careers to this risky business of boundary-breaking cross-cultural thinking. Let us formulate that problem through an anecdote. Once, in a small American university, one of us had to co-teach an Introduction to Philosophy class with a well-known Kant-expert American philosopher. When we came to Logic as the foundation of philosophy, there was a request that we should take one class-period to acquaint the Mid-Western American freshmen with the basics of Indian Logic. When that was done, the American Co-teacher's reaction was the following: "Interesting, but, the technical terms are too alien sounding and it does not sound like what we would call 'Logic'! Could you try tomorrow to explain these same rules of reasoning to our students in more recognizably Western terms?" When that too was done the next day, the reaction was: "Well, this is just familiar Aristotelian logic! What is new or different in Indian logic that we should take the trouble of learning it when we already have this kind of logic in the West?" The charge, when formulated abstractly, is this: either we represent an Asian (or African or Islamic or Hawaiian etc.) philosophy in its own original terms, which are utterly alien to Western philosophy, in which case it is not philosophy proper, or we rephrase it in Western terms, in which case it risks ending up as just a repetition of what we already have in the West. Thus we either have no need of comparison with foreign ideas because they are just the same or too similar to our own native ideas, or we cannot allow it to count as hard-core philosophy because it is too different from how philosophy is done in the Western tradition. We have given an American's example, but the same can be the experience when one tries to share Western metaphysics or epistemology or ethics with Sanskrit or Chinese traditional scholars of philosophy. If it is alien it is not philosophy, if it is philosophy we already have it, why bother? This objection has a vague similarity with Meno's Paradox of Inquiry. If one does not know something at all one cannot ask a question about it, but if one already knows what one is asking about, why need one ask? This so-called paradox of inquiry, by the way, has been raised by Śrīharṣa (twelfth century) who could not by any stretch of imagination have had any knowledge of Plato.[34]

Our response to this objection is predictably similar to the standard reply to Meno's Paradox of Inquiry: There can be a state of undetailed knowledge of a topic, which is also a state of ignorance that one can wish to seek relief from. In the present context, though we cannot cater to the uncurious or the exclusivist, there must be a non-flaky "middle way" of doing philosophical comparison, the content and the concerns of which would resonate with the non-comparative analytic or continental philosopher's preexistent conception of what is genuinely philosophical and yet, push the boundaries of any familiar ways of thinking and introduce new ideas not only in the host (in this act of intellectual hospitality), but into the guest cultures themselves. Something like this must have happened in China when early Mahayana Buddhist Tantra was translated *en masse* into Chinese, which changed both Chinese philosophy and Indian Tantra. Whether this happened historically or not, this *space between* unrecognizably and unintelligibly alien and boringly familiar has to be found by any comparative philosopher who wishes to be heard by the mainstreams of both of the traditions that she is trying to bring together, either in conflict or in cooperation, in conversation or contestation.

The second objection has to do with interpreting versus changing. In our own volume, even as Sor-hoon Tan essays to reconcile Rawlsian and Confucian notions of justice, she cautions us against such a distorting influence of cross-cultural comparison. Comparison in philosophizing is often valued for its illuminating effects, but at the same time, cross-cultural comparisons in comparative philosophy risk distortion of the thought of a very different culture and time by imposing alien lenses. When we compare, for example, Japanese Zen Buddhist concepts of "dependent" social self and the American pragmatist concept of relational "I-Me" self (as Steve Odin does in his magisterial study on Nishida Kitaro, Doi Takeo, and G. H. Mead—a paradigm example of what we describe below as the third stage of comparative philosophy), are we not thereby changing both the *comparanda*, in the name of interpreting them? The best response to this charge is to welcome transformation as a healthy rather than repugnant consequence of interpretation. Both Steve Odin and Karl Jaspers (in his small but insightful chapter on Nagarjuna) have tried to draw analogies and disanalogies between their *comparanda,* but end up taking a position of candidly biased preference. To quote the last lines of Odin's Chapter 10: "For Nishida the I-Thou relation is symmetrical, while for Mead the I-Me relation is asymmetrical in character. . . . In the evolutionary process cosmology of Whitehead and Mead, then, it is this notion of *asymmetrical* theory of becoming *in the arrow of time* which . . . constitutes the autonomous nature of selfhood as a creative advance into novelty."[35] The fusion here results not only in a Zen that is recognizably Whiteheadian, but even a Mead whose progressive and creative I-Me dialectic has been transformed in a subtle way into a "dependently arising" self that strives to be less and less egocentric.

A third objection could go as follows: Either you are interested in objective truth, in which case, you will have to evaluate and grade different views coming, let us say, from Christian Europe, Buddhist Japan, and Islamic Arabia about the relation of human actions and the moral status of the world, and end up exposing the errors or relative inferiority of some traditions in comparison to others. If you are not a believer in such realist absolutist appeal to truth, all you can do is juxtapose an anthropological account of all these "ethno-philosophies" of other cultures, which each of them—it is often assumed—can do anyway with better justice, entitlement, and accuracy. In the first case, you are encouraging a destructive contest or clash of civilizations and in the second case, you are not doing philosophy at all. Since there appears to be no third option, comparative philosophy is either odious, as is sarcastically said of comparison more generally, or perniciously anti-cosmopolitan. We would like to think of fusion philosophy as a third option, in which one neither risks the pitfall of supposing that one tradition has reached the truth (or could possibly have reached the truth) nor references back to different traditions in a manner that leads to unwelcome destructive consequences. Fusion philosophy makes use of different traditions (or rather different philosophical standpoints) in a consciously methodological or instrumental fashion. The imputation of definite philosophical standpoints might help add clarity about the exact problem at hand and certainly encourages disagreements of all sorts. If the reference is to entities such as "traditions" or "cultures," it is to be expected that there is already enough internal disagreement on any philosophical question, which undermines the unitary thrust of the respective reference itself. In that sense, the comparative exercise with the aim of doing fusion philosophy comes to propel rather than dispel the project of truth. In fusion philosophy, given the emphasis on the comparer, it is, furthermore, more than evident that the interest in objective truth lies with the comparer and his or her argument and not with what tradition or school got it right. The comparer appropriates the variety of philosophical standpoints—and eventually transcends the borders between them. In the end, far from arguing for one tradition or the other, the comparer is arguing his or her own case. And it would seem odd if in some sense or another *that* case would not aim at truth, however provisionary or pragmatist it may be fashioned.

Three stages of comparative philosophy

It is time to say something about the narrative that informs our advocacy of fusion philosophy. We believe that the history of comparative philosophy can be divided roughly into three stages.

The imperative at the first stage amounted to something like: modern Western philosophy has sophisticated debates about, say, freedom of the will, so let us find in Indian philosophy something similar. The bottom line of this exercise resulted in statements such as "we/they had something similar (but something which had to be looked for, retrieved)." From another point of view, there might have been a more strategic motivation in finding various resemblances, overlaps, anticipations, namely to draw attention to non-Western traditions in the first place. It was thus happily and often apologetically claimed that Chinese thinkers *also* had philosophy and ethics in the Greek sense, that there was *also* logic and phenomenology in India! More boldly (with the arrogance of cultural insecurity), some asserted that "we said all of that long ago," and "we said it much better long before you." The basic idea at this stage is universalism.

At the second stage of comparative philosophy, the impetus was more to find contrasts and context-dependent culture-immanent peculiarities in non-Western philosophies, and to detect specific lacks compared to the Western tradition. The resulting lack-discourse ran a gamut of asserting that there was no possibility, no propositions, no deductive validity, no free will or apriori in Indian philosophy, no ontology, no logic and no truth claims in Chinese philosophy, no formal logic in African philosophy and so on and so forth. The moderate version drew the conclusion that these missing elements had to be introduced and adapted into Indian, Chinese or African philosophy. A more strident version of the second stage had it that these philosophies, if they were to retain their unique character, are better off without this Western theoretical stuff. Indian philosophy can easily do without the idea of "possible worlds," which shows that it is far from being a necessary or compelling topic to discuss. It thus became an intellectual option to assert with confidence the lack of this or that, that there was no notion of correspondence truth or a creator God transcending the empirical world in Chinese philosophy and no notion of logical necessity or deductive validity in Indian logic. That was in fact not a lack, but a major strength. The implication was that Western philosophy should question these notions because there could be such rich traditions eschewing such notions altogether. The basic idea here is localism.

The third stage comprises some of the best comparative philosophy written today, that is, at the critical conjuncture between universalism and localism. The imperative is to re-interpret Indian, Chinese, or Japanese philosophy in terms of (oppositionally or positively) Western philosophical ideas as much as contributing back into English-language philosophy by bringing in elements of Asian or African or Hawaiian philosophy. Such crisscrossing comparative philosophy harks back to the regional or intra-traditional philosophical traditions, the Western analytic, the Continental phenomenological, the Indian analytic, the Indian sociocultural, the Asian literary, the Feminist European, the historical-political, the literary aesthetic, and enriches them with the lessons of comparison. When we ask "how would a rasa-theorist explain the beauty of Goya's painting 'Saturn Eating his own Child?,'" a prior question is likely to arise. "Is it legitimate," asks a closet-Orientalist of sorts, "to take an ancient or medieval Indian theory of art-experience and try to explain a modern European painting in its terms? Is the cultural baggage of the former not totally incommensurable to the complex semiotic milieu of the latter?" Without entering the larger issue of cultural relativism within the hermeneutics of art, we want simply to point out that the reverse has been done often, perhaps too often. For centuries, thanks to epistemological colonization, Oriental literary or artistic practices have been "interpreted" through Occidental theories, partly because it was regarded as a truism that any "theory" worthy of its name would have to be European. Even negatively it seems more apt to call the architecture of Dilwara Temple, in Mount Abu, similar to but not quite Baroque, than to judge Hamlet as not a dhirodatta nayaka. Besides anthroplogy and sociology, the histories of which in the West are histories of explaining Oriental raw data with the help of Western pure theories—did Husserl not remark that the Oriental mind is too crude and practical to fashion pure theories? Right now, even the postcolonial experts apply Sigmund Freud, Karl Marx, Michel Foucault, Walter Benjamin, Max Weber, Antonio Gramsci, Julia Kristeva and Giorgio Agamben in order to understand Indian art, mysticism, politics, philosophy, poetry and purity-pollution taboos etc. In principle there is nothing wrong with this, but it is about time that we also try the cross-cultural enterprise the other way. An earlier generation of "admirers" of the East believed or at least would have us believe that there simply is no dry complicated theories of aesthetics in India: there are only those juicy uncensored poetry, voluptuous erotic sculptures on the temple walls and cave-frescos of full-bodied damsels in Ajanta, and a bunch of blissed out Tantrics and Yogis who tell us to transcend all theoretical disputes and pass straight from Kamasutra postures and Tantric rituals to Nirvana or Samadhi, skipping all "why" questions! We now certainly know better. If we have to test and rejuvenate by creative criticism and adaptation those numerous intricate theories of making, communicating, enjoying, suffering, interpreting and assessing art that are already available in Sanskrit theoretical literature, then we must try it out on the literally outlandish examples and see if they work. The cultural difference between Elizabethan England and ancient Greece did not stop anyone from trying out Aristotle's theory of catharsis or mimesis on King Lear! Of course, the theories need to be changed and enriched to fit examples undreamt of by the original philosophers of art living in radically different times and places. But that is no reason to freeze the ancient theories with their own local and contemporary examples or to be skeptical about the point of assessing Yeates's work by the interpretive tools of Anandavardhana. Especially at a time when philosophers have loosened up considerably about finding the "correct meaning" of a work of art and are not always looking for what the poet or artist herself meant, a South Asian theory may very well throw new light on the meaning of European art. This, a ramified rasa-theory of disgust, may well unravel the mystery of how a creepy face of an obese man made of skinned dead chicken be the subject of a masterly painting by Giuseppe Arcimboldo.

In this volume, we want to put a spin on the practice of comparative philosophy at the third, current stage, which eventually might lead us to a fourth stage. The spin would take us beyond comparative philosophy. It would amount to just doing philosophy as one thinks fit for getting to the truth about an issue or set of issues, by appropriating elements from all philosophical views and traditions one knows of but making no claim of "correct exposition," but just solving hitherto unsolved problems possibly raising issues never raised before anywhere.

In this fourth stage, comparative philosophy can become truly borderless and eventually drop its epithet "comparative," although one should anticipate strong resistance against this last phase of dropping the qualifier "comparative." Good creative philosophy in a globalized world should spontaneously straddle geographical areas and cultures, temperaments and time-periods (mixing classical, medieval, modern, and postmodern), styles and subdisciplines of philosophy, as well as mix methods, sprinkling phenomenology, and political economic analysis into analytic logico-linguistic or hermeneutic, or culture studies or literary or narrative methods—whatever comes handy. The result would be either very flaky mishmash or first-rate original work. Philosophers, especially those who strive for clarity and truth, have to live with more confusions than clear and distinct ideas, when they welcome fusion philosophy as their preferred genre.

Celebrating the collaborative philosophical eclecticism of this collection

Such healthy eclecticism shows up at three levels in our collection of essays: At the level of choice of topics, which do not fit into any special branch of philosophy; at the level of choice of method, let us say of Patton's, Weber's and Nusseibeh's essays, which adopt entirely different methods, at the level of proportion or ratio between Western and non-Western philosophical preoccupations and contexts. Where Weber's essay is based on mostly modern European materials, Patton or Ho are mainly dealing with ancient Indian and Chinese texts.

Beyond all suspected philosophical borders between branches of philosophy, different methods, and Western and non-Western philosophical preoccupations and contexts, the problem of philosophy in different languages, and translation among them, has been a key concern for long. And if every language has its own unique, albeit changing, conceptual scheme, and no two languages share these basic conceptual schemes, then philosophically responsible translation across them should be impossible. Of course, Chinese and Tibetan Buddhism originally arose out of centuries of translation projects from Sanskrit and Pali. But now when we translate Sanskrit, Chinese, or Tibetan into English, the conceptual scheme which draws sharp distinction between, let us say "a cow" (indefinite article and count noun), "the cow" (definite description), "cows/all cows" gets into confusions and misunderstandings not only appearing weird and implausible but also doing injustice to the originals. In Tibetan *Collected Topics* arguments, subject terms are quite frequently not translatable by the count nouns they would apparently require in a Western target language, with the result that such count-noun translations would seem not to preserve truth. Some of our chapters engage with such meta-methodological issues of translation, albeit by way of an exemplary discussion of the very possibility of translating into an African or classical South Asian language some key-terms in philosophy such as "truth."

Tom J. F. Tillemans, in his chapter on "Count Nouns, Mass Nouns, and Translatability: The Case of Tibetan Buddhist Logical Literature," engages the primary and secondary literature on Tibetan *Collected Topics* (*bsdus grwa*) arguments in light of the now classic arguments on intertranslatability and its philosophical limits proffered by W. V. Quine and Donald Davidson. He thus sets into conversation two different philosophical traditions. There are even more fusions undertaken in his text. Tillemans additionally weaves into his discussion some of the arguments made in the parallel debate regarding the Tibetan cousin, that is Chinese language, both arguments of long-standing (Christoph Harbsmeier, Chad Hansen) and more recent contributions (Chris Fraser, Dan Robins). Finally, there is also fusion between the philologist's care for linguistic and textual matters of detail—which may serve as helpful hindrances forestalling too-swift philosophical conclusions, but also as hints toward philosophically important distinctions and therefore potentially important conclusions. Thus the philosopher's concern for clarity and an argument that can stand on its own is addressed. Tillemans shows how the philological game must not ultimately come to stand in the way of the philosophical aim, but can be fruitfully combined to form what is perhaps a more substantial philosophical argument. Tillemans defends the argument that languages themselves do not have inherent features that would limit their inter-translation, but he adds and showcases an important exception at the level of theoretical writings about language. Pushing the effort at fusion philosophy one step further, Tillemans offers a short appendix with a comparison to Gongsun Longzi's white horse dialogue and the question of a possible entanglement with the Tibetan *Collected Topics* literature.

Finding also a point of departure in the work of Quine, Barry Hallen sets out in his chapter "Translation, Interpretation, and Alternative Epistemologies" to examine, compare, and, in terms of topic, fuse the philosophy retrieved from the semantics of the West African languages of the Akan of Ghana, the Yoruba of Nigeria and of the English language (apparently and interestingly in no need of an indication of a particular people or a particular country) with regard to the underlying problematique of intertranslatability. Hallen especially focuses on the criteria for "truth" in ordinary language, which—he argues—differ fundamentally and may be productively exploited to tackle, and even resolve, some epistemological problems. There are at least three different interventions evident in Hallen's chapter. He unmistakably contributes to the many efforts underway to correct and balance some earlier sweeping characterizations (and more often than not disqualifications) of African philosophy, as when he emphasizes that "Yoruba discourse does employ terminology and systematic criteria for the evaluation of any type of information." Moving beyond issues of African philosophy to comparative philosophy, Hallen offers a series of meta-reflections on comparative and intercultural philosophy including on the very project of fusion philosophy. Finally, Hallen offers an interesting example of fusion philosophy when relating and using Yoruba epistemology to question the paradigm of propositional knowledge and also to problematize and reject one of Gettier's famous counterexamples.

Straddling over Indian Buddhist, Chinese Buddhist, and Hindu philosophical materials is Chien-hsing Ho's method in his chapter on "Resolving the Ineffability

Paradox." Ho's text has a very clear and focused topic that put in form of a question would read: how can one *say* that something is *unspeakable* without getting irretrievably implicated in paradox or self-refutation? This is what Ho terms the "ineffability paradox." Section after section, in a double movement of encircling and closing in on his topic, Ho rehearses positions defended in contemporary philosophy, such as the common division of the functions of human language into cognitive and noncognitive, or positions represented, for instance, by Graham Priest or Ludwig Wittgenstein. Ho then sets out to complicate and elucidate the issue. To do this, he alludes to an impressive array of texts from thinkers that all lived between the fourth and eighth century CE and include—keeping the exact wording used by Ho—the prominent Indian Buddhist epistemologist Dignāga, the Chinese Yogācāra thinker Kuiji, his pupil Huizhao, the two Chinese Mādhyamika philosophers Sengzhao and Jizang, the Huayan master Fazang, and the Hindu grammarian-philosopher Bhartṛhari. Here, the descriptive vocabulary demonstrates the borders that separate the different thinkers beyond the fact that they are different thinkers, such as Indian/Chinese as two different Buddhisms and Yogācāra/Mādhyamika/Huayan as different Buddhisms cutting through the Indian/Chinese border, while the Hindu grammarian-philosopher is presented as a distinct point of reference outside the Buddhist borders. The vocabulary of master-pupil indicates further the strong sense of philosophical *traditions* that conventionally inform such discussions. This is the constellation of different philosophical traditions that Ho fuses to resolve the paradox by way of introducing "indication" as a mode of expression.

Laurie L. Patton practices comparative philosophy crossing boundaries both of cultures as well as time-periods, using the most contemporary "philosophy of instruments" (Daniel Rothbart) to interpret the hymns to weapons one finds in one of the most ancient mystical poems—the *Ṛg Veda*—in the history of human literature. "The Bowstring is Like a Woman Humming: The Vedic Hymn to the Weapons and the Transformative Properties of Tools" straddles in a most creative way two newer branches of philosophy, namely the philosophy of literature and the emerging field of philosophy of technology. The question might sound rather specific, but it is straightforward: What kind of practice is the blessing of weapons and what might it say about culture? If one expands one's vision from weapons to tools, "from spears to computer algorithms" (Patton's example), the question loses some of its specificity and the general philosophical implications become manifest. Tools, far from being "mere" instruments, so Patton argues (with Rothbart), may constitutively change our understanding of our own agency and help develop our capacity to act in the world. Patton's chapter, in this regard not unlike Tilleman's, also simultaneously deploys and fuses the methods of philology and philosophy, while keeping an ear for the poetic qualities of language.

The practice of reading culturally "other" texts may share deeper problems with the universal human practice of reading other's feelings. Without presupposing the thick metaphysical claim that people are texts, Arindam Chakrabarti raises the question "How Do We Read Others' Feelings? Strawson and Zhuangzi Speak to Dharmakirti, Ratnakīrti and Abhinavagupta." We humans cannot live without forming criss-crossing groups of "we" which require us to know or at least act as if we know what another conscious being is feeling. Yet, philosophers in European, Indian, and Chinese traditions have been skeptical about the very possibility of knowing other minds. Using insights from Zhuangzi's brief but exemplary disputation with Hui Shi on his alleged knowledge of the happiness of the fish swimming in a river, and the debate between two Buddhist epistemologists, Dharmakirti and Ratnakirti, who prove and disprove the existence of other mind-streams, Chakrabarti makes these Asian engagements with the problem of other minds speak to the contemporary question of how we read others' minds. Apart from the complex and deep ideas of Abhinavagupta, an eleventh-century philosopher of the Kashmir Shaiva Recognition school, the arguments proffered by the late-twentieth-century Oxford philosopher P. F. Strawson and his student, the Indian philosopher R. C. Gandhi on the close connection between our self-awareness and our capacity to address and access other persons are deployed to suggest a theory of direct perceptual empathy that underlies the very possibility of dialogue.

In his "The Geography of Perception: Japanese Philosophy in the External World." Masato Ishida delves into the depths of an enactive realist theory of perception. Japanese philosophy in Ishida's text is articulated on the one hand directly through the voices of Dōgen and the twentieth-century philosophers Watsuji Tetsurō, Nishida Kitarō, and Ōmori Shōzō. On the other hand, in a formidable series of pertinent mini-comparisons with positions held by "Western" philosophers—some comparisons brought up by Ishida himself, others invoked by the Japanese philosophers—the articulation becomes further refined and increasingly appropriated. The mini-comparisons run the gamut of Western philosophy, stretching across Hume, Fichte, Nietzsche, Heidegger, and Sartre, but also including classical American philosophy, French phenomenology, contemporary analytic philosophy, and even ecological psychology. In one paragraph, Ishida (like Chakrabarti) even finds pleasure and incitement in the Zhuangzi-Huizi exchange about the happiness of fish. That the impressiveness of this scope of philosophical positions and traditions does not slide into superficial mishmash is ensured by the pertinence of each mini-comparison at a clearly defined juncture of a no-less clearly structured argument. Beyond all comparison and juxtaposition of Japanese and Western philosophers, Ishida advances an argument that is neither a Japanese argument nor an argument set against Western philosophy, but an argument about (or rather a philosophy of) visual perception that proves to be embodied in a complex geography of another kind, namely that any perceptual system that responds to visual properties is at least potentially an *eye*.

When in doubt about the truth of a judgment, report or belief, common people get a second opinion, or check whether many experts agree with it or not. Yet, Socrates laughed at the idea that truth should be determined by majority opinion, when in the *Theaetetus* someone suggested that whether currently we are dreaming or awake could be decided by intersubjective corroboration. Of course Plato disliked democracy, and perhaps in case of dream-reality distinction, the majority principle has little epistemic value, but in many, especially normative and political matters, the authority of the opinion of a large number of people cannot be ignored especially in contemporary democratic societies. In his chapter "Authority: Of German Rhinos and Chinese Tigers," Ralph Weber raises the question "What is authority?" from three nonnormative angles, that is, the logic of authority (Bocheński), its phenomenology (Kojève), and its conceptual history (Eschenburg). These accounts are then expanded and complicated by way of two anecdotes. The first anecdote is an early encounter between Wittgenstein and Russell, which is read in the context of Miranda Fricker's recent discussion on epistemic injustice in order to reflect on epistemic authority in ethical and political terms. The second anecdote is reported in the early Chinese classic *Han Feizi* and helps bring into focus a sort of authority which turns on number and which plays—so Weber argues—a fundamental role in understanding what is normatively at stake when theorizing democracy. Weber's chapter offers a fusion between two styles or methods of doing philosophy, conceptual analysis, and anecdotal or narrative phenomenology, between several branches of philosophy, namely epistemology, logic, ethics and political philosophy, and between some few elements taken from Chinese philosophy and a huge junk of modern European philosophy. Zooming in on the latter would of course bring to light quite another fusion, as German, French, and English philosophical traditions are made to speak to the question of authority generally and to the discourse in contemporary political philosophy specifically, something all too readily subsumed under that pernicious label "European."

Weber's chapter works as a bridge between the broadly epistemological part of our anthology to the broadly political and final part, which consists of two chapters by Sari Nusseibeh and Sor-hoon Tan. Reviewing different approaches to the definition of justice, Nusseibeh argues in his "To Justice with Love" in favor of viewing the natural human instinct of love (for the other) as constituting not only the cornerstone of a community factually, but also of the arrangement of a best human order normatively. Nusseibeh's fusion relates the famous concept of *asabiyyah* (compassion or affection) extracted from Ibn Khaldun's *Muqaddimah* with the liberal-communitarian debate and particularly with John Rawls's theory of justice. Here, hence, we witness no encompassing reference to the Arabian or Islamic philosophical tradition, but to a careful and well-dissected concept, which is then woven into modern (distributive and social) justice theory with its dominant focus on rationality. Pitting love against modern justice theory is not to contest a minor detail in the Rawlsian account; it means to put the entire project on a new footing. But Nusseibeh still works with and through Rawls when he finally comes to propose an approach based on two principles, an *overlapping* principle delineating individuals' wants, and a (reformulated) *difference* principle delineating limits of wants. The upshot of this approach is equality as a primary individual want, rather than a secondary function between different individuals' wants: "the 'primariness' of the equality want is finally interpreted in terms of the love instinct." Finally, compared with all other chapters, Nusseibeh's is probably offering the most concentrated attempt at a fusion between philosophical thought, pressing contemporary political problems and a just system of world order. It is hence no surprise that in his text there is hardly any talk of cultures, but the focus is consequentially set on societies.

The last chapter is written by Sor-hoon Tan. Her "Justice and Social Change" takes yet a different route than all the other chapters. It begins with a discussion of contemporary efforts at reconstructing an account of Confucian justice culminating in a comparison between Mencian and Confucian positions, on the one, and Aristotle, on the other side, as found in the contemporary research literature. What is the point of such comparison? That is the starting and perhaps startling question, to which

Tan adds some interesting second-level thoughts on the purpose of comparative philosophy. Still, in her discussion of justice and social change, she of course also engages in manifold comparisons and her chapter comes to fuse Mencius and Harry Frankfurt ("Mencius would certainly agree with Harry Frankfurt that . . ."), Confucian meritocracy (to each according to his ability?) with the phrase "from each according to his ability, to each according to his need" (nowadays most remembered for Karl Marx), but also Aristotle and Marx on the link between justice and law, and so on. Tan (not unlike Nusseibeh) aims at the reconstruction or development of a philosophy that could impact contemporary societies and their problems. She does so from a decidedly pragmatic/pragmatist standpoint—as well as from a decidedly Confucian standpoint. For this matter, Tan's chapter is unique in this collection. Although fusion philosophy is far from claiming some neutral ground or a view from nowhere, it is adamant about that the resulting philosophical argument should be standing on its own, that is, be the argument of the fusion philosopher. Tan reminds us that that fusion philosopher might still be motivated by a self-understanding of belonging to a tradition, even if and no less if positions from within that tradition are woven into the philosophical argument. Is such an argument still the fusion philosopher's argument or rather the tradition's perspective on a given problem? Does the goal of developing one's tradition (by offering, in Tan's case, a needs-based Confucian conception of justice) square with the goals of fusion philosophy and its insistence on an argument that can stand on its own? It probably depends on what is meant by "standing on its own." The worry of fusion philosophy is that an argument from authority might be camouflaged as a philosophical argument. But "standing on its own" might of course also mean and presuppose a self-conscious and self-critical awareness of one's hermeneutical standpoint, one's position in time and place, and even (but perhaps not necessarily) one's belonging to an identifiable tradition.

Recommending fusion philosophy goes hand in hand with an understanding of texts as eclectic attempts directed at forming philosophical arguments that can stand independently of the sources they draw on. Looking at the results of fusion philosophy from the perspective of how the fusions have been conducted brings up a set of (self-) critical questions. Are the fusions well done? What frictions and tensions have been ignored or leveled out for the sake of fusion? Could these same frictions and tensions be further exploited to add more depth and sophistication to the philosophical argument? One might also reflect on fusion philosophy from the perspective of what has been fused with what. Fusion seems to imply the tearing down of borders, but the philosophical gain comes from initially assuming the validity of these borders. If a text elegantly fuses Aristotelian-Thomistic scholastic philosophy and the philosophy of Nishida Kitarō, there seems to be posited at some level a claim that Aristotelian Thomism and Nishida Kitarō form or are part of two different philosophical traditions, that "philosophical traditions" is a useful *tertium comparationis*, that a border runs between the *comparanda* (while the eventual fusion posits the further claim that they speak about the same subject matter that the fusion philosopher is interested in and hence cannot be so different as to be incommensurable or even incomparable). From this point of view, a focus on the fusions undertaken in a text might also serve to highlight assumptions about pre-fused entities and the set of conventionally or methodologically established borders separating philosophical traditions. How persuasive are these borders and the pre-fused entities, both as juxtaposed against each other as well as each internally? What if Nishida Kitarō has studied scholastic philosophy and here and there might have come to form his own views against the views he found in Aristotelian Thomism? Would that sort of entanglement crucially undermine the effort at fusion philosophy and the borders that it (artificially) erects and eventually overcomes? Or would it inversely rather corroborate the possibility of fusion and add further credibility to the approach?

Concluding hopes and warnings: Futures of fusion thinking

In his major work *Empty Words: Buddhist Philosophy and Cross-Cultural Interpretation*, Jay Garfield goes beyond comparison.[36] Whether it was predominantly a history of knowledge-looting, or of conversion in the name of civilization or of systematic erasure of non-European intellectual traditions by means of deletion and distortion of indigenous cultural memories, the history of colonialism and its dream of Europeanization of the globe, has changed the global research-imperative in the Humanities. Under and immediately after colonialism, comparison has been done, somewhat anthropologically, merely for the sake of understanding other cultures or for the sake of finding "fascinating" resemblances and disanalogies. Jay Garfield's comments in this context especially merit our attention. Garfield himself has had, as it were, three successive intellectual careers: first as a Sellarsian analytical philosopher of mind, language, and knowledge, then as a diligent English translator from Tibetan Buddhist philosophical texts, and finally as a comparative philosopher of confessedly Madhyamika persuasion. In one of his chapters, he traces the development of Western idealism, from Berkeley, through Kant, to Schopenhauer, but through the CittamAtra lens of Vasubandhu, a Yogacara Buddhist subjective idealist from the fifth century. At the end of this Sanskrit/Buddhist critique of modern Western idealisms, he expresses the hope that this has been an example of comparative philosophy "done right."[37] This "rightness" is what we allude to when we talk about global research imperative. What makes it "right" *philosophically* is not the scholarly accuracy of the history of ideas or the "scientific historical" correctness in discovering who said what first, or who influenced whom across the cultures, but "the motivation, the intended next step"—where one wants to go with the comparison.[38] A philosophical comparison is right-minded if it is aimed at doing good philosophy, ideally, better philosophy than could be done in either of the compared traditions when they are secluded from the other. This telos of cross-cultural history of ideas becomes clear in his following remarks:

> Philosophy is, however, a live enterprise, both in the West and in the East, and if cross-cultural philosophy is to mean anything and to contribute anything to philosophical progress, it must do so with a view toward ideas and their development.... The task is to provide a common horizon that can be a background for genuine collaboration and conversation in a joint philosophical venture.

> The possibilities for such a venture are enormous. The enlargement of the world's scholarly community and the range of texts and resources, on which it can draw portends a greater philosophical depth and rate of progress. But the condition of the possibility of such progress and of such a future is the establishment of genuine collegiality and conversation, as opposed to contact and the interrogation of informants. And the condition of the possibility of conversation is taking seriously the standpoint and hermeneutic method of one's interlocutor as well as his or her ideas themselves, and taking seriously one's own tradition not as a lens to view another's but also as specimen under one's colleagues' lens at particular moments in the dialectic. . . . But the danger of abuse is not an argument against careful use. I have urged here that such careful use is not only possible, but desirable. In part this is true because of the essential role of comparative philosophy as a rung in a ladder to be discarded by our descendants, whose interlocution it may some day be seen to have enabled.[39]

Of course, there are risks. Even if concealed or vicarious cultural supremacist undertones are avoided, there is the risk of an insatiably encyclopedic (Borges-like) erudition for ever postponing creative, original, or committed thinking. There is also the risk of culture-hopping with no interest in finding a correct and coherent answer to the deepest philosophical questions. Then there is the risk that one would get abetted into in a back-lash of nativist revivalism or intellectual identity-politics after encountering enduring non-reaction of the Western academic establishment which may dig its purist (insular) heel in response to the increasing popularity of fusion philosophy.

Notes

1 "*Weil der Mensch das verbindende Wesen ist, das immer trennen muß und ohne zu trennen nicht verbinden kann—darum müssen wir das bloße indifferente Dasein zweier Ufer erst geistig als eine Getrenntheit auffassen, um sie durch eine Brücke zu verbinden. Und ebenso ist der Mensch das Grenzwesen, das keine Grenze hat.*" See Georg Simmel, "Brücke und Tür" (1909), translated in: David Frisby and Mike Featherstone (eds), *Simmel on Culture* (London: Sage Publications, 1997), p. 174.

2 Aaron Stalnaker, *Overcoming Our Evil: Human Nature and Spiritual Exercises in Xunzi and Augustine* (Washington, DC: Georgetown University Press, 2006), p. 17.

3 Bhoja, *Šṛngāra-prakāśa of Bhojaraja* (1–25, 26–36 Prakasa; Vol. I & II), ed. Rewa Prasad Dwivedi, New Delhi: IGNCA and Varanasi: Kalidasa Sansthan, 2007.

4 Bhoja, *Šṛngāra-prakāśa of Bhojaraja*, Vol II, p. 1202.

5 Archie Bahm, *Comparative Philosophy: Western, Indian and Chinese Philosophies Compared*, revised edition (Albuquerque: World Books, 1995), p. 25.

6 See, for some examples: *Society for Asian & Comparative Philosophy* (est. 1967: http://www.sacpweb.org/), *Wiener Gesellschaft für interkulturelle Philosophie* (WiGiP, est. 1994: http://www.wigip.org), *Gesellschaft für interkulturelle Philosophie* (GIP, est. 1992: http://www.int-gip.de), *Académie du Midi* (est. 1988: http://www.uni-trier.de/index.php?id=32709&L=2), *International Society for Comparative Studies of Chinese and Western Philosophy* (ISCWP, est. 2002: http://www.iscwp.org), *The Columbia*

Society for Comparative Philosophy (CSCP, est. 2006: http://www.cbs.columbia.edu/cscp/), *Simplegadi: rivista di filosofia interculturale* (est. 1996, ceased its activities in 2009).

7 The most successful in terms of output has been the one on *Chinese Philosophy and Culture* (and its explicit component of work in comparative East-West philosophy) at State University of New York Press. Among German-speaking publishing houses, Verlag Karl Alber and its series *Welten der Philosophie* has gained much prominence since its inception in 2009.

8 The most prestigious journals in the field are *Philosophy East and West* (est. 1951), *polylog: Zeitschrift für interkulturelles Philosophieren* (est. 1998), *Dao: A Journal of Comparative Philosophy* (est. 2001), *Comparative and Continental Philosophy* (est. 2009), *Comparative Philosophy* (est. 2010), and *Confluence: Online Journal of World Philosophies* (est. 2014). Journals with an area of focus but featuring many articles on comparative philosophy are *Journal of Indian Philosophy* (est. 1970), *Journal of Chinese Philosophy* (est. 1973), *Asian Philosophy: An International Journal of the Philosophical Traditions of the East* (est. 1991), and *Frontiers of Philosophy in China* (est. 2006). Articles on comparative philosophy are, of course, also occasionally found in general journals of philosophy, such as *International Philosophical Quarterly* (est. 1961) or *Allgemeine Zeitschrift für Philosophie* (est. 1976).

9 Ronnie Littlejohn, "Comparative Philosophy," http://www.iep.utm.edu/comparat/ (accessed December 27, 2014).

10 Robert E. Allinson, "The Myth of Comparative Philosophy or the Comparative Philosophy Malgré Lui," in *Two Roads to Wisdom? Chinese and Analytical Philosophical Traditions*, ed. Bo Mou (Chicago: Open Court, 2001), pp. 269–92; Dunhua Zhao (ed.), *Dialogue of Philosophies, Religions and Civilizations in the Era of Globalization* (Washington, DC: The Council for Research in Values and Philosophy, 2007).

11 Littlejohn, "Comparative Philosophy."

12 David Wong, "Comparative Philosophy: Chinese and Western," http://plato.stanford.edu/entries/comparphil-chiwes/ (accessed December 27, 2014).

13 P. T. Raju, *Introduction to Comparative Philosophy* (Delhi: Motilal Banarsidass, 1992), p. vii.

14 K. Tanaka, "Davidson and Chinese Conceptual Scheme," in *Davidson's Philosophy and Chinese Philosophy: Constructive Engagement*, ed. Bo Mou (Leiden: Brill, 2006), p. 55.

15 See also T. Itzutsu, *Sufism and Taoism: A Comparative Study of Key Philosophical Concepts* (Berkeley: University of California Press, 1983); Stephen C. Angle, "The Minimal Definition and Methodology of Comparative Philosophy: A Report from a Conference," *Comparative Philosophy* 1, no. 1 (2010), pp. 106–10; Monika Kirloskar-Steinbach, Geeta Ramana and James Maffie, "Introducing Confluence: A Thematic Essay," *Confluence* 1, no. 1 (2014), pp. 7–63.

16 Tanaka, "Davidson and Chinese Conceptual Scheme", p. 55.

17 William Edelglass and Jay L. Garfield, "Introduction," in *The Oxford Handbook of World Philosophy*, ed. William Edelglass and Jay L. Garfield (Oxford: Oxford University Press, 2011), p. 4.

18 Allinson, "The Myth of Comparative Philosophy", p. 270.

19 Ibid., p. 281. A similar sort of wrangling between admitting that all philosophy is comparative and carving out a realm for comparative philosophy as intercultural philosophy is visible in Raimundo Panikkar's meta-discussion of "comparative

philosophy": Raimundo Panikkar, "What Is Comparative Philosophy Comparing?," in *Interpreting Across Boundaries: New Essays in Comparative Philosophy*, ed. Gerry J. Larson and Eliot Deutsch (Princeton: Princeton University Press, 1988), pp. 116–36. See also: Ralph Weber, "Raimon Panikkar, and What 'Philosophy' is Comparative Philosophy Comparing," *Cirpit Review*, no. 4 (2013), pp. 167–76.

20 J. F. Staal, *Advaita and Neoplatonism. A Critical Study in Comparative Philosophy* (Madras: University of Madras, 1961), p. 16.

21 See Ralph Weber, "Comparative Philosophy and the Tertium: Comparing What with What, and in What Regard?," *Dao: A Journal of Comparative Philosophy* 13, no. 2 (2014), pp. 151–71; Ralph Weber, "'How to Compare?'—On the Methodological State of Comparative Philosophy," *Philosophy Compass* 8, no. 7 (2013), pp. 593–603.

22 Charles Taylor writes: "There is a set of problems about comparison. These invariably arise for any group of people engaged in understanding a culture or religion which is not theirs. How does the home culture obtrude? Can we neutralize it altogether, and ought we to try? Or are we always engaged in some implicit, if not explicit, comparison when we try to understand another culture? If so, where do we get the language in which this can be non-distortively carried out? If it is just our home language, then the enterprise looks vitiated by ethnocentrism from the start." See Charles Taylor, "Comparison, History, Truth," in *Philosophical Arguments* (Cambridge, MA: Harvard University Press, 1995), pp. 146–47.

23 Bina Gupta and J. N. Mohanty, "General Introduction," in *Philosophical Questions: East and West* (Lanham: Rowman & Littlefield, 2000), p. xii.

24 Merle Johnson (ed.), *More Maxims of Mark*, privately published in November 1927. See: Mark Twain, *Collected Tales, Sketches, Speeches and Essays*, vol. 2, 1891-1910, edited by Louis J. Budd (New York: Library of America, 1992), p. 942.

25 Alisdair MacIntyre, "Books in Review," *Political Theory* 11, no. 4 (1983), p. 623.

26 Michel Foucault, *The Order of Things: An Archeology of the Human Sciences* (New York: Pantheon, 1970), p. xv.

27 Rorty, certainly not shy to use provocation whenever it served his purposes, later came to state some "hunches" that seem to contradict his earlier views: "My hunch is that our sense of where to connect up Indian and Western texts will change dramatically when and if people who have read quite a few of both begin to write books which are not clearly identifiable as belonging to any particular genre, and are not clearly identifiable as either Western or Eastern. . . . My hunch is that the best vehicle for such imaginative flights will be texts which are neither comparisons and contrasts between previously-delimited domains within traditions, nor comparisons between traditions as a whole, but works of brilliant bricolage." Richard Rorty, "Letter 4: Richard Rorty to Anindita Balslev," in *Cultural Otherness: A Correspondence with Richard Rorty*, 2nd edn., ed. Anindita Balslev (Atlanta: Scholars Press, 1999), pp. 68–69. We would, of course, add that Rorty simply was ignorant of those people who were already writing the sort of "brilliant bricolages" he was expecting in the future.

28 For a recent account amply showcasing the difficulty of coming up with a rough-and-ready notion of analytic philosophy, see Hans-Johann Glock, *What is Analytic Philosophy?* (Cambridge: Cambridge University Press, 2008).

29 We have responded to each of these arguments separately in some detail elsewhere, see Arindam Chakrabarti, "Rationality in Indian Thought," in *A Companion to World Philosophies*, ed. Eliot Deutsch and Ron Bontekoe (Oxford: Blackwell Publishers, 1997), pp. 259–78.

30 Stephen Phillips, "Counter Matilal's Bias: The Philosophically Respectable in Indian Spiritual Thought," *Studies in Humanities and Social Sciences* 3, no. 2 (1996), pp. 173–84.
31 Paul Bernier, "Dignāga on Reflexive Consciousness," *Philosophy East and West* 65, no. 1 (2015), pp. 125–56. The same issue has three other explicit engagements with the problems of comparing Chinese and European philosophies.
32 Abhinavagupta (*Īśvara-Pratyabhijnā-Vimarśinī* 1/5/19).
33 John McDowell, *Mind and World* (Cambridge, MA: Harvard University Press, 1996), pp. 56–57.
34 See Amber Carpenter and Jonardon Ganeri, "Can You Seek the Answer to this Question?," *Australasian Journal of Philosophy* 88, no. 4 (2010), pp. 571–94.
35 Steve Odin, *The Social Self in Zen and American Pragmatism* (Albany: State University of New York Press, 1996), p. 349.
36 Jay L. Garfield, *Empty Words: Buddhist Philosophy and Cross-Cultural Interpretation* (Oxford: Oxford University Press, 2002).
37 Garfield, *Empty Words*, p. 168.
38 Ibid.
39 Ibid., pp. 168–69.

References

Allinson, R. E. (2001), "The Myth of Comparative Philosophy or the Comparative Philosophy Malgré Lui," in B. Mou (ed.), *Two Roads to Wisdom? Chinese and Analytical Philosophical Traditions*, Chicago: Open Court, pp. 269–92.

Angle, S. C. (2010), "The Minimal Definition and Methodology of Comparative Philosophy: A Report from a Conference," *Comparative Philosophy*, 1 (1), pp. 106–10.

Bahm, A. (1995), *Comparative Philosophy: Western, Indian and Chinese Philosophies Compared*, rev. edn, Albuquerque: World Books.

Bernier, P. (2015), "Dignāga on Reflexive Consciousness," *Philosophy East and West*, 65 (1), pp. 125–56.

Bhoja (2007), *Śṛngāra-prakāśa of Bhojaraja* (1–25, 26–36 Prakasa; Vol. I & II), ed. R. P. Dwivedi, New Delhi: IGNCA and Varanasi: Kalidasa Sansthan.

Carpenter, A. and Ganeri, J. (2010), "Can You Seek the Answer to this Question?," *Australasian Journal of Philosophy*, 88 (4), pp. 571–94.

Chakrabarti, A. (1997), "Rationality in Indian Thought," in E. Deutsch and R. Bontekoe (eds), *A Companion to World Philosophies*, Oxford: Blackwell Publishers, pp. 259–78.

Edelglass, W. and Garfield, J. L. (2011), "Introduction," in W. Edelglass and J. L. Garfield (eds), *The Oxford Handbook of World Philosophy*, Oxford: Oxford University Press.

Foucault, M. (1970), *The Order of Things: An Archeology of the Human Sciences*, New York: Pantheon.

Frisby, D. and Featherstone, M., eds (1997), *Simmel on Culture*, London: Sage Publications.

Garfield, J. L. (2002), *Empty Words: Buddhist Philosophy and Cross-Cultural Interpretation*, Oxford: Oxford University Press.

Glock, H.-J. (2008), *What is Analytic Philosophy?* Cambridge: Cambridge University Press.

Gupta, B. and Mohanty, J. N. (2000), "General Introduction," in *Philosophical Questions: East and West*, Lanham: Rowman & Littlefield.

Itzutsu, T. (1983), *Sufism and Taoism: A Comparative Study of Key Philosophical Concepts*, Berkeley: University of California Press.

Kirloskar-Steinbach, M., Ramana, G., and Maffie, J. (2014), "Introducing Confluence: A Thematic Essay," *Confluence*, 1 (1), pp. 7–63.
Littlejohn, R., "Comparative Philosophy," http://www.iep.utm.edu/comparat/ (accessed December 27, 2014).
MacIntyre, A. (1983), "Books in Review," *Political Theory*, 11 (4), pp. 623–26.
McDowell, J. (1996), *Mind and World*, Cambridge, MA: Harvard University Press.
Odin, S. (1996), *The Social Self in Zen and American Pragmatism*, Albany: State University of New York Press.
Panikkar, R. (1988), "What Is Comparative Philosophy Comparing?," in G. J. Larson and E. Deutsch (eds), *Interpreting Across Boundaries: New Essays in Comparative Philosophy*, Princeton: Princeton University Press.
Phillips, S. (1996), "Counter Matilal's Bias: The Philosophically Respectable in Indian Spiritual Thought", *Studies in Humanities and Social Sciences*, 3 (2), pp. 173–84.
Raju, P. T. (1992), *Introduction to Comparative Philosophy*, Delhi: Motilal Banarsidass.
Rorty, R. (1999), "Letter 4: Richard Rorty to Anindita Balslev," in Anindita Balslev (ed.), *Cultural Otherness: A Correspondence with Richard Rorty*, 2nd edn, Atlanta: Scholars Press, pp. 67–74.
Staal, J. F. (1961), *Advaita and Neoplatonism. A Critical Study in Comparative Philosophy*, Madras: University of Madras.
Stalnaker, A. (2006), *Overcoming Our Evil: Human Nature and Spiritual Exercises in Xunzi and Augustine*, Washington, DC: Georgetown University Press.
Tanaka, K. (2006), "Davidson and Chinese Conceptual Scheme," in B. Mou (ed.), *Davidson's Philosophy and Chinese Philosophy: Constructive Engagement*, Leiden: Brill, pp. 55–71.
Taylor, C. (1995), "Comparison, History, Truth," in *Philosophical Arguments*, Cambridge, MA: Harvard University Press.
Twain, M. (1992), *Collected Tales, Sketches, Speeches and Essays*, vol. 2, 1891-1910, edited by L. J. Budd, New York: Library of America.
Weber, R. (2013a), "'How to Compare?'—On the Methodological State of Comparative Philosophy," *Philosophy Compass*, 8 (7), pp. 593–603.
Weber, R. (2013b), "Raimon Panikkar, and What 'Philosophy' is Comparative Philosophy Comparing," *Cirpit Review*, 4, pp. 167–76.
Weber, R. (2014), "Comparative Philosophy and the Tertium: Comparing What with What, and in What Regard?," *Dao: A Journal of Comparative Philosophy*, 13 (2), pp. 151–71.
Wong, D. (2001), "Comparative Philosophy: Chinese and Western," http://plato.stanford.edu/entries/comparphil-chiwes/ (accessed December 27, 2014).
Zhao, D., ed. (2007), *Dialogue of Philosophies, Religions and Civilizations in the Era of Globalization*, Washington, DC: The Council for Research in Values and Philosophy.

1

Count Nouns, Mass Nouns, and Translatability: The Case of Tibetan Buddhist Logical Literature

Tom J. F. Tillemans

The difference between count nouns and mass nouns is usually first approached as a difference in word classes recognizable in terms of syntax: the former are words like "table" that can take numerals, vary in singular and plural, be qualified by adjectives like "many," and have other such morphosyntactic tags, while the latter are words like "water" that do not take numerals, do not vary in grammatical number, take adjectives like "much," etc. We also like to think that there is a semantic and a corresponding ontological distinction. Words that refer to things have clear boundaries of individuation while those that refer to stuffs do not have such boundaries—this too is supposedly captured by count-mass noun distinctions. None of these criteria, even in their more sophisticated elaborations, seem to be watertight across languages. Precision falters for many reasons. Some Asian languages, like Chinese and Tibetan, arguably have count-mass distinctions, but without many of the usual morphosyntactic tags. As for the thing-stuff distinction, it becomes problematic even with common English mass nouns like "furniture," where obviously each piece of furniture is a thing and not an amorphous stuff like water. And, crucially, the idea of neat word classes in one language or across languages fails. In many languages there are uses of nouns as count or mass in different contexts ("Waiter, three coffees please!," "Coffee spilt all over her new carpet." "She heard several loud sounds." "Sound is everywhere"). In some languages, like Chinese, any noun can be used as a mass noun,[1] while in many other languages specific nouns may not exhibit that same variability of use at all. Finally, what is count in one language may be mass in another (the French count noun "baggage" has a corresponding English mass noun "luggage"), so that establishing clear classes across languages proves to be impossible. Probably the most adequate approach for our purposes is a semantic one turning on uses and functions rather than word classes: nouns are used as count nouns in a specific language when they divide their reference into distinguishable and countable objects; they are used as mass nouns when they do not.

Are mass-and count-noun distinctions in source languages important when one translates Buddhist texts into English? Let me begin with a commonly cited position that I think is *not* an answer to that question for translators of Sino-Tibetan languages. This is the view that there simply is no distinction at all between mass and count nouns in these Asian languages, and that there are hence only the "impositions" of translators—the formulation is that of the philosopher W. V. Quine (1968) in his work on indeterminacy of translation and ontological relativity.[2] Indeed, Quine had famously suggested that Chinese and Japanese were arbitrary in precisely this way. He made much of the fact that classifiers (=Chin. *liang ci* 量詞) are used with all common nouns and that it is therefore impossible to decide whether a phrase like *yi tou niu* 一頭牛 should be translated as "one cow" or "one head of cattle."[3] As he said bluntly, "Between the two accounts of Japanese classifiers there is no question of right and wrong."[4]

This is hard to defend as a description of actual language usage. Sinologists muster ample textual data that show that there are mass and count nouns in Chinese, using what seem to me both syntactic and semantic criteria. They may have differences on how that mass-count noun distinction unpacks in particular periods, whether it needs to be supplemented, whether mass nouns predominate, etc., but the very applicability of a mass versus count noun distinction to Chinese or Japanese is hardly in question.[5] The obscurity of some classifiers is not generalizable to all uses of nouns. First, classifiers are often not used in classical Chinese; *yi niu* 一牛 (one cow) seems, uncontroversially, a count-noun usage. Moreover, in modern Chinese, there is evidence that children learn the difference between sortal and mensural classifiers, and that this difference in types of classifiers more or less mirrors the count-mass distinction.[6] Finally, taking a straightforward linguistic perspective, one could say that *you niu* 有牛 (literally, "There exists *cow*") is a mass-noun usage of "cow" and *yi niu* 一牛 (one cow) is a count-noun. Such a version of mass-and count-noun usage is not just restricted to Chinese. It is largely mirrored in Tibetan. Although Tibetan does not use classifiers, neither in the modern nor in the classical language, it is certainly fair to say that *ba lang yod* (Cow exists, There exists *cow.*) is a mass noun usage and *ba lang gcig* (one cow) is a count noun usage, and so on in general for common nouns in Tibetan, be it *rta* (horse), *khang pa* (house), *mi* (people), *mo ṭa* (car), and so forth. We will return to parallels between Tibetan and Chinese in more detail later.

Interestingly enough, however, Quine did not adopt a straightforward linguistic perspective on the usage of nouns in Asian languages. Instead, he seductively combined the linguistic/philological problems in describing the usage of nouns in particular languages with the philosophical issues that arise in interpreting reference in *any* language. His real point was that we cannot determine the *sorts of entities people talk about* (in Chinese or any other language) among equivalent possibilities, be it individual oxen versus heads of cattle, particular instances of properties versus distributions of a stuff or fusion (horses vs. discontinuous distributions of horsey stuff or the fusion of all horses), or even mathematical expressions versus their corresponding Gödel numbers. The type of entities referred to, or in other terms, "the inherent ontology of the language," is inscrutable. Now, this is a different issue from the question as to whether a given language just simply has mass and count nouns. One could very well say that there are determinate answers to the existence of mass and count nouns in many languages and that *yi niu, ba lang gcig*, and the like are best translated as "one cow," but also say that the sort of entities the mass or count nouns refer to remains indeterminate and inscrutable. Indeed, *that* is a point of view I would defend, not just with regard to Asian languages like Chinese and Tibetan, but across the board.

Let us grant that there are count nouns and mass nouns in Sino-Tibetan languages and that reading a Tibetan or Chinese sentence as having mass or count nouns is not just an arbitrary imposition of the European translator. Let us also grant that Sino-Tibetan languages use mass nouns much much more frequently than European languages do, but that European translators are generally unfazed and adopt strategies of reformulation (We will see the details of these strategies below). That much should be a nonissue. What *is*, however, a genuine issue for translators and philosophers is whether there are, at least sometimes, uses of mass nouns in the Asian source languages that *preclude* any adequate translation or reformulation in a European language. Are there such uses that are more than quirks and that a translator of Buddhist texts fundamentally cannot translate, reformulate, nor, perhaps, even satisfactorily paraphrase? In what follows, I will frame the problems largely in terms of translation into English, but one can no doubt make the same arguments for other European languages.

Nowhere, in my opinion, is *that* issue of translatability of mass nouns more urgent than in the indigenous Tibetan Buddhist literature of *bsdus grwa* (Collected Topics). This type of Tibetan Epistemological, or *tshad ma (*=Skt. *pramāṇa),* literature starts in the fifteenth century and is often said to stem from the earlier Epistemological Summaries (*tshad ma bsdus pa*) of Phya pa Chos kyi seng ge (1109–1169) and his school, although the ancestry is actually quite unclear.[7] The earliest work of Collected Topics is the *Rwa bstod bsdus grwa* of the dGe lugs pa writer 'Jam dbyangs mchog lha 'od zer (1429–1500). Several other authors subsequently took up the genre of *bsdus grwa*.[8] 'Jam dbyangs bzhad pa (1648–1722), of Bla brang monastery, wrote a small Collected Topics in verse, and four other works concerned, in one way or another, with subjects in *bsdus grwa*. There are works of varying sizes and affiliated with different dGe lugs pa monastic colleges—for example, the Collected Topics of bSe Ngag dbang bkra shis (1678–1738) representing the tradition of Bla brang, or those of Yongs 'dzin Phur bu lcog byams pa tshul khrims rgya mtsho (1825–1901), representing, especially, Se ra.[9] Although the Sa skya tradition is known to have engaged in very vigorous polemics against the "Epistemological Summaries" (*tshad ma bsdus pa*) of the Phya-tradition, there are also, curiously enough, Sa skya pa "Summaries"[10] and there even seems to be a seventeenth-century Sa skya pa *bsdus grw*a, the *Chos rnam rgyal gi bsdus grwa*.[11] The sources I use for reasonings from Collected Topics are essentially the *Yongs 'dzin bsdus grwa, bSe bsdus grwa, Rwa stod bsdus grwa*, and the *bsDus grwa brjed tho* of dGe bshes Ngag nyi ma (twentieth century).[12] Note, too, that the present article builds upon and to some degree presupposes Tillemans, "On the so-called Difficult Point of the Apoha Theory" (1999).[13] Many of the supporting explanations and detailed translations from Tibetan works can be found there and will not be repeated here.

bsDus grwa semantic problems do not just remain in *bsdus grwa* texts: as argued in Tillemans (1999), they spread to indigenous commentaries on Pramāṇa, Abhidharma, and Madhyamaka that use *bsdus grwa* notions, and they make various philosophical debates notoriously hard to translate into acceptable English. What are these seemingly intractable semantic issues? Puns and equivocations in Tibetan—and

Collected Topics is certainly rich with them—are *not* intractable issues, nor are the many syntactic tricks in Collected Topics that involve plays on Tibetan grammatical cases, such as the genitive used in relative clauses. Unpacking puns and exposing syntactic sleight of hand may be more or less laborious, but in the end there is nothing that cannot be rendered adequately. The problems that interest us turn on a peculiar use of mass nouns. These semantic issues will be my focus here as they pose problems for which we have no solution now, nor in the easily foreseeable future. They are very different from the many *bsdus grwa* brainteasers that turn on *double entendre* and devious syntax.

The problem is the following: Subject terms (*chos can*) in Tibetan Collected Topics arguments, like *vase* (*bum pa*), *tree* (*shing*), *knowable thing* (*shes bya*), *non-red* (*dmar po ma yin pa*), *good reason* (*rtags yang dag*), and many others are often not translatable by the count nouns they would seem to require in a Western target language—"a vase," "some/all vases," "this vase," "some/all/a/the good reason," "some/all/a/one/the knowable thing," "some/all/a/one non-red thing," and so on. Such count-noun translations would not preserve truth. Two examples will have to suffice. Here and in what follows I have put the grammatically problematic English terms in italics:

(1) "*Non-red* (*dmar po ma yin pa*) is permanent, because there are common bases between *permanent* and it (*khyod dang rtag pa'i gzhi mthun yod pa'i phyir*)"
Comment: The same example can be constructed with *knowable thing*, *good reason*, and many other entities; the reason is a usual one in *bsdus grwa* to prove that something is permanent. The point of "Y having a common basis with X" is that there are cases of Y that are also cases of X. There are non-red things that are permanent, for example, space (*nam mkha'* = Skt. *ākāśa*).[14]

(2) "*Defining characteristic* (*mtshan nyid* = Skt. *lakṣaṇa*) [of anything] is not a defining characteristic (*mtshan nyid mtshan nyid ma yin*), because it has a defining characteristic and is thus a definiendum (*mtshon bya* = Skt. *lakṣya*)."[15]
Comment: *Defining characteristic* itself is defined as *what satisfies the three criteria for a substantial property* (*rdzas yod chos gsum tshang ba*) and is thus itself something that can be defined, that is, a *mtshon bya*.

Here, in more detail, is the problem in translating (1) and (2) if we use available English renderings involving "all," "some," "a," "the/this." Sentences like (1) will be false in the philosophy of Collected Topics when *dmar po ma yin pa* or *shes bya* are rendered as "all non-red things" or "all knowable things," just as (2) is also false if one renders *mtshan nyid* as "all defining characteristics." A sentence like (1) becomes trivially true if we render *dmar po ma yin pa* or *shes bya* as "some non-red things," "some knowable things," "a non-red/knowable thing," and it is perhaps true when rendered as "the or this non-red/knowable thing." In fact, in Collected Topics, (1) is *not* a trivial truth or just a possible truth: it is held to be true, but nonobvious and needing justification—hence the reason about common bases.

What is more dramatic for translation than (1) is (2): it becomes false if *mtshan nyid* is taken as "some" or "all" defining characteristics or even "a/the/this defining characteristic." These renderings would all be false because Collected Topics holds that every defining characteristic is, indeed, a defining characteristic: to say that some, all, or the/a, defining characteristics, are not defining characteristics would lead to howls of derision—it would be said to be absurd (*ha cang thal* = Skt. *atiprasaṅga*) because of being a flat-out contradiction.[16] If we use a generic "the" we get no further, as "the defining characteristic is not a defining characteristic" remains false, and, indeed, it is not at all clear that the generic knowable thing would be permanent for an adept of *bsdus grwa.*

Finally, one cannot say that subject terms in Tibetan are actually veiled uses of an abstract term, as if we should simply translate *bum pa* by "vaseness" and *shes bya* by "knowable thingness" much as if it were the Tibetan *bum pa nyid* and *shes bya nyid* (= the Sanskrit *ghaṭatva* and *jñeyatva*). It is a cliché in Tibetan philosophical texts to say "*vase* is bulbous, splay-bottomed and able to perform the function of carrying water" (*bum pa lto ldir zhabs zhum chu skyor kyi don byed nus pa yin*): vaseness, as an abstract entity or a property, is obviously not able to carry water, and is thus *not* what is being talked about. One can come up with many other such examples to show that terms do not designate such abstract entities.[17]

What is left as a plausible English translation? The problem in (1) and (2) and in other such cases is that they seem to need some sort of a mass noun rendering, along the lines of "knowable thing," "defining characteristic," "vase," "good reason," etc., if our translation of the Tibetan argument is to both preserve truth and not fall into triviality. But, of course, "vase," "good reason," "knowable thing" and the like are not used as mass nouns in English, French, Dutch, etc., that is, they do not behave like "snow," "water," and the like. "Vase" does divide its reference into readily distinguishable and countable objects. It would usually be considered a solecism in English to speak of *vase* (or French *cruche,* Dutch *vaas,* German *Vase,* etc.) or *knowable thing* as being found here, here, and here—one naturally understands the sentence "Vases are found in the museum," but not "*Vase* is found the museum,"—and it makes no sense to speak of a collection of *vase* or a set of *knowable thing,* although a collection of vases and a set of knowable things are, of course, perfectly fine. The result is this: we are, so it seems, forced to translate many philosophical passages in a way we fundamentally do not understand in our own languages, and there is no unpacking in English that would preserve the rationality, and hence comprehensibility, of the Tibetan philosophical discussion.

Tibetans themselves were aware that the meaning of *bum pa* (vase) was not the same as the meaning of *bum pa 'ga' zhig* (some vases), *bum pa thams cad* (all vases), *bum pa 'di* (this vase), *bum pa zhig* (a vase), etc.—they saw that difference as applying mutatis mutandis to "good reason" (*rtags yang dag*) versus "a/some/all good reasons" and numerous other terms, and thought that it was an important difference with philosophical consequences. Indeed, it was emphasized by a figure no less than Tsong kha pa (1357–1419) himself, in his *Tshad ma'i brjed byang chen mo,* that although something may be true of X itself, that is, *reason, positive phenomenon, universal* etc., it need not be true of all x's (all reasons, universals, etc.). Tsong kha pa says that when we get this subtlety wrong, it is a major obstacle (*gegs*) because of which the rest of our thinking goes astray—he applies his diagnosis across the board to metaphysics, philosophy of logic, and philosophy of language.[18] The problem supposedly arises when we fail to reconcile two key propositions in Buddhist nominalism:

> *rtog pa'i yul rang mtshan ma yin pa dang rang mtshan rtog pa'i yul yin pa gnyis 'gal bar 'dzin pa nyid yin no/.* [The obstacle] is precisely to grasp as contradictory the pair [of propositions] that *object of thought* (*rtog pa'i yul*) is not a particular and that particulars are [nonetheless] objects of thought.[19]

lCang skya Rol pa'i rdo rje (1717–1786) elaborates the solution:

> *de'i rgyu mtshan yang rtog pa'i dngos yul gyi rang ldog rang mtshan ma yin kyang rang mtshan rtog pa'i dngos yul du 'gyur ba mi 'gal bas . . .* Now, the reason behind this is that there would be no contradiction [in the fact] that the property *per se* (*rang ldog*, Skt. **svavyāvṛtti*) *explicit object of thought* is not a particular, but that particulars are explicit objects of thought.[20]

On Tsong kha pa's diagnosis, then, people supposedly fail to understand nominalism because they cannot see the compatibility between the fact that *object of thought* itself is a fictional creation and, hence, not a real particular (*rang mtshan* = Skt. *svalakṣaṇa*) and the fact that there are objects of thought that are particulars (e.g., vases, tables, chairs, etc. are real particulars and also objects of thought simply in that we do think about them). The solution is that we need to be able to properly differentiate *object of thought per se* (i.e., X itself) and objects of thought (i.e., the individual x's)—while the former is a fictional universal, the latter need not be fictions at all.

His disciple rGyal tshab rje (1364–1432), in *rNam 'grel thar lam gsal byed*, called this X versus x's differentiation, somewhat bombastically, the "supreme main difficult point which is difficult to understand in this philosophical tradition [i.e., Buddhist logic]" (*gzhung lugs 'di'i rtogs dka' ba'i gnad gyi gtso bo dam pa*), in short, the hard point in the Buddhist's philosophy of language and logic.[21] It becomes a recurring dGe lugs pa position, one that is regularly invoked in key arguments by textbook writers such as Paṇchen bSod nams grags pa (1478–1554), Se ra rje btsun Chos kyi rgyal mtshan (1469–1546), lCang skya Rol pa'i rdo rje, and others, and is known as the "main difficult to understand point of the anyāpoha [theory of language]" (*gzhan sel gyi rtogs dkar ba'i gnad kyi gtso bo*).[22] It is what lies behind the *bsdus grwa* arguments that we see represented by (1) and (2). In other terms, (1) and (2) are just the tip of an iceberg!

Where does this "difficult point" leave translators? The supposed difference between talking of X itself (*vase, reason, object of thought,* etc.) and talk of x's (vases, reasons, objects of thought, etc.) was no minor matter for these thinkers. Like it or not, it is, for a dGe lugs pa, nothing short of essential to doing philosophy. If Tsong kha pa and rGyal tshab rje are right and we do have to talk of X itself as opposed to x's, or if we simply want to translate their theories, we would have to translate solecistically to render their philosophical thinking in English.

Now, at this point, it might well be replied that this philosophical thinking and writing in Tibetan about X itself versus x's is, indeed, unintelligible to us; the conclusion to draw is not that it is interesting, but that it is just better confined to the scrap-heap of bad philosophy. Tibetan writers' uses of terms in the sense of X itself, so it might be argued, are confused and would regularly need disambiguation to be explained away. If we are to avoid unintelligibility in English, a term like *bum pa* (vase) or *shes bya* (knowable thing) would sometimes have to be interpreted to refer to some or all individual things, sometimes to an abstract universal property, like vaseness, or knowable thinghood, or perhaps even the generic vase, but never to the mysterious *vase itself* or *knowable thing itself*.

However, the proposed disambiguation of troublesome contexts would be extremely inelegant and complex, necessitating *ad hoc* decisions for many arguments: it is generally simpler, and hence desirable, to find a univocal semantics where possible, even if that is not the semantics of a Western language. Worse, it is a type of uncharity to maintain that because such and such a semantics leads to problems when "translating up" into a prestigious language, it *must* be wrong and hence demand complex disambiguation, as if it were simply a muddle. It is remarkable that many very intelligent Tibetan traditional scholars do not feel that talk of X itself is problematic at all. In explaining Collected Topics, they will often insist that the subject terms (*chos can*) in most debates refer to "vase itself" (*bum pa kho rang*), "knowable thing itself" (*shes bya kho rang*), or "defining characteristic itself" (*mtshan nyid kho rang*), or equivalently, they will use the terms *bum pa rang ldog, shes bya rang ldog, mtshan nyid rang ldog* ("vase, the property per se," etc.).[23] What is striking is that for many Tibetans, *bum pa, shes bya,* etc. *are felt to be univocal and perfectly clear*, needing no disambiguation in terms of vaseness and vases. In my vivid personal experience of learning Collected Topics, my teachers frequently felt puzzlement and even exasperation that something so obvious would be so inexplicably difficult and suspect to their foreign student. In fact, their linguistic intuitions probably deserve greater weight than our nagging feeling that something is going wrong in their Tibetan and hence needs the disambiguation that a European supposedly can, and should, provide.[24]

Would a parallel with Chinese be of help in understanding the problematic Tibetan uses of mass nouns? The specific Tibetan debates in Collected Topics are not, as far as we can see, of Chinese ancestry, with the likely exception of a Tibetan version of the white horse argument (see Appendix). Could one perhaps get some support from common syntactic and semantic features of the Sino-Tibetan family of languages? In Tibetan, as in Chinese, mass and count are not rigid word classes, but more like functions of words. There is no clear *inherent or essential feature* of the Tibetan language that fixes nouns as mass nouns by word class; there are uses of nouns as mass nouns and uses as count nouns—one says *sgra mi rtag pa yin pa* ("Sound is impermanent"), but also *sgra gnyis thos pa* ("She heard two sounds"). Moreover, Tibetan is like Chinese in that all nouns, including "horse" (Tib. *rta*, Chin. *ma* 馬), "person" (Tib. *mi*, Chin. *ren* 人) and the like, can be used as mass nouns and are also used thus frequently. To take an unphilosophical and very simple example, just as in modern Chinese, it is normal in colloquial Tibetan to say, literally, "in Lhasa, *car* exists. In Lhasa *car* is many" (*lha sa la mo ṭa yod. lha sa la mo ṭa mang po ('dug/yod)* = Chin. *zai Lasa you che* 在拉薩有車; *zai Lasa che duo* 在拉薩車多). It is thus not surprising that the possibilities of using Tibetan nouns as mass nouns are much greater than in English, French, and other European languages and that nouns like *bum pa* can easily be mass nouns while the English noun *vase*, French *cruche* or Dutch *vaas* cannot.

Is *that* all there is to the translational issues in Tibetan philosophical writing turning on uses of mass nouns, that is, the so-called "difficult point"? No. The translational problems in the "difficult point" go beyond the fact that Tibetan, like Chinese, regularly uses mass nouns that we would not countenance as mass nouns in an English translation. Reformulation of those Tibetan or Chinese mass nouns as English count nouns is usually banal, and yields English sentences *salva veritate*, that is, with no change in truth value—Tibetan *mo ṭa mang po* and Chinese *che duo* 車多 (Car [is] many) are rendered as "There are many cars" routinely and unproblematically. I would see this as support for a position with regard to Tibetan like that of Chris Fraser with regard to Chinese, namely, that usage of mass nouns or count nouns has no implications about what kind of entities people are speaking about.[25] Indeed, one could well deflate much Tibetan similarly. Most uses of mass nouns—for example, in colloquial speech, in history texts, in opera and epics, in Marxist or Buddhist tracts, what have you—would not have *any* implications for whether one is speaking of particulars, manifestations of universals, distributions of fusions, and other such ontologies. There would be no semantic and metaphysical issues at stake in such cases, only verbal usage. To supplement Fraser a bit, we could say that there certainly are mass and count nouns, but that their reference remains inscrutable. One can apply a one-to-one permutation function to the referents of nouns and predicates so that the inherent ontology of the language in question is not only unknowable but immaterial to its statements being true or false.[26] Inscrutability of reference, if right, puts paid to a myriad of modern views about inherent metaphysics of languages and ways of thinking supposedly peculiar to their speakers alone.[27]

That said, the specific problem of understanding *bsdus grwa* and the "difficult point" is very different from the grand-scale discussion about inherent semantics. It is certainly not resolved by simply saying that statements about facts that we understand are interpretable indifferently, *salva veritate*, in terms of several sorts of entities, so that we could, for example, just as well be talking about distributions of the rabbit fusion (or instantiations of an abstract entity, rabbithood) being furry instead of individual rabbits. Rather, the point in bringing up (1) and (2), as we saw, is that we do not understand why these particular kinds of Tibetan statements and their English translations are supposedly true; we do not adequately understand the facts the Tibetan theoreticians are talking about *at all* when they talk about *vase* itself or *knowable thing* itself nor the reasons why they assert what they do of them. Usual translational strategies to come up with reformulations in English *salva veritate* are thus simply not available here. More specifically, we are confronted with a dilemma. On the one hand, when the reformulations of (1) and (2) are in proper, clear English, they do not conserve truth value, but, on the other hand, if we seek to conserve truth value, we are forced into using a badly obscure English, so odd that certain terms are in italics and scare-quotes, suggesting unintelligibility. This is a problem of the philosophical implications of the Tibetan "difficult point." They leave (1) and (2) with specific problems of intelligibility and translatability that more ordinary Tibetan does not have.

This dGe lugs theoretical position on Tibetan subject terms was important in Tibetan theorizing about language, but not surprisingly it was also contested by many non-dGe lugs thinkers. Sa skya pa thinkers like Kun dga' rgyal mtshan (1182–1251), Go rams pa bSod nams seng ge (1429–1489), and gSer mdog Paṇchen Śākya mchog ldan (1428–1507) were oriented more toward a more Indian Buddhist semantics where words either had to refer to real individual things, that is, particulars (*rang mtshan* = Skt. *svalakṣaṇa*), or to fictional universals (*spyi mtshan* = Skt. *sāmānyalakṣaṇa*), with no middle ground of a universal that would also be a real thing (*spyi dngos po ba*). They were thus often very skeptical about interpretations of their own language in accordance with the "difficult point." Talk of X itself along the lines of the "difficult point" theorists would, so they thought, lead to a kind of realism about universal properties. *Vase, tree,* and the like would be fully fledged universals present in several particulars, but also fully real as they would possess the ability to perform functions (*don byed nus pa* = Skt. *arthakriyā*). That intra-Tibetan debate took on major importance in contrasting dGe lugs pa/gSang phu versus Sa skya pa Tibetan approaches to the problem of universals and philosophy of language. Go rams pa polemically insisted that talk of "mere tree" (*shing tsam*) as being a real universal (*spyi dngos po ba*) present in particulars was just "verbal obfuscation" (*tshig gi sgrib g.yog*) and an invention of "the snowy Tibetans" (*bod gangs can pa*).[28] The main motivation of these Sa skya thinkers was not so much the mere usage of terms like *tree* (*shing*)—they used those terms too—but the un-Indian aspect of accepting *tree* or *tree itself* as a real universal somehow to be contrasted with trees.

Were Go rams pa and others fair to the dGe lugs pa? They thought, probably rightly in many respects, that the dGe lugs-Phya pa semantic theories and, especially, the resultant metaphysics were out of step with mainstream Indian Buddhist nominalist positions such as what one would find in Dignāga and Dharmakīrti, and they cited *Pramāṇavārttika* commentators like Śākyabuddhi to show that Buddhists should *never* accept universals. Georges Dreyfus and I, in a number of separate publications, have taken up the theories of *spyi dngos po ba* (real universals) in Tibetan thought and the slim Indian antecedents for this theory that might be found in 10th–12th century Kashmiri philosophers like Śaṅkaranandana (=Tib. Bram ze chen po; ca. 940/50–1020/30) and perhaps Bhavyarāja (=Tib. sKal ldan rgyal po).[29] It is certainly arguable that the *spyi dngos po ba* that the dGe lugs pa accepted was not *simply* the universal of non-Buddhist schools, and that it would thus be unfair to accuse them of wholesale betrayal of Buddhist nominalism. Instead, *vase* is a concrete real entity able to perform functions like carrying water, and it is of the same substance (*rdzas gcig* = Skt. *ekadravya*) as the particulars; it is not a universal vaseness (Skt. *ghaṭatva*) that is separate from particulars and instantiated (Skt. *samaveta*) in them, along the lines of the non-Buddhist Nyāya-Vaiśeṣika school (or for that matter, Platonism). It may even be more like a recurring stuff (although certainly not amorphous) than a universal or a thing—one that is found here, here, and here, and that has no existence apart from those distributions. So far, perhaps, so good. Adding the peculiar details of the dGe lugs pa X versus x's distinction, however, would yield entities for which we seem to have no readily available ontological category.[30]

Let me conclude on a nuanced note, taking some distance from the usual discussions about translation and translatability that one finds in analytic philosophy post-W. V. Quine and Donald Davidson. As should be clear, I subscribe to much of the Quine-Davidson position on the inscrutability of reference. I am thus certainly *not* advocating a strong thesis, along the lines of Benjamin Lee Whorf, to the effect that a language has its own inherent ontology and is incommensurable with some or all other languages.[31] I do *not* think that Sino-Tibetan languages have an inherent ontology because of their extensive use of mass nouns. However, I *do* think that philosophical Tibetan as used and interpreted by many indigenous authors presents important problems of translatability because of *their* uses of mass nouns and their promotion of a certain set of problematic truths involving them. The authors I am speaking of represent the school of Buddhism that has been dominant in Tibet since the fifteenth century. When they think the "difficult point" is key to understanding philosophy of language, that is, in a sense, the official Tibetan line. There is a significant problem in translating their writings and the philosophy of their school; there is hence a problem in translating much influential Tibetan philosophy *tout court.*

Some, following Davidson, might say that natural languages are intertranslatable, or that untranslatability is an incoherent notion. And, indeed, it is often repeated, since "On the Very Idea of a Conceptual Scheme," that a culture that did not share with us a common endorsement of a very large number of truths would be thoroughly unintelligible to us—even its difference and foreignness, and for that matter, whether it has a language, would be obscure.[32] However, a Davidsonian *a priori* argument against untranslatability would be overkill in the case at hand. It is clear we do share a very great number of truths with Tibetans and that understanding Tibetan culture is not the type of radically foreign encounter Davidson criticizes as unintelligible. We may not understand the whys and wherefores of utterances in "difficult point" debates, but we easily know that they are utterances, and, indeed, we know quite a lot about the underlying background to them, just as we do about Tibetan medical and pharmacological terms that are often untranslatable in the present state of our scientific terminology.

No doubt, there is often *de facto*, or practical, untranslatability given a current state of knowledge—the language of the Indus Valley civilization, the Minoan Linear A, and Egyptian hieroglyphics before J. F. Champollion come to mind. The Davidsonian arguments, however, are best seen as directed against a much stronger thesis: untranslatability *in principle*, because of inherent features in languages that imply a conceptual scheme incommensurable with that of the translator.[33] It is this *necessary, essential,* or *inherent* untranslatability of languages and the resultant relativity of truth to a language's inherent conceptual scheme that inspired Whorf and repelled Davidson. However, in that case, it is unlikely that the Davidson argument applies if one does not subscribe to inherent linguistic features or cognitive limitations and hence to essential untranslatability.

Essential untranslatability aside, the "difficult point" is, nonetheless, more than a usual practical problem that will be cleared up with new discoveries and more information. What we *can* say in the case at hand is that we see no way out of the translational problems of the "difficult point" given the current requirements of English, and that old Tibet hands who study *bsdus grwa* and related dGe lugs pa thinking in depth will continue, as far as we can foresee, to develop a divided mind, learn how to reason in Tibetan persuasively to Tibetans, but be unable to translate and explain that reasoning satisfactorily in English.[34] That does not entail that truth varies from Tibetan to English, only the recognition that the truths at stake are sometimes very obscure. But it is *enough* untranslatability to be a major obstacle to a cross-cultural dialogue on the predominant Tibetan philosophy of language and logic.

Appendix

Might the debates in Collected Topics have Chinese origins? While at least one Indian *pramāṇa* text was translated into Tibetan from Chinese—for example, the *Nyāyapraveśa* from the translation of Xuanzang[35]—there are no logic commentaries that I know of by Chinese authors of, for example, the Xuanzang school, that made their way into Tibetan. We do find an important commentary on the *Saṃdhinirmocanasūtra* by a student of Xuanzang, Yuan Ce 圓測, that was translated into Tibetan and had a significant influence in Tibet, often being discussed by writers like Tsong kha pa. However, this is not a work on logic and *pramāṇa*: it is a work on hermeneutics and the interpretation of the three cycles of Buddhist teaching.

There is, however, a "white horse" argument found in the Tibetan Collected Topics literature that seems like the strongest candidate for Chinese influence and origins. The debate is very well known among people educated in the dGe lugs pa curriculum, for whom it is typically taken as showing an important Buddhist point, the unfindability of entities under analysis, the impossibility that any macroscopic entity can be localized or identified with one or more of its constituent dharmas/tropes. Here is a representative version as found in *Yongs 'dzin bsdus grwa:*

> *kha cig na re/chos dung dkar po chos can/kha dog yin par thal/dkar po yin pa'i phyir/ma grub na/de chos can/der thal/chos dung dkar po yin pa'i phyir na/'gal khyab la 'bud/'o na kho rang la/rta dkar po chos can/dkar po yin par thal/rta dkar po yin pa'i phyir/khyab pa 'grig/'dod mi nus te/bem po ma yin pa'i phyir te/gang zag yin pa'i phyir te/rta yin pa'i phyir.* (*Yongs 'dzin bsdus grwa chung* ed. Kelsang and Onoda, f. 4a)

> A certain [debater] might say: A white conch, the subject; it follows that it would be a color, because it is white. If [his opponent says that the reason] is not established [i.e., that a white conch is not white] [then the debater could argue to him as follows:] Take that [white conch as] subject; it follows that it is [white], because it is a white conch. If [this debater] says that, then [one should force upon him the opposing pervasion (*'gal khyab*) [i.e., that if something is a white conch, it is pervaded by not being white] as follows: Well then, for him, take a white horse, the subject; it follows that it would be white, because it is a white horse. The pervasion would be the same [i.e., in the first case the debater had argued that all white conches are pervaded by being white and in the second case he similarly should argue that all white horses are pervaded by being white]. But [actually] he cannot agree [that a white horse is white], because it is [in fact] not matter (*bem po* = Skt. *jaḍa*). Why? Because it is a living personality (*gang zag* = Skt. *pudgala*). Why? Because it is a horse.

How would this compare with the famous debate of Gongsun Long 公孫龍 (325–250 BCE.) that concludes *bai ma fei ma ke* 白馬非馬可 (One can say that *white horse* is not [a] horse)?[36] The differences are considerable. The first and most obvious thing to note is that the conclusions are not the same: Collected Topics seeks to show that *white horse* is not white and not that *white horse* is not a horse! Second, while the debate does not figure in Indian Buddhist sources, as far as I can see, the underlying reasoning relies on Abhidharma metaphysics rather than indigenous non-Buddhist Chinese ideas. The point of the white horse not being white is that the white horse cannot be identified with one of the many tropes that constitute it. The fundamental idea in Indo-Tibetan Abhidharma is that a macroscopic entity is always composed of dharmas, that is, what would nowadays be termed quality-particulars or tropes.[37] In short, a horse, or any other living being, cannot be identified with its shape, its color, its weight, its mental features, or any other material or mental trope. On the other hand, the debate in the *Gong sun long zi* 公孫龍子, as I understand it, does not turn on Abhidharmic trope metaphysics and the resultant impossibility to identify an entity with one of its constituent tropes, but rather, to take Chad Hansen's analysis, on issues of interpretation of Chinese compound terms like "white horse" (*bai ma* 白馬), that is, either as a sum of all white and horse entities, or as a product, the entity that is both a horse and white. The white horse not being a horse is assertable if (for philosophical reasons about language) we say that "white horse" is to be taken along the lines of "ox horse" (*niu ma* 牛馬), that is, as a sum, rather than along the lines of a product like "hard white" (*jian bai* 堅 白). However, the Confucian semantical principle, the rectification of names, precludes that one and the same thing should be referred to by two different words, and hence rules out the product reading of "white horse."[38]

The white horse argument is not findable, as far as I can see, in Indian discussions—it is not an Abhidharma debate in India. I would tentatively submit that what may have happened is that the white horse debate in Collected Topics is derived from the Chinese, but that in any case, if it is so derived, it changed significantly, philosophically speaking, in its use in Tibet. Note that there are other discussions in Collected Topics that are thoroughly un-Indian and somewhat suggestive of Chinese views on language. For example, Collected Topics has a whole "lesson" (*rnam bzhag*) concerning X being or not being an x,[39] and there are also discussions about products (impermanent sound) and sums (pillar vase) that do and do not, respectively, admit "instances" (*yin pa srid pa/yin pa mi srid pa*).[40] The contents of these discussions are, as far as I can see, not due to Indian sources (although some terms have Indian antecedents), so that one might look to Chinese sources for their origins, or one might well say that these are original Tibetan developments. A minimalist hypothesis is that there is no "smoking gun" clearly establishing *specific* Chinese origins of debates in Collected Topics.

Notes

1 See Dan Robins, "Mass Nouns and Count Nouns in Classical Chinese," *Early China* 25 (2000), pp. 147–84.

2 W. V. Quine, *Word and Object* (Cambridge, MA: MIT Press, 1960) is the classic source for the thesis of indeterminacy of translation—namely, that there could be mutually incompatible, but equally adequate, translations of nouns in a source language—which has probably made more of a splash in sinological circles than in Tibetan studies. Hansen, for example, mentions it approvingly in connection with his mass-noun hypothesis for Chinese, see C. Hansen, *Language and Logic in Ancient China* (Ann Arbor, MI: University of Michigan Press, 1983), pp. 140–41, 188. Cf. also

Christoph Harbsmeier, *Science and Civilisation in China, volume 7, part 1: Language and Logic* (Cambridge: Cambridge University Press, 1998), p. 311.

3 Cf. W. V. Quine, "Ontological Relativity," *Journal of Philosophy* 65, no. 7 (April 4, 1968), pp. 191–3.

4 Ibid., p. 193.

5 See, for example, Robins, "Mass Nouns and Count Nouns," and Chris Fraser, "Language and Ontology in Early Chinese Thought," *Philosophy East and West* 57, no. 4 (2007), pp. 420–56. Harbsmeier, *Language and Logic*, pp. 313–21, divides Chinese nouns into count, mass, and generic and gives rules for when they are to be taken in one or in another fashion. Note, too, that the strong mass-noun hypothesis for Chinese in Hansen, *Language and Logic*, if right, would have to be taken as opposed to Quine, "Ontological Relativity," as it would maintain that Chinese *is* a mass-noun language that does talk of mass stuffs, that is, horsey stuffs, rabbity stuffs, and the like.

6 See Peggy Li and Pierina Cheung, "Acquisition of Classifiers and Count-Mass Distinction (Mandarin)," in *Encyclopedia of Chinese Language and Linguistics*, eds. Rint Sybesma, Wolfgang Behr, Yueguo Gu, Zev Handel, C.-T. James Huang, James Myers (Brill: Leiden, forthcoming in November, 2015).

7 For an idea of early Tibetan epistemology and logic (*tshad ma*) and Phya pa's place in it, see Leonard W. J. van der Kuijp, *Contributions to the Development of Tibetan Buddhist Epistemology* (Wiesbaden: Franz Steiner, 1979).

8 In fact, the Tibetan term *bsdus grwa* is not an easy one to translate. Shunzo Onoda, *Monastic Debate in Tibet. A Study on the History and Structures of bsDus grwa Logic*, Wiener Studien zur Tibetologie und Buddhismuskunde 27 (Vienna: Arbeitskreis für Tibetische und Buddhistische Studien Universität Wien, 1992), p. 87 gives what may be the most thorough explanation, taking it as probably *bsdus pa slob pa'i sde tshan gyi grwa*, "the schools or classes in which [primary students] learn *bsdus pa* or summarized topics [of logic or dialectics]," and then quoting a later etymological explanation according to which the word *bsdus grwa* meant "the class where many arguments are summarized together" (*rigs pa'i rnam grangs du ma phyog gcig tu bsdus pa'i grwa*).

9 bSe Ngag dbang bkra shis was a student of 'Jam dbyangs bzhad pa (1648–1722) and also an abbot of Bla brang bkra shis 'khyil monastery in present-day Gansu. The *bSe bsdus grwa* is particularly a text of Gomang (*sgo mang*) college of Drepung (*'bras spungs*) monastery near Lhasa. Few of these texts have been studied in publications by contemporary scholars—the exception being the many Japanese articles of Shunzo Onoda, and the English study summarizing their results, Onoda, *Monastic Debate in Tibet*, and Shunzo Onoda, "bsDus grwa Literature," in *Tibetan Literature: Studies in Genre*, eds. Jose Ignacio Cabezón and Roger R. Jackson (Ithaca, NY: Snow Lion, 1996), chapter X, pp. 187–201. See also the publications of Fokke Sierksma, "Rtsod-Pa: The Monachal Disputations in Tibet," *Indo-Iranian Journal* 8 (1964), pp. 130–52; Kenneth Liberman, *Dialectical Practice in Tibetan Philosophical Culture: An Ethnomethodological Inquiry into Formal Reasoning* (Lanham, MD: Rowan and Littlefield, 2007); Margaret Goldberg, "Entity and Antinomy in Tibetan Bsdus grwa Logic (Part I)," *Journal of Indian Philosophy* 13 (1985a), pp. 153–99; Margaret Goldberg, "Entity and Antinomy in Tibetan Bsdus grwa Logic (Part II)," *Journal of Indian Philosophy* 13 (1985b), pp. 273–304; Georges Dreyfus, *The Sound of Two Hands Clapping* (Berkeley: University of California Press, 2003); Daniel E. Perdue, *Debate in Tibetan Buddhism* (Ithaca, NY: Snow Lion, 1992); Daniel E. Perdue, *The Course in Buddhist Reasoning and Debate. An Asian Approach to Analytical Thinking Drawn From Indian and Tibetan Sources* (Boston: Shambhala Publications, 2014);

and Tom. J. F. Tillemans, *Scripture, Logic, Language. Essays on Dharmakīrti and his Tibetan Successors. Studies in Indian and Tibetan Buddhism* (Boston: Wisdom Publications, 1999). For handy access to Onoda, *Monastic Debate in Tibet*, see the site of the Tibetan and Himalayan Library, http://www.thlib.org/encyclopedias/literary/genres/genres-book.php#!book=/studies-in-genres/b10/dn1/.

10 See Onoda, "bsDus grwa Literature"; David P. Jackson, *The Entrance Gate for the Wise (Section III). Sa-skya Paṇḍita on Indian and Tibetan Traditions of Pramāṇa and Philosophical Debate*, Wiener Studien zur Tibetologie und Buddhismuskunde 17.1 and 17.2 (Vienna: Arbeitskreis für Tibetische und Buddhistische Studien Universität Wien, 1987), pp. 128–31; Leonard W. J. van der Kuijp, *Introduction to Gtsang-nag-pa's Tshad-ma rnam-par nges-pa'i ṭī-kā legs-bshad bsdus-pa. An Ancient Commentary on Dharmakīrti's Pramāṇaviniścaya*, Otani University Collection no. 13971. Otani University Tibetan Works Series, Volume II (Kyoto: Rinsen Book Co, 1989), p. 17.

11 Onoda, "bsDus grwa Literature," is careful to say that he personally has not seen this text, but that it is preserved in the Library of Tibetan Works and Archives in Dharamsala.

12 Collected Topics continue to be studied and even composed in the Tibetan cultural community, in both the Tibetan Autonomous Region and the diaspora. Indeed, debate is still widely practiced as a study technique in the dGe lugs curriculum. Perhaps the most extraordinary recent record of actual Tibetan debates and sophisms is the "Mnemonic Notes on the Collected Topics" (*bsdus grwa brjed tho*) composed in Tibetan by the twentieth-century Buryat abbot of sGo mang college of Drepung monastery, the late dGe bshes Ngag dbang nyi ma. Collected Topics is regularly studied in Dharamsala in the dGe lugs pa "School of Dialectics" (*mtshan nyid slob grwa*) and in Sarnath at the Central University for Tibetan Studies, as well as in some modern Sa skya pa institutions. In short, Collected Topics and its logic are alive and well in communities both within and outside Tibet. Shunzo Onoda, myself, and several others had the good fortune to study *bsdus grwa* and related *tshad ma* texts with a number of remarkable teachers in the 1970s and 1980s, notably, dGe bshes lTa mdin rab brtan and dGe bshes bKa' dbyangs of Se ra, and dGe bshes Ngag dbang nyi ma himself. My initial discovery of Collected Topics was in Dharamsala, with dGe bshes bKra shis dbang rgyal in the early 1970's.

13 Tillemans, *Scripture, Logic, Language*.

14 See, for example, *bsDus grwa brjed tho*, p. 5: *dmar po ma yin pa chos can/rtag pa yin par thal/khyod dang rtag pa'i gzhi mthun yod pa'i phyir*, "Take *non-red* as the subject; it follows that it is permanent, because there is a common basis between *permanent* and it." Cf. *Rwa stod bsdus grwa*, p. 116: *ma byas pa chos can/der thal/rtag pa yin na/khyod dang rtag pa'i gzhi mthun yod pa'i phyir*, "Take *non-produced* as the subject; it follows that there is a common basis between permanent and it, because if anything is permanent, then there is a common basis between it and *permanent*."

15 See, for example, *Yongs 'dzin bsdus grwa (chung)* f. 9b: *dngos po'i mtshan nyid chos can/mtshan nyid ma yin par thal/mtshon bya yin pa'i phyir/*'Take *defining characteristic of entity* as the subject; it follows that it is not a defining characteristic, because it is a definiendum [i.e., something to be defined].'

16 Let there be no mistake: Collected Topics, and Tibetan *tshad ma* texts in general, do not accept true contradictions. The "difficult point" cases that we are discussing are not suggestive of dialetheism.

17 For example, when it is repeatedly said in *bsdus grwa* that *entity itself* (*dngos po*) is a nonassociated conditioned thing (*ldan min 'du byed* = Skt. *viprayuktasaṃskāra*), one is *not* asserting that entityness (*dngos po nyid*) is a conditioned thing, as entityness

would be permanent, while any conditioned thing is impermanent. Note that the term *viprayuktasaṃskāra* is in the *Abhidharmakośa* of Vasubandhu, but what the dGe lugs pa do with it is not. The dGe lugs pa are asserting that *entity itself* is neither a material nor a conscious thing, but is, nonetheless, a real entity (*dngos po*). Hence, it belongs to the third category, *viprayuktasaṃskāra.*

18 See Tillemans, *Scripture, Logic, Language*, pp. 214–15.

19 *Tshad ma'i brjed byang chen mo* f. 19a (= p. 188). For the full passage, see Tillemans, *Scripture, Logic, Language*, p. 231, n. 12. An astute reader will notice that I have translated *rang msthan rtog pa'i yul yin pa* as "particulars are [nonetheless] objects of thought," and might well claim that to be consistent my translation should be "*particular* is [nonetheless] an object of thought." Fair enough, one could have that, strictly speaking. But the reason I have translated *rang mtshan* here as "particulars" rather than *particular* is that it is one of those many occurrences that lend themselves to easy reformulation. See the discussion below about reformulating Chinese and Tibetan mass nouns. The sentence *rtog pa'i yul rang mtshan ma yin pa*, "*object of thought* is not a particular," however, does not lend itself to that kind of reformulation at all.

20 *lCang skya grub mtha'* p. 71 ed. rDo rje rgyal po.

21 *rNam 'gel thar lam gsal byed* vol 1., p. 76 translated in Tillemans, *Scripture, Logic, Language*, pp. 232–4, n. 4.

22 See Tillemans, *Scripture, Logic, Language*, p. 230, n. 10 for the use of this phrase by Paṇ chen bSod nams grags pa and Se ra rje bstun Chos kyi rgyal mtshan. On *apoha*, see Mark Siderits, Tom Tillemans, and Arindam Chakrabarti (eds), *Apoha. Buddhist Nominalism and Human Cognition* (New York: Columbia University Press, 2011).

23 See Pascale Hugon, *Trésors du Raisonnement. Sa skya Paṇḍita et ses prédécesseurs tibétains sur les modes de fonctionnement de la pensée et le fondement de l'inférence. Édition et traduction annotée du quatrième chapitre et d'une section du dixième chapitre du Tshad ma rigs pa'i gter*, Wiener Studien zur Tibetologie und Buddhismuskunde 69.1 and 69.2 (Vienna: Arbeitskreis für Tibetische und Buddhistische Studien Universität Wien, 2008), pp. 45, 326–29 et sq. on the Phya pa school's development of the notion of *rang ldog*, property per se. Often, it does not matter much that one refers to X itself, as there is no significant contrast with x's: the predicate will unproblematically apply to both the property per se and its loci (*gzhi ldog*). Thus, for example, in *bum pa mi rtag pa yin* "*vase* is impermanent," impermanence does apply to *vase* itself and the various vases. dGe lugs pa do recognize that in certain debates a subject term may refer only to the individual loci or bases, but these are relatively rare.

24 Cf. David Bellos, *Is That a Fish in Your Ear? Translation and the Meaning of Everything* (New York: Faber and Faber, 2011), pp. 212–13: "The feeling that a difficult foreign text makes real and proper sense only when it's been put into the language we prefer to use for thinking hard thoughts can easily ambush an otherwise sensible mind. . . .We should always resist the false conclusion that the target language—whatever language it is—is 'better' at expressing this or that kind of thought."

25 Fraser, "Language and Ontology in Early Chinese Thought."

26 Here is how the argument goes if we follow Donald Davidson in his article "The Inscrutability of Reference," included in Donald Davidson, *Inquiries into Truth and Interpretation* (Oxford: Clarendon Press, 1984). Inscrutability of reference comes down to an important point in formal semantics that there is always a permutation function Φ that maps one reference scheme for a language onto another scheme, so that when, on the first scheme, a name refers to an object x, then on the second it

refers to $\Phi(x)$ and when a predicate *F* refers to the *x*'s of which it is true that *x* is *F*, then on the second scheme *F* will refer to the *x*'s of which it is true that $\Phi(x)$ is *F*. See Davidson, *Inquiries into Truth and Interpretation*, pp. 229–30. If we grant, as I think we surely must, that every rabbit is an instance of rabbitness, a distribution of the rabbit fusion entity, and vice versa, and that there is thus a permutation function, then it is not only easily shown that "*a* is a rabbit" is true if and only if *a* is a rabbit, but also that "*a* is a rabbit" is true if and only if *a* is an instance of rabbitness. And so on for rabbit fusions and the like. The truth conditions become equivalent and there is only one fact of the matter needed for the sentences to be true. Whether that fact is *a*'s being an instance of rabbitness, a distribution of the rabbit fusion, or being a particular individual rabbit, is inscrutable and immaterial to truth.

27 Not only does it put paid to such hypotheses famously formulated about Hopi and aboriginal languages, but it would also seem to undermine the strong versions of the mass-noun hypothesis for Chinese that we find in Hansen, *Language and Logic*, according to which the Chinese language itself is said to have a stuff-semantics, rather than a semantics of universals and instantiations. See Hansen, *Language and Logic*, p. 35: "The question, 'Of what is *ma* 'horse' the name?' has a natural answer: the mereological set of horses. 'Horse-stuff' is thus an object (substance or thing-kind) scattered in space-time."

28 See Tillemans, *Scripture, Logic, Language*, p. 212 et sq and pp. 229–30, no. 6.

29 See Georges Dreyfus, "Universals in Indo-Tibetan Buddhism," in *Tibetan Studies: Proceedings the 5th Seminar of the International Association for Tibetan Studies*, eds. Shoren Ihara and Zuiho Yamaguchi (Narita: Naritasan Shinshoji, 1992), pp. 29–46; Georges Dreyfus, *Recognizing Reality: Dharmakīrti's Philosophy and its Tibetan Interpretations* (Albany: State University of New York Press, 1997), chapter 9, p. 171 et sq.; Tillemans, *Scripture, Logic, Language*, pp. 212–20; Tom J. F. Tillemans, "On a Recent Work on Tibetan Buddhist Epistemology," *Asiatische Studien/Études asiatiques* 38, no. 1 (1984), pp. 64–65, fn. 5. The dates for Śaṅkaranandana are those of H. Krasser, *Śaṅkaranandanas Īsvarāpākaraṇasaṅkṣepa, mit einem anonymen Kommentar und weiteren Materialien zur buddhistischen Gottespolemik*, 2 volumes (Vienna: Verlag der Österreichischen Akademie der Wissenschaften, 2002).

30 One could experiment with a semantics of discontinuously distributed fusions, that is, entities composed by adding all the world's snow to make a sum, and (why not?) adding the world's rabbits or horses, what have you, to make their respective sums. See David Nicolas, "The Logic of Mass Expressions," *Stanford Encyclopedia of Philosophy*, http://plato.stanford.edu/entries/logic-massexpress/ (2013), section 2, on mereological sums as reference for mass expressions. This might even be something like the stuff-semantics Hansen, *Language and Logic*, hypothesizes on a grand scale for Chinese. Would such a semantics, after all, help rationalize the "difficult point" theory that is promoted by dGe lugs pa philosophers, even if there is no reason to think that it is somehow inherent to Tibetan language generally or that the mere use of mass nouns makes it necessary? It may seem possible for horses, rabbits, and vases, but becomes increasingly weird for knowable things and good reasons. The big problem, however, is that we would somehow have to learn to argue in English why the non-red fusion *itself* and knowable thing fusion *itself* and finally, the good reason fusion *itself*, would supposedly have properties that they do and that their distributions quite often do not. A very daunting task.

31 See Benjamin Lee Whorf, *Language, Thought and Reality: Selected Writings of Benjamin Lee Whorf*, edited by John B. Carroll (Cambridge, MA: MIT Press, 1956).

32 See Davidson, *Inquiries into Truth and Interpretation*, chapter 13; see also Jeff E. Malpas, "The Intertranslatability of Natural Languages," *Synthese* 78 (1989), pp. 233–64.
33 That distinction and interpretation of Davidson is emphasized in Malpas, "The Intertranslatability," pp. 248–9.
34 One could, of course, speculate that on the very odd chance that future analytic philosophers came to prize Collected Topics, legitimized English mass-noun usage of *vase, knowable thing*, etc., and learned to reason persuasively about them, the untranslatability that I have been discussing might disappear. However, it is obscure how this would happen rationally. We do not yet have a clue as to what information or insights we would need.
35 Tōhoku 4208.
36 On this debate, see Harbsmeier, *Language and Logic*, p. 298 et sq.
37 Tropes are particular occurrences of being brown, being heavy, being square, etc. They are localized in a unique region of space and time and are thus particulars rather than universals. The notion has been recently used in Western thought by philosophers like David Armstrong; Jonardon Ganeri and Charles Goodman have interpreted Buddhist dharmas in this fashion.
38 See Hansen, *Language and Logic*.
39 This is the *rdzas ldog gi rnam bzhag* "The lesson on substances and properties (lit. 'exclusions'. ldog pa = Skt. *vyāvṛtti*). See Goldberg, 'Entity and Antinomy (Part I)', and Goldberg, 'Entity and Antinomy (Part II)'."
40 *Yongs 'dzin bsdus grwa chung* f. 4b et sq., *gzhi grub kyi rnam bzhag*, "the lesson on real bases [i.e., ontology]."

References

Bellos, D. (2011), *Is That a Fish in Your Ear? Translation and the Meaning of Everything*, New York: Faber and Faber.

bSe ngag dbang bkra shis. *bSe bsdus grwa = Tshad ma'i dgongs 'grel gyi bstan bcos chen po rnam 'grel gyi don gcig tu dril ba blo rab 'bring tha gsum du ston pa legs bshad chen po mkhas pa'i mul rgyan skal bzang re ba kun skong*. In *Kun mkhyen 'jam dbyangs bzhad pa'i thugs sras ngag dbang bkra shis kyis mdzad pa'i bsdus grwa*. Drespung Gomang College text ('bras spungs sgo mang grwa tshang yig cha), printed in South India in 1972.

Davidson, D. (1984), *Inquiries into Truth and Interpretation*, Oxford: Clarendon Press.

dGe bshes ngag dbang nyi ma. *bsDus grwa brjed tho*. Leiden, 1970's. This handwritten text records a large number of orally passed on debates, sophisms, definitions, etc., many of them not appearing in other *bsdus grwa* texts.

Dreyfus, G. (1992), "Universals in Indo-Tibetan Buddhism," in S. Ihara and Z. Yamaguchi (eds), *Tibetan Studies: Proceedings of the 5th Seminar of the International Association for Tibetan Studies*, Narita: Naritasan Shinshoji, pp. 29–46.

Dreyfus, G. (1997), *Recognizing Reality: Dharmakīrti's Philosophy and its Tibetan Interpretations*, Albany: State University of New York Press.

Dreyfus, G. (2003), *The Sound of Two Hands Clapping*, Berkeley: University of California Press.

Fraser, C. (2007), "Language and Ontology in Early Chinese Thought," *Philosophy East and West*, 57 (4), pp. 420–56.

Goldberg, M. (1985a), "Entity and Antinomy in Tibetan Bsdus grwa Logic (Part I)," *Journal of Indian Philosophy*, 13, pp. 153–99.

Goldberg, M. (1985b), "Entity and Antinomy in Tibetan Bsdus grwa Logic (Part II)," *Journal of Indian Philosophy*, 13, pp. 273–304.

Hansen, C. (1983), *Language and Logic in Ancient* China, Ann Arbor, MI: University of Michigan Press.

Harbsmeier, C. (1998), *Science and Civilisation in China*, vol. 7, part 1, *Language and* Logic, Cambridge: Cambridge University Press.

Hugon, P. (2008), *Trésors du Raisonnement. Sa skya Paṇḍita et ses prédécesseurs tibétains sur les modes de fonctionnement de la pensée et le fondement de l'inférence.* Édition et traduction annotée du quatrième chapitre et d'une section du dixième chapitre du *Tshad ma rigs pa'i gter.* Wiener Studien zur Tibetologie und Buddhismusknde 69.1 and 69.2, Vienna: Arbeitskreis für Tibetische und Buddhistische Studien Universität Wien.

Jackson, D. P. (1987), *The Entrance Gate for the Wise (Section III). Sa-skya Paṇḍita on Indian and Tibetan Traditions of* Pramāṇa *and Philosophical Debate.* Wiener Studien zur Tibetologie und Buddhismuskunde 17.1 and 17.2, Vienna: Arbeitskreis für Tibetische und Buddhistische Studien Universität Wien.

'Jam dbyangs mchog lha 'od zer. *Rwa stod bsdus grwa dang de'i dogs gcod.* Tibetan text published under the title *The Logic Primer of Rato. Text and Commentary,* Rato Datsang Tibetan Monastic University, Mundgod, South India, 1992.

Kelsang, T. and Onoda, S., eds (1985), *Textbooks of Se-ra Monastery for the Primary Course of Studies.* Biblia Tibetica 1, Kyoto: Nagata Bunshodo.

Krasser, H. (2002), *Śaṅkaranandanas Īśvarāpākaraṇasaṅkṣepa, mit einem anonymen Kommentar und weiteren Materialien zur buddhistischen Gottespolemik.* 2 volumes, Vienna: Verlag der Österreichischen Akademie der Wissenschaften.

lCang skya Rol pa'i rdo rje (1989), *lCang skya grub mtha' = Grub pa'i mtha' rnam par bzhag pa gsal bar bshad pa thub bstan lhun po'i mdzes rgyan.* Ed. rDo rje gyal po. Qinghai: mTsho sngon mi rigs par khang.

Li, P. and Cheung, P. (forthcoming in November, 2015), "Acquisition of Classifiers and Count-Mass Distinction (Mandarin)," in R. Sybesma, W. Behr, Y. Gu, Z. Handel, J. Huang and J. Myers (eds), *Encyclopedia of Chinese Language and Linguistics*, Brill: Leiden.

Liberman, K. (2007), *Dialectical Practice in Tibetan Philosophical Culture: An Ethnomethodological Inquiry into Formal Reasoning*, Lanham, MD: Rowan and Littlefield.

Malpas, J. E. (1989), "The Intertranslatability of Natural Languages," *Synthese*, 78, pp. 233–64.

Nicolas, D. (2013), "The Logic of Mass Expressions," *Stanford Encyclopedia of Philosophy.* http://plato.stanford.edu/entries/logic-massexpress/.

Onoda, S. (1992), *Monastic Debate in Tibet. A Study on the History and Structures of* bsDus grwa *Logic.* Wiener Studien zur Tibetologie und Buddhismuskunde 27. Vienna: Arbeitskreis für Tibetische und Buddhistische Studien Universität Wien.

Onoda, S. (1996), "*bsDus grwa* Literature," in J. Cabezón and R. Jackson (eds), *Tibetan Literature: Studies in Genre*, chapter X, pp. 187–201, Ithaca NY: Snow Lion.

Perdue, D. E. (1992), *Debate in Tibetan Buddhism*, Ithaca, NY: Snow Lion.

Perdue, D. E. (2014), *The Course in Buddhist Reasoning and Debate. An Asian Approach to Analytical Thinking Drawn From Indian and Tibetan Sources*, Boston: Shambhala Publications.

Quine, W. V. (1960), *Word and Object*, Cambridge, MA: MIT Press.

Quine, W. V. (1968), "Ontological Relativity," *Journal of Philosophy*, 65 (7), pp. 185–212.
rGyal tshab Dar ma rin chen (rGyal tshab rje) (1974), *rNam 'grel thar lam gsal byed = Tshad ma rnam 'grel gyi tshig le'ur byas pa'i rnam bshad thar lam phin ci ma log par gsal bar byed pa*, 2 volumes, Sarnath: Pleasure of Elegant Sayings Press.
Robins, D. (2000), "Mass Nouns and Count Nouns in Classical Chinese," *Early China*, 25, pp. 147–84.
Siderits, M., Tillemans, T., and Chakrabarti, A., eds (2011), *Apoha. Buddhist Nominalism and Human Cognition*, New York: Columbia University Press.
Sierksma, F. (1964), "Rtsod-Pa: The Monachal Disputations in Tibet," *Indo-Iranian Journal*, 8, pp. 130–52.
Tillemans, T. J. F. (1984), "On a Recent Work on Tibetan Buddhist Epistemology," *Asiatische Studien/Études asiatiques*, 38 (1), pp. 59–66.
Tillemans, T. J. F. (1999), *Scripture, Logic, Language. Essays on Dharmakīrti and his Tibetan Successors*, Studies in Indian and Tibetan Buddhism, Boston: Wisdom Publications.
Tsong kha pa Blo bzang grags pa. *Tshad ma'i brjed byang chen mo = rGyal tshab chos rjes rje'i drung du gsan pa'i tshad ma'i brjed byang chen mo.* In *Collected Works*, vol. pha, pp. 152–245. Tashi lhun po edition, published by Ngag dbang dge legs bde mo in the Ge den sung rab mi nyam gyun phel series 79–105. Delhi, 1975–1979.
Whorf, B. L. (1956), *Language, Thought and Reality: Selected Writings of Benjamin Lee* Whorf, edited by J. B. Carroll, Cambridge, MA: MIT Press, 1956.
van der Kuijp, L. W. J. (1979), *Contributions to the Development of Tibetan Buddhist Epistemology*, Wiesbaden: Franz Steiner.
van der Kuijp, L. W. J. (1989), Introduction to Gtsang-nag-pa's *Tshad-ma rnam-par nges-pa'i ṭī-kā legs-bshad bsdus-pa. An Ancient Commentary on Dharmakīrti's Pramāṇaviniścaya. Otani University Collection no. 13971,* Otani University Tibetan Works Series, Volume II, pp. 1–39, Kyoto: Rinsen Book Co.
Yongs 'dzin Phur bu lcog byams pa tshul khrims rgya mtsho (1985). *Yongs 'dzin bsdus grwa = Tshad ma'i gzhung don 'byed pa'i bsdus grwa'i rnam bzhag rigs lam 'phrul gyi lde'u mig* (3 volumes: *chung, 'bring, che ba*). Included in Kelsang T. and S. Onoda, eds.

2

Translation, Interpretation, and Alternative Epistemologies

Barry Hallen

Introduction

The notion of "fusion" introduces something new to comparative philosophy. "Conjoining" or "integrating" elements of different cultures' philosophical thought is an intriguing idea. But as Chakrabarti and Weber indicate, it is a process that must be nuanced. Simply throwing diverse notions derived from different cultures into some crude intellectual blender would not do their methodology justice. Inherent to fusion philosophy is the additional notion that too much is still made of the *differences* that are presumed to demarcate cultural identities, so that they end up estranging cultures from one another in an artificial and counterproductive manner. A fusion orientation suggests that such appearances are deceptive and relatively superficial. If scholars were to take a closer look at what are supposedly the "unique" notions that distinguish cultures from one another, they will find that there are deeper and more profound commonalities or similarities between those same cultures.

Much of modern African philosophy began from a defensive posture. In the African context, certainly, differences in appearance and behavior were presumed to indicate fundamentally different forms of cognition. The characterization of Africa's indigenous cultures as "traditional," in itself, was meant to indicate that, when their inhabitants were asked to justify a belief or practice, the justification would amount to an appeal to tradition, that is, along the lines of "because this is what we inherited from the forefathers." An appeal to tradition to justify tradition—elementary circular reasoning. Additional characterizations of indigenous African thought as "prelogical," "precritical," "protorational," and "prescientific" reinforced what was to become a demeaning and false stereotype.

The fact that this stereotype was largely the product of Western scholarship did not go unnoticed. As a result, African scholars became disenchanted with translation exercises between African and Western languages. Why should languages that might not share a single cognate in common be taken as semantically compatible? The philosopher W. V. O. Quine[1] uses the phrase "radical translation" to characterize such exercises. And the Ghanaian philosopher, Kwasi Wiredu, remarks, "As for 'radical translation,' God knows that Africa has suffered enough from it"[2]; "there is a need to unravel the conceptual distortions that have accumulated in accounts of African traditional thought through the legacy of years of a self-assumed Western spokesmanship."[3]

Whether on an analytical, phenomenological, or original basis, philosophers in the African context have been concerned to challenge the "traditional" stereotype and present accounts of indigenous thought systems that are somehow non-Western and yet have integrity as far as comparative standards of rationality are concerned.[4] As Anthony Appiah puts it when writing about postmodernism, African intellectuals may need "to clear a space in which one is distinguished from other producers and products—and one does this by construction and the marking of differences."[5] If that motivates African philosophers to emphasize the distinctiveness, even the uniqueness, of their cultures, then so be it.[6]

It seems that fusion philosophy would be sympathetic to appreciating the circumstances that lead to this response on the part of African philosophers. But, again, that remonstrance from a fusion approach kicks in to suggest that, in their efforts to respond to and refute negative portrayals of the African intellect—think of Leopold Senghor's Negritude—these African philosophers might be emphasizing some of that uniqueness as a consequence of the *desire* to be, rather than the *reality* of being, different. This could mean that Africans too may promote misrepresentations of their cultures because they too have, without sufficient justification, bought into the idea that those cultures must not only be distinctive—they must be unique.[7]

Truth in the Twi language of the Akan of Ghana

A number of African philosophers have therefore become concerned to refocus attention on better understandings of the meanings of philosophically prepossessive concepts internal to the discourse of indigenous languages. This should also hopefully open the way to more precise interpretations, aka translations, of African meanings in Western languages. Kwasi Wiredu is a pioneer in this regard. Wiredu is not a relativist, in that he is committed to a form of universal rationalism from the outset. Otherwise, he warns, rationality in the African context tends to become not just different, but inferior and second-rate to its Western counterpart. One extensive analysis and translation exercise Wiredu has been engaged in for the past twenty-five years involves Akan culture's Twi language conceptual equivalent of the English-language "truth."

In an early essay where he discusses Akan discourse relevant to the notion of cognitive truth, Wiredu is concerned to elucidate the Twi phrase that he renders into English as something's being "so." "We render the cognitive concept of truth by some such phrase as '*nea ate saa*,' 'that which is so.'"[8] The *Concise Oxford Dictionary* records this form of usage for the word "so" *in the English language* as "In that state or condition, actually the case" and cites as one example, "God said 'Let there be light' and it was so."[9] As far as Wiredu is concerned, that "p is so" in the Twi language of Akan culture means that "p is true." He acknowledges that in order to be clear about the philosophical prepossessions of this Akan expression, more information about its usage is required. For what precisely is being claimed in Twi when someone says that something *is* so? Philosophical analysis may beckon, but he points out that there are some issues that ordinary discourse and usage do not address because there is no need for human beings to be so technically precise on the level of everyday discourse.

Nevertheless, one may still ask whether the Akan distinguish between the "so" in "it/that is so" [statements] and the "so" in "what is so" [facts]. In Western epistemology, as Wiredu is well aware, the issue most relevant to this question is the relationship said to hold between a statement or proposition purportedly claiming to be true, and the fact or real-world situation to which reference is being made that enables it to be true (or false), a statement such as, "The Empire State building is in New York City." In Western epistemology, the so-called correspondence theory of truth is frequently introduced at this point, with its stricture that the key to truth is whether the proposition or statement that is being made actually corresponds to or "pictures" something that really is the case. The common-sense notion underlying this is that what should make a statement true or false is whether it does or does not correspond to something beyond itself, a "fact," for example.

Wiredu continues his own analysis as follows: "To say that something is true, the Akan simply say that it is so, and truth is rendered as what is so. No undue sophistication is required to understand that although the Akan do not have *a single word* for truth, they do have the concept of truth."[10] The phrase "a single word" turns out to be significant. For there is no one-to-one equivalence between the English-language "truth" relevant to correspondence theory and a term in the Twi language. The same expression, *nea ete saa*, does double duty in the Twi language in that it is used to refer both to *statements* that are true and to the "independent" *facts* that would make those statements true.

If these two meanings, of statement and of fact, are interchangeable or conflated, this could be interpreted to suggest that the Akan are epistemologically naïve because they assume that any statement made somehow records a fact, and that facts somehow justify every imaginable statement. But this would be precisely the kind of "radical" translation or misinterpretation of meanings Wiredu condemns in the strongest terms. This kind of mistake would be made by an outsider not entirely familiar with the linguistic conventions of the culture concerned, but persuaded, nevertheless, that such people's cognition must somehow be defective.[11]

Wiredu's own analysis pursues more realistic and philosophically interesting possibilities. There are at least three that deserve specific mention. (1) That statements refer to something beyond themselves is understandably a universal assumption. "The need itself for some reference to reality in our thought is genuine."[12] But it would be a mistake to assume that the conventions prescribed by Western epistemology are universal. *Western* philosophy's correspondence theory may bifurcate understanding, so that truth is viewed as a consequence of a relationship between statements and facts: "a true sentence *refers* to a 'nonlinguistic' reality."[13] Numerous *Western* philosophical texts address themselves to this notion of a statement's referring. But Twi discourse does not replicate this bifurcation. The expression for something's being "so" applies across the board.

> In Akan the notions of *truth* and *fact* may be rendered by means of one notion, namely, the notion of what is so, *nea ete saa*. The sentence "'p' is true" may be

> expressed as "'p' *te saa*" and "It is a fact that p" as *Nea ete ne se* p. The expressions *(e)te saa* and *nea ete ne se* are just grammatical variants for rendering the idea of being so. In the upshot, the Akan version of the formula amounts, roughly, to saying something like "'p' is so if and only if what is so is that p," which is an unconcealed tautology. To be sure, all tautologies are splendid truths. But some are conceptually informative, and others are not; and certainly this one is not. From it, therefore, *no philosophical enlightenment can be anticipated* . . . although the equivalence "'p' is true if and only if it is a fact that p" is correct and philosophically interesting in English, it is truistic in Akan but of *no philosophical interest*.[14]

Western correspondence theory, therefore, does not apply to Akan discourse.[15] From the standpoint of an epistemology grounded in correspondence theory, Akan discourse has nothing to say about the so-called problem of reference. But saying the Twi language is of no *philosophical* interest on this subject does not mean the Akan cannot talk about whatever in English is said to be true or a fact. They certainly can even if, in their discourse, the two English-language meanings in Twi are one, in that they are conveyed by the same expression. What they cannot talk about, as if they were two separate kinds of things, are true statements as entirely distinct from "facts" that make those statements true.

(2) That Akan culture is silent on the problem of reference generated by English-language discourse does not imply that the culture is somehow intellectually or philosophically underdeveloped. What this does indicate is that the vocabulary and grammatical structures of an indigenous language (English, Twi or, as we shall see, Yoruba) and its meanings may have philosophical consequences.[16] By concluding that Twi-language usage does not replicate the referential terminology that gives rise to English-language epistemology's correspondence theory, Wiredu is able to argue that some "problems" of philosophy are culturally relative.

> When the determining factor is language, I have called this dependency *tongue-dependency*. Of such a nature is the equivalence thesis relating truth to fact, and the language involved is English. Probably, all languages generate some tongue-dependent problems and theses. It therefore behooves every philosopher, whatever his or her language, to watch and pray lest he or she confuse tongue-dependency issues with universal ones.[17]

(3) Wiredu's renderings of Akan meanings into English indicate that the Akan do not, specifically, distinguish between a knowledge claim or statement and the corresponding fact that makes that claim or statement true. This does not make it difficult for the Akan to make knowledge claims about the world, but it does make their language less interesting from an epistemological point of view. However, this lack on the part of Twi discourse, again according to Wiredu, suggests that some epistemological concerns—such as the problem of reference—may arise from the terminology and usage taken as conventional by a particular language culture. In which case, some "problems" of philosophy are not truly universal and become relative to particular language cultures.[18]

Truth in Western epistemology

In Western epistemology, the most problematic and controversial sub-category of information is what has come to be known as secondhand (testimonial) propositional knowledge, knowledge "that" something is the case ("I know *that* there are eight planets orbiting the sun."). Generally this is associated with information in written or oral propositional (sentential) form that is supposed to be knowledge and therefore true, but which the individual recipient is in no position to test or to verify in a firsthand manner. When one reflects upon what a member of Western society may "learn" in the course of a lifetime, it becomes clear that most people's "knowledge" consists of information they will never ever be in a position to confirm in a firsthand or direct manner. What they "find out" from a history book, "see" via the evening news on television, or "confirm" about a natural law on the basis of one elementary experiment in a high-school physics laboratory—all could be (and sometimes are!) subject to error, distortion, or outright fabrication.

Secondhand propositional knowledge is therefore generally characterized as information that cannot be tested or proved in a decisive manner by most people who have it, and therefore has to be *accepted as true* because it "agrees" with common sense or because it "corresponds" to or "coheres" with the very limited amount of information that people are able to test and confirm in a firsthand or direct manner. As has been mentioned, exactly how this coherence or correspondence is to be defined and ascertained are still subjects of endless wrangling in (Western) epistemological theory. What is relevant to the present discussion is that this wrangling is evidence of the intellectual concern and discomfort (in academic parlance, it becomes one of the "problems" of philosophy) on the part of (Western) philosophers about the evidential basis of so much information that people in that culture are conditioned to regard as knowledge, as true.

Western epistemology has formulated three basic criteria that must be satisfied if secondhand propositional information is to qualify as knowledge—*justified, true, belief.*[19] The consequences of each of these criteria for the conventions governing such "knowledge" may be summarized as follows: First, is it the case that what a person claims to know must be *true*? Consider the alternative—that it would be possible for us to have false knowledge. It might seem to be the case that this does, indeed, frequently happen, as when I assume that a certain article I read in today's newspaper is true, only to find out later that it was an outright fabrication. But, in such cases, would we not prefer to say that we were mistaken, and that what we thought we "knew" was in fact false from the very beginning? In other words, for a piece of information to be, in fact, regarded as knowledge it must, indeed, qualify as *true*.

Second, in conventional English-language usage we must *believe* what we say we know. To say, "I know it but I don't believe it," may make metaphorical sense in some extraordinary situations (winning the lottery, for example). Yet, surely the conventions of ordinary usage stipulate that we must believe what we say we know.

Last, but far from least, is the criterion of *justification*. Imagine you were invited to a friend's home for dinner, and found yourself seated next to her eleven-year-old daughter. During the course of the meal you happened to ask that proverbial question,

"And what do you want to be when you grow up, young lady?" What if the eleven-year-old looked you straight in the eye and, dead serious, said, "When I am 21 years old I will have a million dollars in the bank." Let's fast forward and say it so happens that ten years later, when that daughter is twenty-one years old, she does, in fact, have a million dollars in her bank account. The crucial question then becomes, was she somehow *justified* in making that original statement when you first met her? Obviously not, because, for one thing, how was the girl to presume she would still be alive at age twenty-one, much less have a million dollars at her disposal? What this indicates, then, is how important it is to have solid *evidence* for a knowledge claim if it is to be taken seriously.

Truth in the language of the Yoruba of Nigeria

The Hallen-Sodipo approach[20] to the philosophical analysis of Yoruba discourse begins from the knowledge-belief distinction as portrayed in English-language philosophical analysis, and explicitly sets out to investigate whether there is anything with which to compare it in Yoruba discourse. Although the Yoruba of southwestern Nigeria affirm the epistemic importance of all sensory perception, they single out visual perception (*ìríran*)—seeing something for yourself—as clearer and more reliable. Persons are said to "know" or to have "knowledge" only of experience they have witnessed in a firsthand or personal manner. The example most frequently cited by discussants, virtually as a paradigm, is visual perception of a scene or an event as it is taking place.

"Knowledge" is said to apply to sensory perception generally, even if what may be experienced directly by touch is more limited than is the case with visual perception. In Western philosophy, this is conventionally described as "firsthand" experience. "Knowledge" in a Yoruba context implies a good deal more than mere sensation, of course. Perception implies cognition as well, meaning that the persons concerned must comprehend that and what they are experiencing. When conjoined with cognitive comprehension (*ẹ̀rí okàn*; literally "the witnessing of the mind") *that* one is seeing and *of what* one is seeing, the two sufficient conditions for *ìmọ̀*, usually translated into English as "knowledge," are fulfilled. Experience that fulfills these two conditions and propositions that recount such experience are both characterized as *òótọ́*. When "*òótọ́*" is predicated of statements, the appropriate English-language equivalent would seem to be "true." However, in Yoruba "*òótọ́*" may be a property of both *propositions* and *forms of experience*. Therefore, in some contexts it is better rendered into English as being "certain" or "certainty."[21] In other words, the appropriate English-language equivalent would appear to be *experience* that is "certain."

The terms "*òótọ́*"/"*òtítọ́*" are therefore associated with "knowledge" in at least one respect that parallels the manner in which "true"/"truth" are paired with "know"/"knowledge" in the English language. However, in the English language "truth" is principally a property of propositional knowledge, of statements human beings make about something. The emphasis placed upon propositions being *òótọ́* because they presumably report firsthand experience accurately indicates elements of a correspondence theory of truth in Yoruba discourse as well.

The distinction made in Yoruba-language culture between putative "knowledge" (*ìmọ̀*) and putative "belief" (*ìgbàgbọ́*) indicates a systematic concern about the evidential status of firsthand versus secondhand information. The Yoruba noun form that is being translated as "belief," "*ìgbàgbọ́*" (and its verb form "*gbàgbọ́*"), does, in fact, arise from the conflation of "*gbà*" and "*gbọ́*."[22] The two components are themselves verbs, the former conventionally translated into English as "receive" or "agree to," and the latter as "hear" or "understand." Yoruba linguistic conventions suggest that treating this complex term as a synthesis of the English-language "understand" (in the sense of cognitive comprehension) and of "agree to" (in the sense of affirming or accepting new information one comprehends as part of one's own store of secondhand information) is perhaps the best way to render its core meaning. *Ìgbàgbọ́* encompasses what one is not able "to see for oneself" or to experience in a direct, firsthand manner. For the most part this involves things we are told about or informed of—this is the most conventional sense of "information"—by others.

What makes it different from the English-language "believe"/"belief" is that *ìgbàgbọ́* can apply to *everything* that might be construed as *secondhand* information. This would apply to most of what in English-language culture is regarded as propositional knowledge: the things one is taught in the course of a formal education, what one learns from books, from other people, and, of particular interest in the special case of the Yoruba, from oral traditions. While English-language culture decrees that propositional or secondhand information, if classified as "knowledge," should be accepted as *true*, Yoruba usage is equally insistent that, since classified as *ìgbàgbọ́* (putative "belief"), it can only be accepted as *possibly* true (*ó ṣe é ṣe*) or untrue (*ko ṣe é ṣe*).

The cross-cultural ramifications of these differing viewpoints on the truth status of propositional or secondhand knowledge are worth considering. Yoruba-language speakers would likely regard members of English-language culture, who are willing to assign so much certainty to and put so much trust in information that they can never test or verify, as perilously naïve and perhaps even ignorant. Members of English-language culture might criticize their Yoruba counterparts' identification of optimal knowledge with "you can only know what you can see" as indicative of a people who have yet to discover the benefits of institutionalized knowledge and formal education.[23]

The criteria that define the respective extents of and the interrelations between "knowledge" (*ìmọ̀*) and "belief" (*ìgbàgbọ́*) in Yoruba stipulate that any experience or information that is not firsthand, personal, and direct must by definition fall under the heading of "belief" (*ìgbàgbọ́*). The sense of "belief" (*ìgbàgbọ́*) may therefore be paraphrased as "comprehending, and deciding to accept as possible (as 'possibly true'—*ó ṣe é ṣe/ko ṣe é ṣe*, rather than as 'true'—*òótọ́*), information that one receives in a secondhand manner." "Knowledge" (*ìmọ̀*; firsthand experience) and "belief" (*ìgbàgbọ́*; information gained on the basis of secondhand experience) together exhaust all of the information that human beings have at their disposal.

Following up on Wiredu's ideas about tongue-dependency, might this be interpreted to mean that the distinction between firsthand and secondhand experience became an issue for Yoruba epistemology because of the language's introduction of the two categories for classifying information and experience information—*ìmọ̀* and *ìgbàgbọ́*? That distinction seems to have been foundational to the meanings of these two terms from the beginning. Yoruba meanings in translation become philosophically interesting when linked to English-language notions of knowledge and belief, to that language-culture's distinction between firsthand and secondhand experience, and to the propositions that arise from those experiences.[24] Wiredu's analyses of Twi discourse do not pursue a similar path, in that he does not discuss terminology that may be used to characterize statements that are less than cognitively true.

If and when my "knowledge" (*ìmọ̀*) is challenged (*àríyàn jiyàn*) by other persons who have not undergone a similar firsthand experience and who therefore doubt what I say I actually saw happen, the best way to convince them would be to arrange for some kind of test whereby they would be able to see the thing happen for themselves.[25] If I cannot arrange for this kind of direct testing, the next best I can do is to ask any others who may have personally witnessed my own or a similar experience to come forward and testify. In this case my firsthand experience cannot become the challengers' own "knowledge" (*ìmò*), but if they are influenced by the combined testimony, they may decide to "believe" me/us and accept the information on a secondhand basis, as "belief" (*ìgbàgbọ́*).

A simple example may serve to clarify things. If I claim I have seen for myself (*ìmọ̀*) that a certain friend drives a specific make and model of car and another friend challenges my claim, the best way to resolve the dispute is to visit the friend and see (*ìmọ̀*) what kind of car she actually has. If the friend lives a thousand miles away, a more practical solution would be to ask other mutual friends who have seen (*ìmọ̀*) the car themselves to tell us (*ìgbàgbọ́*) what kind it is. Or perhaps to telephone my friend directly and ask her to tell us (*ìgbàgbọ́*) what kind of car she is driving. Speaking to her directly by telephone would still not be firsthand "knowledge" of the car because one is not actually seeing it. One is only hearing a further form of secondhand information about the car, another form of testimony—albeit a particularly relevant one given the circumstances.

If and when my "belief" (*ìgbàgbọ́*) is challenged by another person, again the best solution would be to arrange some form of empirical test. In this case since this is information I myself only know secondhand, the most reliable solution for all concerned would be to test it directly, so that the information would progress from being "belief" (*ìgbàgbọ́*) to being "knowledge" (*ìmọ̀*) for all concerned, myself included. Next best would again be to call upon all relevant witnesses who may have heard the same or similar secondhand information (*ìgbàgbọ́*) or, even more definitively, have firsthand (*ìmọ̀*) experience of what I can only claim to know on a secondhand (*ìgbàgbọ́*) basis.

When agreement or a consensus among disputants is reached on the level of "belief" (*ìgbàgbọ́*), the applicable term (comparable to the role of "truth" with reference to knowledge, or of "*òótọ́*" with regard to *ìmọ̀*) is "*papọ̀*," which may be rendered colloquially as "the words have come together."[26] The antecedent process of testimony, discussion, and reflection on the basis of which the consensus is reached is described as "*nwádi*"—an expression whose meaning may be compared to the English language "let's get to the bottom of this matter."[27]

The system that emerges from these criteria appears to be three-tiered. "Knowledge" (*ìmọ̀*) is the sole category of experience or of propositions entitled to be regarded as certain or as true (*òótọ́*). "Belief" (*ìgbàgbọ́*) that is in principle open to empirical testing, verification, and thereby transformed into "knowledge" (*ìmọ̀* that is *òótọ́*) is the next best. "Belief" (*ìgbàgbọ́*) that can never be verified and can only be evaluated on the basis of testimony, explanation, discussion, and reflection (*nwádì*) is the least certain.

Comparative philosophy

The significance of all this for comparative philosophy is complex. The most obvious and perhaps most important point is that Yoruba discourse does employ terminology and systematic criteria for the evaluation of any type of information. This is a priority to which African systems of thought were once said not to attach special importance or about which they were said to be unclear.[28]

A more intriguing philosophical consequence of this Yoruba epistemology arises from its ramifications for conventional Western paradigms of *propositional knowledge*—sentences expressing *secondhand information* in the form of "I know that X" statements—and their relation to the legitimizing epistemic criteria routinely specified as "justified, true, belief." What is of particular interest here is that knowledge (*ìmọ̀*) in Yoruba terms would seem to make two of the three English-language criteria that determine whether a piece of information qualifies *as* knowledge, irrelevant, or certainly unnecessary. The criterion of *belief* (Yoruba "*ìgbàgbọ́*") would no longer apply, since it would be pointless and confusing to say that one had secondhand, *possibly* true, information about what one *already* "knew" to be true on the basis of firsthand experience. Also, the notion of *justification* would seem to lose much of its significance since one would not be obliged to provide the kinds of evidence associated with that criterion for information or experience that has already been validated directly in a firsthand manner. Only the *true* criterion would carry over, as is indicated by the previous discussion regarding the Yoruba terms "*òótọ́*"/"*òtítọ́*."

A further and equally interesting consideration is whether this alternative Yoruba epistemic system would serve to "counter" the epistemologically infamous Gettier counterexamples.[29] They involve a number of imaginary situations, created by the American philosopher Edmund Gettier, designed to illustrate how a person could be said to have knowledge in English-language terms despite the fact that the three criteria (justified, true, belief) were *not* satisfied.

Perhaps the best known of these examples involves one Mr. Smith who works in an office with one Mr. Jones. Mr. Smith is in possession of relatively *secondhand* information (having overheard a remark made by a person in authority) that Mr. Jones is about to receive a promotion (for which, in Smith's opinion, he is fully qualified). By chance, Smith also had the opportunity *firsthand* to observe Jones carefully counting the number of coins in his pocket that day—ten. On the basis of this information, Smith perfectly correctly arrives at the further conclusion (via deduction) that the person who receives the promotion will have ten coins in his pocket. But, as it turns out, the person who is promoted later that day is one Mr. Robinson, not Mr. Jones. Yet, it just so happens that Mr. Robinson also has precisely ten coins in his pocket.

If evaluated from the standpoint of English-language epistemology, Smith was *justified* in *believing* that Jones would get the promotion, even if this important piece of information eventually turned out to be *not* true. But his second conclusion—that the person receiving the promotion would have ten coins in his pocket—does turn out to be *true*, as well as deduced from information that, at the time, Smith was justified in believing. Yet, English-language epistemology most certainly would not want to label it, given the circumstances, as *knowledge*! If anything, some sort of *coincidence* or *accident* has occurred. Yet, Gettier's point was that, if such coincidences or accidents can actually occur (as certainly seems reasonable), then justified, true, belief—as criteria—are not *sufficient* to guarantee that a piece of information be rated as knowledge.

The point of particular relevance here is that the Yoruba insistence on *firsthand* experience as a basis for all information that is to qualify as knowledge would appear to rule out the possibility of such apparently irreconcilable deductions because *all* of the information that they were based upon would have to have been obtained initially on a rigorously firsthand basis. Smith would have had to have a firsthand encounter directly with Jones' promotion itself, rather than relying on a comparatively secondhand remark. And this would then make the status of Gettier's secondary conclusion about the ten coins relatively uninteresting—in fact, irrelevant.

Further conclusions

The Yoruba alternative summarized above would also suggest the novel thesis that what philosophers conventionally refer to as universal propositional attitudes are, in fact, culturally relative. Such attitudes are indicated by the various verbs used to indicate a speaker's predisposition with respect to a particular statement she makes. In English-language discourse such attitudes are expressed by "I *know* that . . ."; "I *believe* that . . ."; "I *hope* that . . ."; "I *doubt* that . . ."; "I *fear* that . . .," and so forth. The point being that, if the criteria intrinsic to a natural language (English) that govern such expressions as "I know" or "I believe" can be very different from those of another natural language (Yoruba)—most obviously as indicated by the very different status of firsthand versus secondhand experience—the possibility should be raised that perhaps other words taken to refer to universal "mental" states or verbal dispositions may be unique and culturally relatively defined as well.[30]

According to Wiredu, in English-language epistemology, arising from English-language usage, "truth" is most often defined on the basis of correspondence theory. A statement is said to be true when it *corresponds to* a fact or a situation in the "real" world. Again according to Wiredu, the Twi-language phrase, *nea ete ne*, is said to be somewhat equivalent to the English-language "truth," since it is used to characterize *both* propositions and facts. Such usage has no further implication for any privileged relationship that should supposedly obtain between propositions and facts. This is not an issue for Twi discourse.

This does not result in Twi discourse being regarded as epistemologically underdeveloped. It does, however, indicate that idiosyncratic language usage alone may give rise to culturally relative "problems" of epistemology. This is further evidenced by the fact that the Yoruba-language "*òótó*" is used to characterize forms of experience as well as propositions (though, for coherent translation purposes, the

English-language meaning must shift to something like the English-language "certain" or "certainty").

Do the Yoruba, as well, use *òótó* to claim that certain things are "true" of the world independently of human experience (akin to English-language "facts")? Or does the emphasis the culture seems to place upon firsthand experience as the foundation of all knowledge dissuade its members from making such statements? Once again, there are some issues that ordinary discourse and usage do not address because there is no need for people to deal with them on the level of everyday discourse.

The skepticism implied by the Yoruba emphasis upon firsthand experience as the exclusive basis for knowledge is noteworthy. If that skepticism was to be implanted in English-language discourse, one wonders what the practical consequences might be. Apparently, no information would be lost if all secondhand propositional knowledge was reclassified as belief—as information whose truth status is only possible rather than clearly determined. But would such a step generate a form of cognitive insecurity that would be counterproductive? Ordinary language usage may be silent about such an issue, but this is, perhaps, the kind of consequence fusion philosophy would be interested in considering.

Linguistic or conceptual philosophy in the African context began with innumerable papers that had titles along the lines of, "The So-and-So's Concept of 'X.'" For "So-and-So" substitute the name of any African culture. For "X" substitute an indigenous term of apparent philosophical prepossession. Eventually, the emphasis shifted to more systemic concerns and entire fields of discourse rather than isolated concepts. Philosophers undertook outlining networks of concepts in African languages that were linked on the basis of epistemology, ethics, aesthetics, etc.[31] Highlighting the systematic basis of such systems of thought had very positive consequences, insofar as it illuminated the systematic character of African conceptual networks. Today there remain approximately 800 distinct language-cultures in sub-Saharan Africa. Most have yet to receive the attention of analytic philosophers, so it is likely there will be other interesting and intriguing discoveries about African meanings as African philosophy progresses.

African philosophers might be unhappy to see their fusion colleagues surgically removing individual components of those conceptual networks as they endeavor to link or integrate them with other components derived from non-African cultures. But they should be reassured by another very positive consideration that is implied by such "thought experiments," namely that all of the world's cultures and their indigenous languages are being treated as potential players and contributors to the fusion process. The playing field, finally, is becoming level and all participants are being granted intellectual integrity.

Notes

1 W. V. O. Quine, *Word and Object* (Cambridge, MA: MIT Press, 1960).

2 Kwasi Wiredu, "On Defining African Philosophy," in *African Philosophy: The Essential Readings*, ed. Tsenay Serequeberhan (New York: Paragon House, 1991), p. 109, fn. 42.

3 Kwasi Wiredu, *Cultural Universals and Particulars: An African Perspective* (Bloomington: Indiana University Press, 1996), p. 118.
4 D. A. Masolo, "Critical Rationalism and Cultural Traditions in African Philosophy," *New Political Science* 21, no. 1 (1999), pp. 59–72.
5 Kwame Anthony Appiah, "Inventing an African Practice in Philosophy: Epistemological Issues," in *The Surreptitious Speech*, ed. Valentin-Yves Mudimbe (Chicago: University of Chicago Press, 1992a), pp. 227–37.
6 Kwame Anthony Appiah, *In My Father's House: Africa in the Philosophy of Culture* (Oxford: Oxford University Press, 1992b), p. 143.
7 See: Helen Verran, *Science and an African Logic* (Chicago: University of Chicago Press, 2001); and Paulin Hountondji, "The Pitfalls of Being Different," *Diogenes* 131 (1985), pp. 46–56.
8 K. Wiredu, *Philosophy and an African Culture* (Cambridge and New York: Cambridge University Press, 1980), p. 213.
9 Henry Watson Fowler and Francis George Fowler, *Concise Oxford Dictionary* (Oxford: Clarendon Press, 1964), p. 1213.
10 Kwasi Wiredu, "The Concept of Truth in the Akan Language," in *Philosophy in Africa: Trends and Perspectives*, ed. Peter O. Bodunrin (Ife: University of Ife Press, 1985), p. 46 (my italics).
11 Valentin-Yves Mudimbe, *The Invention of Africa: Gnosis, Philosophy, and the Order of Knowledge* (Bloomington: Indiana University Press, 1988).
12 Kwasi Wiredu, "Truth and an African Language," in *African Philosophy: New and Traditional Perspectives*, ed. Lee M. Brown (Oxford: Oxford University Press, 2004), p. 47.
13 Ibid., p. 37.
14 Ibid., p. 48 (my italics).
15 Kwasi Wiredu, "Truth: The Correspondence Theory of Judgment," *African Philosophical Inquiry* (January, 1987), pp. 1–17.
16 Kwasi Wiredu, "Formulating Modern Thought in African Languages. Some Theoretical Considerations," in *The Surreptitious Speech*, ed. Valentin-Yves Mudimbe (Chicago: University of Chicago Press, 1992), pp. 301–32.
17 Ibid., p. 49.
18 Benjamin L. Whorf, *Language, Thought and Reality: Selected Writings of Benjamin Lee Whorf*, edited by John B. Carroll (Cambridge, MA: MIT Press, 1964); Kwasi Wiredu, "Are There Cultural Universals?" *The Monist* 78, no. 1 (1995), pp. 52–64.
19 Richard Feldman, *Epistemology* (Upper Saddle River, NJ: Prentice Hall, 2003), pp. 8–24.
20 J. Olubi Sodipo, my late colleague, coauthor, and friend was instrumental to all of the research relating to Yoruba epistemology. See: Barry Hallen and J. Olubi Sodipo, *Knowledge, Belief, and Witchcraft: Analytic Experiments in African Philosophy* (Stanford: Stanford University Press, 1997).
21 I am grateful to W. V. O. Quine for this suggestion.
22 The *Dictionary of Modern Yoruba* compiled by R. C. Abraham (1958) usually serves as the standard reference for Yoruba-English translations of this variety. Abraham misleadingly treats "*òótọ́*" as a straightforward equivalent of the English-language "truth," and the same is the case with "*ìgbgàbọ́*"/"*gbàgbọ́*" (p. 233) and the English-language "belief"/"believe." Both are examples of the apparently "loose" translation equivalences that are a necessary evil for the conventional, cross-cultural translation of everyday matters, and which cannot afford to take account of all semantic

differences, even if they happen to be more than nuances. See: Roy Clive Abraham, *Dictionary of Modern Yoruba* (London: University of London Press, 1958).

23 Barry Hallen, "Moral Epistemology. When Propositions Come Out of Mouths," *International Philosophical Quarterly* 38, no. 2 (1998), pp. 187–204.

24 See: Susan Haack, *Evidence and Inquiry: Towards Reconstruction in Epistemology* (Oxford: Blackwell, 1993), p. 233, where she compares this aspect of Yoruba epistemology to positions taken by Bertrand Russell, *The Problems of Philosophy* (Oxford: Oxford University Press, 1912).

25 One expression used regularly for testing was *dánwò* ("try to do").

26 Since it may now be said that the various disputants are reconciled.

27 According to Abraham, "*nwádi*" is a participial conflation of the verb for "looking" or "seeking" with the noun "*ìdí*" for "bottom," "base," "reason," or "cause," see: Abraham, *Dictionary of Modern Yoruba*, p. 272.

28 Ernest Gellner, *Legitimation of Belief* (Cambridge: Cambridge University Press, 1974); Rodney Needham, *Belief, Language and Experience* (Oxford: Blackwell, 1972); W. Newton-Smith, "Relativism and the Possibility of Interpretation," in *Rationality and Relativism*, ed. Martin Hollis and Steven Lukes (Oxford: Blackwell, 1982), pp. 106–22.

29 See: Edmund Gettier, "Is Justified True Belief Knowledge?" *Analysis* 23, no. 6 (1963), pp. 121–3.

30 Barry Hallen, "African Meanings, Western Words," *African Studies Review* 40, no. 1 (1997), pp. 1–11.

31 See: Rowland Abiodun, *Yoruba Art and Language: Seeking the African in African Art* (New York: Cambridge University Press, 2014); Barry Hallen, *African Philosophy: The Analytic Approach* (Trenton, NJ: Africa World Press, 2006).

References

Abiodun, R. (2014), *Yoruba Art and Language: Seeking the African in African Art*, New York: Cambridge University Press.

Abraham, R. C. (1958), *Dictionary of Modern Yoruba*, London: University of London Press.

Appiah, K. A. (1992a), "Inventing an African Practice in Philosophy: Epistemological Issues," in V. Y. Mudimbe (ed.), *The Surreptitious Speech: Presence Africaine and the Politics of Otherness 1947-1987*, Chicago: University of Chicago Press, 1992.

Appiah, K. A. (1992b), *In My Father's House: Africa in the Philosophy of Culture*, Oxford: Oxford University Press.

Feldman, R. (2003), *Epistemology*, Upper Saddle River, NJ: Prentice Hall.

Fowler, H. W. and Fowler, F. G. (1964), *Concise Oxford Dictionary*, Oxford: Clarendon Press.

Gellner, E. (1974), *Legitimation of Belief*, Cambridge: Cambridge University Press.

Gettier, E. (1963), "Is Justified True Belief Knowledge?" *Analysis*, 23 (6), pp. 121–3.

Haack, S. (1993), *Evidence and Inquiry: Towards Reconstruction in Epistemology*, Oxford: Blackwell.

Hallen, B. (1997), "African Meanings, Western Words," *African Studies Review*, 40 (1), pp. 1–11.

Hallen, B. (June, 1998), "Moral Epistemology: When Propositions Come Out of Mouths," *International Philosophical Quarterly*, 38 (2), pp. 187–204.

Hallen, B. (2006), *African Philosophy: The Analytic Approach*, Trenton, NJ: Africa World Press.
Hallen, B. and Sodipo, J. O. (1997), *Knowledge, Belief, and Witchcraft: Analytic Experiments in African Philosophy*, Stanford: Stanford University Press.
Hountondji, P. (1985), "The Pitfalls of Being Different," *Diogenes*, 131 (Fall), pp. 46–56.
Masolo, D. A. (1999), "Critical Rationalism and Cultural Traditions in African Philosophy," *New Political Science*, 21 (1), pp. 59–72.
Mudimbe, V. Y. (1988), *The Invention of Africa: Gnosis, Philosophy, and the Order of Knowledge*, Bloomington: Indiana University Press.
Needham, R. (1972), *Belief, Language, and Experience*, Oxford: Blackwell.
Newton-Smith, W. (1982), "Relativism and the Possibility of Interpretation," in M. Hollis and S. Lukes (eds), *Rationality and Relativism*, Oxford: Blackwell, pp. 106–22.
Quine, W. V. O. (1960), *Word and Object*, Cambridge, MA: MIT Press.
Russell, B. (1912), *The Problems of Philosophy*, Oxford: Oxford University Press.
Verran, H. (2001), *Science and an African Logic*, Chicago: University of Chicago Press.
Whorf, B. L. (1964), *Language, Thought and Reality: Selected Writings of Benjamin Lee Whorf*, edited by J. B. Carroll, Cambridge, MA: MIT Press.
Wiredu, K. (1980), *Philosophy and an African Culture*, Cambridge and New York: Cambridge University Press.
Wiredu, K. (1985), "The Concept of Truth in the Akan Language," in P. O. Bodunrin (ed.), *Philosophy in Africa: Trends and Perspectives*, Ife: University of Ife Press, pp. 43–54.
Wiredu, K. (January, 1987), "Truth: The Correspondence Theory of Judgment," *African Philosophical Inquiry*.
Wiredu, K. (1991), "On Defining African Philosophy," in T. Serequeberhan (ed.), *African Philosophy: The Essential Readings*, New York: Paragon House, pp. 87–110.
Wiredu, K. (1992), "Formulating Modern Thought in African Languages: Some Theoretical Considerations," in V. Y. Mudimbe (ed.), *The Surreptitious Speech: Presence Africaine and the Politics of Otherness 1947-1987*, Chicago: University of Chicago Press, pp. 301–32.
Wiredu, K. (January, 1995), "Are There Cultural Universals?," *The Monist*, 78 (1), pp. 52–64.
Wiredu, K. (1996), *Cultural Universals and Particulars: An African Perspective*, Bloomington: Indiana University Press.
Wiredu, K. (2004), "Truth and an African Language," in L. M. Brown (ed.), *African Philosophy: New and Traditional Perspectives*, Oxford: Oxford University Press, pp. 33–50.

3

Resolving the Ineffability Paradox

Chien-hsing Ho

Prologue

If I believe that a certain item X is ineffable for the reason that X cannot be expressed as it truly is by human concepts and words, questions arise as to how I can make this known to others *in words*, how words can be used to gesture toward X. I cannot even say X is unsayable,[1] because in *saying* so, I would have made X *sayable*. This is a time-honored conundrum known to many philosophers and religious thinkers in the East and the West. Confronting this conundrum, Augustine thinks it is better to evade the concerned verbal conflict silently than to quell it disputatiously, and early Wittgenstein famously asks us to pass over the ineffable in silence.

Indeed, a number of contemporary philosophers would agree that the unqualified statement "X is unspeakable" faces the danger of self-referential absurdity: if this statement is true, it must at the same time be false, given that X is speakable by the predicate word "unspeakable."[2] This predicament can be formulated as the following argument, which I shall term the "ineffability paradox":

P1: X is unspeakable.
P2: The statement "X is unspeakable" is true. (From P1)
P3: X is speakable by the predicate word "unspeakable." (From P2)
P4: The statement "X is unspeakable" is not true. (From P3)
∴ The statement "X is unspeakable" is both true and not true. (From P2 and P4)

Palpably, the conclusion of this argument is a contradiction. Recently, Graham Priest has reiterated that speaking of the ineffable does involve a real contradiction. However, his strategy for tackling something like the ineffability paradox, besides using the techniques of contemporary paraconsistent logic, is to aver that some contradictions are true in that they have their cause in the nature of reality, a nature that is contradictory. There are then, for Priest, contradictory statements that are true, and the statement "X is unspeakable" can well be both true and contradictory.[3] Nevertheless, most of us would find it hard to swallow the idea of the contradictoriness of reality. Consequently, we need to come up with a different strategy for resolving the paradox.

After the linguistic turn in the early twentieth century, with so much emphasis placed on the ubiquity and significance of language, the notion of ineffability may, for many philosophers, become somewhat obsolescent, perhaps something to be left to mystics and old school metaphysicians. Then, why do we need to bother with the notion? With all due respect to language, however, we must not think that language knows no limits, as we must not think we can capture the fresh gust of present actuality in the box of past convention. It is *not* true that each and every aspect of reality is speakable in the sense of being directly and properly expressible in words. If so, the notion of ineffability can still be of relevance to contemporary philosophizing.

To explain—in its use of general terms, such as "tree" and "squirrel," language operates in the realms of resemblance or commonness. It relies for its operation on the application of a general term to many particular objects that are held to be subsumed under the concept that corresponds to that term. For example, the word "tree" can be used, on the grounds of different trees' resemblance to one another, to refer to any one tree or all trees. Yet, features that are really specific to a particular tree *qua* tree do not fall within the semantic range of the word. It helps little to appeal to more specific words such as "maple" or "sugar maple," because they, as general terms, also function on the grounds of resemblance. Thus, such features can be so concrete, specific, and fine-grained that the tree evades complete linguistic determination, which must be abstract, generic, and coarse-grained. Given that words do not match the features, the tree is ineffable in at least some of its aspects.[4]

Furthermore, if one's repertoire of realities does not include universals and resemblances (more or less generic features that may be believed by others to inhere in things of the world), then concrete particulars such as maples and apples are wholly ineffable insofar as they are taken to be devoid of objective universals and real resemblances. Dignāga (c. 480–540 CE), a prominent Indian Buddhist epistemologist, basically takes such a stance.[5] For him, universals and resemblances are conceptually constructed and imposed onto real particulars, which are, in themselves, beyond the grip of words and concepts. The point for us is that the notion of ineffability may even concern objects of sense perception.

Now, if concrete particulars are ineffable, how are we to use words to refer to them? In the fifth chapter of his magnum opus, the *Pramāṇasamuccaya*, Dignāga puts forth a semantic theory of meaning known as the *apoha* (exclusion) theory, according to which a nominal word functions by excluding objects other than its own referent. The meaning of the word "maple" would then be the exclusion of non-maples. Dignāga does not explicitly address the aforesaid conundrum. However, the Chinese Yogācāra thinker Kuiji (窺基, 632–682) applies the theory to tackle the conundrum. As a first step toward resolving the ineffability paradox, I shall in the next (second) section discuss Dignāga's and Kuiji's relevant views on the issue.

In section 3, I first cope with the predicament of setting a limit to language. Then, I attend to a few passages in the works of the two Chinese Mādhyamika philosophers, Sengzhao (僧肇, 374?–414) and Jizang (吉藏, 549–623), and of the fifth-century Hindu grammarian-philosopher Bhartṛhari to reconstruct a strategy for showing how we can gesture toward the ineffable without making contradictions. A key notion here is that of *indication* as an indirect mode of expression, the mechanism and functioning of which will be clarified. In section 4, I contrast indication with description while introducing the notion of correctness in order to resolve the ineffability paradox. Thereafter, I discuss and dismiss three other approaches for tackling the conundrum as well as two likely objections against my strategy. Section 5 presents the conclusion.

A preliminary approach

Indian philosophers generally think that to apply a nominal word properly to a thing, a basis for the application is needed, that when one cognizes in a thing the basis for the application of a word, one is justified in using the word to refer to that thing. A universal inherent in a thing would for many serve as the basis: when I cognize in a tree the universal mapleness, I am justified in applying the word "maple" to that tree. Alternatively, some may hold that things of the same kind bear a family resemblance between them, which can well serve as the basis.

Dignāga repudiates the reality of universals and resemblances.[6] Instead, he brings in *apoha* or exclusion of others as a substitute for universals. The exclusion is only a conceptual-semantic item, to be reckoned with whenever we use words, but in no way truly inherent in a particular. Presumably, for him, the basis for the application of the word "maple" to particular maples is not the universal mapleness, but the exclusion of things other than maples, in short, non-maples, such as pines, breadfruits, rabbits, squirrels, hills, rivers, and so forth. The exclusion of non-maples is what all the particular maples have in common, on the basis of which one can use the word to refer to them. Incidentally, we can also use the term *apoha* operationally by saying that the word "maple" functions by excluding non-maples or by differentiating the maples from other things.

For Dignāga, a nominal word directly and properly expresses exclusion of others *qua* its basis of application. However, he also takes the word to directly and properly express something else. To cite two relevant statements[7]:

> S1: A word says (*āha*) those things that are qualified by exclusion of others.
> S2: The word "tree" . . . presents its own object (*svārtha*) as possessing the feature of being a tree. Thus, the object of a word is a thing qualified by exclusion, but not merely exclusion.

The word "tree" conventionally expresses and refers to all particular trees; it may, given contextual factors, be used to refer to a given tree. One may take S1 to mean that the word *says* (viz., directly and properly expresses) particular trees by excluding non-trees. However, on account of the ineffability of particulars, the word cannot really say any particular tree or any of the latter's intrinsic features. In addition, the qualifier-qualificand distinction is for Dignāga conceptually constructed. Thus, a conceptually unqualified particular tree must be distinguished from the tree qualified by the exclusion of non-trees. Meanwhile, the own object of the word, as noted in S2, is a thing qualified by the exclusion of non-trees. The exclusion is conventionally none other than the generic feature of being a tree, which the thing is linguistically presented as possessing. In any case, the word "tree" directly and properly expresses a conceptually qualified, generic tree as well as the exclusion of non-trees.

As such a qualified generic something is what a word *semantically* refers to, it may be termed the "semantic referent." In contrast, the real particular concerned may be termed the "intended referent," because it is what the language user intends to refer to but has difficulty putting into words. Of course, under normal circumstances, no one would use the word "maple" to refer to a conceptual-semantic item as the semantic referent. Given the ineffability of a particular maple *qua* the intended referent, however, we need to reckon with a generic maple as an individual thing taken precisely as conceptually qualified by the exclusion of non-maples.

Intriguingly, before the time of Dignāga, ideas similar to the notion of *apoha* were present in Chinese Madhyamaka. Sengzhao asserts that, in Mahayana Buddhist scriptures, the use of the word "existent" (*you* 有) with respect to a thing is to show that the thing is *not* nonexistent, whereas that of the word "nonexistent" (*wu* 無) is to make explicit that the thing is *not* existent.[8] The words function by differentiating their referents from what the referents are not, rather than denoting something definitively existent or nonexistent. However, the rationale behind the assertion differs from Dignāga's. It concerns Sengzhao's own Mādhyamika view, which he thinks is implied in the scriptures, that the myriad things are *empty* in the sense of being void of any determinate form or nature.

Although the *apoha* theory was set forth to explain how nominal words function given the ineffability of particulars, Dignāga did not explicitly address the conundrum of saying the unsayable. Yet, the Chinese Yogācāra thinker Kuiji does apply the theory to offer a noteworthy solution[9]:

> A particular cannot be reached by word and speech. . . . [Question:] If so, all real things being unspeakable, wouldn't it be inappropriate as well to speak the word "unspeakable"? [Answer:] The word is spoken in order to exclude the speakables. It is not meant that the word "unspeakable" matches the substances of things (*fati* 法體), for the latter are not [what one would take to be by the concept of] *unspeakable.*

The question posed is that if one uses the word "unspeakable" to *speak* of particulars as unspeakable, one would self-contradictorily make them speakable. To resolve the problem, Kuiji applies the *apoha* operation to the word "unspeakable." The word here does not really *reach* or speak of the unspeakable; it does not predicate of the latter the intrinsic property of being unspeakable. Instead, the word functions by excluding speakable items such as unreal universals. Meanwhile, Kuiji implies that we must distinguish between an unspeakable thing in itself and what we understand it to be by the concept of "unspeakable," a distinction that corresponds to that between intended referent and semantic referent.

Kuiji's ingenious solution is helpful, but it does not explain how words used can refer, or direct one's attention, to the ineffable.[10] Elsewhere, he claims that nominal words both exclude and signify.[11] We may clarify this terse claim by considering the view of his pupil Huizhao (惠沼, 650–714), who appears to think something like this: as the word, say, "maple" was formed and learned by people's perceiving particular maples in the past, although it mainly excludes non-maples, one can use it provisionally to refer to what one intends to signify, namely, particular maples.[12] Presumably, both convention and causation play a role here. Still, this view does not explain the mechanism of linguistic reference, so it is far from being satisfactory.

The mechanism of indication

In the preface to his *Tractatus*, Wittgenstein writes thus: "In order to be able to draw a limit to thought, we should have to find both sides of the limit thinkable (i.e., we should have to be able to think what cannot be thought)."[13] Similarly, it may be said, to set a limit to language, we should have to find both sides of the limit sayable and so the unsayable would turn out to be sayable. We can understand this by considering an analogical example in actual life. In order to draw a line as a limit on any surface, our eyes would have to look at both sides of the line. Then, the two sides of the line are on a par, equally visible or cognizable to us; in *this* sense, the limit ceases to be a limit. However, there is a line or limit that is an exception to this: the horizon.

Suppose, on a countryside, someone asks me about the location of village X, which is somewhere beyond our visible horizon. Although I can *point out* the roads to X, which we both can see, I can only *point toward* X, of which neither of us can have a glimpse, while saying something like "It is over there above the horizon." Clearly, X and the roads to X, on the two sides of the horizon, are not equally cognized. Still, with the information conveyed, the person can roughly locate X and know how to reach it. Likewise, things on the near side of our *semantic* horizon (the limits to sayability) can be spoken of or described, whereas those on the far side can only be gestured toward or indicated. The sayable and the unsayable, on the two sides of the horizon, are surely different. Even though words cannot describe the unsayable, they can gesture toward it, locating it on the far side of a segment of the semantic horizon.

Gesturing toward is an indirect mode of expression, and so I am assuming that the ineffable is indirectly expressible. As far as I can tell, when an Eastern ineffabilist asserts that a certain item X is ineffable, he or she is mostly denying any conformity between words and X, but not X's indirect expressibility too. In this regard, we may attend to Sengzhao again[14]:

> As this [sagely mind] is nameless, it cannot be spoken of in words. Yet, though it cannot be spoken of in words, it cannot be transmitted without the use of words. Thus, the sages speak all day without having spoken.

Sengzhao clearly implies that though sagely mind is unspeakable, it is linguistically transmittable. Words can be used to transmit information about the mind and thereby indirectly express it. Meanwhile, the paradoxical expression "the sages speak all day without having spoken" presumably means that the sages do not use words to *speak* the unspeakable. The words used are provisional,[15] indirectly expressive, and to be negated if one takes them to represent the unspeakable as it is.

Elsewhere, Sengzhao explains why anything is said to be ineffable[16]:

> A speech arises from names, names arise because of forms (*xiang* 相), and a form arises owing to the mind's cognizing a form [in its object]. What is formless is nameless, what is nameless is speechless.

The term "form" is related to the Indian notion of the basis for the application of a word. If one conceptually cognizes a generic or coarse-grained form in an object, one can adequately apply the corresponding word to the object, and the object is deemed sayable. However, if the object is not endowed with any such cognizable form, as sagely mind is for Sengzhao, then, being formless, it is nameless and unsayable.

Now, if X is formless and unsayable, how can we use words to refer to it? Sengzhao suggests that words used to identify the unsayable are provisional external appellations. According to Jizang, all the Buddha's teachings "are similar in trying provisionally to apply names and forms to that which is nameless and formless, in order that sentient beings realize the speechless by means of speech."[17] Then, to let others understand the formless and unsayable X, we should provisionally apply the word "unsayable" to it. For this provisional application, a provisional form as the basis is needed. The form can be the state of being unsayable, or simply unsayability, which is what the word directly and properly expresses. Although X is formless, we can conceive this form of unsayability and apply or superimpose it onto X such that one understands that X is unsayable.

Something like this can be rationally reconstructed from the following passage by the Hindu grammarian-philosopher Bhartṛhari in his attempt to resolve the conundrum of saying the unsayable[18]:

> If a thing is said to be unsayable, someway or another or in all ways, by some words, then its state of being unsayable [i.e., its unsayability] is *not* denied by those words. Indeed, a doubt with regard to an object does not function toward the dubiousness attached [to that object] without giving up its own nature.

Suppose for some reason I am doubting someone, I do not simultaneously doubt her dubiousness. If, instead, I come to doubt her dubiousness, then she is made free from doubt and my doubt gives up its original nature of rendering her dubious. Likewise, we can thus construe the functioning of the word "unsayable" in the statement "X is unsayable." The word *denies* only X itself, but not X's unsayability; that is, the word conveys that X is *not* sayable, but not that X's unsayability is not sayable. To put it the other way, the word *says* only X's unsayability, but not X itself. Significantly, this unsayability is not an intrinsic feature or property of X. It is only provisionally conceived and does not really inhere in X. Yet, by being superimposed on X, it makes known that X is unsayable. As X is *not* said, it is not made sayable. As the unsayability is said, by being superimposed on X, one comprehends the unsayability *of* X. Thus, the purpose of making known that X is unsayable is achieved, without thereby making X sayable.

The notion of superimposition plays a key role here as it helps to relate that which is said to what is unsayable and show how words can be used to direct one's attention to the unsayable. On the one hand, the superimposition has the function of revealing, because the superimposed unsayability shows X to be unsayable. It performs the function of concealing on the other, for it covers up the real nature of X, which is *not* unsayable in the way we understand X through the concept of unsayability (recall the above quotation from Kuiji). Then, we need to negate the superimposition, taking it as simply a provisional application, not a real attribution. In the provisional use of the word "unsayable," we cognize the unsayable through the superimposition on it of unsayability and the negation of this superimposition. Without the superimposition nothing about the unsayable would be intimated; without the negation the unsayable may erroneously become sayable.[19]

Let us use the term "indicate" in this technical sense: the word "unsayable" *says* the form of unsayability and so, with the unsayability being superimposed on X, *indicates* X such that one comprehends that X is unsayable. Hence, indication is an indirect mode of expression that consists of two phases: the saying phase and the imposition phase. An indicative expression can indirectly express the unsayable without actually saying it.

In respect of the word "unsayable," we have so far focused on the form of unsayability. Yet, our discussions on Dignāga's *apoha* theory suggest that the word also directly and properly expresses a generic something qualified by the unsayability. It is a qualified generic X *qua* the word's semantic referent. The semantic referent is then superimposed on the unsayable X *qua* the intended referent such that one knows X to be *something* unsayable. However, we can generally neglect this aspect of the functioning of a word. In addition, while we have been mainly concerned with a word in the context of a sentence, the mechanism of indication can, *mutatis mutandis*, be applied to a sentence as well, allowing us to speak of an indicative sentence or statement.

Finally, indication can broadly be regarded as a gestural language. It helps to reconstrue, and is reinforced by, the horizon simile. Here, my pointing gesture, as it were, *tells* the direction for reaching village X. This direction is superimposed onto what lies beyond a segment of the horizon, the result of which is the rough location of the village. The location may need implicitly to be negated as it is not truly an intrinsic feature of the village. In any case, the point for us is that we can gesture toward the ineffable without making contradictions.

Resolving the paradox

It is widely thought in contemporary philosophy that human language has both cognitive (referential) and noncognitive (nonreferential) functions. In its cognitive function, language is meant primarily to convey information about, or express factual descriptions of, the world. In its noncognitive function, language is used not primarily to convey information but to make a request, give an order, elicit feelings, evoke experiences, and so forth. Yet, I think it is unconvincing to hold that language has only one cognitive function, that is, to describe objects or states of affairs. Suppose X is unspeakable and the statement "X is unspeakable" truly describes what the case is, namely, the state of affairs of X's being unspeakable. Then, as X can be spoken of by the statement, the statement is both true and not true. The ineffability paradox ensues!

Indication as an indirect mode of expression is broadly cognitive in that it conveys information about its intended referent. Unlike a description, however, an indication is not meant to, and does not actually, match the referent. Since the notion of truth is often understood to imply a correspondence between language (words, propositions) and reality (objects, states of affairs), we should not take an indicative sentence to be a truth-bearer: it is *not* either true or false. However, not only can an indication meaningfully, informatively gesture toward something beyond our semantic horizon, but the information transmitted can be correct or otherwise (In showing where village X is, my pointing would be correct if I point in the right direction, incorrect if otherwise.). Therefore, I suggest that we, instead, speak of an indication as correct or incorrect, where the notion of correctness does not imply the aforesaid correspondence.

Now, recall the argument I termed the ineffability paradox. The argument embodies a legitimate logical paradox if we treat its premises as descriptive statements, which are all plausibly true. However, if we treat P1, "X is unspeakable," as an indicative statement, then, even if the statement "X is unspeakable" is correct, it is not true that the statement is true. Therefore, P2 is false. Consequently, the argument turns out to be fallacious and fails to be a legitimate paradox. We have thus resolved the ineffability paradox. The point, then, depends on whether we use the words of the statement indicatively or descriptively.

There are, of course, other possible ways of responding to the conundrum of saying the unsayable or the ineffability paradox. To keep this chapter focused, I shall briefly discuss only three approaches that are pertinent here. The first approach distinguishes first-order from second-order use of words and treats the word "unspeakable" in the above statement as a second-order word that refers to first-order words. For instance, two verses after the above-quoted passage Bhartṛhari writes: "What functions as a signifier cannot be signified. That which expresses something else cannot in the same context be expressed."[20] Thus, the word "unspeakable" functions to convey that X cannot be spoken of by any first-order words, the word not being one of them. It is a mistake, and goes against the language user's intention, to assert that the use of the word in respect of X would result in self-referential absurdity. Meanwhile, in the paradox argument, the statement "X is unspeakable" ought to be qualified one way in P2, another way in P4; when this is done, the argument is fallacious and the paradox ceases to arise. One problem with this approach is that it implies that X can be spoken of by the word "unspeakable."[21] This is a bit odd, and anyone who adopts the approach owes us an explanation as to why and *how* X is speakable by second-order words but unspeakable by first-order words (when both are human words).

For similar purposes, the anonymous Chinese Buddhist text *Awakening of the Mahayana Faith* (*Dacheng qishen lun*, 大乘起信論) introduces the phrase "using words to exclude words" (*yin yan qian yan*, 因言遣言) to contend that the term "suchness" (*zhenru*, 真如) is the ultimate term that one can appeal to for intimating the ineffable mind of suchness, and that the term serves the function of excluding all other terms. Unlike the former approach, however, even the term "suchness," the text suggests, is provisional and does not match the ineffable. The commentator and Huayan master Fazang (法藏, 643–712) gives an intriguing analogy. One shouts "Quiet!" in order to stop human noises. Without the shouting, the noises would not be stopped. Yet, if one, to make sure that the order is obeyed, shouts several times, then one makes noises oneself and fails to stop noises. Just as here one must not keep shouting, likewise, the term "suchness" needs to be excluded too.[22] This points to the second approach concerned, in which one negates or *unsays* whatever one has said about the ineffable. Of the paradox argument, one who upholds the approach can challenge even P1 by saying something like "I don't mean to say X is unspeakable" or "X's being unspeakable is also unspeakable."

We already touched on this approach while explaining Sengzhao's expression "the sages speak all day without having spoken." It is partially implicit in the discussion on the notion of superimposition. Like Kuiji's ingenious *apoha* solution, the approach has the advantage of refraining from making the unsayable sayable. Nonetheless, they are both deficient because they do not clearly explain how words can, one way or another, be related to the unsayable: without the relation, the words used are hardly better than meaningless sounds. By contrast, our strategy overcomes this problem by resorting to the notions of superimposition and of gesturing beyond the horizon.

The third approach, the *dialetheist* approach, radically differs from the first two. In their paper on contradictions in Buddhism, Graham Priest, Jay Garfield, and Yasuo Deguchi contend that certain Mahayana Buddhists are committed to the view that some contradictions are true and acceptable, and that modern developments in paraconsistent logics have shown that such a stance can be rational. According to them, for instance, some Buddhists describe certain things about an indescribable reality such that the indescribable is described.[23] Then, the paradox argument would have the conclusion that the statement "X is unspeakable" is both true and contradictory, which they would say is rationally acceptable.

If the Buddhist simply means to transmit indirectly certain information about an indescribable reality, then, as we have seen, to state that the reality is indescribable is *not* to describe it. There is no irresoluble contradiction here. It is, instead, gesturing beyond our semantic horizon by telling something about the direction across the horizon. To the best of my knowledge, Mahayana Buddhist thinkers never explicitly assert that some contradictions are true. Whereas some Buddhists are keen on using paradoxical or figurative expressions, this usually has to do with the perceived limitations of descriptive language. As an additional note, Priest's claim that reality is contradictory in the sense that it is such as to render certain contradictory statements true squares poorly with the Chinese Mādhyamika position that reality is *empty* of any describable determinate structure.[24] A contradiction is as determinate as a tautology. Correspondingly, to claim that reality is contradictory is to predicate of reality a determinate, though contradictory, structure describable in words or logical symbols. Yet, what if reality is indescribable and, somewhat like an amorphous lump, empty of any determinate structure? Perhaps, the idea of a contradictory reality fits better with a logically possible world, but not the concrete world of lived experience.

To complete this section, let me examine two likely objections against my strategy. First, some may object that I, like many others, have unnecessarily complicated the issue of referring to the ineffable. After all, one can use nominal words simply as proper names that designate and refer to the ineffable. Since few would take a proper name to have any conceptual meaning or content, the use of such names would not result in the aforesaid conundrum. Second, it may be charged that my strategy is based on the problematic assumption that the ineffable is indirectly expressible. In actual fact, the objector may say, some ineffabilists claim or imply that the ineffable is indirectly inexpressible as well. Thus, even if we rephrase P2 of the paradox argument as "The statement 'X is unspeakable' is correct" (where the word "unspeakable" implies indirect inexpressibility), the argument would still have the contradictory conclusion to the effect that the statement is both correct and not correct. Then, the strategy fails to resolve the ineffability paradox.

In responding to the first objection, we may appeal to William Alston's views against a tactic for resolving the predicament of referring to the ineffable. For Alston, although the word "God" in the statement "God is ineffable" may be regarded as a proper name not standing for any concept, we would not count anyone as understanding the statement if he or she is unable to use some identifying phrase, for example "the first cause" or "the father of Jesus Christ," to explain the word. Yet, any such phrase would constitute a characterization of God and so make God factually speakable.[25] The use or understanding of a proper name thus presupposes a certain expressible knowledge of the object named, but this inevitably implies the expression of the so-called ineffable. In addition, we also wonder how anyone can use the word "unspeakable" in the statement "X is unspeakable" as a proper name at all. Hence, the issue cannot be resolved so easily as is believed by the objector.

I agree with the second objection that if the ineffable X is directly and indirectly inexpressible, then one cannot express it without making contradictions. When asked any question about X, the ineffabilist cannot but remain in silence. To make matters worse, if remaining in silence counts as a body language, which in turn counts as a form of language, then one cannot even stay silent.[26] There would be no escape from self-contradiction. Nonetheless, it is never my intention to defend such an ineffabilist. In addition, to my knowledge, no Eastern ineffabilist referred to above asserts that his ineffable X is indirectly inexpressible. Consequently, our assumption is not problematic, and the objection may simply miss its target.

Epilogue

We began this chapter with the time-honored linguistic-philosophical conundrum of saying the unsayable and the related ineffability paradox. For many, this issue is unresolvable, which casts doubts on the viability of the notion of ineffability. After examining the Buddhist semantic theory of *apoha* and an *apoha* solution to the issue, we resorted to certain Buddhist and non-Buddhist philosophical materials to rationally reconstruct a strategy for coping with the conundrum and, especially, resolving the paradox. By introducing the mode of expression termed "indication," together with the relevant notions of superimposition and of gesturing beyond the horizon, I wish to have shown that expressing the ineffable does not necessarily involve irresoluble contradiction. It is also hoped that our philosophical exercise, unusual in conjoining Chinese Buddhism and Hindu philosophy, points to a constructive way forward for comparative philosophy.

If our strategy is on the whole persuasive, if we cannot adequately capture the fresh gust of actuality in the box of convention, then philosophers may need to recognize the limitations of language and acknowledge the relevance of the notion of ineffability for contemporary philosophizing. Instead of belittling language, this recognition may induce one to value even more various possibly nondescriptive modes of expression such as metaphor, negation, paradox, indication, parable, poetic language, and so on. It might also prompt philosophers to attend more than is normal to the concrete, fine-grained, and tacit aspects of human life and experience, which have tended to be filtered out by abstract philosophical thinking.

Notes

1 In this chapter, the words "ineffable," "unsayable," and "unspeakable" are used interchangeably.

2 Cf. William Alston, "Ineffability," *Philosophical Review* 65, no. 4 (1956), pp. 506–22; Keith E. Yandell, "Some Varieties of Ineffability," *International Journal for Philosophy of Religion* 6, no. 3 (1975), pp. 167–79; and Walter Terrence Stace, *Mysticism and Philosophy* (Los Angeles: Jeremy P. Tarcher, 1987). Correlatively, Plantinga contends that the "view that our concepts don't apply to God is fatally ensnared in self-referential absurdity." See: Alvin Plantinga, *Does God Have a Nature?* (Milwaukee: Marquette University Press, 1980), p. 26.

3 Graham Priest, *Beyond the Limits of Thought* (Oxford: Oxford University Press, 2002), pp. 294–5; Graham Priest, "Speaking of the Ineffable . . .," in *Nothingness in Asian Philosophy*, ed. JeeLoo Liu and Douglas L. Berger (New York: Routledge, 2014), pp. 91–103.

4 I understand the notion of ineffability somewhat broadly. An item is ineffable (viz., directly and properly inexpressible) if it or its texture does not conform to the semantic structure of any words one may use to denote or describe it. Roughly something like this nonconformity or mismatch between language and reality is behind many Eastern thinkers' assertion of ineffability.

5 It is disputable whether Dignāga's notion of particular (*svalakṣaṇa*) covers such medium-sized objects as maples and apples. However, we can here neglect this technical issue.

6 Richard P. Hayes, *Dignāga on the Interpretation of Signs* (Dordrecht: Kluwer Academic Publishers, 1988), p. 246. For a recent exposition of Dignāga's *apoha* theory, see: O. Pind, "Dignāga's Apoha Theory: Its Presuppositions and Main Theoretical Implications," in *Apoha: Buddhist Nominalism and Human Cognition*, ed. Mark Siderits, Tom Tillemans, and Arindam Chakrabarti (New York: Columbia University Press, 2011), pp. 64–83.

7 Hayes, *Dignāga on the Interpretation of Signs*, p. 308: "*śabdo 'rthāntaranivṛttiviśiṣṭān eva bhāvān āha*"; Pind, "Dignāga's Apoha Theory," p. 83: "*vṛkṣaśabdo . . . svārthaṁ vṛkṣalakṣaṇaṁ pratyāyayati . . ., evaṁ ca nivṛttiviśiṣṭaṁ vastu śabdārthaḥ, na nivṛttimātram*." In this chapter, all translations from Sanskrit and Chinese are mine.

8 *Zhaolun*, *T* 45: 152c12–14, 159b11; cf. 151b13–15. All references taken from *Taishō shinshū daizōkyō* 大正新脩大藏經 (abbreviated as *T*). In CBETA Chinese Electronic Tripiṭaka Version April 2014. Taipei: Chinese Buddhist Electronic Text Association.

9 *Cheng weishi lun shuji*, *T* 43: 288a21–b1: "言說不及是自相。 . . . 若爾，即一切法不可言，不可言言亦不稱理？遮可言故，言不可言；非不可言即稱法體，法體亦非不可言故."

10 As Priest puts it, "If one wishes to explain why something is ineffable, one *must* refer to it and say something about it. To refer to something *else*, about which one *can* talk, is just to change the subject." See: Priest, "Speaking of the Ineffable . . .", p. 98. It is surely not enough just to take the word "unspeakable" to exclude speakables.

11 *Yinming ru zhengli lunshu*, *T* 44: 138a26–28. This claim is to explain why, by uttering the word "fire," one would obtain fire, but not water, when the particulars of both fire and water are unspeakable.

12 *Cheng weishi lun liaoyi deng*, *T* 43: 716b9–14. See also *Cheng weishi lun shuji*, *T* 43: 296c15–17.

13 Ludwig Wittgenstein, *Tractatus Logico-Philosophicus*, translated by D. F. Pears and B. F. McGuinness (London: Routledge and Kegan Paul, 1963), p. 3.

14 *Zhaolun*, *T* 45: 153c24–26: "斯則無名之法，故非言所能言也。言雖不能言，然非言無以傳，是以聖人終日言而未嘗言也."

15 The words are *provisional* in that they are used provisionally in the sense that they are not meant to say or match the intended referent and need to be negated, especially if one takes them to represent the way the referent truly is.

16 *Zhaolun*, *T* 45: 159b20–21: "夫言由名起，名以相生，相因可相。無相無名，無名無說." In Chinese Buddhism, the word "name" (*ming* 名) normally means a nominal word, but not a proper name.

17 *Shengman baoku*, *T* 37: 5b18–19: "同是無名相中強名相說，欲令眾生因言以悟無言也." Also, *Jingming xuanlun*, *T* 38: 856b7–8.

18 Wilhelm Rau, ed., *Bhartṛharis Vākyapadīya: Die Mūlakārikās nach den Handschriften herausgegeben und mit einem Pāda-Index versehen* (Wiesbaden: Franz Steiner, 1977), p. 120: "*tathānyathā sarvathā ca yasyāvācyatvam ucyate, tatrāpi naiva sāvasthā taiḥ śabdaiḥ pratiṣidhyate. na hi saṁśayarūpe'rthe śeṣatvena vyavasthite, avyudāse svarūpasya saṁśayo'nyaḥ pravartate.*" Bhartṛhari's notion of superimposition (*adhyāropa, samāropa*) can be found in Rau, *Bhartṛharis Vākyapadīya*, pp. 123, 132.

19 For a related paper of mine that focuses on Bhartṛhari's approach, see: Chien-hsing Ho, "Saying the Unsayable," *Philosophy East and West* 56, no. 3 (2006), pp. 409–27. To my knowledge, the Mādhyamika philosopher Candrakīrti (c. 600–650) and the Hindu Vedantic philosopher Śaṅkara (c. 788–820) have both employed the notion of superimposition to show how we can use words to refer to the ineffable. However, they did not elaborate further the way I have done.

20 Rau, *Bhartṛharis Vākyapadīya*, p. 120: "*na ca vācakarūpeṇa pravṛttasyāsti vācyatā, pratipādyaṁ na tat tatra yenānyat pratipadyate.*" Before this verse, Bhartṛhari states that if someone claims that "all what I say is false," the person does not intend to take this claim to be false. That Bhartṛhari mentions such examples may indicate that our aforesaid strategy is a reconstruction rather than an interpretation of his proposed solution.

21 If, however, the word "unspeakable" refers solely to first-order words, not to X, then the problem would be similar to the one faced by Kuiji's *apoha* solution.

22 See *Dacheng qishen lun yiji* (大乘起信論義記), *T* 44: 252c11–253a2.

23 Yasuo Deguchi, Jay L. Garfield, and Graham Priest, "The Way of the Dialetheist: Contradictions in Buddhism," *Philosophy East and West* 58, no. 3 (2008), pp. 399–401. We have mentioned above Priest's strategy.

24 For Sengzhao's position on the issue, see: C. Ho, "Emptiness as Subject-Object Unity: Sengzhao on the Way Things Truly Are," in *Nothingness in Asian Philosophy*, ed. JeeLoo Liu and Douglas L. Berger (New York: Routledge, 2014), pp. 104–18.

25 Alston, "Ineffability," pp. 511–17.

26 In the *Vimalakīrtinirdeśa Sūtra*, when asked about his own way of transcending duality, unlike other Bodhisattvas around who spoke their views, Vimalakīrti, the main character of the sutra, wisely remained silent. He was then praised for his *sacred silence*. Commenting on this narrative, Jizang remarks that while other Bodhisattvas provisionally applied names to show the nameless and formless, Vimalakīrti provisionally applied the *forms* of silence to make explicit the nameless and formless. Then, Vimalakīrti's silence is none other than a provisional *bodily* expression. See *Jingming Xuanlun*, *T* 38: 856b6–11.

References

Alston, W. (1956), "Ineffability," *Philosophical Review*, 65 (4), pp. 506–22.

Cheng weishi lun liaoyi deng 成唯識論了義燈 [*A Lamp for Illuminating the Meaning of the Vijñaptimātratāsiddhi Śāstra*]. By Huizhao. In *T*, vol. 43, no. 1832.

Cheng weishi lun shuji 成唯識論述記 [*Commentary Notes on the Vijñaptimātratāsiddhi Śāstra*]. By Kuiji. In *T*, vol. 43, no. 1830.

Dacheng qishen lun yiji 大乘起信論義記 [*Notes on the Meaning of the Awakening of the Mahayana Faith*]. By Fazang. In *T*, vol. 44, no. 1846.

Deguchi, Y., Garfield, J. L., and Priest, G. (2008), "The Way of the Dialetheist: Contradictions in Buddhism," *Philosophy East and West*, 58 (3), pp. 395–402.

Hayes, R. P. (1988), *Dignāga on the Interpretation of Signs*, Dordrecht: Kluwer Academic Publishers.

Ho, C.-H. (2006), "Saying the Unsayable," *Philosophy East and West*, 56 (3), pp. 409–27.

Ho, C.-H. (2014), "Emptiness as Subject-Object Unity: Sengzhao on the Way Things Truly Are," in JeeLoo Liu and Douglas L. Berger (eds), *Nothingness in Asian Philosophy*, New York: Routledge, pp. 104–118.

Jingming xuanlun 淨名玄論 [*A Treatise on the Profound Teaching of Vimalakīrti*]. By Jizang. In *T*, vol. 38, no. 1780.

Pind, O. (2011), "Dignāga's Apoha Theory: Its Presuppositions and Main Theoretical Implications," in M. Siderits, T. Tillemans, and A. Chakrabarti (eds), *Apoha: Buddhist Nominalism and Human Cognition*, New York: Columbia University Press, pp. 64–83.

Plantinga, A. (1980), *Does God Have a Nature*? Milwaukee: Marquette University Press.

Priest, G. (2002), *Beyond the Limits of Thought*, Oxford: Oxford University Press.

Priest, G. (2014), "Speaking of the Ineffable . . .," in J.-L. Liu and D. L. Berger (eds), *Nothingness in Asian Philosophy*, New York: Routledge, pp. 91–103.

Rau, W., ed. (1977), *Bhartṛharis Vākyapadīya: Die Mūlakārikās nach den Handschriften herausgegeben und mit einem Pāda-Index versehen*, Wiesbaden: Franz Steiner.

Shengman baoku 勝鬘寶窟 [*The Jewel Cave of the Śrīmālā Sūtra*]. By Jizang. In *T*, vol. 37, no. 1744.

Stace, W. T. (1987), *Mysticism and Philosophy*, Los Angeles: Jeremy P. Tarcher.

Taishō shinshū daizōkyō 大正新脩大藏經 (abbreviated as *T*). In CBETA Chinese Electronic Tripiṭaka Version April 2014. Taipei: Chinese Buddhist Electronic Text Association.

Wittgenstein, L. (1963), *Tractatus Logico-Philosophicus*, translated by D. F. Pears and B. F. McGuinness, London: Routledge and Kegan Paul.
Yandell, K. E. (1975), "Some Varieties of Ineffability," *International Journal for Philosophy of Religion*, 6 (3), pp. 167–79.
Yinming ru zhengli lunshu 因明入正理論疏 [*A Commentary on the Nyāyapraveśa*]. By Kuiji. In *T*, vol. 44, no. 1840.
Zhaolun 肇論 [*The Treatise of Sengzhao*]. By Sengzhao. In *T*, vol. 45, no. 1858.

4

The Bowstring is Like a Woman Humming: The Vedic Hymn to the Weapons and the Transformative Properties of Tools

Laurie L. Patton

The questions

A much-ignored early Vedic hymn (*Ṛg Veda* [RV] 6.75) not only blesses weapons before battle, but in its ebullience it compares the bowstring to a woman humming.[1] Why would one engage in the practice of blessing a weapon, and spend time describing it in such intimate detail? Would a weapon's efficacy not speak for itself? Recently, on a blog by a Cuban Orthodox priest there was a discussion about whether it was appropriate at all for the priests of the Russian Orthodox Church to bless weapons, including photos and a description of the service. The defense of such a practice looked at a series of earlier precedents, such as in the 1920s and 1930s, when most of the Russian Orthodox clergy had been executed and the church and its followers needed a way to defend themselves. Surely this, the interlocutor asked, was a situation where the blessing of weapons was needed?

And lest we think that this is only a debate between pacifist and non-pacifist Christians, we might remind ourselves of the twenty-first-century video and Internet game called Mabinogi, where there is an entire protocol about the development and blessing of weapons. And, of course, there are the very powerful stories from India itself. Indra's magical weapons include a thunderbolt and other celestial implements of deadly sharpness. We see weapons frequently in the great Indian epic of the *Mahābhārata*. In one famous episode, after taking the form of the mountaineer Kirāṭa, Śiva does battle with the Pāṇḍava warrior Arjuna, and conquers him. After the battle, Śiva gives Arjuna a whole host of magical weapons that he seeks. The epic heroes, Paraśurāma, Bhīṣma, Droṇa, Karṇa, Kṛpa, Aśvatthāma, Arjuna, and even the dharmic king Yudhiṣṭhira, all possess the knowledge of *brahmāstra*, the weapon with the head of Brahma at its tip, capable of destroying whole hosts at once.

But these more well-known contexts aside, what kind of practice is the blessing of weapons? And what are the contexts of its use? In this chapter I argue that we can think about the blessing of weapons even before the epic tradition in India and beyond the more well-known Vedic example of Indra. We can turn particularly to lesser known works in the oldest of Indian traditions. In analyzing this understudied hymn RV 6.75, dating from the late second millennium BCE, we might be able to get at some of the dynamics that would inspire such a practice, and think about its philosophical (yes, philosophical) implications.

The hymn: Background

RV 6.75 explodes all the stereotypes anyone could have about a peaceful ancient India: it is a hymn to the weapons before setting out for war. Its *ṛṣi*, or sage and composer, is called Pāyu Bhāradvāja. The Bhāradvāja clan is mentioned in the *Atharva Veda*, a Veda of the Atharva clan that includes both sacrificial and "everyday" mantras from the world of the household, in hymn 18.36, as well as in 4.29.5.

As Indologist Thaneshwar Sarmah explains, the *ṛṣi* Pāyu is also known for other hymns of battle.[2] He is said to be the author of the singular *saṃgrama* hymn, the hymn that contains blessings in battle. And *Ṛg Veda* 6.47.24 is also the hymn that mentions Pāyu as a *ṛṣi* and an author in his own right. *Ṛg Veda* 6.47 states that Aśvatha gave Pāyu and the followers of the Atharvans chariots with the best horses and a hundred cows. Pāyu is also named as a composer in the *Yajur Veda*, a Veda focused on ritual rules and procedures. In the Yajur Vedic text *Vājansaneyi Saṃhitā* 29.38–60, fourteen verses repeat the Ṛg Vedic hymn itself. The rest of Pāyu Bhāradvāja's hymn in the *Vājansaneyi Saṃhitā* is also a repetition, and based on the Ṛg Vedic verses that honor the war drum, or *dundubhi*, 6.47.26–31.

What else might we learn about Pāyu? The great Vedic commentator Sāyaṇa, in the fourteenth century CE, argues that he is Prastoka, the son of Sṛñjaya. Nineteenth-century Indologist Ralph Griffiths thought he was the great king Divodāsa, and understands the Atharvans as the Aṅgirasas, of the Atharvan lineage. The Vedic commentarial texts the *Bṛhaddevatā* (5.124–42) and the *Sarvānukramaṇī* (2.6.75) give us more information, as they always do, about the *ṛṣi*. They indicate that Bhāradvāja helped Prastoka and Abhyāvartin (son of Cāyamāna) to gain victory over the demon Varaśikha on the banks of the Hariyūpīyā.[3] His father then consecrated all the war materials and weapons in the verses of our hymn, RV 6.75. And after their victory, they gave gifts to their family priest, called Bhāradvāja, whose power (*brahma*) had lifted their morale in battle. While they were returning home with gifts from the palace, Bhāradvāja and his son Garga met Indra. They told Indra about the wealth bestowed upon them by Prastoka and Abhyāvartin. These are the verses 6.27.8, which mention the gifts of Prastoka and Divodāsa. And in RV 6.47.22, Cāyamāna and Prastoka are praised. Sthaneshwar conjectures that there were two Bhāradvājas—one, the priest of Divodāsa, and the other, the Bhāradvāja Bārhaspatya. These two and their descendants were intimately connected with the Bhāratas, and may well have been responsible for many of the hymns of Maṇḍala 6 of the *Ṛg Veda*.

It is also clear from these and other sources that the Bhāradvājas were an old family with great knowledge about war, weaponry, and statecraft. Bhāradvāja the sage's opinion is frequently cited in the *Mahābhārata*. Kauṭilya, in the *Arthaśāstra*, cites him positively as an authority on warfare and statecraft on seven different occasions. Clearly, if one wanted someone on one's side in inter-*janapada* conflict, one wanted the Bhāradvājas, whose ideas about weaponry hail from this oldest of strata. Bhāradvāja often opines on the role of ministers and what makes them vulnerable, as well as the role of secrecy and the power of the king's ministers in times of emergency.

The hymn: Interpretation

This tradition of Bhāradvājas is old and complex enough to suggest that their hymns are also more subtle than the simple ebullience of the victory of war. And hymn 6.75 might be a good example of such subtlety. Jamison and Brereton call it one of the more delightful hymns of the *Ṛg Veda*.[4] In addition, they see the internal structure as a riddle hymn, where each weapon is described in one verse. The weapon is named at either the beginning or the end of the verse, and it is preceded or followed by a riddling definition.[5] As they also observe, "The final verse calls down the destruction on every type of enemy and affirm the primacy of the protective sacred formulation—as 'inner armor,' thus paired with the outer armor (the same word *várman*) found in the first verse of the hymn. Thus, whether secondarily or not, the hymn has a faint ring structure."[6] In addition, RV 6.75 switches meter three times—from *triṣṭubh* to *jagati* to *anuṣṭubh*. Following Paul Thieme's[7] suggestion that Vedic meters are switched to indicate different ritual moments, perhaps these three meters occur because different parts of the hymn were sung in different moments of preparation for battle.

Let us turn again to the contents of the hymn.[8] It has been traditionally read (if it has been read at all) straightforwardly as a source of evidence for the practice of cattle raiding and organized warfare in the Vedic period.

1. When the armored warrior goes in front of the battle, he takes the form of a cloud. Conquer, with no wounds on your body! May the strength of the armor defend you!
2. With the bow may we conquer cattle; with the bow may we be victorious in battle. With the bow may we overcome those who are fiercely violent. The bow makes the enemy horrified; may we conquer in all directions.
3. Going into battle, drawn tight on the bow, the bowstring again and again goes up to the ear, as if embracing a friend. Stretched out, the bowstring is like a woman humming, and protects us in battle.
4. The two ends of the bow act together, like a woman in embrace, or like a mother who nurses her son on her lap. Going together, may they pierce the foe, scattering the enemies.
5. The quiver is the father of many, and one who has many sons. It makes a noise as it enters into the battle. Fastened on the back, prolific, it overcomes all armies and bands.
6. Standing on the cart, the skillful charioteer drives his horses ahead of him exactly as he wishes. Praise the power of the reins. From behind, the reins follow the sense of the driver.

7. The horses make a loud roar with their dusty hooves; with the chariots, they show their strength. With their forefeet, they trample on the enemies. Relentlessly, they destroy them.
8. The name of his oblation is the chariot-vehicle, where the weapons and armor are laid. Therefore, let us daily praise that helpful chariot with joy.
9. The guards (also fathers, *pitaraḥ*) are a pleasant company. They possess strength, and are serious protectors in trouble. Armed with spears, they are invincible, well-arranged, heroically brave, and robust, and conquerors of many armies.
10. Brahmans, the fathers, are the offerers of Soma and the guardians of truth. May heaven and earth, which are without fault, be kind to us. Pusan, protect us from calamity. May no one who wishes us ill conquer us.
11. The arrow is dressed in feather, the deer is its tooth. It is bound with the hide of a cow. It lands where it is directed. Wherever strong heroes come together or move apart, there let the arrows land for our protection.
12. May the arrow, which flies straight, spare us. Let our bodies be stone. Let Soma encourage us; let Aditi give us protection.
13. May the whip, who lashes the backs and whips the flanks, urge the bright horses to the battle!
14. Like a snake [the brace] encircles the arm with its rings, protecting it from the impact of the bowstring. May the brace, who knows all the rules, heroically protect the man all around.
15. Let praise be given to the arrow, from Parjanya's seed, whose head is a deer, whose neck is of iron, and whose point is poison.
16. Fly away, Arrow, speeded by the power of the word. Go, reach the enemies; let not one of those remain alive.
17. Where the arrows alight, like boys with shaved heads, may Brahmaṇaspati and Aditi give us protection; give protection always.
18. I cover your vital parts with armor, may King Soma cover you with his nectar of immortality. May Varuṇa make your plenitude even greater. May the gods rejoice with you in your triumph.
19. If a relative or a hostile stranger wants us dead, so shall all the gods bring him down. The power of the word is my inner armor.

Let us think first about the images of the weapons and how they progress throughout the hymn. The verses progress from the shield (1) to the bow (2), to the bow tip (3), the quiver (5), the charioteer (6a), the reins (6b), the horses (7), the chariot (8), the chariot guards (9), the *liṅgotadevatas*—presumably deities who help in battles (10), the arrows (11, 12, 15, 16), the goad (13), the wrist guard (14), and the *liṅgotadevatas* again (17–19). The movement of the poem, then, is from the armor, close to the person of the warrior, and progresses outward through the bows, the quivers, and the charioteer and his chariot, and the horses. It returns briefly to the arm of the warrior in verse 14, but then ends on a celestial note with arrows in the air, as well as the gods rejoicing at the well-covered warrior's triumph, his vital parts protected and his faith in the power of words his ultimate weapon.

The eye, then, moves over the ever-widening landscape of battle as each of the accoutrements of battle is praised. The imagination is extended across an expanse, beginning with the body of the warrior and ending with the extended arc of the arrow and the voices of the gods. If we are to believe the *Bṛhaddevatā*, this praise occurs after victory in battle, which would suggest a memory of the expanded arena. The voices of the poem itself, though, suggest a near future or present, thus anticipating a battle that is about to come, and expands out in front of the warrior as part of the future. In a sense, this is what John Measors and Benjamin Muller call the visual aesthetics of war, in which visualization of a field is part of the larger understanding of strategy in battle.[9]

We would also benefit by looking closely at the imagery and metaphors used to describe the weapons being blessed and the actors in the anticipated battle. Here, we see even more intriguing linguistic usages. Three themes emerge: intimate domestic imagery, ritual imagery, and animal imagery. Each of these themes ground the battle and link, through deft use of metaphor, the field of battle with sacrificial fires of home and hearth.

First, much of the imagery is reminiscent of other intimate metaphors in the more ritually oriented hymns, used to describe sacrificial implements, as well as deities who motivate and inspire the sacrificial actors. Verse 3 states:

3. Going into battle, drawn tight on the bow, the bowstring again and again goes up to the ear, as if embracing a friend. Stretched out, the bowstring is like a woman humming, and protects us in battle.

And verse 4 says:

4. The two ends of the bow act together, like a woman in embrace, or like a mother who nurses her son on her lap. Going together, may they pierce the foe, scattering the enemies.

The effect of these two verses is to ground the violent but exhilarating aspects of war in highly domestic, intimate, and even eroticized context—an embracing friend, a woman humming, a mother nursing a child upon her lap. The acts of war become almost friendly acts that are guaranteed by the safety of the women in the picture. In addition, to complete the domestic, familial picture, in verse 5 the quiver is described as "the father of many, and one who has many sons" (*bahvīnā̃m pitā̃ bahúr asya putrā́ś*).

Many of these erotic images of domestic life are similar to the ones used in the hymn to the Dawn, RV 1.92.3, where the dawn sings like a woman busy at her tasks, and in RV 1.92.4, she puts on ornaments like a dancing girl, and uncovers her breasts as a cow her udder. So too, in RV 10.71.4, the goddess of speech reveals herself in the same erotic way, showing herself to discerning sacrificers as a loving bride to her husband.

The idea of the erotics and intimacy of battle is not new; it has been noted by Patricia Simpson in German romantic idealist movements.[10] We can find traces of it certainly as early as the Bible in the literary treatment of the battle between David and Goliath. The erotics of the battle between David and Goliath feature in Richard Howard's poem "The Giant on Giant Killing" in his book *Fellow Feelings*.[11]

Relatedly, the weapons in the battle are also described in the same powerful ritual way as some potent sacrificial substances, such as Soma, are described in other hymns. In verse 10, the Brahmans are invoked as protectors and presenters of Soma.

10. Brahmans, the fathers, are the offerers of Soma and the guardians of truth. May heaven and earth, which are without fault, be kind to us. May Pūṣan protect us from calamity. May no one who wishes us ill conquer us.

So too in Verse 12, Soma is asked to speak words of encouragement to the warriors. And in verse 18, Soma is understood as royal, and asked to invest the warrior with *amṛta*.

18. I cover your vital parts with armor, may King Soma cover you with his nectar of immortality. May Varuṇa make your plenitude even greater. May the gods rejoice with you in your triumph.

So, too, in verse 8: the spoils born in the chariot where his weapons and armor are left, is the proper oblation of the warrior. Thus the poet asks us to honor this car as one honors a deity with an oblation of weapons.

8. The name of his oblation is the chariot-vehicle, where the weapons and armor are laid. So let us daily praise that helpful chariot with joy.

And perhaps the most compelling sacrificial imagery is in verse 17, where Aditis alight like boys, or to be more specific: *kumārā́ viśikhā́ iva* "like boys without the lock of hair left at shaving."

17. Where the arrows alight, like boys with shaved heads, may Brahmaṇaspati and Aditi give us protection; give protection always.

Sāyaṇa suggests they are *munditā mundāḥ*, or shorn-headed. This suggests that the arrows fall where they might, as boys might also play wherever they like, before they are left only with the single lock of hair in their *upanayana* ceremony.

While the idea of war as sacrifice in the *Mahābhārata* has been amply discussed recently,[12] this hymn lays the groundwork for that idea in a very different way that focuses as much on the aesthetics of ritual procedure as it does on the aesthetics of violent offerings, *per se*. All of these images, even when they are explicitly sacrificial, are startling in their domesticity. There is no violent fiery conflagration, as there is in the *Mahābhārata*. There is no reference to the shedding of blood. Rather, the chariot is the recipient of an oblation; the arrows are boys just before the *upanayana* ceremony, and Soma is asked to guard in the same way that it guards and inspires the sacrifice. Each metaphor of praise for the weapons is almost comforting in its everydayness, even when the content is explicitly erotic. Finally, RV 6.75 is replete with the imagery of animals. In terms of actual animals, we encounter, not surprisingly, the ever-present horse in Vedic mythology in verses 6 and 7.

6. Standing on the cart, the skillful charioteer drives his horses ahead of him exactly as he wishes. Praise the power of the reins. From behind, the reins follow the sense of the driver.
7. The horses make a loud roar with their dusty hooves; with the chariots, they show their strength. With their forefeet they trample on the enemies. Relentlessly, they destroy them.

Note the dynamic in verse 6: just as the horses are animate, so too the reins have their own agency and drive, following as they do the sense of the driver. Later in that verse, the poet asks us to "praise the power of the reins." And in verse 7, the horses are described like weapons in their own right, making a loud roar, in alliance with the chariots, and trampling on the enemies with their forefeet.

Going beyond the actual animals, we see metaphorical strategies in this hymn as well. In verse 11, the arrow is described with a multitude of animal metaphors:

11. The arrow is dressed in feather, the deer is its tooth. It is bound with the hide of a cow. It lands where it is directed. Wherever strong heroes come together or move apart, there let the arrows land for our protection.

Three animals are invoked both directly and indirectly to describe the arrow: a bird, who gives the arrow its feathers; the deer, because the horn is its tooth; and the cow, whose hide binds it. (The imagery of the deer is repeated again in verse 15.) The arrows' power derives from all three of these animals as they are slung in the battlefield.

A similar strategy is used in Verse 14, only this time for the brace.

14. Like a snake [the brace] encircles the arm with its rings, protecting it from the impact of the bowstring. May the brace, who knows all the rules [of battle], manfully protect the man all around.

The imagery of a snake, even in this early Vedic stage of Indian mythology, is auspicious and protective. And the brace fulfills the typical activity of a snake, only this time in battle, in that it is the protector of the arm.

Weapons, orientation, and the expansion of agency

So why not just praise weapons and their power to destroy? Surely, as we have seen above, RV 6.75 does just that, but it also does something more. In its crafting of the hymn, we see a movement outward in orientation, and expansion of the horizons. We see multiple, complex uses of imagery—domestic, erotic, sacrificial, and animal.

We can see, in the contemplative power of many of these verses as they think about weapons, echoes of what Hermann Usener wrote about in the nineteenth century when he described the magical power of tools.[13] While in an earlier work, I have argued against the use of the term "magic" to describe some of these dynamics,[14] his larger point is quite powerful even today. For Usener, the tool was not separate from the person, caught up in an attitude of instrumentality, but rather an extension of the person, and a form of power that expanded the person's power. Ernst Cassirer picked up on this idea in his classical study, *Language and Myth*, (1946) showing the power of presence not only in the natural world but also in the human-made world. As Cassirer writes, "As soon as man [sic] employs a tool, he views it not as a mere artifact of which he is the recognized maker, but as a Being in its own right, endowed with powers of its own."[15] He points out the ways in which various implements, such as the hammer, the axe, the hoe, the fishhook, the spear, and the sword, have attained this religious significance. The weapons in RV 6.75 also are described with this perspective; in each case, the weapons (as tools) are actors in their own right, and have their own dynamics.

Daniel Rothbart creates a wonderful link between ancient views of tools and contemporary ones in his recent work: *Philosophical Instruments: Tools and Minds at Work.*[16] Citing Suzanne Langer's work,[17] he argues:

> Some of the greatest human achievements are found in the symbols that govern general orientation in nature, on the earth, and in society. Such symbols can take many forms: drawings, stories, principles, or theories. In indigenous societies, purification rituals provide orientation in a spiritual world. The ritualistic uses of water, fire, or food function as concrete embodiment of ideals, beliefs, and values associated with the cosmic order. The participant's presence here and now is located securely within that order, providing an effective remedy to the fear of a chaotic world.[18]

Here Rothbart is referring to the symbolic nature of tools, not their instrumentality. And ritual tools are also ritual symbols, as we see in the cases of the ways in which weapons of battle are compared to the instruments of the Vedic sacrifice in RV 6.75.

Moving even more close to our own subject, Rothbart goes on to discuss the ways in which instruments, in a post-Enlightenment scientific lab or a pre-Enlightenment ritual, "are symbols of orientation, of finding one's place through a process of knowing."[19] He goes on:

> For example, a spear is not a microscope, but in many ways the differences between these artifacts are fewer than one might imagine. Like a microscope, a spear is an instrument for knowing one's place in the world. Our first tool-making ancestors who fashioned lengths of wood, bone and flint into weapons utilized more than mere animal strength and hand-eye coordination when they set out to hunt. The feel of the spear in the hand as it pierced the animal's hide, its effective (and ineffective) deployment against various prey, and a host of other forms of feedback made the hunter-spear unit an efficient and deadly combination.[20]

Rothbart concludes by arguing that the spear as a weapon "enhanced the hunters' potency of action—a spear could be thrown to increase the reach of the arm, and its sharp edge could pierce tough hides impervious to fists and small human teeth."[21]

Rothbart's point tells us something more general, and quite powerful, about our experience of instruments, in that "the skilled use of any tool enhances and re-establishes its user's particular orientation of the world in various contexts."[22] In these contexts, tool-users gain extensive knowledge about the behavior of materials through the skilled use of tools, and those that are used *in situ*.

We can view the imagery of RV 6.75 in exactly the same light. Poetic contemplation is also a way of becoming familiar with, and passing on familiarity about, the behavior of tools in contexts—in this case, the behavior of weapons in battle contexts. The use of intimate imagery might be a way of understanding the weapon's relationship to the body. The use of sacrificial imagery might be a way of connecting the power of ritual tools to the power of battle weapons, and grounding those weapons in cosmological meaning. And the use of animal imagery might be a way of reflecting the natural world's physical power, which is present in the weapons. Weapons enhance the composer's and the listener's orientation to the world, and increase their agency. These compelling similes are a way of showing that enhancement.

Thus we return to the bowstring that is like a woman humming. We might find in this imagery not only an erotic sensibility within a poem of war, but also a means of knowing. The Vedic hymn to the weapons can be read as a means of deepening the experience of the bowstring as a weapon, which, in turn, extends human agency. Each simile, whether it is the armband compared to a snake or the arrows compared to fathers and sons, is a figure of speech that teaches about tools, and how they might expand the capacity to act in the world. Thus, like the weapons themselves, Vedic similes might be understood as instruments of the most transformative, non-instrumental kind.

Notes

1 The verb, *śiñj*, can mean tinkling, or jangling, as in a woman's bracelets, or a humming, rattling sound.
2 Thaneshwar Sarmah, *The Bhāradvājas in Ancient India* (Delhi: Motilal Banarsidass, 1991), p. 134.
3 RV 6.27.4–5.
4 Stephanie Jamison and Joel P. Brereton, *The Rigveda: The Earliest Religious Poetry of India*, vol. II (New York and London: Oxford University Press, 2014), p. 876.
5 Ibid.
6 Ibid.
7 Thieme's conjecture occurs in a broader discussion of the versification and dialogical structure of the Vedic hymn 10.179, the conversation between the *ṛṣi* Agastya and his wife Lopāmudrā. See: P. Thieme, "Agastya und Lopāmudrá," *Kleine Schriften*, vol. 1 (Wiesbaden: Franz Steiner Verlag, 1971).
8 The translation is my own, after consulting with Jamison and Brereton, *The Rigveda*:

6.075.01a	jīmū́tasyeva bhavati prátīkam
6.075.01b	yád varmī́ yā́ti samádām upásthe
6.075.01c	ánāviddhayā tanúvā jaya tvám
6.075.01d	sá tvā vármaṇo mahimā́ pipartu
6.075.02a	dhánvanā gā́ dhánvanājím jayema
6.075.02b	dhánvanā tīvrā́ḥ samádo jayema
6.075.02c	dhánuḥ śátror apakāmám kṛṇoti
6.075.02d	dhánvanā sárvāḥ pradíśo jayema
6.075.03a	vakṣyántīvéd ā́ ganīganti kárṇam
6.075.03b	priyám sákhāyam pariṣasvajānā́
6.075.03c	yóṣeva śiṅkte vítatā́dhi dhánvañ
6.075.03d	jiyā́ iyám sámane pāráyantī
6.075.04a	té ācárantī sámaneva yóṣā
6.075.04b	mātéva putrám bibhṛtām upásthe
6.075.04c	ápa śátrūn vidhyatām saṃvidāné
6.075.04d	ā́rtnī imé viṣphurántī amítrān
6.075.05a	bahvīnā́m pitā́ bahúr asya putrā́ś
6.075.05b	ciścā́ kṛṇoti sámanāvagátya

6.075.05c iṣudhíḥ sáṅkāḥ pŕ̥tanāś ca sárvāḥ
6.075.05d pr̥ṣṭhé nínaddho jayati prásūtaḥ

6.075.06a ráthe tíṣṭhan nayati vājínaḥ puró
6.075.06b yátra-yatra kāmáyate suṣārathíḥ
6.075.06c abhī́śūnām mahimā́nam panāyata
6.075.06d mánaḥ paścā́d ánu yachanti raśmáyaḥ

6.075.07a tīvrā́n ghóṣān kr̥ṇvate vŕ̥ṣapāṇayo
6.075.07b áśvā ráthebhiḥ sahá vājáyantaḥ
6.075.07c avakrā́mantaḥ prápadair amítrān
6.075.07d kṣiṇánti śátrūm̐r ánapavyayantaḥ

6.075.08a rathavā́hanam havír asya nāma
6.075.08b yátrā́yudham níhitam asya várma
6.075.08c tátrā rátham úpa śagmám sadema
6.075.08d viśvā́hā vayám sumanasyámānāḥ

6.075.09a svāduṣaṃsádaḥ pitáro vayodhā́ḥ
6.075.09b kr̥chreśrítaḥ śáktīvanto gabhīrā́ḥ
6.075.09c citrásenā íṣubalā ámr̥dhrāḥ
6.075.09d satóvīrā urávo vrātasāhā́ḥ

6.075.10a brā́hmaṇāsaḥ pítaraḥ sómiyāsaḥ
6.075.10b śivé no dyā́vāpr̥thivī́ anehásā
6.075.10c pūṣā́ naḥ pātu duritā́d r̥tāvr̥dho
6.075.10d rákṣā mā́kir no aghá́śaṃsa īśata

6.075.11a suparṇám vaste mr̥gó asyā dánto
6.075.11b góbhiḥ sáṃnaddhā patati prásūtā
6.075.11c yátrā náraḥ sám ca ví ca drávanti
6.075.11d tátrāsmábhyam íṣavaḥ śárma yaṃsan

6.075.12a ŕ̥jīte pári vr̥ṅdhi no
6.075.12b áśmā bhavatu nas tanū́ḥ
6.075.12c sómo ádhi bravītu no
6.075.12d áditiḥ śárma yachatu

6.075.13a ā́ jaṅghanti sā́nu eṣām
6.075.13b jaghánām̐ úpa jighnate
6.075.13c áśvājani prácetaso
6.075.13d áśvān samátsu codaya

6.075.14a áhir 'va° bhogaíḥ pári eti bāhúm
6.075.14b jiyā́yā hetím paribā́dhamānaḥ
6.075.14c hastaghnó víśvā vayúnāni vidvā́n
6.075.14d púmān púmāṃsam pári pātu viśvátaḥ

6.075.15a ā́lāktā yā́ rúruśīrṣṇi
6.075.15b átho yásyā áyo múkham
6.075.15c idám parjányaretasa
6.075.15d íṣvai devyaí br̥hán námaḥ

6.075.16a ávasr̥ṣṭā párā pata
6.075.16b śáravye bráhmasaṃśite
6.075.16c gáchāmítrān prá padyasva
6.075.16d mā́mī́ṣām kám canóc chiṣaḥ

6.075.17a	yátra bāṇā́ḥ sampátanti
6.075.17b	kumārā́ viśikhā́ iva
6.075.17c	tátrā no bráhmaṇas pátir
6.075.17d	áditiḥ śárma yachatu
6.075.17e	viśvā́hā śárma yachatu
6.075.18a	mármāṇi te vármaṇā chādayāmi
6.075.18b	sómas tvā rā́jāmŕ̥tenā́nu vastām
6.075.18c	urór várīyo váruṇas te kr̥ṇotu
6.075.18d	jáyantaṃ tvā ánu devā́ madantu
6.075.19a	yó naḥ suvó árano
6.075.19b	yáś ca níṣṭyo jíghāṃsati
6.075.19c	devā́s táṃ sárve dhūrvantu
6.075.19d	bráhma várma mámā́ntaram

9 John Measors and Benjamin Muller, "'Theatres of War': Visual Technologies and Identities in the Iraq Wars," *Geopolitics* 16, no. 2 (2011), pp. 389–409.

10 Patricia Anne Simpson, *The Erotics of War in German Romanticism* (Lewisburg: Bucknell University Press, 2006).

11 Richard Howard, *Fellow Feelings: Poems* (New York: Atheneum Press, 1976).

12 For an overview of these authors, see: Laurie L. Patton, "Telling Stories about Harm: An Overview of Early Indian Narratives," in *Religion and Violence in South Asia: Theory and Practice*, ed. John Hinnells and Richard King (London: Routledge, 2007), pp. 10–39.

13 Herman Usener, *Götternamen: Versuch einer Lehre von der Religiösen Begriffsbildung* (Bonn: Friedrich Cohen, 1896).

14 See: Laurie Patton, *Bringing the Gods to Mind: Mantra and Sacrifice in Early Indian Ritual* (Berkeley: University of California Press, 2005).

15 Ernst Cassirer, *Language and Myth*, translated by Suzanne K. Langer (New York and London: Harper & Bros., 1946), p. 59.

16 Daniel Rothbart, *Philosophical Instruments: Minds and Tools at Work* (Urbana and Chicago: University of Illinois Press, 2007).

17 Suzanne K. Langer, *Philosophy in a New Key: A Study in the Symbolism of Reason, Rite, and Art* (Cambridge, MA: Harvard University Press, 1942).

18 Rothbart, *Philosophical Instruments*, p. 8.

19 Ibid.

20 Ibid.

21 Ibid., p. 9.

22 Ibid., p. 8.

References

Atharva Veda Saṃhitā, 4 vols, edited by V. Bandhu, Hoshiarpur: Vishveshavaranand Vedic Research Institute, 1960–62.

Atharva Veda Saṃhitā, 2 vols, translated by W. D. Whitney, Harvard Oriental Series, vols. 7 and 8. Cambridge, MA: Harvard University Press, 1905.

Cassirer, E. (1946), *Language and Myth*, translated by Suzanne K. Langer, New York and London: Harper & Bros.

Howard, R. (1976), *Fellow Feelings: Poems*, New York: Atheneum Press.

Jamison, S. and Brereton, J. P. (2014), *The Rigveda: The Earliest Religious Poetry of India*, vol. II, New York and London: Oxford University Press.
Kātyāyana (1886), *Kātyāyana's Sarvānukramaṇī of the Ṛgveda, with extracts from Ṣaḍguruśiṣya's commentary entitled Vedārthadīpikā*; ed. with critical notes and appendices, by A. A. Macdonell, Oxford: The Clarendon Press.
Langer, S. K. (1942), *Philosophy in a New Key: A Study in the Symbolism of Reason, Rite, and Art*, Cambridge, MA: Harvard University Press.
Macdonnell, A. A. (1904), *Bṛhaddevatā*, 2 vols. Harvard Oriental Series, 5-6, edited and translated by A. A. Macdonell, Cambridge, MA: Harvard University Press.
The Mahābhārata, 19 vols, edited by V. S. Sukthankar, Poona: Bhandarkar, Oriental Research Institute, 1933–60.
The Mahābhārata, 3 vols, edited and translated by J. A. B. Van Buitenen, Chicago: University of Chicago Press, 1973–78.
Measors, J. and Muller, B. (2011), "'Theatres of War': Visual Technologies and Identities in the Iraq Wars," *Geopolitics*, 16 (2), pp. 389–409.
Patton, L. (1996), *Myth as Argument: The Bṛhaddevatā as Canonical Commentary*, Berlin and New York: Degruyter Mouton.
Patton, L. (2005), *Bringing the Gods to Mind: Mantra and Sacrifice in Early Indian Ritual*, Berkeley: University of California Press.
Patton, L. (2007), "Telling Stories about Harm: An Overview of Early Indian Narratives," in J. Hinnells and R. King (eds), *Religion and Violence in South Asia: Theory and Practice*, London: Routledge, pp. 11–40.
Ṛg Veda Saṃhitā, together with the Commentary of Sāyaṇa Ācārya, 5 vols, Poona: Vaidika Samshodana Maṇḍala, 1951–84.
Rothbart, D. (2007), *Philosophical Instruments: Minds and Tools at Work*, Urbana and Chicago: University of Illinois Press.
Sarmah, T. (1991), *The Bhāradvājas in Ancient India*, Delhi: Motilal Banarsidass.
Simpson, P. A. (2006), *The Erotics of War in German Romanticism*, Lewisburg: Bucknell University Press.
Thieme, P. (1971), "Agastya und Lopāmudrá," *Kleine Schriften*, Teil 1, Wiesbaden: Franz Steiner Verlag.
Usener, H. (1896), *Götternamen: Versuch einer Lehre von der Religiösen Begriffsbildung*, Bonn: Friedrich Cohen.
Van Nooten, B. and Holland, G., eds (1994), *Ṛgveda: A Metrically Restored Text with an Introduction and Notes*, Harvard Oriental Series, vol. 50, Cambridge, MA: Harvard University Press, 1994.

5

How Do We Read Others' Feelings? Strawson and Zhuangzi Speak to Dharmakirti, Ratnakīrti, and Abhinavagupta

Arindam Chakrabarti

We understood / Her by her sight: her pure and eloquent blood / Spoke in her cheeks, and so distinctly wrought, / That one might almost say, her body thought

John Donne[1]

It is as if he became transparent *to us through a human facial expression.*

Wittgenstein[2]

As used, the term (I) has a uniquely singular reference; but as understood, it is general in the sense the term unique *is general. . . . You are individual to me primarily through my act of addressing and only secondarily through what appears to my imagination as your identification with or appropriation of your body.*

K. C. Bhattacharya[3]

Our feelings, their feelings

Philosophers in nearly all traditions have spent millennia formulating and solving issues around the use, meaning, and reference of the first-person singular pronoun. But the first-person *plural* is no less mysterious and puzzling. The concept of a collective (therefore non-individual) subject could turn out to be even more primordial than "I," for rational social creatures like "us." It is definitely more politically potent. The most baffling problem of the first-person plural—"we"—is that it seems to demand a complementary contrast class of third-person plural others—"they"—whereas inside its own extension each of the multiple first persons can be as distinct from one another as "they" are from "us." We are not they.

And yet, the multiple alternative ways in which collectivities are formed by thinking-feeling-willing creatures begin to break the boundaries between us and them no sooner than they have been drawn up. The understanding and solidarity that we university teachers feel toward each other is sometimes trumped and ruptured by the closeness that we South Asians, academic and nonacademic alike, feel toward one another. Those of us who belong to the same chess or square-dancing club may lump together a bunch of professors and south Asians as those awkward non-square-dancers.

These crisscrossings of sometimes conflicting we-identities, used as a justification for lack of empathy or fellow-feeling, are all neglected or transcended in two opposite extreme contexts: (A) the context of my singular self versus the rest of the world, and (B) the context of we human beings versus all the other sub- or non-humans. While no one can deny a certain special directness and authority with which one feels and knows one's own pleasures and pains, drives, and desires, one cannot plead ignorance or complete opacity of the other. As Zhuangzi (dialectically) pointed out, in a much-commented-upon passage, if we cannot know when the fish are happy because we are not fish, how can you know whether I (another human being) do not know about fish happiness, as long as you are not I?

Marcel Proust wrote:

> it was she [Françoise] who first gave me the idea that a person . . . is a shadow which we can never succeed in penetrating, of which there can be no such thing as direct knowledge, . . . a shadow behind which we can alternatively imagine with equal justification, that there burns the flame of hatred and of love.[4]

But notice how the authorial voice gets the very idea that no one knows directly the ideas in the mind of another, from another person!

The logical culmination of skepticism about other minds (or about the very possibility of knowing the feelings of creatures of other species) is solipsism. And solipsism is not only untenable; it refutes itself as soon as it is stated in any language. Whether one believes in a same-staying self across different changing bodily and mental states and processes or not, for any conversing human being it is impossible to think honestly that the only intelligible self is myself, that the only stream of consciousness is this first-person subject's stream of consciousness. Yet, the idea of "another self" or "another stream of subjective states" is deeply problematic. When, through empathy with another human being who looks different, talks, eats, and interacts differently from me, I try to imagine what it would be like to be she, I seem to be stuck with being myself even in all imagined situations.

Similarly, at a different species level, when we try to imagine what it is like to be a bat, how a bat must be feeling in a totally dark cave, for example, the best we can do is to have the existentially quantified belief that *there must exist some way that it feels*. But how do we know what exactly it feels like to be this alien creature? The best I can do is to imagine *how I would feel if I were a bat*. During that mental simulation, if I had to remain myself, I could not possibly be a bat, so we are back to our original problem of never being able to know how the bat feels. In his famous long story "Metamorphosis," Kafka managed to imagine what it would be like if a human being suddenly turned into a cockroach, but who is to tell if his fictional thought-experiment could access any part of what an average cockroach actually feels. Does that mean that I cannot know (at all) how another person or a creature of another kind is feeling unless I am that person or a creature of that very kind?

That is exactly what Huizi, most probably a Chinese counterpart of a sophist dialectician, seems to assume when he questions Zhuangzi's simple statement that the fish are happy. We are not the fish that is frolicking inside the fish tank, so we cannot understand fish-feelings or the meanings of fish-movements.

Or can we? When a fish squirms and flops about caught on a hook, do we need any extraordinary powers or do we have to master additional bits of fish-physiology to know that it is in pain? Can we use our scientific knowledge of fish-brains to assure ourselves that that is mere pain-behavior without any pain behind it? Can we use this alleged incomprehension of fish behavior or this rational doubt as to whether or not it can feel pain at all to justify our frying and eating the fish? As long as frying and eating a certain life-form is the form of life we are accustomed to, the question of fish-subjectivity does not arise for us; just as, so long as American slave-holders used African people as tools of production, the question of how Africans feel was at best an academic question. You do not eat or beat, fry or brand, or chain a fellow-feeler with whom you communicate socially.

But what if someone argues as follows: we, Indians, are not British, African, or Chinese. So we cannot understand the feeling of the British, African, or Chinese people, and cannot always divine the meanings of their gestures or movements. Yet we can, somehow, using translation and the basic belief that we are all human (though we could include the fish in the first-person plural feeling that we are all suffering/enjoying living beings), tell this to the British and the Chinese and hope to be understood. So, we do not fry them or eat them up. But to go up to someone and tell them, "You can never understand what I am thinking or feeling" smells of a pragmatic self-refutation insofar as to tell anything to anyone is to expect to be understood and believed.

The opposition between native and alien is, roughly, the collective counterpart of the opposition between oneself and the other one is facing, between I and you. The love-hate that a formerly colonized person or culture feels toward their own "native" culture is counterbalanced by and perhaps traceable to the repulsion and attraction one feels toward the foreign. Colonization ruptures the cultural subject into a strife between insecure revivalist reactionary nativism and shameless re-colonization or one-upping the historical successors of the colonizer community. At the time of repairing centuries of political, economic, epistemic, and, above all, cultural injustice between one community and another, the need, and therefore the problem, of understanding what the foreign collective consciousness feels, needs, desires, remembers, thinks, perceives, and knows looms large. Without that understanding, no fair redistribution of epistemic power or cultural prestige is possible. But this problem of trans-communal understanding is rooted in the more fundamental problem of the seemingly unbridgeable gap between my feelings, which I more often than not know unmistakably, and your feelings, which I apparently can never be sure about.

I am not You: Zhuangzi and Huizi wrangle about how to know that the fish are happy

The very idea of a second self is logically and phenomenologically troublesome. The idea of a self is derived from the first-person singular, which demands a uniqueness that it cannot rationally refuse to share with other similar uniqueness-demanding subjects. Yet, what could it mean to *share a uniqueness*? If both you and I have to be unique with respect to the single property of being "the self"—like none other—there seem to be only two alternatives, Non-dualism or Solipsism. Either strictly, numerically, equate you with I, because such identity follows from both of us being equated to a single Self, or take turns, sometimes recognizing the Ego alone and sometimes the Other/Thou alone to be the only self. But neither of these would constitute a genuine "sharing," let alone a "facing each other," whatever that seductive verb-noun means.

Zhuangzi reports a conversation with Huizi, an academic skeptic about other minds, and especially about radically other kinds of creatures as far removed from humans as fish. Let us assign numbers to the six sentences of this profoundly puzzling text as Wan-Chuan Fang[5] has done, while engaging with Chad Hansen[6] and Xiaoqiang Han's[7] interpretations of them.

1. Zhuangzi and Huizi were strolling on the bridge above the Hao river.
2. "Out swim the minnows, so free and easy," said Zhuangzi. "This is fish happiness."
3. "You are not a fish. Whence do you know that the fish are happy?"
4. "You are not I. How do you know that I don't know that the fish are happy?"
5. "Let us grant that not being you, I don't know about you. You will grant that you are not a fish, and that completes the case that you don't know that the fish are happy."
6. "Let us go back to where we started. When you said, 'Whence do you know that the fish are happy?' you had asked me the question already knowing that I knew. I knew it from up above the Hao."

Zhuangzi, who himself comes across as a skeptical relativist in the famous second chapter called "Making All Things Equal," in this dialogue, holds up the naturalist, almost a descriptive ordinary language, position by making three crucial moves to dissipate Huizi's skepticism. Adopting the symbolism of writing "x knows y," when y could be another person, species, or a proposition, as "Kxy," Huizi's first move was:

> If z is not f then ~Kzf (If Zhuangzi is not a fish then he does not know that the fish are happy).

In response, first Zhuangzi makes what is called—according to "*The Lesser Pick*" (the *Xiaoqu*), the ancient Chinese manual of disputation-techniques—a "parallelizing" move:

> If ~(z = f) entails ~Kzf, then ~(h = z) should entail ~(Kh(~Kzf)).

Second, Zhuangzi points out that, paying close attention to Huizi's initial phrasing of the question, "Whence do you know" (possibly meant as a rhetorical question), we could notice how, literally, that question presupposes that Zhuangzi knew that the fish were happy, and Huizi only wanted to know his method or means of knowledge.

Third, he "goes back to the ordinary" starting point where there was no knowledge claim, but only an observation of the fish. Indeed, one says "I am sure P" or "I know that P" either when one is uncertain, or when one is attacked by external or internal doubt. If I see a dog running in front of me, it would be odd to describe that by saying "I know that the dog is running." The more natural thing to say would be "The dog is running." But this time, directly answering Huizi's question "Whence do you know?" but giving it an ecological twist, he takes the "Whence" almost geographically. He says "I know that the fish are happy from here, on the bridge above the river Hao." By recalling the physical place from where he observed fish happiness, he reminds Huizi that in an ordinary day-to-day life what matters is the location of the knower, and that it is perverse to presume that one cannot know about a certain kind of creature unless one is of that same kind. Like all words, "know" also has a conventional, contextual, "situated" meaning. If one sees that the fish are frolicking in water, the normal thing to say is that the fish are playing happily, where "happily" refers to a certain way in which the minnows are darting about, but not to any special inner mental state or brain-state of the fish.

Here, an objection would naturally arise against my use of the *Zhuangzi* story in the context of "the typically Western" problem of other human minds. I seem to be deliberately conflating three utterly different kinds of questions:

- Can one individual human being know what another individual human being is feeling currently?
- Can people of one (e.g., Israeli) community know what people of another (e.g., Palestinian) community feel in a certain situation?
- Can a human being know if and when a leopard, or a fish, or a worm is happy or agitated?

Of course, all of them could be brought under one rubric "The problem of reading the minds of the other" (though the idea of a worm having a mind or an anxiety should sound bizarre). But (as Ralph Weber has reminded me) not being fish and not being British or African are so different that it may be a category mistake to bring these two kinds of "otherness" under the same rubric. It is hard to imagine that one day, say after having lived for thirty years in a fish pond, a human being would come to say that he now feels more fish than human (the fable of the wolf living among the sheep notwithstanding). But after having lived for thirty years in the UK, an Indian could perhaps to some extent consider herself to be British (though skin color is almost as hard to ignore as the presence or absence of scales on your body). The objector's point is that although we could include fish within our first-person plural we-feeling, there is a more basic difference between not being a fish and not being Indian or British. Of course, while one can conceptually play with gender, race, species classifications, and exclusions, taking the foreignness of an alien to be a more general case of the distinction between self and other, I and you smacks of a category mistake. For example, I can stop considering myself an Indian, not simply by taking American citizenship but also by thinking, talking, feeling, and, above all, borrowing and buying like an American, but I cannot likewise stop considering myself as being myself.

That grave objection can be answered in stages. I concede that there is an indexicality about the "You are not I" distinction that is not there between being Austrian and being Californian. An Austrian can become a Hollywood actor, or a governor, and thus more American than Austrian, whereas even as a no-self-ist Buddhist he cannot cease to be "I" in his own eyes. In response I would say that "I" could also be a disguised definite description. Except for the contentless, and according to Wittgenstein merely grammatical, specialty of the first-person singular pronoun, all that there is to being and feeling like a certain particular person, with the added affective attachment that makes that person "myself", can, through spiritual and aesthetic exercise of detachment and practice of other-directed compassion, be so overcome that one can look at one's ego as that clot of descriptions one used to be intimately emotionally attached to, but what has now stopped being. Elsewhere,[8] in the context of giving phenomenological plausibility to the idea of aesthetic transcendence of the ego, I have spoken of experiencing ownerless emotions. We shall see below how Max Scheler[9] endorses the idea of perceiving a feeling without caring to ascribe it to oneself or another, and Paul Ricouer[10] has explored the idea of treating oneself as another from many points of view. Here I would still like to uphold the view that the problem of intercultural understanding is rooted in the more fundamental problem of the seemingly unbridgeable gap between my feelings and your feelings.

Our unsocial sociability and the trouble with "you"

In contemporary Western analytic philosophy, the classic analogical argument explaining our knowledge of other minds has been mostly discredited. But at least three alternative positive theories of our knowledge of the second person have been formulated: the theory-theory, the simulation theory, and the theory of direct empathic perception. After sketching out the problems faced by these accounts of the ego's access to the contents of the mind of a "second ego," I shall try to recreate one argument proposed by Abhinavagupta (Shaiva philosopher of recognition) to the effect that even in another's body, one must feel and recognize one's own self, if one is able to address that embodied person as a "You." The otherness of you does not take away from the second person's subjectivity. In that sense, just as every second person to whom one could speak is, *first*, a person, she is also a *first person*. Even as I regret that I do not know exactly how, for example, my closest friend who is right in front of me is feeling right now, I must have some general access to the subjective experience of that other person, for otherwise what is it that I feel so painfully ignorant about? My subjective world is mine only to the extent that I recognize its continuity with a sharable subjective world where other I-s can make a You out of me, and we (you and I) could perceive, and transact with, objects and events in a common world outside.

Still, even at the emotional level, the I is in "trouble" insofar as it, at once, desires and detests a You. Both the ancient Indian Upanishads and the great mentor of European modernity Immanuel Kant give voice to this logico-emotional dilemma of needing and yet fearing a second, of craving the company of those very others from whom one wants to be independent. Kant calls this inherent "antagonism" or "the unsocial sociability" of man. In his words:

> By "antagonism" I mean the unsocial sociability of men, i.e., their propensity to enter into society, bound together with a mutual opposition which constantly threatens to break up the society. Man has an inclination to associate with others, because in society he feels himself to be more than man, i.e., as more than the developed form of his natural capacities. But he also has a strong propensity to isolate himself from others, because he finds in himself at the same time the unsocial characteristic of wishing to have everything go according to his own wish. Thus he expects opposition on all sides because, in knowing himself, he knows that he, on his own part, is inclined to oppose others.[11]

The Upanishads call this the self-imposed self-othering veil of ignorance of the self.

In certain kinds of suffering, I feel so alone in the world that I have to befriend others just to confide in them that I have no friends. This may sound incoherent, at best deliberately paradoxical. But the basic trouble is that I understand you best when I stand next to you in your troubled times and confess to you, in all humility, that I, as long as I remain myself, fail to understand you fully. I somehow open myself to your wound just when I feel most acutely and painfully that it does not hurt me quite the way it hurts you. Even to feel your separateness from me, I need to imaginatively try to fill up the hollow of your foreignness with the kernel of my subjectivity and face you as if I am facing myself, emptying myself from my first-person-ness and giving all my I-ness to you.

It is well known that solipsism is one view that can neither expect endorsement from a fellow-solipsist nor acknowledge disagreement with another. Yet, in spite of such logical awkwardness, do not each of us, independently of the use of the first-person singular pronoun, at least in certain pensive situations, feel imprisoned in a solitary bubble?

I would not be anyone at all, I would not even be myself, without you, unless I recognize my qualitative identity with, and numerical distinction from, you. I am not just a thinking being; I am essentially an addressable person. I need you to speak to and listen to me. You are someone whom I can noticeably stop talking to. I can treat you as someone who may or may not ignore me. I learned calling myself "I" from your calling me "you." So there must be some translation rules from the word "you" to the word "I." Yet I am not one with you (in the singular), and I am not one-of-you (in the plural).

We are distinct as ego and nonego, but we are the same as self or subject, and that is why when I refer jointly to you and I, I do not say "you" in the plural, or "the two of you," but I say "we" or "the two of us." Together we are two first persons; but apart, I alone am I and you are another. Much of this may well be a linguistic muddle. But not all of it.

The other connected epistemological trouble with you is that when you are angry or happy, sometimes I know vividly *that* you are, but I still do not quite feel your anger or happiness, because if I did feel them they would be my anger and happiness, and therefore not yours. Sometimes I can see that you are feeling an emotion when you really are, without myself having those emotions. Yet, the only emotions I seem to directly experience are emotions I have. It seems perfectly possible for me to see your nose without having your nose, but somehow not so easy for me to experientially and immediately feel your rage without myself having that rage too.

The analogical argument from J. S. Mill (1872) and back-tracking to Dharmakirti (seventh century CE)

How do I know that another person is overjoyed or outraged, bored or anxious, has a wish or a belief? The classical answer, repeated by Dharmakirti (in *Santānāntarasiddhi*) is the Argument from Analogy. His formulation is slightly different from John Stuart Mill's classic formulation of the argument. Mill's formulation in "An Examination of Sir William Hamilton's Philosophy," went as follows:

> I am conscious in myself of a series of facts connected by an uniform sequence, of which the beginning is modifications of my body, the middle is feelings, the end is outward demeanour. In the case of other human beings I have the evidence of my senses for the first and last links of the series, but not for the intermediate link. I find, however, that the sequence between the first and last is as regular and constant in those other cases as it is in mine. In my own case I know that the first link produces the last through the intermediate link, and could not produce it without. Experience, therefore, obliges me to conclude that there must be an intermediate link . . . by supposing the link to be of the same nature as in the case of which I have experience, and which is in all other respects similar, I bring other human beings, as phenomena, under the same generalisations which I know by experience to be the true story of my own existence. And in doing so I conform to the legitimate rules of experimental enquiry.[12]

This inference simply says that since my own bodily changes and actions are correlated with my introspected inner feelings, the other's observed bodily changes must also be inferred to be preceded by inner stirrings of desire and feelings; since when I run to get some object, I first feel a desire for the object, the other must be feeling a similar desire when she is running.

The seventh-century Buddhist epistemologist Dharmakirti's general thrust is the same, as has been stated in a couplet in his major epistemology text *Pramāṇa-Vārttikam* III, verse 68: "It is well-established that two means of knowledge are available for our knowledge of other minds. The existence of the feelings of others is proved in utterance of words (avowals) and from their actions."[13] Basically, the claim is that by denying the existence of external material bodies, the Buddhist idealist has *not* committed himself to solipsism. He can use the same analogical inference as the realists do. In "Establishment of Other Mind-Streams," Dharmakirti makes the claim: "Just as the external world-realist infers conscious awareness in others, by noticing voluntary action (*kriyā*) in one's own body, preceded by a cognition, the same reasoning should work with the [idealist doctrine of] 'consciousness only' (*cittamātra*) as well." We only have to replace "bodily behavior and utterance of words" with "*appearance of* bodily behavior and *experience of* utterances coming out of what appears to be another body." The more cautious inference is then laid out roughly as follows:

> Since the movements and actions experienced in another body are not caused by any will or cognition within my/this stream of consciousness, they would either be uncaused, or caused by a will or intelligence which is outside this stream of consciousness, belonging to another stream. Since we cannot coherently call such observed actions uncaused, there must exist other streams of awareness. (*Santānāntarasiddhi*, verses 7–26)[14]

Refutation of the analogical argument: Ratnakīrti's rigorous defense of solipsism

Four hundred years after Dharmakirti, within the same sub-school of Yogācāra Buddhism, Ratnakīrti's *Refutation of the Other Stream-of-Consciousness* (*Santānāntara-dūṣaṇa*)[15] exposes fatal fallacies in any attempt at justifying a claim about another mind on the basis of an inference. The refutation is extremely sophisticated and complex. We are running a simplified version of it here.

In Indian logic, all inferences from the sign F to the unobserved property G have to be based on a prior knowledge of a universal concomitance of the form: *wherever there is an F there is a G, such that F cannot be present (must be absent) where G is absent.* Now, what exactly is the prover-sign (*hetu*) for my inference that there is another stream of beliefs and desires in you? It has to be my own mental impression of your talk, your tone of voice, your facial expressions, your movements. What is the basis for the supporting universal concomitance of the form "Wherever there is a frown-sensation, as its cause, there must be an annoyance-experience"? Well, it must be the concomitance both in presence and absence, which I observe in my own case. In myself, when I hear myself talk or catch myself raising my hand voluntarily, I find inside me beliefs and desires, feelings and attitudes. It is in order to convey these beliefs, desires and sentiments that I use words or raise my hand. When I do not introspectively find any intentional mental states within myself, I do not see any corresponding conversation or voluntary movements of my body either. Now, *any failure to perceive something is not a proof of its nonexistence.* Only the non-perception of that which would be perceived under normal conditions, had it been there, is taken as a proof of absence. We could then argue: "Had it been there, we would have seen it, but we don't see it, so it must not be there." Now Ratnakīrti asks a tough question to the I-to-someone-else extrapolator. This desiring mind that I wish to prove, outside my body, but inside your body—the so-called "other stream of consciousness"—is it visible or invisible?

Ratnakīrti's refutation proceeds in the typical destructive dilemmatic (*vaitandika*) fashion by a downward tree of bifurcating options, each of which is closed with a modus tollens. First of all, let us take the target of the alleged inference (*probandum*), as a cause of the appearance of actions in those other bodies. Is that intention, that particular wish-to-act, in principle perceptible by one who infers the mental states in another stream of psychophysical processes, or is it intrinsically imperceptible to all but that other mental-event series itself (which has not yet been proved to exist), or does the inference use wish-to-act in general, not qualified by perceptibility or imperceptibility?

If it is assumed to be visible, and yet, I have never directly seen or felt it, then by the method of non-perception-of-that-which-is-fit-to-be-perceived, I could have proven such states as your pain or your desire to be nonexistent when there was no movement in your body or no utterance issuing from it. If, on the other hand, we regard it as intrinsically and in principle invisible, like an electron (Ratnakīrti's example is the "digestive fire," which, as a theoretical posit to explain metabolism, no one ever expects to see), then merely the fact that I do not see it will never prove that it is not there.

But if we can never be sure of the absence of the target-property to be inferred (in known cases of the absence of the reason-property), we would not be able to establish the concomitant correlation between (absence of) these mental states and (absence of) another's conduct and conversation. So how could we be certain that *wherever*—not just in my case—there is sure absence of a desire and cognition, there is absence of movement and talk? Remember that unless the absence of the target property is known to be necessarily colocated with the absence of the reason property, the reason property loses all its probative power. Accidental agreement in the presence of the two factors is to be eliminated in this fashion by its negative counterpart: wherever the target-property is absent, the reason-property has to be absent too. The only way I could claim to confirm the universal concomitance between the external signs and the internal states to be inferred is by claiming to observe the presence and absence of internal states in many cases, even outside myself, in the presence and absence of the external signs. But to claim that is to claim clairvoyance—a direct perception of the inner states of others—which renders this entire analogical inference process redundant!

As if this death-blow to the inference to another mind was not enough, Ratnakīrti then proceeds to show the intrinsic incoherence of the very idea of a phenomenal subjective state that is not of the first person. This is where, as Ganeri rightly emphasizes,[16] Ratnakīrti's refutation of other mind-streams goes way beyond the mere epistemological skepticism or a lament that we can never be sure about what others are feeling and thinking. It goes on to reduce the very idea of *other mind-streams* to be as incoherent as the idea of a married bachelor. If the other stream of mind-states were even possible, I would observe myself, always, as either distinct or non-distinct or as neither distinct-nor-non-distinct from these other streams. But surely the last two options are unacceptable. I do not perceive myself to be non-distinct from you. My very being myself consists in not being you or he or she. And to be neither distinct nor non-distinct is a logical contradiction, which I cannot ascribe to your mind-stream.

So, the first option is the only plausible one: I perceive the series of my own mental states as distinct from your series. But a distinction between one thing and another cannot appear unless both the things appear distinctly. Yet, by our own admission, I can only see or feel my own stream of perceptions, emotions, desires, pleasures, and pains, which is only one side of the distinction. I have never seen any other stream. I can never see yours. Thus the distinction between my stream or its psychic waves and your stream or its psychic waves cannot clearly appear to me. Since none of the three possible consequences of its assumption can be accepted, the Other Stream of mental states is not even a coherent possibility. You not only do not exist, as a conscious being other than me, you (a non-first-person mind-stream) are not even consistently conceivable!

But the point of this exercise was not to prove solipsism. Who would Ratnakīrti be trying to prove it to? The point was to show how useless any attempted inference for the existence of another feeling and desiring mind would be, so that one can move closer to the Jñānaśri-Ratnakīrti view of Variegated Non-Dualism of Consciousness Only.

Peter Strawson and a certain peculiarity of P-predicates

In his book *Individuals: An Essay in Descriptive Metaphysics*, Sir Peter Strawson raised the most constructive objections against the Analogical Argument for other minds.[17] To say that the Analogical Inference is a weak inductive argument from a single case, he pointed out, would be too mild a complaint. Even in the single case of myself, the mental predicate cannot be coherently applied, Strawson insisted, unless I already know how to apply it to others. In order to be a predicate, "... wishes" must be capable of occurring with more than one singular term filling up the subject-blank. If only I could have wishes, wishing would not be a general property. If the idea of a mental state or P-predicate were somehow uniquely egocentric then it would not be a general predicate at all. The skeptical question, which is answered by Dharmakirti by the analogical argument, cannot even be coherently posed, because the concept of a person—a "santāna" or "Mind-stream" (a five-component set-and-series) in the Yogācāra Buddhist case—would not be a concept unless there were more than one instances of it. We can put this Strawsonian point even more strongly using Dharmakirti's own theory of the meaning of predicates. When we say "This wish or that pain is mine," according to Dignāga-Dharmakirti's *exclusion (apoha) theory of the meaning of general terms* "mine" means "not belonging to others." The consciousness predicates, in order to be self-ascribed, have to be other-ascribable, because of the generality constraint on any intelligible predicate.

Strawson is neither a behaviorist nor a Cartesian dualist. His *persons* are located in space and time; they are living bodies with both material predicates (M-predicates, e.g., 6-foot tall) and psychological predicates (P-predicates, e.g., "is happy," "worries"). Strawson shows how we do not need to reduce your inner state of depression to your episodic or dispositional depressed behavior in a crude or Rylean behaviorist fashion. But neither should we be skeptical like the typical dualist, obsessed with first-person privileged access, as to whether anyone other than myself ever suffers the very same property of depression or elation. Although I know that I am depressed by direct first-person introspection, whereas I know that you are depressed by using your depressed behavior as the "criterion" for my ascription of that predicate to you, the predicate "... is morose" retains its sameness of meaning across these two sorts of application-rules. If it did not, it would not be a P-predicate. "If psychological predicates were only mine, then they would not even be mine," says Strawson, coining one memorable maxim in his chapter on Persons in *Individuals*.[18]

I could not tell others that I am depressed in, as it were, my private language—and expect to be understood—if somehow my depression was mine alone. "X is depressed" is a predicate that I feel from inside when I attach it to myself, but observe from outside in you, and you feel from inside in you but observe in me. Yet, the sort of property that being sad or wishing to speak is remains the same whether a certain instance of it is directly, first-personally felt or vicariously ascribed from outside to another. Just as the speaker and the hearer can "experience" the same utterance from two ends, one as "I wished to say this and did" and the other as "I heard this and understood what the speaker wished to say," the same process of wishing to speak, leading one to breathe out and move one's vocal chords to make sounds, can be seamlessly, continuously received as an auditory experience of a verbal act preceded by a wish that is not mine.

The concept of a person, or the more capacious category of a living being, is as basic to our common conceptual scheme, part of which contemporary eliminative materialists or mental fictionalists tolerate as folk psychology, as the category of an external physical object is tolerated as a useful fiction by staunch phenomenalists. For all his intolerance of "Ghost in the Machine"—"inside stories" of human behavior—Wittgenstein predicts that we would fail to look upon children playing over there as a bunch of automata with no feelings whatsoever, even if we tried to do this gestalt switch (P.I. #420).[19] The living human body and face, thus, simply demand out of us a treatment different from how we look upon machinery or puppets. As the poet John Donne says, it is as if, when we look upon a live human being as an alive human being we are perceptually convinced that the blood in "her cheeks" speaks to us, that "her body thinks."

Two contemporary routes to reading others' feelings

The contemporary Western scene in cognitive science and philosophy of mind, roughly, is an ongoing tussle between two competing theories of our apprehension of the second person's mind. The first theory, continuous with the analogical inference account we have rejected above, is the *Theory-of-mind Theory* (TT). According to this theory, mental states are *theoretical posits* like electrons or magnetic fields, and equally unobservable. Around the age of four, a (non-autistic) child starts manifesting his or her tacit knowledge of a set of causal-explanatory conditionals, connecting current behavior with future or past or current behavior or mental states. For example:

> "If she is so red in the face, she is going to cry."
> "If he came back from the door, he must have forgotten to take his keys."
> "If she got up in the middle of dinner, she must have needed to use the toilet."

Hundreds of such conditional interpretation rules constitute the child's pre-theoretical (tacit) rough-and-ready theory of mind, which is also known as a "folk psychology." One major rift within the TT camp is between empiricists such as Churchland who claim that a folk psychology is entirely learned, confirmed, and corrected empirically by the child from its human environment (which seems, eventually, to beg the question, since experience never yields any of these inference rules, since the other's mental/neuro-cerebral property to be inferred is inaccessible to experience) and those innatists such as Carruthers who argue that unless the child is born with a core Theory of Mind it could not pick up more such law-like connections by observing and interacting with its similar others.

Against TT, a very strong candidate is *Simulation Theory (ST)*. Simulation theory claims to be a "hot," as against a "cold," theory of mind-reading. It makes mind-reading not a propositional intellectual job, but a more touchy-feely and participatory act of immersing oneself in a make-believe role playing in order to come up with a "warmer" empathic mind-reading. The core idea is enshrined in the popular idiom of oneself getting into someone else's shoes in order to figure out how she feels. If A notices B in a certain condition and "understands" that B is nervous, anxious, or embarrassed, the steps of simulation are supposed to be:

A observes B in an uncomfortable position with certain bodily changes.
A imagines himself in B's (bodily-contextual) position and imagines having such overt changes.
A simulates, impersonates, pretends that he is B.
A (in the role of B) undergoes some feelings, experiences, beliefs, desires etc., as if they are A's own.
A goes "off-line"—de-linking these mental states from his own ego-involvement.
The outputs of this simulation process are taken and tagged on to B.
A knows or has some justification to believe that B feels afraid, anxious, embarrassed, etc.

If we ignore the big and small internal differences within this camp, what is the most vital distinction between these two accounts of mind-reading? It seems that they have split between themselves the two insights that originally prompted the analogical inference view. That view was rooted in the idea that we need to figure out or use some general premise to infer the current mental states of another, and that, in the process, our sense of possibly being in a similar position has some role to play. Now, TT seems to have taken the inferential figuring-out part seriously but ignored the analogical "what if I were you" part. Thus there is no need to look within and feel the emotions that one is going to ascribe to the other for a folk-psychologist who is completely uninvolvedly giving a theoretical explanation of the other's behavior, in the form: "She would not have cried if she was not upset," "He would not have stuck to her in the party unless he was attracted," etc. The mind-reader does not need to introspect or play at introspecting in this account. But, my similarity to you is crucial in the simulation theory and it goes through the "let's see what I would have felt had I been in a similar position" in a spontaneous mimicking process. To the extent I can make you myself, in this make-believe re-enactment, the rest of the inner story is supposed to automatically unroll—following no set of theoretically articulable connections—as a detachable narrative of my own pretend-branching-out life. In their basic outlooks, Theory Theorists treat others as live objects of explanation, studying them in interaction with each other but objectively, ascribing them mental states in the functionalist sense of the term, whereas Simulationists are still under the common Cartesian spell that primarily subjective mental states are best apprehended in oneself, and then grafted on to others.

At the turn of the twenty-first century, the most popular view among cognitive scientists and philosophers of mind was a punch of the two. This is known as "Interaction theory". Inspired by the work on *empathy* done by Max Scheler and Edith Stein[20] and the work done by Simon Baron-Cohen on Autism,[21] Shaun Gallagher[22] and Evan Thompson[23] have come up with this integration of the best elements of both

TT and ST. Incorporating evidence from the neonatal imitation of others, one could summarize this theory as follows.

In our natural process of mind-reading, elements of all the following six seem to be involved. Based on these processes, we (normal adults) seem routinely to read others' feelings, quite easily, reliably though fallibly:

1. (innate) facial and muscular mimicry and emotional contagion
2. eye-direction detection
3. shared attention mechanism
4. face-reading cues
5. theory-deployment
6. simulation (imaginative role-reversal)

Perhaps we should propose a newly recognized but perennially used knowledge-source or *pramāṇa*: EMPATHY, which is a mixture of all six of these. That solves the epistemological problem.

But, in spite of the emergence of such a synthetic view, the basic conceptual issue—the trouble with YOU—still remains unsolved. How can I directly and subjectively "experience" your pain or anger or desire, without making it my pain, anger, or desire? This is where I would like to derive new insights from the tenth-century Indian phenomenologist of emotions and consciousness, Abhinavagupta, of the Kashmir Shaiva tradition.

Abhinavagupta refutes Dharmakirti's "Proof of the Other Mind-Stream"

Abhinavagupta first reconstructs Dharmakirti's version of the Analogical Inference for the existence of other minds:

> It could be said that in myself I observe voluntary actions such as utterance of words, invariably pervaded by a wish of the form: "let me speak" assuming the causal role; now such actions as speaking must therefore be preceded by such inner wish even in the body of Chaitra—the body which is not mine. By self-awareness I have established the connection between my will and my action. From the other's action I can infer back a will outside the stream of my consciousness; therefore the existence of another stream of consciousness is easily established. Couldn't we say that?[24]

Then he goes on to expose a fatal logical error in it:

> Here, one who infers has two types of experience of utterance of words. At the time of establishing the rule of universal concomitance (*vyāpti*), the drawer of the inference correlates the experience or phenomenon describable as "I am uttering words" with the subjective experience "I have a desire to communicate," which is unsevered from one's self-awareness. But in applying the rule of *vyāpti* to the case of the other body, he at best has the experience or the sense-datum: "That

> other body is emitting words." Now, this new phenomenon, "that body utters" severed from the subjectivity of the one who draws the inference, is quite distinct from the sign which has been established as concomitant with an inner desire, since that sign was "I am uttering." The first person cause: *my inner desire*, could explain the occurrence of the first person effect: *my utterance*. How can it explain the distinct type of third person effect: *his utterance*? And, if I know that what I have to infer from your utterance is not my inner desire but your desire to speak, then I must have already formed the concept of you as another person capable of having desires, and the whole inference to the existence of the other stream of consciousness is rendered redundant.[25]

So Abhinavagupta is threatening the classical analogical inference with a dangerous dilemma. Either the sign or the premise of the inference "uttering of words by the other body" is inconclusive because it has no preestablished general connection with the inner states of wish etc. Being based in one's own case, the inductively generalizable sign would have to be "uttering of words by me" connected to "my wish to mean something." The alleged inferential sign "emission of word-sounds from that other body" is entirely unlike the felt first-person phenomenon of my uttering words. And the inference fails. Or, alternatively, one has already learned to treat "he utters words" as a special case of "I utter words" (said with an "I," which is a mere place-marker for general subjectivity), in which case one has already established the existence of a first person—a self—in the other body and one does not need this kind of analogical inference. So the so-called proof of other minds is either inconclusive or circular (*iha anumātuḥ vyāptigrahanakāle . . . vyāpter eva asiddhiḥ*).[26]

Modern Western (Post-Cartesian) thought not only finds the problem of the Other Mind hard to solve, but it also ends up finding the very presence of the other as existentially constraining and self-annihilating as "Hell" (Sartre: *No Exit*). Abhinavagupta, on the other hand, finds the You to be a foundational middle-reality between the pure Self and the apparent Non-Self in contrast and community with which the Self discovers its own playful knower-hood. He insists that even if we try to look upon the other person's body as a mere physical object, the moment "this body" is addressed in communication—even when we say such dramatic things as: "Listen, you stones, you mountains!"—it is completely enveloped with the I-feeling of the addresser. Every speaker-subject is ultimately the I, *aham* (*Shiva*–the Supreme Divine). The this, *idam* (*nara*–the mundane object-man), that is addressed as a you becomes an I-this, *aham-idam* (*śakti*–the feminine power). This Tantric principle of deriving the second person through making an I out of the This is beautifully reflected in the transformations of the German verb to-be: the "*ist*" of the third person, when immersed in the "*bin*" of the first person, becomes "*bist*." (Taking out the contrasting "m" from "*asmi*," and the contrasting "t" from "*asti*," the second person *śakti* only retains what is common between Shiva and Nara: "*asi*") The principle of addressing demands that when I say: "Hey you! standing there," I mean that just as I stand and feel my cognition-will-action manifest itself as standing, you are standing too, thus assimilating your this-ness into my I-ness, and together creating an uninterrupted relishing of subjectivity. This is very far from a Being-With or *Mitsein* that the existentialist could come up with in overcoming the problem of alterity: "The sense in which the addressor and the addressee, though different, become one in the addressing is indicative of the *parāpara* Goddess, whose characteristic is identity in difference."[27]

With similar non-dualistic insight, Professor Ramchandra Gandhi has characterized addressing as a uniquely non-coercive, nonreferential, quintessentially linguistic non-causal invitation of the attention of the other person, while giving notice of his or her freedom not to respond.[28] Abhinavagupta tells us that in addressing the other I address the self in the other, and thereby imagine myself to be addressed. In friendship and love we get an empathic re-discovery of the original unity of all apperception: "The second person which is characteristic of Shakti, shedding its standard divisive use, acquires the aspect of the first person which is characteristic of Shiva, when, for instance, one feels: 'My dear friend! You indeed am I.'"[29]

Both Abhinavagupta and Ramchandra Gandhi tell us about the convertibility of the I into you and the you into I, through linguistic acts such as addressing and speaking of oneself as another, such as in "Look at me, this is myself! Fie on me" (*dhik mām*!).This may prove that all that a single person comes to apprehend and imagine is somehow woven into a single self-enjoying creative I-consciousness, into some sort of unity that is tolerant of a projected plurality of times—my past, my present, and my future. But what about the distinction between one cognitive emotive agent and another, between myself and others?

Abhinavagupta gives a very subtle argument[30] to overcome even that basic otherness: First, let it be admitted that my own consciousness is known to me directly. I know what it is like to be self-aware and aware of outer objects from inhere. And if, say in the context of an effort at empathy with a friend, I feel acutely that I am not feeling this friend's own emotions, as a missed feeling, do not I have to subjectively be aware of those emotions, in however inadequate a fashion?

In that sense, could the unfelt pleasures and pains of another person not become objects of my direct awareness *as what I fail to feel* just as a remembered event is experienced by the same experiencer as what is not now happening?

My self-awareness manifests itself through my bodily activities, and I notice others' bodily activities just as immediately as I notice my own, though there are differences of access set up by our habitual walls of individuality. Observable actions of sentient beings are quite distinct from mere physical movements. As Abhinavagupta remarks in IPVV,[31] the going of a living being is not like the movement of water, neither is the motionless sitting by a person similar to the motionlessness of a stone. Everywhere it is undeniable that we notice the actions of others as actions enlivened by self-sentient "feelings." Just as "He knows" is said as an abbreviation of "He is in a position to say 'I know,'" similarly, "He walks" is said in the sense that he is able to make himself aware that "I am walking." Thus even others' actions are observed (not inferred) by us to be shimmering with the same subjectivity that I feel behind my voluntary actions. We must reject the suggestion that our knowledge of other minds is merely an analogical inference. The word used by Utpala in the context (IPK 1, I, 4) of our awareness of consciousness in other bodies is "*uhyate*." And Abhinavagupta clarifies:

> "*uhyate*" does not mean that others' sensations are merely inferred. To do "*ūha*" is to intuitively extrapolate, directly postulate from "otherwise inexplicability," to make it highly likely. Here, the process is partly a function of our sense organs—we see

> that the other is in pain, we can feel their pleasure (sometimes more than at other times)—thus the word "*ūha*" signifies "direct acquaintance": *atra amśe indriya-vayāparanam api asti . . . tataśca sākṣātkāram upalakṣayati* "*ūhaḥ*" (Distinguishing itself presupposes knowledge of the distinguished, thereby bringing it within the light of I-ness).[32]

When we are thus directly aware of the power of activity in others' bodies as something cognitive and conscious, this awareness inside others does not appear to us as a "this," as a mere inert material property. To be a "this," it has to be noncognitive, non-conscious. Whatever the modern brain-mind identity theorist may say, when I say and *see* that my friend is in pain or my daughter is singing happily, I do not mean that she is undergoing some physical objective event in her C-fibers or in her amygdala or somewhere else in her body. I mean (even if I do not feel it as mine) exactly the same sort of thing that I mean when I say that I am in pain or I am singing (something as subjectively feelable as that). If a state of consciousness appears as a "this thing out there," then it is not appearing as a state of consciousness at all, hence it is as good as not appearing. But others' states of consciousness are "seen" in their faces and postures (to make a Wittgensteinian point, minus Wittgenstein's allergy against the "inner"), not like inert pictures or puppet shows, but as parts of the same life-world in which my embodied consciousness is also immersed. Therefore even others' mental states appear to us as subjective, as connected to the I. The otherness only belongs to the adjuncts and dividers such as these outer bodies, but the consciousness ascribed to them, qua consciousness, rests on the I-ness of the knower-in-general, as much as my own consciousness rests on the I-ness. Thus even the awareness in/of the other is, indeed, awareness in/of one's own Self![33]

It is on the basis of such a passionate and playful I-ing and You-ing of discursive consciousness that Abhinavagupta could write:

> The free power of self-consciousness (*vimarśa*) can do everything. It can turn the other into its own self, it can turn the self into an other, it can identify the two, and it can leave aside and ignore even this unification of the self and the other . . . and this self-synthesis is nothing other than inner dialogue—a speech that is not ruled by artificial semantic conventions, but is an uninterruptedly self-relishing use of natural signs like inward noddings[34]

The Shaiva-Non-Dualist takes the lesson from this debate between the externalist and internalist Buddhists (whose denial of a permanent self, in any case, is unacceptable to the Shaiva) that the other subject can only be established when the other's action is perceived both by him/her (in the form: "I want to speak/spit/dance" followed by "Now I am speaking/spitting/dancing") and by me in the form ("He is speaking/spitting/dancing,") from the assumption that *one and the same action* is then apprehended in these two different forms. For, "we have to make this assumption in order to justify the unity of the sphere of human practice."[35] The world my own subjective representations are about would not be an objective world unless it is a shared world, and in order to share a world, I need other equally active-conscious "I" users (third persons to me, first persons to themselves) to share it with.[36]

Abhinavagupta's own view, if there is any, in these extraordinarily complex and allusive passages recording the hot debate between a world-denying internalist idealist, an externalist realist, and a world-affirming dynamic Pan-psychist Non-Dualist appears to be the following:

The final court of appeal for any philosophical dispute is the practice of everyday life, public affairs (*loka-yātrā*) where communication and pragmatic transactions go on "really" among many conscious active persons. While constructing a transcendental argument from the otherwise inexplicability of this "common public practice," we must first note that any attempt to base our knowledge of other people's minds (desires, feelings, motivations, beliefs) on an analogical inference starting from a first-person correlation of inner states and outer expressions would be hopelessly circular. Our perception of other active expressive beings spontaneously takes them to be alive, and to take something else as living is—to use a Kantian turn of phrase—to recognize its actions as capable of being smeared with a first-person ambiance, with an "I think, I feel, I intend," as continuous with that sole subjectivity that I am in touch with, of a universal spatiotemporally indivisible original Unity of Consciousness.

So, when representations of the physical expressions and movements of another live body appear to one embodied Self #1, the subjective appearance of an action in another living body spontaneously (but not infallibly) gets interpreted as tingling with the same continuous subjectivity and intentionality that enlivens the body of Self #1 directed at a common world. Indeed, the objectivity of this common co-perceived world presupposes that at the back of those bodily movements operates a dynamics of "apparently another" center of consciousness. To take Max Scheler's example, the "clasped hands" appearance seen by Self #1 as "not in this body but in that other body," is thus "interpretively seen as" the front-face of the same appearance of which the back is an inner wish to implore, to say "please," which must be of Self #2.[37] The act of spitting is seen sense-makingly as generated by the desire to spit, with or without the wish to be seen spitting by another. Eventually, through these facts of successful interpersonal communication and quotidian common world-negotiation, one is supposed to get clued into the transcendental identity between Self #1 and Self #2, as they both "recognize" or rediscover themselves to be none other than Shiva at play.

Under IPK 1.2.8, Abhinavagupta offers his complex mirroring theory of perception, where even hearing the sound made by an external body is possible because the perceiver generates an echo inside himself; hearing thus turns into a sort of act of "re-sonating." Even tasting is possible because of the gustatory mirroring we find in the act of salivation (*dantodaka*) and touching consists in the act of hair standing on end because of a mirroring thrill inside. At this point, Abhinavagupta gives the example of an attentive sensitive woman who starts quivering with pain when she sees a sharp thorn being touched by another stranger.[38] It is extremely tempting to conjecture that the aesthete philosopher was unwittingly anticipating the recently discovered close developmental link between mirror-neurons responsible for gestural mimicry and language ability in a child, between the sense of self and empathy, between action, interpersonal affect, and conscious cognition. He was surely embracing a more Max Scheler-type "direct perception" view of our knowledge of other toward a transcendental argument from the very possibility of genuine empathy and interpersonal communication to the underlying unity of all sentience.

Objectivity/intersubjectivity within a unity of consciousness and public practice

Vāmanadatta in *Seventy Verses on the Self* (also called *Samvitprakāśa*), comments:

> (the common-sense position:) "This person is other than myself, and I am distinct from this person," cannot stay in conflict even for a moment against the Oneness we are arguing for. We cannot even assign otherness to the other as long as the other is not selved or absorbed in the subjectivity of the self because only that which is understood and perceived as other is an other. What is comprehended cannot be spoken of as utterly separated from and unconnected with awareness; if such unconnected entities could be called "comprehended" then anything and everything would be comprehended. In that case, these poor external objects which are quite content in their self-contained existence and are apparently independent of our awareness, what crime have they committed for you, so that you set them aside as mere objects of knowledge?[39, 40]

If the thought "No one understands what another person wants to say" cannot be put into a public language, it is not even a thought, hence cannot be true (or false). If it can be put into a *public* language, then it must be possible for at least this thought to be understood by others, people distinct from the speaker/thinker. Therefore this thought must be false, if it is a thought at all. So it is possible, albeit fallibly, for one to know that the fish are swimming happily without being a fish. It is possible for a Hindu or a Jew to see that a Muslim is suffering without being or becoming a Muslim.[41]

To assume that we can translate exactly and exhaustively one cultural language into another would amount to a naïve universalism about common meanings and perfect transparency across languages, unlike traditions and communities. To be cynically certain that the individual other or cultural alien is always totally opaque to the self or native culture would be to degenerate into a radical localism and incommensurabilism claiming impossibility of communication. Though one needs to be equally wary of wholesale naïve universalism, this chapter is against the latter extreme.

Initially, it may seem plausible to say "I cannot read the mind of a British or a Malayali person the way I can know the feelings of another Bengali, because I am not French or Malayali, but grew up as a Bengali." Yet, if this other Bengali turns out to be a woman from a village of Bangladesh or Birbhum, when I am a Kolkata urban man, I may be able to understand the feelings of the British philosophy professor with whom I studied at Oxford much better than the feelings of the rustic Bengali lady. Once we indulge in radical localism about language/culture sharing communities, the domino-effect lands us in the absurdity of "private languages" of individuals. I may, that way, forget and fail to make sense of my own feelings or emotional behavior when I was a child, at the age of sixty. Once I give in to localism of this sort, even the self of a year ago would become an incomprehensible stranger to me (although a Buddhist moral meditator could make good use of such diachronic self-alienation!)

Since there is no cut-off point until which we can allow the possibility of intersubjective or intergroup or diachronic empathic knowledge of each other, the transparent availability of my kind of joy or anguish, belief or desire would have to stop right at the frontiers of my own mind/body at the present time. Any consciousness beyond my skin would have to be subject to an academic skepticism of possible mindlessness, or, at least, incomprehensibility. Cocooned inside my current psychophysical boundaries, would I then even understand my own "current" self (since even the current happens across moments)? My language would then become a strictly presentist private language. No dialogue—not even a soliloquy[42]—is possible in such a private language. If it is a language, it must be a bridge between me and you, between my self and your self.

This brings us back to the bridge from where Zhuangzi could see fish happiness down below. He could know that the fish were happy from his own place—not even having to engage in simulative imagination or analogical inference. The only twist that Abhinavagupta adds is that the non-dual ocean of consciousness swallows both the bridge above where Zhuangzi and Huizi are engaging in their peripatetic wrangling and the river below where the fish are swimming happily.

Notes

1 John Donne, "Of the Progress of the Soul: Second Anniversary," in *The Poems of John Donne*, Vol. 1, ed. Herbert Grierson (Oxford: Clarendon Press, 1912), Ll. 242–245, p. 258.
2 Ludwig Wittgenstein, *Last Writings on Philosophy of Psychology*. Vol. II, 67b, ed. G. H. Von Wright and H. Nyman (Oxford: Basil Blackwell, 1982).
3 K. C. Bhattacharya, *Studies in Philosophy* (Delhi: Motilal Banarsidass, 1983), pp. 282–3.
4 Quoted by John Wisdom in his book *Other Minds* (Oxford: Blackwell, 1952), p. 206.
5 Wan-Chuan Fang, "Going Back to the Ordinary: The Case of the Happy Fish in the *Zhuangzi*."
6 Chad Hansen, "The Relatively Happy Fish," *Asian Philosophy* 13, no. 2/3 (2003), pp. 145–64.
7 Xiaoqiang Han, "The Happy Fish of the Disputers," *Asian Philosophy* 22, no. 3 (2012), pp. 239–56.
8 Arindam Chakrabarti, "Play, Pleasure, Pain: Ownerless Emotions in Rasa Aesthetics," in *History of Science, Philosophy, and Culture in Indian Civilization*, Vol. XV Part III, ed. D. P. Chattopadhyaya and Amiya Dev (New Delhi: Centre for Study in Civilizations, 2009).
9 Max Scheler, *The Nature of Sympathy* (London and New Brunswick: Transaction Publishers, 2008).
10 Paul Ricoeur, *Oneself as Another*, translated by K. Blamey (Chicago: Chicago University Press, 1992).
11 Immanuel Kant, "Idea for a Universal History from a Cosmopolitan Point of View" (1784), in *Kant: On History*, trans. L. W. Beck (Indianapolis: The Bobbs-Merrill Co., 1963), Fourth Thesis.

12 John Stuart Mill, *An Examination of Sir William Hamilton's Philosophy* (London: Longman, Green, Reader, and Dryer, 1872), pp. 243–44.
13 Dharmakirti, *Pramāṇavārttikam*, ed. R. C. Pandey (Delhi: Motilal Banarsidass, 1989) http://www.dsbcproject.org/node/7047, P. III. 68.
14 Theodore Stcherbatsky, "Establishment of the Existence of Other Minds" (*Saṃtānāntarasiddhi*), in *Papers of Th. Stcherbatsky*, ed. Debiprasad Chattopadhyaya and trans. H. C. Gupta, Soviet Indology Series. No. 2 (Calcutta: R.K. Maitra, 1975), pp. 87–93 (vv. 7–26).
15 Yuichi Kajiyama, "Buddhist Solipsism: A Free Translation of Ratnakīrti's *Saṃtānāntaradūṣaṇa*," *Journal of Indian and Buddhist Studies/Indogaku Bukkyōgaku Kenkyū* 13, no. 1 (1965), pp. 435–20.
16 Jonardon Ganeri, *The Self: Naturalism, Consciousness, and the First-Person Stance* (Oxford: Oxford University Press, 2012), pp. 206–11.
17 See: Peter Strawson, *Individuals: An Essay in Descriptive Metaphysics* (London: Methuen, 1959).
18 Ibid., pp. 97–100.
19 Ludwig Wittgenstein, *Philosophical Investigations*, trans. G. E. M. Anscombe (Oxford: Basil Blackwell, Ltd, 1958), p. 126.
20 Edith Stein, *On the Problem of Empathy*, trans. Waltraut Stein (Washington: ICS Publications, 1989).
21 Simon Baron-Cohen, *Mindblindness: An Essay on Autism and Theory of Mind* (Cambridge, MA: MIT Press, 1997).
22 Shaun Gallagher, *How the Body Shapes the Mind* (Oxford: Oxford University Press, 2005).
23 Evan Thompson, ed., *Between Ourselves: Second-person Issues in the Study of Consciousness* (Charlottesville: Imprint Academic, 2001).
24 Abhinavagupta, *Īśvarapratyabhijñāvimarśinī: Bhāskarīsaṃvalitā*. (IPV), ed. Iyer, Subramania, Padeya, Kanti Chandra (Delhi: Motilal Banarsidass, 1986), vol. 1, p. 216.
25 Abhinavagupta, *Īśvarapratyabhijñāvimarśinī*, vol. I, pp. 217–18.
26 Ibid., pp. 217–19.
27 Abhinavagupta, *Parātrimśikāvivaranam*: The Secret of Tantric Mysticism. (PTK) Bettina Bäumer, ed. J. Singh (Delhi: Motilal Banarsidass, 1988), pp. 70–71.
28 R. Gandhi, *Availability of Religious Ideas* (London: Macmillan, 1985).
29 Abhinavagupta, *Parātrimśikāvivaranam*, p. 27.
30 Abhinavagupta, *Īśvarapratyabhijñāvimarśinī*, vol. I, pp. 75–76.
31 Abhinavagupta, *Īśvarapratyabhijñāvimarśinī*, vol. I, p. 105.
32 Abhinavagupta, *Īśvarapratyabhijñāvimarśinī*, vol. I, p. 101.
33 *sa ca para-śarīrādisāhityena avagatam svam svabhāvam jñānātmakam avagamayati, na ca jñānam idantayā bhāti . . . bhāti ca yat tadeva aham ityasya vapuḥ iti parajñānam api svātmā eva*. Abhinavagupta, *Īśvarapratyabhijñāvimarśinī*, vol. I, p. 76.
34 Abhinavagupta, *Īśvarapratyabhijñāvimarśinī*, vol. I p. 252.
35 Isabelle Ratié, "Some Hitherto Unknown Fragments of Utpaladeva's *Vivṛti* (I): On the Buddhist Controversy Over the Existence of other Conscious Streams," in *Utpaladeva: Philosopher of Recognition*, ed. B. Bäumer and R. Torella (Delhi: DK Printworld, forthcoming 2015), p. 8.
36 Utpaladeva and Abhinavagupta take advantage of the Buddhists' internal dispute between mind-only idealism and externalist realism.
37 Scheler, *The Nature of Sympathy*, p. 10.
38 See Abhinavagupta, *Isvarapratyabhinjnavivrtivimarsini* (Delhi: Akay Book Corporation 1987) (IPVV), pp. 145–59.

39 *mattaḥ paro'yam etasmād anyo'ham iti yāpi dhīḥ |neyam aikyavirodhena sthātuṃ kṣaṇam api kṣamā || 31 || paravyavasthāpi pare yāvan nātmīkṛtaḥ paraḥ |tāvan na śakyate kartuṃ yato buddhaḥ paraḥ paraḥ || 32 || buddhaś ca bodha bhedena bhaven na vyavahārabhāk |vyatiriktasya buddhatve sarvaṃ buddhaṃ na kiṃ bhavet || 33 || svasattāmātrasaṃtuṣṭair anapekṣair svabhāvataḥ |bhāvaiḥ kim aparāddhaṃ vo yena meyatvam āpitāḥ || 34 ||* Vāmanadatta, *Samvitprakāśa* (Vārāṇasi: Sampūrṇānanda Saṃskṛta Viśvavidyālaye, 1993) vv. 31–34.

40 Abhinavagupta, *Parātrimśikāvivaranam*, p. 27.

41 See: Xiaojing Xu, Xiangyu Zuo, Xiaoying Wang, and Shihui Han, "Do You Feel My Pain? Racial Group Membership Modulates Emphatic Neural Responses," *The Journal of Neuroscience* 29, no. 26 (2009), pp. 8525–29.

42 In a brilliantly insightful recent essay, Sundar Sarukkai, unwittingly echoing Abhinavagupta's point about self-consciousness being of the nature of internal dialogue with oneself in a preconventional language as it were of inward head-nodding for or against oneself, makes the point that our moral sensibility may spring from the natural capacity for self-conversation. See "On Quiet Conversation: Ethics and the Art of Self-Conversation," chapter 8 of *Grounding Morality: Freedom, Knowledge and the Plurality of Cultures*, ed. Jyotirmaya Sharma and A. Raghuramaraju (Delhi: Routledge, 2010).

References

Abhinavagupta (1986), *Īśvarapratyabhijñāvimarśinī: Bhāskarīsaṃvalitā*, edited by Iyer, Subramania, Padeya, Kanti Chandra, Delhi: Motilal Banarsidass.

Abhinavagupta (1987), *Isvarapratyabhinjnavivrtivimarsini*, Delhi: Akay Book Corporation.

Abhinavagupta (1988), *Parātrimśikāvivaranam*: The Secret of Tantric Mysticism, Bettina Bäumer, edited by J. Singh, Delhi: Motilal Banarsidass.

Baron-Cohen, S. (1997), *Mindblindness: An Essay on Autism and Theory of Mind*, Cambridge, MA: MIT Press.

Bhattacharya, K. C. (1983), *Studies in Philosophy*, Delhi: Motilal Banarsidass.

Chakrabarti, A. (2009), "Play, Pleasure, Pain: Ownerless Emotions in Rasa Aesthetics," in D. P. Chattopadhyaya and Amiya Dev (eds), *History of Science, Philosophy, and Culture in Indian Civilization*, Vol. XV Part III, New Delhi: Centre for Study in Civilizations, pp. 189–202.

Dharmakirti (1989), *Pramāṇavārttikam*, edited by R. C. Pandey, Delhi: Motilal Banarsidass, http://www.dsbcproject.org/node/7047.

Donne, J. (1912), "Of the Progress of the Soul: Second Anniversary," in Herbert Grierson (ed.), Vol. 1, *The Poems of John Donne*, Oxford: Clarendon Press, pp. 249–66.

Fang, W., "Going Back to the Ordinary: The Case of the Happy Fish in the *Zhuangzi*." (unpublished manuscript of keynote lecture delivered at SACP and ASACP joint session annual meeting in Singapore, July 10, 2013).

Gallagher, S. (2005), *How the Body Shapes the Mind*, Oxford: Oxford University Press.

Gandhi, R. (1985), *Availability of Religious Ideas*, London: Macmillan.

Ganeri, J. (2012), *The Self: Naturalism, Consciousness, and the First-Person Stance*, Oxford: Oxford University Press.

Han, X. (2012), "The Happy Fish of the Disputers," *Asian Philosophy*, 22 (3), pp. 239–56.

Hansen, C. (2003), "The Relatively Happy Fish," *Asian Philosophy*, 13 (2/3), pp. 145–64.
Kajiyama, Y. (1965), "Buddhist Solipsism: A Free Translation of Ratnakīrti's *Saṃtānāntaradūṣaṇa*," *Journal of Indian and Buddhist Studies/Indogaku Bukkyōgaku Kenkyū*, 13 (1), pp. 435–20.
Kant, I. (1963), "Idea for a Universal History from a Cosmopolitan Point of View" (1784), in *Kant: On History*, translated by L. W. Beck, Indianapolis: The Bobbs-Merrill Co.
Mill, J. S. (1872), *An Examination of Sir William Hamilton's Philosophy*, London: Longman, Green, Reader, and Dryer.
Ratié, I. (forthcoming 2015), "Some Hitherto Unknown Fragments of Utpaladeva's *Vivṛti* (I): On the Buddhist Controversy Over the Existence of other Conscious Streams," in B. Bäumer and R. Torella (eds), *Utpaladeva: Philosopher of Recognition*, Delhi: DK Printworld.
Sarukkai, S. (2010), "On Quiet Conversation: Ethics and the Art of Self-Conversation," chapter 8 of *Grounding Morality: Freedom, Knowledge and the Plurality of Cultures*, edited by Jyotirmaya Sharma and A. Raghuramaraju, Delhi: Routledge, pp. 130–42.
Scheler, M. (2008), *The Nature of Sympathy*, London and New Brunswick: Transaction Publishers.
Stcherbatsky, T. (1975), "Establishment of the Existence of Other Minds" (*Saṃtānāntarasiddhi*), in *Papers of Th. Stcherbatsky* edited by Debiprasad Chattopadhyaya and translated by H. C. Gupta, Soviet Indology Series. No. 2, Calcutta: R.K. Maitra, 1975.
Stein, E. (1989), *On the Problem of Empathy*, translated by W. Stein, Washington: ICS Publications.
Strawson, P. (1959), *Individuals: An Essay in Descriptive Metaphysics*, London: Methuen.
Thompson, E., ed. (2001), *Between Ourselves: Second-person Issues in the Study of Consciousness*, Charlottesville: Imprint Academic.
Vāmanadatta (1993), *Samvitprakāśa*, Vārāṇasi: Sampūrṇānanda Saṃskṛta Viśvavidyālaye.
Wisdom, J. (1852), *Other Minds*, Oxford: Blackwell.
Wittgenstein, L. (1958), *Philosophical Investigations*, translated by G. E. M. Anscombe, Oxford: Basil Blackwell, Ltd.
Wittgenstein, L. (1982), *Last Writings on Philosophy of Psychology*, edited by G. H. Von Wright and H. Nyman, Oxford: Basil Blackwell.
Xu, X., Zuo, X., Wang, X., and Han, S. (2009), "Do You Feel My Pain? Racial Group Membership Modulates Emphatic Neural Responses," *The Journal of Neuroscience*, 29 (26), pp. 8525–29.

6

The Geography of Perception: Japanese Philosophy in the External World

Masato Ishida

Introduction

Vision, or visual perception, constitutes the central focus of this chapter. My general thesis is that perception incorporates a complex *geography* associated with the body, where the body is understood as including the entire *action-space* for organisms. I take perception to be *direct*. As I shall argue below, this makes it different from sensation. In terms of tradition, Japanese philosophy has always tended toward theories of *direct perception*. It is, therefore, unsurprising that modern Japanese philosophy has found proponents of this position such as Watsuji Testurō (1889–1960) and Ōmori Shōzō (1921–1997). Since comparative perspectives can be found in classical American philosophy, this chapter draws on the works of C. S. Peirce (1839–1914), John Dewey (1859–1952), and Alfred N. Whitehead (1861–1947) as well.

Another prominent aspect of Japanese philosophy is its emphasis on *phenomenalism*. I will bring the philosophy of Nishida Kitarō (1870–1945), the founder of modern Japanese philosophy, into dialogue with David Hume (1711–1776) and J.-P. Sartre (1905–1980). The latter two represent, in this chapter, classical phenomenalism and phenomenology in the West. Moving beyond traditional borders, I propose a generalized conception of *vision*, the source of which idea I attribute to Dōgen (1200–1253), the founding father of Japanese Sōtō Zen, and, to a slightly lesser degree, to Nishida Kitarō mentioned above. My argument is that any perceptual system that responds to visual properties is, at least potentially, an *eye*. The chapter concludes with the proposition that a similar analysis can be applied to other forms of perception, each exemplifying a complex *geography*.

Blinking the eyes

When I perceive a red apple on a table several feet away, why is it that the *apple* appears red to me, not my eyes or brain, let alone my belief about the apple? Our nervous system, the brain in particular, processes information that was initially received through the optical eyes, the result of which is the recognition of the red apple on the table. But if information processing takes place in the brain, as it actually does, why is it that its *output* is found in the external object that I am staring at from a distance? In contrast, if a computer processes information, the output is stored in its internal memory. However, the red color does belong to the *apple* if I am *perceiving* it before me—it would be counter-intuitive to consider that the vivid red color is stored in my mind, even if I conceded, reluctantly, that the *belief* about the red apple might be stored in my brain.

So blink your eyes a few times. The perceived apple vanishes from the visual field when the eyes are closed, and it reappears when the eyes open again. Let us note that an *afterimage* is perceived immediately after the eyes are closed. The afterimage is felt nearer, the redness felt more internal to consciousness, as the world loses much of its perceived extension each time the eyes blink. I also wish to observe that there is no measurable distance between our mind, on the one hand, and the redness felt in the *afterimage*, on the other, whereas in *perception* we have a much more concrete sense of the physical distance between our eyes and the object we perceive. Thus we can easily reach out to the object and grab it with our hand. To anticipate one of the main points of this chapter, visual perception is always *geographically informed*, which is why it differs from mere *sensation*.

This is, however, not an altogether new view. A useful description can be found in the words of Henri Bergson (1859–1941). "I only have to shut my eyes for my visual universe to vanish," he writes, also pointing out that in closing our eyes "we pass, with insensible degrees, from the representational state that occupies space, to the affective state that appears unextended."[1] We lose, in short, *spatial extension* as perception turns into a more internal, affective state. Further, "the *given* of our different senses are the qualities of things perceived first in the things rather than in ourselves."[2] Hence the *given*, if we retain this classic vocabulary for a moment, is not "sense-data" for Bergson—they are aspectual appearances of *things*. The important point to begin with is that *spatial extension* is no longer there in internalized states of sensory experience.

Qualia in space: Where geography begins

On the other hand, when our eyes reopen, objects *and* their attributes are *simultaneously* pushed back into the spatial environment, as it were. There is a sense of instant visual expansion. Figuratively speaking, the characteristic qualities that were felt internal to us when the eyes were closed now "fly back" into the world. The redness becomes the redness of the apple, not that of the afterimage in our mind. To be more precise, however, the internally felt redness does not "travel outward" into space from within the mind, as if a red fire line ran across the visual field all the way back to the apple. As one can verify through each blink, the sense of distance, the object, and its redness, *all appear at once*, as occurring in one perceptual event.

So blink again. You should see that objects of visual perception literally "jump into" the eyes when the eyelids are lifted. Pushing Bergson a step further, I suggest that perception is not only *spatial* but also *geographical*, which I will consider in greater detail below. At the same time, it remains important to bear in mind that perceptual objects located in space are accompanied by *subjectively felt qualities*, such as the vivid red of the apple. I shall call them *qualia* in the usual way. They are immediately felt phenomenal qualities. Yet, where I diverge from common accounts of qualia is that, in my view, qualia in perception are *actually spread out in space.*

To keep the projectile of this chapter clear, I have no trouble regarding qualia as *subjective* in the sense that they are accessible only to a particular perceiver, hence making them *first-person* properties irreducible to third-person properties. However, I shall have great enough trouble if *qualia* are considered to be introspective reports of the perceiver, suggesting that they only refer to subjective modifications of consciousness. For it is the *redness-of-the-apple* that I perceive, not my *consciousness-here-in-me*. That is, I gain information about an *object-in-the-environment,* not about myself, when I perceive a red apple in the ordinary way. I will argue in a moment that perceptual qualia thus spread out in space provide us with a geography that forms our *action space.*

Geographically located qualia

Now, if it is argued that the quality of the *afterimage* of the apple belongs to—or is felt internal to—the mind, I may not object too fervently. A moment of "reflection" often gives rise to an enhanced or slightly exaggerated sense of afterimages. But the only reason I would not object would be that qualities perceived in this manner do not constitute an attribute of a thing disclosed in a concrete location relative to, and distinct from, where my optical eyes are located. The very fact that the afterimage has lost its original geographical information makes me feel that the associated qualities somehow belong to my consciousness, though there is nothing like an *insideness* of the mind, a point I also wish to underscore. Likewise, *imagined* objects, not *perceived* ones, lack geographical information—one of the essential differences between dreaming and perceiving is that the former has no definite location in our action space.

As a clarificatory remark, I am not concerned with the *causes* of perception. We can always say that the mental "supervenes" upon the physical without being too specific about causal relations. In other words, the concept of supervenience can be retained as a permissible explanatory vocabulary. Then the question closer to my concern is this: *Where* does the mental supervene upon the physical? In the philosophy of mind, mental states are commonly assumed to supervene upon physical brain states such as "C-fiber firing" taking place in the brain. Strictly speaking, however, the standard concept of supervenience does not specify exactly *where* mental properties are supposed to manifest themselves, given the relevant physical base properties. The "where" question is worth addressing. My response is that perceptual qualia supervene on the entire action space.

Continuing to speak of supervenience, I hold that some supervenient mental properties are real aspects of objects perceived in the environment. As is the case with the perceived apple, or a melody flowing from a violin on stage, phenomenally felt qualities appear with *things in space* whereby different features of the environment are marked up for salience. In this way, perceptual qualia have locations. I may assume that qualia generally supervene on physical properties, but to be cautious, I do not need to assume that they must be where the *brain* is—the quale of *redness* is found *with* the apple, not with my brain. Thus I am informed about *objects-within-a-geographical-context* when I perceive things. This does not appear to be quite the case with *sensation*, since sensation, as touched upon earlier, loses much of the original geographical information.

Being-cold-in-the-world: Watsuji Tetsurō

Turning to Japanese philosophy, one can easily find an observation relevant to this line of thinking in the opening pages of *Climaticity* (*Fūdo*), a classical work by Watsuji Tetsurō (1889–1960) published in 1935. The work intends to reveal the fundamental structure of human existence from a phenomenological point of view, and in relation to climate and culture, but a brief passage on perception is already illuminating enough for the purpose of our discussion. Suppose we go out into the cold on a winter's day. Watsuji describes our average or everyday perceptual experience as follows:

> We directly *feel*, not the "sensation" of the cold, but the "coldness of the open air," or we *feel* the cold air itself. . . . When we *feel* the cold, we are ourselves already abiding in the chillness of the air outside. That we relate ourselves to the coldness means nothing but ourselves *having [our] being outside* in the cold. In this sense, our mode of being, as Heidegger emphasizes, characterizes itself by our being outside (ex-sistere), and therefore by intentionality.[3]

As the passage makes clear, Watsuji rejects the notion of "sensation"—there is no sensory medium that lies between the perceiver and the perceived. Prior to being conscious of individual sensory objects, reflective mental acts, and so on, which are all abstractions from more fundamental experience in Watsuji's view, we are most directly aware of the cold weather. Our experience is, Watsuji argues, that of being "outside" in space.

There is more to Watsuji's point, though, which is echoed in his mention of *intentionality*. As we may recall, Heidegger's *Dasein* has an irreducibly triadic temporal structure. Human existence, which is essentially a being toward *future* for Heidegger, should be understood as having assumed its own *past*, whence an authentic self can be called for in the *present*. Hence, our being spans future, past, and present *at once*, without which its very structure falls. In particular, *Dasein* does not dwell in the present and takes an imaginative journey into the past and future when it experiences time. Quite the contrary, its fundamental mode of being is that of temporal *ex-sistence*, that is, *being outside*. Hence the *present* is nothing but a product of abstraction if singled out as a disconnected instant.

Watsuji applies a similar though wider analysis to the *spatial* nature of human *ex-sistence*. Not necessarily contradicting Heidegger's analysis of temporality, he thinks that human existence in its *spatial* dimension spans the entire living space, which must ultimately include the community. On the smaller end of the scale, perception does not take place inside this or that mind, nor does the mind reach out for objects from within. Just as *Dasein* is never containable in the present but exists across future, past, and present, human existence is not contained in a point of space. In this manner, Watsuji boldly generalized Heidegger's idea of temporal *ex-sistence* in explaining how we are *spatially* "outside" in the world. In his view, perception is *direct*, *extended*, and *outside*, as opposed to veiled within sense-data somehow sitting inside the mind.

Where is perception?: It's not where the head is

To enhance the idea and language of this chapter, *qualia* are self-active markers of subjectivity, but they are more generally first-person properties distributed throughout the environment. This means that subjectivity itself is spread out in the world. I do not consider this unnatural. If the perceiving subject is revealed where the subjective elements of experience are made most immediately manifest, then the perceiving subject, so long as it is seen not as an independent "substance" but as the workings themselves that express the subject, is revealed in the open environment itself. This is not to be confused with the claim that subjectivity is "projected" on things we perceive. Such a view requires that the "subject" exists elsewhere and not in the locations in which subjectivity operates. The argument here is that the subject *is* literally where subjectivity is at work.

Readers might start to wonder, then, whether a perceiving subject can simultaneously exist at multiple locations in the environment. There is no reason to adopt a numeric language in whole numbers, but I say that it can. For example, if my attention is drawn to two red apples held apart, there will be two patches of vividly felt redness before me, and those would be where my subjectivity is. To give a second example, when I talk with two people at the same table, I am often with the two of them at once as much as I am with myself. I am not alone in holding this view. Charles S. Peirce (1839–1914) argues:

> When I communicate my thoughts and my sentiments to a friend with whom I am in full sympathy, so that my feelings pass into him and I am conscious of what he feels, do I not live in his brain as well as in my own—most literally? True, my animal life is not there; but my soul, my feeling, thought, attention are. . . . There is a miserable material and barbarian notion according to which a man cannot be in two places at once; as though he were a *thing*![4]

Without going all the way along Peirce's metaphysics, I still cannot say that my consciousness—which I take as a rough equivalent of subjectivity—is numerically "one" and is located in my brain. I may feel that my physical head is "one" and that it rests upon my cervical vertebra, but the same does not apply to how and where my conscious experience is. Some qualia, such as those associated with the perception of my neck supporting the weight of my head, may be felt very close to where my head is located, but I do not think that readers wish to say that this is also exactly where the phenomenal redness of the apple is perceived.

A number of philosophers have taken similar positions. To continue with the Anglo-American tradition, John Dewey famously wrote, "The qualities never were 'in' the organism," contending that the objectification of qualities does not mean "a miraculous ejection from the organism or soul into external things" nor "an illusory attribution of psychical entities to physical things."[5] Or we may also recall A. N. Whitehead who writes: "It is nonsense to ask if the colour red is real. The colour red is an ingredient in the process of realization."[6] As such, the apple's being red is inseparable from the subject realizing itself. To go a step further with Whitehead, each percipient is "somewhere in the continuum" of the spatio-temporal world, but it is also "everywhere throughout the continuum."[7] What Whitehead means by "continuum" here is the spatio-temporal world itself.

Turning the pocket inside out: Ōmori Shōzō

Another intuitive illustration is given by Ōmori Shōzō (1921–1997), a postwar Japanese analytic philosopher. Ōmori received his undergraduate degree in physics from Tokyo Imperial University and subsequently turned to philosophy. In the preface of his book *A Novel New Theory of Vision*, a work intended as a response to *New Theory of Vision* by George Berkeley (1685–1753), Ōmori writes:

> With the only exception of a dualist pursuing extreme coherence (for instance, a brain physiologist), few people would feel that the perceived landscape, heard and seen by us, is a mental picture "inside the mind." . . . I have attempted in this work to turn the bag of mind inside out, so to speak, and to blow out this "inside the mind" as a self-arising manifestation of the world.[8]

In the foregoing discussion, I have argued that qualia are revealed *with objects* in the environment. I have also remarked that for Watsuji Tetsurō, human existence is characterized by being always "outside." Turning the mentalistic pocket inside out—rather than saying that a perceived world is contained in the mind, Ōmori suggests above that the mind is out there in the world and *is* the direct manifestation of the world. There is no need to eliminate subjectivity or first-person immediate qualities of experience. Nor are there "things" and "minds" that are somehow inseparable. The following words of Ōmori's mirror his training in the analytic tradition:

> It is not that the thing and the mind are two inseparable things, but the very notion of separation is the one senseless thing. . . . white, black, grey, and including transparency, there is no part of our visual field that is "colorless." Just like that, there is, as I might say, nothing that is not mentally colored.[9]

To interpret Omori's point in precise terms, we need to attend to the distinction between *senseless* and *nonsense* in Ludwig Wittgenstein (1889–1951). This is because Ōmori was a well-known Wittgenstein scholar. A helpful example is, in fact, found in Wittgenstein's *Philosophical Grammar*. Here Wittgenstein argues that "bits of an apple" can be meaningfully spoken of but not "bits of the color red."[10] The latter, "bits of the color red," is not total *nonsense* (*unsinnig*) since there is nothing grammatically incorrect about the expression, but it is *senseless* (*sinnlos*) because the color red, in contradistinction from red patches in space, does not have "bits" to refer to.

Ōmori, therefore, considers the "separation" between things and minds as *senseless.* The word "separation" cannot refer to anything since we never perceive things apart from mental properties. The chair we sit in is perceived with a felt hardness of its surface; the air we breathe is felt with warmth, humidity, and so on. As words, "mind" and "thing" can be used separately, of course, but we cannot *refer to* mind or thing as apart from each other, which is why Ōmori writes above that there is nothing in our experience that is not mentally colored. The fact that we are able to use such words as "body," "mind," and "separation" grammatically does not mean that they have independent referents—in fact they do not on Ōmori's account. One might recall here a witty phrase from W. V. Quine (1908–2000): "Don't refer to what isn't."[11]

Classical phenomenalism: Hume on seeing with eyes

Having laid out these points, my argument is not that subjective elements of experience can float about in the world arbitrarily. The immediately felt redness of an apple is to be found *with* the apple—the red surface does not hover in the air detached from the apple itself. Nor does the red color veil a juicy substance as if a mentalistic curtain were drawn between the eye and the fruit. A basic geography is always canvased in actual perception, which classical phenomenalism tends to overlook. Viewed in this light, "impressions" considered by David Hume (1711–1776) are abstractions from things presented in direct perception. The redness in the Humean sense is nearer to the redness of the afterimage that one perceives during a blink.

Yet, there is also a subtler dimension to Hume's interpretation of visual perception. Three noteworthy observations are made by him. First, visual perception involves bodily sensations. Second, there is a distinction between direct perception and the perception of the afterimage. Third, Hume attends to spatial relations, though he does not reveal their full significance. His argument appears in *A Treatise of Human Nature*, where Hume discusses the ideas of space and time, of which we shall consider only space so as to remain focused on the geography of perception. According to Hume, the idea of extension must have a corresponding sensory impression, but more interestingly, the idea of extension derives directly from sight.

"Upon opening my eyes, and turning them to the surrounding objects," Hume writes, "I perceive many visible bodies; and upon shutting them again, and considering the distance betwixt these bodies, I acquire the idea of extension."[12] But since his senses convey only "the impressions of colour'd points, dispos'd in a certain manner," Hume concludes that "the idea of extension is nothing but a copy of these colour'd points, and of the manner of their appearance."[13] Thus Hume admits three things at once. First, *blinking* informs him that his eyes are responsible for visual perception—*seeing* involves the perception of eye movement. Second, he notes how the afterimage gives rise to the idea of extension. Third, a disposition of "colour'd points," such as the spatial arrangement of the points, forms part of visual perception.

Impressions are disposed in "a certain manner," Hume argues. To repeat my example, the redness of an apple is found with the apple, say, ten feet away from me, which I must always view from a *certain angle*. Although Hume does not seem to take notice of the fact that *sensation* quickly loses the perceived distance between the objects and his own eyes—with which the *viewing angle* is also lost—much of the geography of perception can be recovered if the implications of the three aspects of visual perception are pursued in greater depth. The confinement of his observation to spatial relations between objects before his eyes—as if he was contemplating an oil painting on the wall—makes his classical phenomenalism more abstract than it should be.

Recovering the geography: Spatially located qualia

I argue, therefore, that subjectively felt phenomenal qualities are disposed at various distances and angles in space including the small space my body occupies. Moreover, we are at least dimly aware of such geographical information under normal circumstances. For example, there are felt differences between where coenesthetic qualia are felt, on the one hand, and where other sensory qualia, such as visual or auditory qualia, are felt, on the other. The differences among such distinct modes of perceived qualia contribute to the articulation of experience.

To illustrate the point a little further, suppose I gaze at the moon in the dark night sky. My visual qualia, not those of the afterimage, are felt at a fairly large distance and above my normal eye level. In contrast, my coenesthetic qualia are felt at a significantly shorter distance and typically below my eye-level. Unlike sensation, neither of them is felt "inside" my mind. The overlapping effect of the two—which often takes the form of a synthetic feeling arising from the contrast between the two sets of qualia felt at distinct distances and angles—is then felt as intimately connected to my self-consciousness. I perceive my body *here*, the moon *over there*, which gives me a sense of where my body is relative to the moon. In this way, perception maps out our body and other objects in space based on multiple layers of perceptual contrasts, some of which contain saliently felt qualities.

The respect in which my view differs from standard accounts of perception is that I continue to insist on the spatial locations of qualia. I prefer to think with Bergson that perception takes place *with* or *in* things, while sensation tends to lose this geographical dimension of experience. Once again, I am not against regarding the phenomenally felt qualities as "subjective." If the word "subjective" sounds misleading, we may use the more neutral term "first-person." All we mean by "subjective" here is that you do not experience the phenomenal redness of an apple in the same way I do, and I may, accordingly, define "subjectivity" in terms of the direct accessibility to first-person features of experience. This is, of course, a common way to characterize qualia.

The first-person body: From Hume to Nishida

As we saw a moment ago, Hume believes that he sees *with* his eyes. In my language, visual qualia are accompanied by a wide spectrum of somatic qualia. Changing the angle of one's head, for example, implies change in the immediately felt qualities associated with the visual field. We thus move our eyes or turn our heads around to see things better or in different ways. In Japanese philosophy, Nishida Kitarō, the founder of the Kyoto school of philosophy, shared similar insights with Hume. *Inquiry into the Good*, Nishida's early celebrated work, does not inherit Hume's skepticism, but the central strength of Hume's argument is observed by Nishida as follows:

> It is commonly thought as if the law of causality immediately required the existence of fixed things behind phenomena, but this is a mistaken view. As Hume said, the correct significance the law of causality bears is that in the arising of a given phenomenon there are certain phenomena that precede it, and that this does not require the existence of things beyond phenomena.[14]

In a quick move Nishida suggests a few things here, but the central point is clear. There is nothing behind phenomenal manifestations—nothing in the backstairs. In view of perception, the only world, for Nishida, is that of direct knowing, a standpoint reflected in his famous term *pure experience* (*juinsui keiken*). Our body is always phenomenally lived, a flux of qualities incessantly presencing for the first-person experiencer and constituting her from within.

We must note here that *phenomenalism* in the ordinary sense becomes impossible on Nishida's account. What I mean by phenomenalism is the view that phenomenal entities such as sense data, ideas, and images stand between the perceiver and the things perceived as media of perception. No medium is necessary for Nishida. Things perceived are aspectual manifestations of things *as they are*. When we taste food, what we taste is not our sensation but the food. Contrary to Hume, therefore, Nishida does not need to accept classical phenomenalism—which tends to become a double-edged sword when it invites skepticism—while interpreting the body in purely phenomenal terms.

In the same work, Nishida also makes an interesting remark on eye movements, which lends force to our previous argument. He writes, "To take an example, when we think we have perceived something in its entirety in a single act of seeing, careful investigation shall reveal that attention shifted automatically through eye movements, which is how we come to know the thing as a whole."[15] To amplify the point, visual perception is not like taking a single snapshot of an object before the eye. The eye vibrates and gropes over the object many times in a brief second even when one believes to have perceived the object in a single glance. As long as we are living organisms, perception is intertwined with complex bodily movements, which, in Nishida's view, includes the rapid movements of the eyeballs.

Brought under this light, what I have been calling the geography of perception refers to the thick fabric of experience resulting from multifold layers of perception that involves ongoing bodily functions within the environment. It is not particularly important to know where Nishida's relatively early philosophy expressed above stands in comparison with his later works. It is beneficial to turn, instead, to an astute remark made by Takizawa Katsumi (1909–1984), an important Christian thinker who corresponded with Nishida on multiple occasions: "Even Nishida's early thought regards everything always and only through this actual flesh that is ours."[16] With this in mind, I will pursue the "body" a little further in relation to classical phenomenology.

Classical phenomenology: Perceiving the third-person body

Nishida, considers that a third-person view of the body, which objectifies the body and understands it physiologically as well as materially, emerges out of complex layers of perception. The body is not lurking *behind* perception as if there were an independent reality, but is revealed always through perception. Thus Nishida indicates in *Inquiry into the Good* that even nerve centers, or neural structures in general, should be regarded as phenomenal manifestations:

> Our body is only a part of the phenomena of consciousness of ourselves. It is not that consciousness is within the body, but on the contrary, the body is within consciousness. To say that phenomena of consciousness accompany stimulation to nerve centers only means that one kind of phenomenon of consciousness necessarily occurs together with another kind of phenomenon of consciousness. If we assume that we can know phenomena in the brain directly, the relationship between conscious phenomenon and the stimulation of the brain [observed from a third-person perspective] would be tantamount to the relationship between what one senses as sound to the ear, on the one hand, and what one senses as vibration of a string to the hand or eye, on the other.[17]

The word *consciousness* employed by Nishida here might sound mentalistic, but it does not refer to ego-consciousness. It is better interpreted as a train or flow of immediate perception that replaces materialistic or substantial notions in traditional Western metaphysics. Nishida's analogy toward the end has it that the sound sensed directly in the ear is quite different from the same sound viewed or described as vibration, such as when a string phone is observed with the eye or the vibration is felt with the hand. The sound directly heard by the ear is phenomenally experienced as such—it is auditory perception—while the same sound observed visually or known through touch of the finger is not.

The relationship between the phenomenal first-person body and the material third-person body is then not hard to explain, one of the themes that became central to Western phenomenology. A brief yet vivid description provided by J.-P. Sartre (1905–1980), for example, conveys the idea well. He describes the startling discovery of his own body in a clinic as follows:

> During a radioscopy, I could no doubt see myself on the screen, the image of my vertebrae, but I was precisely *outside* in the midst of the world. I was apprehending an entirely constructed object as a *this* among other *thises*, and it is only by reasoning that I referred it back to being *mine*. It was much more of my *property* than my *being*. It is true that I see and touch my legs and my hands. Further, nothing prevents me from imagining an arrangement of sense organs such that a human being could see one of his eyes while the eye which was seen was directing its glance to the world. But it is to be noted that in this case again, I am *the Other* in relation to my eye.[18]

In short, I can be a conscious viewer objectifying a particular body part as being *mine*. As Sartre writes, my body regarded from the outside is discovered and recognized as such rather than immediately lived. Besides the vertebrae in the spine, there are many organs, tissues, and other structures of the body that I will never see directly with my eyes, though I would *infer* that they are *mine* if my doctor needs to show X-rays of them to me for medical purposes.

The first-person consciousness, inclusive of the consciousness of the body, is not an additional reality for Sartre. It does not lie apart from or beyond the physical body any more than the body is a separate or independent reality for Nishida. In this regard, modern Japanese philosophy after the 1930s and the phenomenological movement in France after the 1940s move in the same direction. In Sartre's words, "There are no 'psychic phenomena' here to be united with the body. There is nothing *behind* the body. Rather the body as a whole is 'psychic.'"[19] We may take "psychic" to mean "mental," "subjective," or "first-person." Naturally, a phenomenologist is not deeply concerned with the body examined and described from a third-person perspective.

Eyes at work: "Looking-at" and "being-looked-at" in different ways

The idea of the lived body, contrasted with the material body, emerges as an important theme in Nishida's mature philosophy, the first-person approach proving conducive to the phenomenology of the body. In his 1937 paper "The Historical Body," a work that appeared several years prior to Sartre's *Being and Nothingness*, Nishida points out that traditional Western philosophy has overlooked the significance of the body:

> . . . . although this has been seldom taken up as a problem, I opine that our *body* awaits considerable study. I don't think traditional [Western] philosophy has given adequate thoughts to the problem of the body. Up to the present, various ways of thinking about the body have been proposed, some viewing it physiologically and others viewing life mechanically such as in the theory of mechanism, the latter attempting to be even more scientific than physiology. However, there has not been a view that thinks of the body philosophically.[20]

Noe Keiichi (1949–), who studied under Ōmori Shōzō, attends to these words and writes: "No doubt, Nishida was the first philosopher in our country to take notice of the relevance of the concept of the 'body' and to give it a central position in his philosophy."[21] What Noe has in mind in saying this is that Nishida's mature philosophy and the writings of E. Husserl (1859–1938) and M. Merleau-Ponty (1908–1961) launch strikingly similar trajectories when it comes to the problem of the body.

Two years after the quotation above was written, Nishida published a well-known 1939 paper titled "Absolutely Contradictory Self-Identity." Compared with his 1911 work *Inquiry into the Good*, the question of the body is more finely tuned and is made integral to the larger framework of his philosophy. He now regards perception more clearly as an *active* mode of experience, which constitutes the creative processes of historical nature. A suggestive passage reads:

> We are present in this world entrusted with a task to bring things into formation. Our life lies therein. . . . We are not born without hands, we are born into this world with a body. The fact that life is born with a body, this tells us that a task

> has already been worked out by historical nature (such as seen in the formation of the insect eye), and, at the same time, infinitely many tasks are further involved as contradictory self-identities. To be born with a body is to be born with infinite tasks to carry out.[22]

In Nishida's view, the task-taker and her tasks form contradictory aspects of one and the same reality, or the "self-identical" reality. There is, on the one hand, the reality that insects, for example, have to carry on tasks to survive. Their eyes develop accordingly. On the other hand, the tasks will not be given as such without the development of the eyes, that is, as tasks to be tackled with the aid of eyes. The eyes *form* tasks in the sense that they selectively and effectively navigate through visual situations, but they are also brought into being by nature that gives endless tasks to life.

It is worth paying attention to the point that Nishida's consideration is not confined to particular eye systems since he is more interested in the mutual formation of the eye and its task, that is, how *vision is at work* in the human and natural world—there are things that are *seen* for which *seeing* is called forth, in his view. An interesting train of thought leaning in this direction can be found in Sartre again. The relationship between eyes as physical objects, on the one hand, and eyes at work or what Sartre calls *the look* (*le regard*), on the other, is illuminated well in the next passage:

> If I apprehend the look, I cease to perceive the ocular globes: They are there, they stay in the field of my perception, as pure *presentations*, but I make no use of them, they are neutralized, out of play, they are no longer objects that form a thesis for me, they remain in the state of a "circuit turned off" in which the world sets itself for a consciousness executing the phenomenological reduction prescribed by Husserl. It is never when eyes are looking at you that you can find them beautiful or ugly, that you can remark on their color. The look of another person masks her ocular globes, the look appears to go *in front of* them.[23]

The rich image contains a simple point. When we are looking into someone's eyes, we are not observing her eyeballs as objects. We make ourselves conscious of the eyebeam, the *look*, whereby the ocular globes recede into concealment. On the other hand, Sartre also notes that the function of *looking at* can be "turned on," as it were, even in the absence of physical eyes. He writes:

> Every look directed toward me manifests itself in connection with the appearance of a sensible form in our perceptive field, but contrarily to what one might believe, it is not connected with any determinate form. Without doubt what *most often* manifests a look is the convergence of two ocular globes toward me. But the look will be given just as well on occasion when there is a rustling of branches, the sound of footstep followed by silence, a half-opening shutter, or a light movement of a curtain.[24]

In Sartre's view, therefore, the *look* is not necessarily linked with the actual presence of eyeballs. A video camera, or even a photograph of a friend on the wall, may suffice. In this sense, *being looked at* is part of everyday perception, whose function is significantly wider than collecting well-defined data through the optical eyes. For such reasons

Sartre remarks, "In one word, what is certain is that *I am looked at*" to which he also adds, "it is never the eyes that look at us: It is the other as subject."[25]

"Looking-At" and "Being-Looked-At" in nature

There is, however, not much need to delve into Sartre's existential analysis of "being-for-others." Plainly put, perception involves our caring about how and what others are looking at in a given situation. For instance, if other customers are looking at the same product on sale that we are looking at, we usually perceive it. Contemporary psychology sometimes associates this with eye-direction detection. Autistic children are not as good at detecting eye-directions of others as children without autism. *Looking-at* works in diverse directions and contexts even if we are rarely conscious of it—people can easily change action by merely feeling watched.

The situation is not too different in nature. A hare needs to know when it is perceived by a fox, and the fox in turn needs to know whether or not it is already perceived by the hare before attempting a chase. If a predator senses that its target has already perceived it, this is often enough to deter a strike. Daniel C. Dennett (1942–) has a lucid paragraph on a hare that has detected a fox from a safe distance:

> But if the hare determines that this fox is unlikely to succeed in its chase, it does a strange and wonderful thing. It stands up on its hind legs, most conspicuously, and stares the fox down! Why? Because it is announcing to the fox that the fox ought to give up. "I've already seen you, and I'm not afraid. Don't waste your precious time and even more precious energy chasing me. Give it up!" And the fox typically draws just this conclusion, turning elsewhere for its supper and leaving the hare, which has thus conserved its own energy, to continue its own feeding.[26]

Besides, it is oftentimes the *potential presence* of a predator that determines behavior. Small animals perceive that an open space without cover renders them exposed and hence vulnerable to predators. They also perceive that positions where predators *might* smell them had better be avoided. In countless ways, the perceived environment is saturated with potentials of all kinds. As Dennett would point out, it is not necessary that creatures *think* about such potentials in the environment, but there is little doubt that the space a living creature perceives is colored with a variety of possibilities on the basis of which qualia emerge.

This is, of course, not new knowledge altogether. If two men take a walk on a river bank and one perceives that the fish in the water are at ease, there is no need for the other to wonder why the first man knows that—every fisherman knows that fish are not taking precautions if they do not dive or hide away upon perceiving human figures or shadows. Hence the famous dialogue between Zhuangzi and Huizi in ancient China. When Zhuangzi sees fish on a bridge over the Hao River and remarks that the fish are at ease, Huizi asks Zhuangzi: "You are not a fish. How do you know that the fish are at ease?"[27] Without recourse to Daoist metaphysics, we can simply say that Zhuangzi perceives how the fish are, just as a heron perceives fish in water when it is searching for food.

In fact, Zhuangzi's reply to Huizi is nearly perfect from the viewpoint of this chapter. He says: "I know it by the Hao River."[28] In other words, the question involved was not originally concerned with *cognition* but with *perception,* which Huizi hastily made a question of *cognition*. At the end of the dialogue, therefore, Zhuangzi translates it back into a question concerning *perception*, whereby he recovers the entire perceptual context. As suggested above, how others perceive or might perceive something is part of the living vision. In addition to physical obstacles, shelters, and the like, the eye or look of potential predators, competitors, mates, preys, and even bystanders are active constituents of the environment. This means that even a hint or sign for a *possible* perspective is an essential feature of action space.

Eye and color: Dōgen's one-sentence argument

In foregoing considerations, I have highlighted the important difference between eyeballs regarded as objects, on the one hand, and eyes at work, on the other. It was also emphasized that the actual working of the eye incorporates a full-scale geography. Furthermore, we have been interpreting this working in strictly *functional* terms. Instead of starting with a list of physiological features of the eyeball and then trying to deduce its contribution to perception, we have tried to understand *what the eye is* in terms of *how vision is at work*. Taken together with Nishida's remark on the formation of insect eyes, I am inclined to consider that nature develops eyes where there is yet only a potential task for visual perception.

The focus on the *working* of the eye is certainly not a recent trend in philosophy. Remote as it may sound, Dōgen (1200–1253), the founder of Sōtō Zen, suggests that seeing, on the one hand, and the physical structure of the eye, on the other, are not to be confused with each other. In one short sentence, Dōgen rejects both the view that visual perception can be explained in terms of the physical structure of the eye and the view that when one contemplates a painting, for example, the physical ingredients of the paint are responsible for the perceived color. With respect to the first rejection, Dōgen writes: "There are no muscles and bones in the eye."[29] "Muscles and bones" generally refer to the physical frame of the body. Of course, Dōgen knows, for instance, that the physical structure of the eye system makes it possible for the eyeballs to move in the eye sockets, but he declares that there are no muscles and bones in the eye because *seeing* is fundamentally different from the working of muscles and bones.

Dōgen's intent becomes clearer in the second rejection. The next half of his sentence reads, "in color, there is no pigment or glue, wherein emancipation is revealed."[30] Again, Dōgen is aware that pigments and glue are used in Zen paintings, but the *color perceived as such* is not the physical pigment attached to canvas—we may glue pigments to canvas, but not qualia. It is *our seeing* and the *painting-being-seen* in one act that achieves visual perception, which is not anything found in the eyeball or the pigment itself. Tereda Tōru (1915–1995), a notable Dōgen scholar, thus comments upon the second half of the sentence as follows:

> What contains glue and thereby attaches itself to the canvas is the pigment, not the color itself. The color releases itself from the binding force of the adhesive agent

> used in the coloring material that holds it, and, as color, it plunges into our vision. Not only that, the color [which is not the pigment] makes visual perception what it is, and thereby itself becomes color.[31]

Color and vision, neither of which is the pigment or the eyeball, are not what they are one without the other, nor can they be reduced to the function of muscles, bones, or coloring material. We do not discover the *color perceived as such* in the physical eyeball or in the chemicals constituting the pigment. To understand what visual perception is, Dōgen thinks we must resist the temptation to reduce it to the eye or the pigment on canvas.

Generalizing vision: The great earth as the manifestation of the eye

Dōgen's philosophy leads to another bold view. It is not that there is the eye first in the world, which then decides to look around for objects, but there is an active eye or vision wherever colors, forms, and shapes are brought into play. In other words, if colors, shapes, forms, light, shadow, and other visual properties are meaningful at all in the world, anything that responds to them is potentially an eye. It is where the working of vision comes to life, as it were, not necessarily where the physical eyeballs are located. Below is a passage from Dōgen expressive of such a view. It draws on the words of Ju-ching (1163–1228) of Song China under whose mentorship Dōgen completed his formal Buddhist apprenticeship:

> My late master, old Buddha of Tendō [i.e., Ju-ching], who was residing as Abbot at Zuiganji Temple, addressed to his assembly in the preaching hall: "Pure is the autumn wind, bright is the autumn moon, the great earth, mountains, and rivers, manifest there is the eye. I blink to meet with it afresh. Sticks and shouts cross each other, testing our patch-robed monks."[32]

The meeting of the eye is meant to work in both directions, from the viewer to the great earth, mountains, and rivers, and from the great earth, mountains, and rivers, to the viewer. Dōgen, aligning himself with Ju-ching, thinks that the eye is already at work in the great earth, mountains, and rivers, though few people may notice it. Day and night, therefore, monks at the temple are urged to cultivate such a vision amidst the blows of sticks and shouts that form part of their daily training.

In order to understand the lines better, we may recall Nishida's consideration of the paradoxical interplay between the eye and the task shaping each other, which are two aspects of one and the same reality. The eye selects and responds to vision-related tasks, but it has also evolved into a specific organ designed to carry out such tasks. No eye system would have evolved, Nishida thinks, had there been no visual properties at work in the world. Aside from the modern evolutionary perspective, Dōgen's intuition moves in a similar direction. In interpreting Ju-ching's words above, he writes: "Such becoming of vision, such lively working, is the eye. The great earth, mountains, and rivers, these are the manifestation of the eye from the indefinite past when there was not even the slightest sign of it."[33]

The idea I am exploring with Dōgen and Nishida is that we consider the *working* of the eyes first and then try to understand what eyes are. There is no need to claim originality along this line. Watsuji Tetsurō reminds us: "It is not an eye if it does not see color, while it is not color if it is not seen by the eye. Therefore, the eye is eye *in being what it is for* color, and color is color *in being what it is for* the eye. The two are interdependent and have no self-nature."[34] In saying this, Watsuji has in mind Nāgārjuna's *Mūlamadhyamakakārikā*, chapter three. Yet, it is to be pointed out that the sense of *geographic perception* is not fleshed out well in Mahāyāna Buddhism. In this regard, Dōgen's statement, "The great earth, mountains, and rivers, these are the manifestation of the eye," differs from common landscape metaphors such as those found in Buddhist mandalas. It is the *actual geography presencing here and now* that Dōgen's statement captures in which the viewer and the viewed constitute a single lively vision.

The landscape: This is not idealism

Moving further in this direction, I must iterate that the world is not made up of psychic material, whether on my account or on Dōgen's account. A useful indication of Dōgen's position can be found in his flat rejection of the view that the mind somehow separates from the body when one dies, and can be reborn in different forms. The following words summarize Dōgen's thinking on this matter:

> Know that Buddhism always teaches that body and mind are one. Then how would it be even possible that the mind alone separates from the body and does not come into being or perish as the body comes into being or perishes? If there are times when the body and mind are one and other times when they are not, the Buddhist doctrine would simply be false.[35]

The separation of body and mind, which Omori Shōzō challenged from a different angle, is completely ruled out by Dōgen. This implies that the mind *is* the body. If the mind *is* the body, however, it immediately follows that, in Dogen's view, we *are* our body. There is, accordingly, nothing behind or beyond the body, a point Nishida and Sartre have also made, as mentioned above. In fact, Dōgen holds that the mind adds nothing to the world:

> The mind concerned with mountains, rivers, and the great earth is nothing but the mountains, rivers, and the great earth themselves. No other wave, wind, or wisp of smoke. The mind concerned with the sun, the moon, and the stars is nothing but the sun, the moon, and the stars themselves. No other fog or mist. The mind concerned with birth and death, coming and going, is nothing but birth and death, coming and going themselves. No other delusion or enlightenment.[36]

The "mind" repeated in this passage is *shin* in the original text. Dōgen eliminates *shin* each time a word compound containing it appears. For example, *san-ga-dai-chi-shin*, whose literal meaning is "mountains-rivers-great-earth-mind," is rendered *san-ga-dai-chi* in its second occurrence. "Mountains-rivers-great-earth-mind" thus becomes "mountains-rivers-great-earth" without *shin* at the end. Dōgen repeats this for all three compounds such that each five-character compound is rendered a four-character compound by losing *shin* or "mind." The effect is almost visual—Dōgen encourages his audience to cast off mind by eliminating the word for *mind* in the text.

Revisiting the first half of this chapter, I do consider that subjectivity is present throughout the world of perception, but I take it to be a feature of the world rather than a feature of the mind. There is no need to eliminate subjectivity or to become an extreme idealist. As a counter-viewpoint, take J. G. Fichte (1762–1814), for example, who wrote "everything you see outside you is yourself."[37] Fichte was convinced that what appears external to us, a colored surface of a table, for example, proceeds from the pure ego, not from the world. By contrast, I consider that perception proceeds from the world. Everything I see inside me *is* the world that has undergone various kinds of modification. As perception structures itself, its content emerges as more filtered and concentrated into my cognitive activities and is thus *felt* as if I had an "internal world," separate from the material world, which I do not in reality.

The sense of internality is a figure of speech. The felt internality, often thought to be characteristic of the introspecting mind, stems largely from how perception, sensation, and other internal stimuli are intertwined and contrasted with each other. Nishida Kitarō's words are helpful in this regard:

> We usually distinguish mental and material phenomena in terms of internal and external, thinking of the former as internal and the latter as external. However, such a view originates from the unwarranted assumption that mind is within the body, and when seen from the perspective of direct experience, they are all phenomena of consciousness of the same kind without the distinction between internal and external.[38]

A stomach ache is normally felt inside the surface of the body, of course, but I may perceive pain outside my body if it is not felt within my bodily boundaries. The analogy of "inside the mind" is a natural one. Nonetheless, phenomenally felt qualities, including that of pain, are revealed with *things* in the world and can thus be spread out in the world. The things revealing qualia can be some part of my body, someone else's body, or they can simply be objects in the environment.

Perception as a unique category

This brings us back to the geography of perception. I take qualia to be spatial properties, but I do not hold that they can be *anywhere*, which makes them more than mere intentional features of experience. In conscious experience, their distribution in space marks up the environment and lures the agent into action, but more generally they inform us of the geographical making of the world, not of my internal mental state. In my view, this is not necessarily the case with sensation, imagination, emotion, recollection, intellectual thought, and so on. Perception, which I continue to interpret as *direct*, is a unique category in this regard. Other forms of cognition contain limited geographical information.

For the sake of clarity, I do not assume that this geography must belong to the bottom layer of experience based on which other cognitive functions are made possible. However, I do contend that it is absolutely integral to the conception of action space. This does not need to be taken as a radically new view, since perceiving and being perceived in the environment is just part of how nature works. Aristotle has already described how the chameleon rotates its eyes to direct vision and changes its body color,[39] but St. Augustine further observes how the colors of the environment enter the chameleon's vision. "We may note," he says, "how the little body of the chameleon varies most easily into the colors that it sees."[40] If features of the environment are considered as *signs*, Peirce would add: "a chamelion [sic] and many kinds of insects and even plants make their livings by uttering signs, and lying signs."[41] How creatures perceive, might be perceived, and may make others perceive in deception, constitute the life of the natural environment.

This chapter has also made some philosophical investment in the generalization of the notion of perception, which I discussed in connection with Dōgen. The eyes, for example, are understood as where the *working* appears, not necessarily where the physiological system is located. Eyespots found on species of insects, fish, and birds—such as the peacock—might be taken as suggestive examples for the modern reader. The view emerging from the observations made along the lines of Dōgen, Nishida, and Bergson, is that the eye emerges where visual properties are functionally active. To repeat, what "causes" perception is not my concern. I suggest, instead, that we consider perception in such general terms in order to see how human perception may eventually fall within the larger philosophical picture.

Ecological and geographical perception

Another point I have made in this chapter is that there is nothing like "inside the mind" for perception. Everything occurs directly in the "external world," to use a common phrase in philosophy, though the Japanese philosophical tradition considers the internal-external distinction more problematic than useful. It is meant to be conceptual clarification as well—the concept of *quale* does not require that of *internality*. What I have called *action-space*, on the other hand, can be interpreted broadly. No organism, perceiver, or agent lives without geographical orientation. Ranging from actions in nearby space, such as reaching out for an object, to large-scale actions, such as the migrations of the monarch butterfly, geese, zebras, and gnus, over thousands of miles across borders, life on earth is geographically constituted.

A passage from J. J. Gibson (1904–1979), well known for his *ecological* approach to visual perception, may help us fine-tune the point. Gibson observes how living creatures orient themselves in a multiplicity of ways and on many different levels. The idea receives illumination in the following words worth citing at some length:

> First, the terrestrial animal maintains permanent orientation to the earth—that is, to gravity and the surface of support, these being the chief constants of the environment. Second, the animal adopts temporary orientations to events and objects whenever he attends to them. The orientation of the head, ears, eyes,

> mouth, nose, and hands depends, however, on the orientation of the body as a whole to the earth as a whole. Third, the animal exhibits from time to time oriented locomotion. This may be a simple tropism to a source of light or it may be an elaborate making of one's way to a goal. . . . Finally, there can occur the remarkable kind of oriented locomotion shown in homing and migration where animals and men find their way to a goal over long distances. This is geographical orientation, the kind we ourselves are aware of when we become "lost."[42]

Gibson's purpose is to distinguish between different perceptual orientations so that he applies the geographical viewpoint only to the fourth level here, but it is clear that all four levels work together in perception. This binds the organism to the earth in multifold ways. The remark Gibson makes at the end is equally astute: We are seldom aware of the geography because we are deeply rooted in the world, a fact that surfaces only when we are "lost."

However, I do not find it necessary to accept Gibson's metaphysics of *affordance*, a seminal idea that gave rise to ecological psychology, where *affordance* refers to an invariant property of the environment as a whole that accounts for the effective ways in which organisms transform given conditions into opportunities for action. The objectivity of affordance is a fundamental tenet for Gibson: "The affordance of something does *not change* as the need of the observer changes. The observer may or may not perceive or attend to the affordance, according to his needs, but the affordance, being invariant, is always there to be perceived."[43] He also argues:

> An important fact about the affordances of the environment is that they are in a sense objective, real, and physical, unlike values and meanings, which are often supposed to be subjective, phenomenal, and mental. But, actually, an affordance is neither an objective property nor a subjective property; or it is both if you like. An affordance cuts across the dichotomy of subjective-objective and helps us to understand its inadequacy. It is equally a fact of the environment and a fact of behavior. It is both physical and psychical, yet neither.[44]

The challenge Gibson takes to overcome "the dichotomy of subjective-objective" by regarding *affordance* as a fact of the environment-and-behavior stands at an interesting crossroad with Japanese philosophy that has traditionally striven to avoid subject-object dualism. For the purpose of this chapter, however, it remains crucially important that the "subjective" or "first-person" properties are given a concrete *place* in experience. This retention of the first-person properties marks a significant departure from Gibson. To put it the other way around, Gibson does not tell us *where* affordances are located, revealed, or expected. I also consider that *optical* analogies are made slightly too strong in Gibson's theory such that his ecological approach invites a particular version of metaphysics that the geographical approach does not.

Familiarity and ubiquity of visual perception

Throughout this chapter, I have tried to trespass on a number of philosophical territories and traditions. To some extent, my considerations center on Japanese philosophy, which commonly endorses theories of *direct* perception, but I hope I have also shown that the ideas explored need not be grounded in any particular genre or school of philosophy. In this regard, it is perhaps worth noting that modern Japanese philosophy has always been *comparative*—it acknowledges and appreciates the achievements of other traditions, while looking for new ways to understand old problems.

Watsuji Tetsurō is a good example. He was among the earliest Japanese scholars to recognize the significance of Heidegger's *Being and Time* when it appeared in 1927, but he was also the first modern Japanese intellectual to revive Dōgen as a *philosopher*, not as a Zen master. He also drew considerable resources from Friedrich Nietzsche (1844–1900) in scrutinizing the mind-body problem. In *A Study of Nietzsche* (1913), Watsuji's first published monograph, he observed how important the body was for Nietzsche:

> Nietzsche repeated, again and again, that the body must receive respect. . . . The remotest and the nearest past of organic change blend into each other in the body producing a complex harmony so as to form a lively, ongoing, concrete activity. . . . True, it is the working of cognition that generated the representation of the body. But cognition is a faculty of the body, not a power belonging to a psychic entity. In the absence of the representation of the body, there still is the body, the power that creates representations.[45]

In the same study, Watsuji points out that the "I" or "ego" for Nietzsche "is nothing but *imagined* to be the subject to which the sense of power belongs" such that the initial sense of the "I" is, in fact, "a faith in the one-and-the-sameness of the body," which is then "immediately dissociated from the body and is made a substance."[46] It is the immediate experiential flow of the body that is ultimately real, out of which a "subject"—and hence a *self*—is constructed. A view like this coheres well with the Buddhist understanding of the self, which Watsuji studied in greater detail in his other works.

Following such a comparativist spirit, I have endeavored to draw wisdom from many different traditions in this chapter, sometimes giving a modern voice to them. Of course, what we wish to learn from philosophical texts of the past may be different from what the authors intended to say in the original context. Yet, going beyond historical borders is part of the journey of comparative philosophy, bringing to life ideas from remote times and places, and making it an opportunity to broaden and deepen our insight. The theme of this chapter, visual perception, offers rich material for comparative philosophy because of its familiarity and ubiquity. We can always stare at an apple, blink a few times, and try to find out what is going on in visual perception whenever it appears to us as an unsolved yet enchanting mystery.

Acknowledgments

The first version of this chapter was delivered as a keynote lecture at the Uehiro Cross Currents Graduate Student Conference on March 10, 2012, at the University of Hawaii at Manoa. I wish to thank the conference organizers and the Uehiro Foundation on Ethics and Education for providing me with the opportunity to develop this theme.

Notes

1 Henri Bergson, *Matière et mémoire* [*Matter and memory*] (Paris: Presses Universitaires de France, 1993), pp. 52 and 254.
2 Ibid., p. 49.
3 Tetsurō Watsuji, *Watsuji Tetsurō Zenshū* [*Complete Works of Watsuji Tetsurō*], 20 vols (Tokyo: Iwanami Shoten, 1961–63), vol. 8, p. 9.
4 Charles Sanders Peirce, *Writings of Charles S. Peirce*, 7 vols (Bloomington: Indiana University Press, 1982f), vol. 1, p. 498.
5 John Dewey, *Experience and Nature* (New York: Dover Publications, 1958), p. 259.
6 Alfred North Whitehead, *Science and the Modern World* (New York: The Free Press, 1967), p. 72.
7 Alfred North Whitehead, *Process and Reality* (New York: The Free Press, 1978), p. 67.
8 Shōzō Ōmori, *Shin-shikakushinron* [*A Novel New Theory of Vision*] (Tokyo: University of Tokyo Press, 1982), pp. ii–iii.
9 Shōzō Ōmori, "Kokoro [Mind]," in *Shinshinno Mondai* [*The Problem of Mind-Body*] (Tokyo: Sangyōtosho, 1980), p. 238.
10 Ludwig Wittgenstein, *Werkausgabe* [*Collected Works Edition*], 8 vols (Frankfurt am Main: Suhrkamp, 1984), vol. 4, p. 126.
11 Willard V. O. Quine, *The Roots of Reference*, The Paul Carus Lectures (La Salle, IL: Open Court, 1974), p. xi.
12 David Hume, *A Treatise of Human Nature* (Oxford: Oxford University Press, 1978), p. 33.
13 Ibid., p. 34.
14 Kitarō Nishida, *Nishida Kitarō Zenshū* [*Complete Works of Nishida Kitarō*], 24 vols (Tokyo: Iwanami Shoten, 2002–09), vol. 1, p. 46.
15 Ibid., p. 12.
16 Takizawa Katsumi, *Nishida Tetsugakuno Konpon Mondai* [*Fundamental Problems of Nishida's Philosophy*] (Tokyo: Kobushi Shobō, 2004), p. 120.
17 Nishida, *Complete Works*, vol. 1, p. 44.
18 Jean-Paul Sartre, *L'Être et le néant* [*Being and nothingness*] (Paris: Gallimard, 1943), pp. 342–43.
19 Ibid., pp. 344–45.
20 Nishida, *Complete Works*, vol. 12, p. 350.
21 Keiichi Noe, "Rekishino Nakano Shintai—Nishida Tetsugakuto Genshōgaku [The Body in History: Nishida Philosophy and Phenomenology]," in *Nishida Tetsugaku: Botsugo Gojūnen Kinenronbunshū* [*Nishida Philosophy: Essays in Commemoration of the 50th Anniversary of Nishida's Death*] (Tokyo: Sōbunsha, 1994), p. 76.
22 Nishida, *Complete Works*, vol. 8, pp. 392–93.
23 Sartre, *L'Être et le néant*, p. 297.
24 Ibid.
25 Ibid., p. 316.
26 Daniel C. Dennett, *Kinds of Minds: Toward an Understanding of Consciousness* (New York: Basic Books, 1996), p. 123.
27 Zhuangzi, *Zhuangzi jishi* [Collection and interpretation of Zhuangzi], vol. 3 (Beijing: Zhonghua Shuju, 1961), p. 607.
28 Ibid.

29 Dōgen, *Dōgenzenji Zenshū* [*Complete Works of Zen Master Dōgen*], vol. 1 (Tokyo: Shunjūsha, 1988–93), p. 272.
30 Ibid.
31 Tōru Tereda, *Dōgenno Gengo-uchū* [*Dōgen's Language Universe*] (Tokyo: Iwanami Shoten, 1974), p .168.
32 Dōgen, *Dōgenzenji Zenshū*, vol. 2, p. 118.
33 Ibid.
34 Watsuji, *Watsuji Tetsurō Zenshū*, vol. 9, p. 473.
35 Dōgen, *Dōgenzenji Zenshū*, vol. 2, p. 474.
36 Dōgen, *Dōgenzenji Zenshū*, vol. 1, p. 57.
37 Johann Gottlieb Fichte, *Fichtes Werke* [*Fichte's Works*], vol. 1 (Berlin: Walter de Gruyter & Co., 1971), p. 228.
38 Nishida, *Complete Works*, vol. 1, p. 77.
39 Aristotle, *Aristotelis Opera* [*Aristotle's Works*], vol. 4 (Oxonii: E Typographaeo Academico, 1837), p. 43.
40 Augustine, *Sancti Aurelii Augustini De Trinitate, libri XV* [*Saint Aurelius Augustine's* On Trinity, *15 books*], vol. 1 (Turnhout: Brepols Publishers, 1968), p. 339.
41 Charles S. Peirce, *The Charles S. Peirce Papers*, manuscript 318 (Cambridge, MA: Harvard University Library Microreproduction Services, 1963), p. 205.
42 James J. Gibson, *The Senses Considered as Perceptual Systems* (Boston: Houghton Mifflin Company, 1966), p. 59.
43 James J. Gibson, *The Ecological Approach to Visual Perception* (New York: Psychology Press, 1986), pp. 138–39.
44 Ibid., p. 129.
45 Watsuji, *Watsuji Tetsurō Zenshū*, vol. 1: p. 123.
46 Ibid., pp. 70–71.

References

Aristotle (1837), *Aristotelis Opera* [*Aristotle's Works*], 11 vols, Oxonii: E Typographaeo Academico.

Augustine (1968), *Sancti Aurelii Augustini De Trinitate, libri XV* [*Saint Aurelius Augustine's* On Trinity, *15 books*], 2 vols, Turnhout: Brepols Publishers.

Bergson, H. (1993), *Matière et mémoire* [*Matter and memory*], Paris: Presses Universitaires de France.

Dennett, D. C. (1996), *Kinds of Minds: Toward an Understanding of Consciousness*, New York: Basic Books.

Dewey, J. (1958), *Experience and Nature*, New York: Dover Publications.

Dōgen (1988–93), *Dōgenzenji Zenshū* [*Complete Works of Zen Master Dōgen*], 7 vols, Tokyo: Shunjūsha.

Fichte, J. G. (1971), *Fichtes Werke* [*Fichte's Works*], 11 vols, Berlin: Walter de Gruyter & Co.

Gibson, J. J. (1966), *The Senses Considered as Perceptual Systems*, Boston: Houghton Mifflin Company.

Gibson, J. J. (1986), *The Ecological Approach to Visual Perception*, New York: Psychology Press.

Hume, D. (1978), *A Treatise of Human Nature*, Oxford: Oxford University Press.

Nishida, K. (2002–9), *Nishida Kitarō Zenshū* [*Complete Works of Nishida Kitarō*], 24 vols, Tokyo: Iwanami Shoten.
Noe, K. (1994), "Rekishino Nakano Shintai—Nishida Tetsugakuto Genshōgaku—[The Body in History: Nishida Philosophy and Phenomenology]," in *Nishida Tetsugaku: Botsugo Gojūnen Kinenronbunshū* [*Nishida Philosophy: Essays in Commemoration of the 50th Anniversary of Nishida's Death*], Tokyo: Sōbunsha, pp. 75–100.
Ōmori, S. (1980), "Kokoro [Mind]," in *Shinshinno Mondai* [*The Problem of Mind-Body*], Tokyo: Sangyōtosho.
Ōmori, S. (1982), *Shin-shikakushinron* [*A Novel New Theory of Vision*], Tokyo: University of Tokyo Press, pp. 191–240.
Peirce, C. S. (1963), *The Charles S. Peirce Papers*, Cambridge, MA: Harvard University Library Microreproduction Services.
Peirce, C. S. (1982f), *Writings of Charles S. Peirce*, 7 vols, Bloomington: Indiana University Press.
Quine, W. V. O. (1974), *The Roots of Reference*, The Paul Carus Lectures, La Salle, IL: Open Court Publishing Co.
Sartre, J.-P. (1943), *L'Être et le néant* [*Being and nothingness*], Paris: Gallimard.
Takizawa, K. (2004), *Nishida Tetsugakuno Konpon Mondai* [*Fundamental Problems of Nishida's Philosophy*], Tokyo: Kobushi Shobō.
Tereda, T. (1974), *Dōgenno Gengo-uchū* [*Dōgen's Language Universe*], Tokyo: Iwanami Shoten.
Watsuji, T. (1961–3), *Watsuji Tetsurō Zenshū* [*Complete Works of Watsuji Tetsurō*], 20 vols, Tokyo: Iwanami Shoten.
Whitehead, A. N. (1967), *Science and the Modern World*, New York: The Free Press.
Whitehead, A. N. (1978), *Process and Reality*, New York: The Free Press.
Wittgenstein, L. (1984), *Werkausgabe* [*Collected Works Edition*], 8 vols, Frankfurt am Main: Suhrkamp.
Zhuangzi (1961), *Zhuangzi jishi* [*Collection and interpretation* of *Zhuangzi*], 4 vols, Beijing: Zhonghua Shuju.

7

Authority: Of German Rhinos and Chinese Tigers

Ralph Weber

The social and political significance of authority can hardly be overestimated. This statement is true enough, it seems, but we would feel more comfortable in asserting this truth if we knew what "authority" means. Certainly, in philosophy literature, the significance of the issue is indisputable, but there exist many, often conflicting, accounts of how best to understand authority. There is no shortage of general theories and fine distinctions in the literature on authority, which stretches beyond philosophy to several related academic fields: from argumentation theory and social epistemology, to psychology and sociology, and ethics and political theory. If anything, there are too many distinctions to choose from. Which of these one decides to focus on can easily make all the difference. I should hence be as clear as possible as regards the distinctions proposed to be employed in the following discussion of authority.

One useful distinction is between *epistemic* and *deontic* authority. If I am told that in Niger there is a city called Zinder, and on that basis come to share that belief, then I have given epistemic authority to the person who told me about Zinder. If that person tells me, instead, that I would do well to stop smoking my two packs of cigarettes a day, and if on that basis I quit smoking, then I have accorded him or her deontic authority. In both cases, I am still free to ignore what I am told, free not to recognize the person as *an authority*; but if I do recognize the person as an authority, then I will not ignore what I am told. This introduces an important second distinction. For there is also a sort of deontic authority, whose instructions I am by no means free to ignore, or which I may ignore only at the cost of facing a sanction, given that the person addressing me is *in authority*. The distinction hinges on the role of force (understood as legitimate violence), that is, on whether authority is conceived as opposed to force or as relying on it in the last instance. The former conception of authority is sometimes called the *authority of expertise* (comprising the epistemic authority and the weak sort of deontic authority); the latter is known as the *authority of command* (comprising the strong sort of deontic-*qua*-enforceable authority).[1]

Of course, these two conceptions of authority can, and sometimes do, come together. For instance, those invested with the authority of expertise in political matters (with *techne politike*) have often in the past been thought, particularly, to assume the authority of command. When these two conceptions do come together, it is not always clear whether political authority is granted because those in power are thought to know or because those who know are in power.

What about political authority? Today, discussions in political philosophy largely focus on state authority, and political philosophers understand the political (or practical) authority as a problem of how to legitimize justified coercion, as the capacity to impose duties, or as the right to rule. The language used is, more often than not, one of *command* and *obedience*. Consider the following three statements, formulated over the past forty years, emphasizing the difference between political authority and epistemic and weak deontic authority:

> Authority yields (authorities issue) commands to be obeyed or rules to be subscribed to, not statements to be believed.[2] (Richard E. Flathman)
>
> Practical authority is thought to be power not just to inspire belief in a deontic proposition, nor simply to influence conduct by providing a new reason for action; rather, it is thought to be the authority to compel action, even in the face of a plethora of good reasons to act otherwise . . . The prescriptions of this authority constitute the strongest sort possible—that of commands.[3] (Heidi M. Hurd)
>
> Authority stands for a right to rule—a right to issue commands and, possibly, to enforce these commands using coercive power.[4] (Fabienne Peter)

In much of the literature, political authority seems to be understood as somehow akin to legitimate (or merely legal) power, exercising the right to command and to sanction disobedience.[5] In light of the different sorts of authority presented above, this seems potentially reductionist (or, indeed, very specialized). There are, it should be noted, contemporary theorists concerned with factoring the authority of expertise back into the authority of command. David Estlund's epistemic proceduralism constitutes one such attempt: it avoids rule by experts or by the most learned, arguing instead for a tendency on the part of democracy to make good decisions, thus putting the people in the position of experts.[6] The present chapter seeks to make a contribution to such endeavors, albeit in its own way, and to our understanding of authority more generally.

In what follows, I first approach the subject matter of authority from three different, explicitly nonnormative angles, each represented by a different author, inquiring into the logic of authority (Bocheński), its phenomenology (Kojève), and its conceptual history (Eschenburg).[7] Throughout, I present understandings of authority that go beyond the understanding dominant in political philosophy to the point of being fundamentally at odds with it. My intention is to add complexity to the distinctions outlined above and to put us in a position to look at political authority afresh and from a critical distance. I then tell two anecdotes, involving the titular German rhinos and Chinese tigers, respectively. The first anecdote is an early encounter between Wittgenstein and Russell, which I read in the context of Fricker's recent discussion on epistemic injustice in order to reflect on epistemic authority in ethical and political terms and to problematize further the understandings thus far presented. The second anecdote is reported in the early Chinese classic *Han Feizi* and helps bring into focus a sort of authority that turns on number (in both quantitative and qualitative terms) and which plays—I argue—a fundamental role in understanding what is at stake when theorizing democracy and the shape and function of forms of authority institutionalized in democracy.

What is authority?

The logic of authority—Joseph Maria Bocheński, Was ist Autorität? (1974)

In logical terms, authority is first and foremost a relation (Bocheński, Satz 1.1). Authority could also be conceived as a personal property, and it is true that we often speak of so-and-so being an authority or having authority *tout court*. Bocheński offers the following sentence to disentangle the two ways of conceiving authority: "Adam, the teacher, is an authority for his pupils because he has authority."[8] Obviously, this is a meaningful statement and wholly unlike the tautological "it rains because it rains." That he *has* personal authority is the reason why he *is* an authority *for* his pupils. Yet, authority as a relation can easily be effective without any involvement of personal authority. Bocheński gives the example of an air-traffic controller whose directions the pilot takes to be authoritative without knowing anything about whether or not the controller *has* any personal authority. Authority understood as a relation, therefore, seems to be more fundamental, or at least more encompassing, than authority understood as a personal property (It goes without saying that the controller also *has* authority to the extent that the pilot follows the directions, but that authority is entirely independent of whether it is X or Y sitting in front of the controller's microphone.).

More precisely, authority is a three-dimensional relation, composed of a bearer of authority (B) who is an authority for a subject (S) with regard to a specific domain (D). In most cases, it seems inconceivable that a bearer of authority could be an authority with regard to all possible domains. In Bocheński's view, it is humanly impossible (Satz 3.7). Every three-dimensional relation consists of three two-dimensional relations, which gives us the following picture (adopted from Bocheński) for authority understood as a relation:

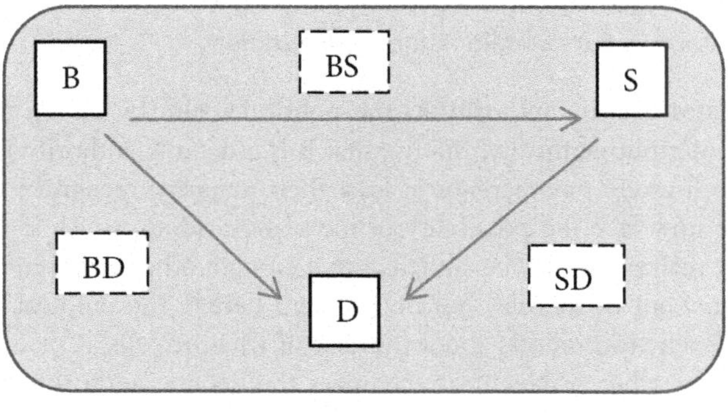

In his logical analysis, Bocheński further characterizes authority as being irreflexive, asymmetrical, and transitive (Sätze 3.1–3.4). Authority is irreflexive because I cannot be, in any domain, an authority for myself; asymmetrical, because if X is an authority for Y in a certain domain, then Y cannot be an authority for X in the same domain; and transitive, because if X is an authority for Y in a certain domain and Y an authority for Z in the same domain, then X must also be an authority for Z in that domain. Referring to the pain that someone experiences, Bocheński also maintains that each person *is* an authority in one domain *for* all other persons (Satz 3.6).

Bocheński distinguishes two basic realms of domains of authority: propositions and instructions or orders, corresponding to epistemic and deontic authority. Each authority is either one or the other, and it is impossible to conceive a third. But one and the same bearer of authority may, of course, exert both epistemic and deontic authority with regard to a certain domain; Bocheński remarks that this would be desirable (Satz 4.4). Epistemic authority, in the last instance, is defined in the following way (Satz 5.2): "B is an epistemic authority for S in domain D if and only if the probability of each proposition within D—with reference to the state of knowledge of S—increases by the disclosure of that proposition from B to S." The recognition of such authority requires that the subject also recognize the greater competence and truthfulness of the bearer of authority. There is a variety of ways how recognition can come about. Bocheński distinguishes between unreasoned and reasoned recognition, the reasons being based either on direct insight or on inferences from experiences about the specific person as the bearer of authority or the specific class (*Klasse*) to which the bearer of authority belongs, for example, the class of physicians, air-traffic controllers, or the clergy. Most recognition, Bocheński emphasizes, is based on reasons, as it ought to be, which for him means that reason (*Vernunft*) and authority are not to be perceived as oppositional.[9]

Deontic authority differs in a variety of regards, the prime difference being the one already mentioned, that is, its specific kind of domain: instructions or orders. Deontic authority is, furthermore, always tied to a practical goal, such as the goal of surviving that leads me to hand over my money to a robber when staring down the barrel of his gun and to follow his instruction (Bocheński's example). Deontic authority is defined in the following way (Satz 7.1):

> B is a deontic authority for S in domain D if and only if there is an event E of such kind that (1) S wishes E to be realized and that (2) S believes that the execution by S of all the instructions, which are received from B with assertion and belong to domain D, is a necessary condition for this realization.

Bocheński relates deontic authority to the political realm by taking up the "more complex case of group-authority," stating that B is a deontic authority for a group G if and only if all group members, or at least their majority, recognize the authority. Obviously, we now face the possibility of moral free-riding, since, for the event in question to be realized, it may be sufficient that enough other group members follow the instructions, but Bocheński sees no problem here.[10] The political realm is also topical when Bocheński reflects about the case of what he calls a "real accumulation of authorities," as when a daughter recognizes the deontic authority of the mother because she believes that this is, indeed, best for her and that this is how it is, since she has an epistemic kind of trust in her mother. It is in this context that Bocheński writes the following remarkable sentence:

> But the application of such nexuses to large, say, political societies should be regarded as dangerous. It seems prudential in that case to give reasons based on inferences for the belief in the necessity of deontic authority that are independent of the epistemic authority of the bearer.[11]

Epistemic authority is not to be the (sole?) reason for granting deontic authority. In Bocheński's analysis of authority, deontic authority is *always* tied to a practical goal.

Wrapping up his logical analysis, Bocheński affirms the point that all deontic authority necessarily takes away some freedom from the subject, inasmuch as that subject no longer decides for himself or herself, but leaves the decision to the bearer of authority. Political liberty, for Bocheński, means the absence of deontic authority, whereby deontic authority in one domain is at the same time claimed to be the condition of liberty in another. In all of this, not once does Bocheński use the notion of political authority.

* * *

Bocheński's analysis of the logic of authority might, of course, be criticized in various ways, and I will offer some criticism (in the context of the Wittgenstein-Russell anecdote). There is only one issue that must presently be raised, not least in view of the phenomenological analysis of authority to follow, since Bocheński seems to gloss over a logically interesting form of the use of authority that is four-dimensional and ubiquitous, that is, arguments from authority. Particularly with regard to the epistemic and the weak forms of deontic authority, this is the more frequent and, logically, the more complicated form of authority, different from a mere delegation of authority (of which Bocheński offers a detailed analysis: see ch. 8). An argument from authority in Bocheński's denotation can be depicted as follows:

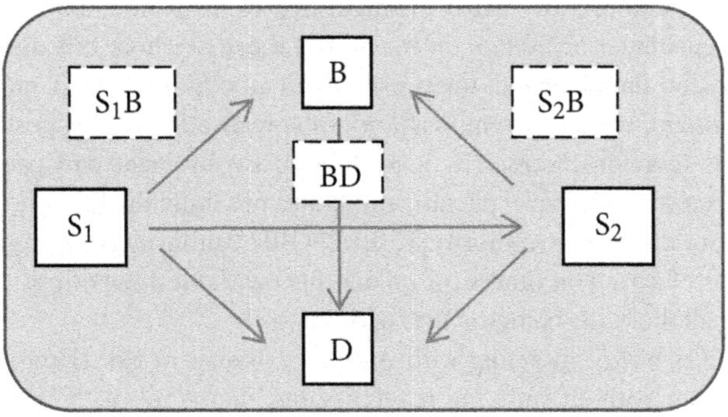

The main difference is that the subject (S_2) is now no longer addressed by the bearer of authority (B), but by a third party (S_1) appealing to the authority invested in the bearer.

This perspective on authority, I argue, opens up a series of interesting questions not covered by Bocheński, but crucial to any claim of grasping the phenomenon of authority. For instance, to what extent, if at all, does S_2 have to recognize S_1 as an authority in the relevant domain for the argument to be successful? Or is recognition rather about the domain of knowing which bearer of authority to appeal to? This would invalidate Sextus Empiricus' skeptical objection about how a nonexpert would have to be an expert to recognize an expert.[12] Another question arises: Does S_1 have to recognize B as an authority, too, or is it sufficient if S_2 recognizes B as an authority? It might seem that the recognition by S_1 is a condition for the argument to be non-fallacious, but that is not quite clear. If I am to persuade a believing Catholic, then not only does it seem effective to appeal to the authority of Pope Francis, even if I myself am not a believing Catholic, but it also seems that it would not render my argument fallacious, say, if I myself subscribed to the proposition in question regardless of what the Pope says, as it seems I should subscribe to it if I honestly want to persuade my interlocutor of *it*.

The phenomenology of authority—Alexandre Kojève, La notion de l'autorité (1942)

A phenomenological analysis has to begin with a general definition of authority to capture all phenomena relevant for the analysis. Kojève's definition is rather extensive and runs as follows:

> There is Authority only where there is movement, change and action (real or at least possible): one has authority only over that which can "react," that is, change depending on the thing or person that represents Authority (incarnates it, realizes it, exercises it). And obviously Authority belongs to the person who makes the change and not to the one who undergoes the change: Authority is essentially *active* and not passive. . . . The authoritative act is always a real act (conscious and free). The authoritative act is distinguished from all others by the fact that it does not encounter *opposition* on the part of those to whom it is directed. This presupposes, on the one hand, the possibility of an opposition and, on the other, the *conscious* and *voluntary* renunciation of the realization of this possibility. . . . Authority is therefore necessarily a relation (between agent and patient): it is therefore an essentially *social* phenomenon (and not individual); there have to be at least *two* for there to be Authority. THEREFORE: Authority is the *possibility* that an agent has of acting on others (or on another) without these others reacting to him or her, all the while being *capable* of doing so.
>
> *Or, in other words*: in acting with Authority, the agent can change the given human exterior without suffering repercussions, that is to say, without him- or herself changing as a result of the action.
>
> *Or, finally*: Authority is the possibility of acting without making a compromise (in the broad sense of the term).[13]

There are some important insights that Kojève draws from this definition of authority. Unlike law, the reaction (the opposition) never leaves the field of pure *possibility* (it is never *actualized*); its *realization* destroys authority. Law may be left untouched by any such reaction. It follows that authority in principle excludes force and *vice versa*, whereas law implies and presupposes it (but never coincides with it). In a general manner, one does not need to *do anything* to exert authority. Moreover, an authoritative act is legal or legitimate by definition, but Kojève is making it wonderfully clear that what is more important is authority, not legality, which he calls the "corpse" or the "mummy" of authority, "a body that endures while being deprived of the soul or life."[14]

If law is different, then "divine 'authority'" (Kojève puts the term in quotation marks for it escapes his definition, but he later includes it . . .) is also different, in an even more radical sense: for, any reaction against the Divine most likely not only leaves the Divine intact, it may even be "absolutely impossible" for humans, whereas it is necessarily possible, although not realized, in the case of (hence slightly pleonastic) human authority. Authority is perishable. In each instance, the possible reaction may be realized and authority destroyed.[15] The exercise of authority, therefore, always implies an element of risk in the sheer act of being exercised and hence possibly being opposed. Consequently, all authority must have some "cause," some "reason," or some "justification," which serves as an explanation for the voluntary renunciation of reacting when facing an act of authority. This is the starting point for Kojève's distinction among four different, pure types of authority, each of which is irreducible to the others, and at least two of them are involved in a mixed form of authority.[16]

	Type of authority	Theory of authority
1.	**The authority of the father (or parents) over the child** Variants: - The authority arising from a large difference in age; the authority of the old over the young - The authority of tradition and those who hold it - The authority of a dead person, the testament - The authority of the "author" over his work	**Scholastics, theological theory** The theological theory of authority would, to some extent, cover all pure types (God being infallible, omniscient, and all-powerful), but it is the only one to make sense of the authority of the father, namely God the father as the creator, the cause, etc. A reaction against this authority is impossible, like a reaction of the effect against its cause.
2.	**The authority of the master over the slave** Variants: - The authority of nobility over villagers - The authority of the military over civilians - The authority of man over woman - The authority of the victorious over the defeated	**Hegel** Life and death struggle for recognition in which the slave cannot master his fear of death, cedes the fight, admitting defeat and recognizing the absolute authority of the master.

(*Continued*)

Type of authority	Theory of authority
3. The authority of the leader over the band Variants: - The authority of the superior (director, officer, etc.) over the inferior (employee, soldier, etc.) - The authority of the teacher over the pupil - The authority of the learned, the technician, etc. - The authority of the soothsayer, prophet, etc.	**Aristotle** The leader has the right to exercise authority over the band members because he or she can foresee, forecast, plan, and project, whereas the members are driven by immediate needs. Acknowledging their inferiority, they let themselves be guided and directed.
4. The authority of the judge Variants: - The authority of the arbiter - The authority of the controller, critic - The authority of the confessor [mixed!] - The authority of the just person, the upright, etc.	**Plato** All authority is—or at least should be—based on justice or fairness. All other forms of authority are illegitimate, that is, unstable, temporary, short-lived, ephemeral, accidental.

(The table summarizes: Kojève 2004, pp. 66–81).

Kojève is aware that the *phenomenon* of authority is always complex—a combination of these pure types.[17] Throughout his analysis, he clearly distinguishes authority from the use of force, and thus rejects what might be seen as a fifth theory of authority, in which authority is "reduced" to force. Such a reduction would amount to denying, or ignoring, the existence of authority.[18] It would be an "erroneous" theory of authority.

But what about authority engendered by elections or justified by reference to some kind of social contract? Are these not forms of authority *sui generis*, distinct from Kojève's four types? Kojève does not think they are. While explaining why he does not think so, Kojève takes the reader through a remarkable sequence of thoughts. His first take on authority derived from being elected is based on something like the Schumpeterian conception of democracy, also formulated in 1942, which, rather than focusing on some public good or other, conceives democracy as a competition among candidates vying for the votes of the electorate, which thus comes to elect not a representative but a political program, what Kojève would call a "project." Hence elections do not *engender* any authority; they only confirm an already existing authority. In Kojève's words, "[the leader] does not have authority because of having been elected, but the leader has been elected because he or she benefits from the authority that arose from the project."[19] In this sense, the election is only an "exterior form of recognition," a "manifestation" of the prior recognition of authority.

By the same token, Kojève finds fault with the (of course, pre-Rawlsian) theory of social contract, which, too, is falsely thought to be about the engendering of authority, but is, in fact, only a confirmation of an already existing authority. The theory presupposes that authority passes from the electorate to those elected. But what authority could that possibly be? Clearly, and by definition, it cannot be the authority that each member of the electorate has over himself or herself, for it makes no sense to react against one's own acts of authority. Moreover, my individual act of electing somebody does not give the elected any authority over me unless there is an authority that I recognize but that is *independent* of my individual election. That is why an election is a collective act. From this point of view, an election only confirms the authority that some majority already has over the minority (or vice versa) and that is already recognized.

If the authority in question is, indeed, an authority *sui generis*, independent of the four types, then that authority, Kojève reasons, must hinge on its *quantitative* aspect, on its relying on parts, parties, or collectives, of which only three constellations are conceivable: the authority-exercising party may be the majority, the minority, or be equal to the other part. If it is equal, then its authority cannot spring from its quantitative aspect, but must be based on one of the four types. If the party is the majority or the minority, then its authority can in principle spring from that fact only. On Kojève's reading, in social contract theory (exempting Rousseau), the majority as such is, generally speaking, granted *sui generis* authority by way of election. Indeed, we often submit to an act of the majority simply because it is the majority. Kojève lists the variants of the authority of public opinion and of hearsay or gossip and points to the desire of not falling out of line and doing as everybody else does. Kojève's emphasis on the authority of the majority stands in a precarious relationship to the opposite case, namely to the authority of the exceptional over the banal, the commonplace, the masses, the populace, the *average* person, etc.

Still, for Kojève, by definition, there really is no such thing as the authority of the majority. The majority cannot exercise authority over itself, and the very existence of a minority proves, if anything, the minority's nonrecognition of an authority. Forming a minority means opposing a majority, reacting in one way or another against it. Lacking authority, the majority can suppress these reactions only by force. A regime relying purely and solely on the quantitative aspect of majority rule, in fact, relies on force alone. Aware of the majority's superior force, the minority often abstains from reacting, and no use of force is required. This conscious renunciation of reaction produces "the illusion" of *sui generis* authority.[20] But the renunciation can hardly be called voluntary. Like the Hobbesian gun pointed at one's head, it is force (or its threat), rather than authority, that is the cause of the renunciation. Kojève puts it picturesquely: "If a box champion tells me to leave the restaurant, I do so without reacting at all, but surely not because he has authority in my eyes."[21]

Returning to Rousseau, Kojève briefly considers the idea of a social contract based on a *volonté générale*, which in his scheme translates into an authority not of parts but of the whole, presupposing some kind of organic view of society but eventually resting on a mixed type of authority, of the father and of the judge. Of the father, because the identity of the organic whole persists by way of claiming a tradition. Of the judge, because the identity is not to be thought of as a unity, but as an "internally complex structure," a whole composed of parts, which are in harmony. "In the human (social or political) world," Kojève adds, "this harmony cannot but be Justice."[22] The authority of the *volonté générale* turns out to be the authority of the father reinforced by the authority of the judge. The point is that, if the authority of the whole cannot be claimed, but only the authority of the majority, then the element of justice drops out of the equation, and the remaining authority is that of the father claiming to represent the authority of the whole, but being a part, not the whole. Kojève concludes that, "to the extent that the majority has authority (drawn even from its number), it intervenes as guardian of the tradition, etc. Its authority is the one of a Senate, of a Confessor [a priest who has been granted the authority to hear confessions, the spiritual father], etc. And this is also the authority of gossip."[23]

A conceptual history of authority—Theodor Eschenburg's Über Autorität (1965)

The English word *authority*, like its equivalents in most European languages, derives from the Latin *auctoritas*, and it is on the early conceptual history and the Latin term that I want to focus, and in particular on the period from the early Roman Republic to the late Principate.[24] This will suffice to highlight a turn of events that we see repeated in later periods over and again in different settings, for instance, in the one from the early Christians to the institutionalized Papal Church.

Eschenburg begins with some etymological notes on the word *auctoritas*. The term derives from *auctor*, which in turn comes from the verb *augere*, meaning to augment, to accumulate, to accrete, and to advance. The early meaning of *auctor* is author, originator, furtherer, augmentor. According to the fifth century BCE *Law of the Twelve Tables*, *auctor* was a vendor who warranted that the good to be sold was indeed his rightful property; the vendor had *auctoritas rerum*, authority over the thing. In Roman law, the guardian's approval of a ward's legal transaction was called the *auctoritas tutoris*, and was understood as the augmentation of a will lacking its full capacity. Beyond such a legal context, to be an *auctor* to somebody else (*alicui auctorem esse*) generally meant having the authority to give advice:

> *Auctoritas* was "more than just an 'advice,'" it was rather a definitive [authoritative] advice or opinion, which the *auctor* was legitimated [authorized] to give due to his or her special insight and to which the other, merely by asking, subordinated from the outset. *Auctoritas* brought about voluntary subordination under somebody else's helping [auxiliary] advice trusting the compelling superiority of that person. One empowered [authorized] another to give an advice. In this act of empowerment [authorization] is the freedom of decision.[25] A command may at the same time be helping advice, but in each case its execution can be enforced. The advice that has *auctoritas* is no command, but it works as if it were a command. It is the nature of *auctoritas* that its advice is helping and hence unselfish. He or she who seeks the advice assesses it less on its contents than on the personality of the advisor; it is sought because of confidence in the advisor.[26]

It is precisely this role of a "helping but eventually quasi-commanding advice" that was already assumed by the early *patres* of the Roman kings (before 510 BCE), forming the king's council and giving the *auctoritas patrum* confirming the decisions of the legislative and elective committees, and that in the Roman Republic translated into the role of the Senate, the *consilium publicum*, advising the magistrates, that is, the consuls and praetors. The Senate was composed of members of patrician families as well as former magistrates, the latter symbolizing governmental experience and forming the center of the Senate. Hence *auctoritas* was the Senate's right of compulsory advice, but it was also the name for the Senate's confirmation of the decisions by the Roman citizenry. In both instances, the idea behind *auctoritas* is the augmentation that the advice or confirmation provides, in both quantitative and qualitative terms. Eschenburg quotes Theodor Mommsen, who draws an analogy between the guardian's augmentation of the ward's will and the Senate's augmentation of the citizens' will, the citizens like the ward being exposed to error and mistake. Mommsen comes to qualify *auctoritas* as "more than an advice and less than a command," as "an advice that cannot be conventionally ignored and that is like the one given by the expert to the layperson or by the leader in parliament to the followers."[27]

In the times of the early Roman Republic, the Senate's *auctoritas* was clearly distinguished from the magistrates' *potestas* and the people's *libertas* (cf. Cicero, *De republica*). *Potestas* referred to the legal power to use force (whereas *potentia* stood for the use of force without legal sanction). The housefather had *patria potestas*, entitling him to all punishment including capital punishment within his family. The Senate had no *potestas*. The consuls were not legally obligated to seek the Senate's advice, and the decisions by the citizenry would have been legally valid without the Senate's confirmation. *Auctoritas* was part of a governmental system that relied, in Eschenburg's felicitous formulation, on the rather ingenious combination of the freedom to decide (*Entscheidungsfreiheit*) and the obligation to consult (*Beratungszwang*). Consultation implies that one's subjective opinion is confronted with other opinions, that one must make oneself aware of what precisely one is seeking advice for and what precisely one's opinion is, and that one gives reasons for it, justifying oneself, becoming responsible. The combination of the freedom to decide and the obligation to consult institutionally therefore lies somewhere between an individual decision, which eludes consultation, and a decision by a majority, which does not elude but on the contrary assumes the responsibility for that which is decided and which might easily bring about non-pertinent decisions.

The use of *auctoritas* as "helpful but ultimately quasi-commanding advice" was not confined to the public, institutional sphere. The institutional *auctoritas* of the Senate continued to rely on the personal *auctoritas* of its members. Likewise, all exemplary persons, but particularly the elders and the ancestors, knowledgeable persons, and persons of distinguished descent were regarded as having *auctoritas*, as being *auctoritas*. Cicero spoke of the *auctoritas* of some great Romans as being exercised with a mere wink. With regard to the Senate, there was a tension that became increasingly exacerbated as the life members of the Senate came to dominate the magistrates, who served one-year terms, leading to institutional authority without personal authority (which also means that the presupposed unselfishness yielded to active defense of interests) and bringing *auctoritas* closer and closer to *potestas*.

Historically, the tension eventually led to a great crisis in the Roman republic, with the Gracchi brothers' attempts at reform, and to the disappearance of the institutional embodiment of the early meaning of *auctoritas*. When Emperor Augustus (69 BCE–14 CE) described himself in his funerary inscription as having had the same *potestas* as his colleagues, the magistrates, but only more *auctoritas*, this was certainly true at the level of personal authority based on his outstanding ability as a leader; institutionally, however, he used the term and its still positive connotations as what Eschenburg calls a "Republican disguise of his factually monarchical position."[28] As a monarch, Augustus could have easily afforded to ignore the Senate altogether, but he still consulted it, with the minor difference that he first "advised" the Senate as to what advice to give to him, which meant that the *auctoritas* of the Senate was, in effect, reduced to the *auctoritas* of Augustus. It also meant that, institutionally, *auctoritas* had become reduced to *potestas*. The successors of Emperor Augustus were unable to match his personal authority, but tried to make up for it by bearing the title of Augustus and by the simple use of force. It is hence fitting that they now adopted the title of *dominus* and later demanded the veneration due to a *deus*: the *auctoritas* that went with the self-understanding of *dominus et deus* is well captured in the expressions *auctoritas imperialis* and *auctoritas maiestatis*, meaning the unconstrained *potestas* of the emperor (his *imperium*) as famously enshrined in Roman law by Ulpian's *lex regia*, which stated that what pleases the *princeps* has the force of law (*quod principi placuit, legis habet vigorem*). In short, if the early meaning of *auctoritas* was "helpful, but ultimately quasi-commanding advice," then its helpful and unselfish impetus had been lost, and the "quasi-" altogether dropped.

* * *

None of the three approaches would warrant the use of the term *authority* as it has come to dominate the discussions in contemporary political philosophy. It appears as if the seemingly slight, but in fact decisive, difference in the extent to which authority should be binding authority (i.e., quasi-commanding vs. commanding) has been lost. The epistemic authority and the weak sort of deontic authority have thus become largely irrelevant for discussions of political authority. Inasmuch as they are discussed, they are made weaker than they are in the accounts presented above, in which authority is understood as an *a priori* reasoned recognition of greater competence or as useful for the realization of a practical goal (Bocheński); a conscious and voluntary renunciation of any opposition (Kojève); or a quasi-commanding advice (Eschenburg). Heidy Hurd, for instance, defines epistemic authority along the lines of a weak form of deontic authority, as a mere advice, that is not really authoritative at all, but only a stand-in "for antecedently existing reasons for action"; an epistemic authority only "affects the balance of reasons for or against an action."[29] The entry in the Stanford Encyclopedia of Philosophy presents the matter in a similar manner, discussing epistemic authority under the rubric of "theoretical authority" whose advice, it is affirmed, one is "free to take or not."[30]

Epistemic authority and injustice

What the British philosopher did not see, and the German engineer did not know

Trusting Bertrand Russell's account (to wit, his epistemic authority), Ludwig Wittgenstein was in Russell's rooms at Trinity College arguing with him and *refusing* to "admit that it was certain that there was not a rhinoceros in the room" (November 1, 1911). In the obituary, written forty years later, Russell would talk of a hippopotamus instead of a rhinoceros and would add the amusing claim that he had even checked under the desk.[31] The title of this section refers to this famous and, certainly at first glance, most entertaining episode, wonderfully captured in Derek Jarman's 1993 movie *Wittgenstein*, but one usually not attributed much philosophical significance, although it is very clear that, at the time, Wittgenstein did not mean to be entertaining at all (all personal accounts tell us that generally he was not much into entertainment), but was trying to advance a philosophical point. In fact, at the time, what was at stake for Wittgenstein was nothing less than finding out "from the horse's mouth—as it were—whether he had any genuine talent for philosophy."[32] In Jarman's movie, Russell gives up—rather anachronistically, as I will argue—by saying: "I thought the next big step in philosophy would be yours. Now I am not so sure."

I have related this episode not because I am out to explain Wittgenstein's philosophical point about the uncertainty of there being a rhino in the room. The explanations that have been given vary from seeing in this anecdote an early version of what would become the first proposition of the *Tractatus*[33]—more specifically the claim that only asserted propositions exist—and a correction of Moore's position in *The Nature of Judgement* (1899) that the world is formed of concepts.[34] The episode was also thought to be about a completely different understanding of the very meaning of "asserted proposition," which would amount to the point that Russell's proposition, that there is no rhinoceros in the room, "only appears to assert something, but in fact does not."[35] Be that as it may, the episode is also interesting in light of the fact that later on Russell would indeed come to see Wittgenstein as having made "the next big step in philosophy"; but at the time, he was very far from considering Wittgenstein as a philosopher, let alone an important one. The reason I have related this episode, then, lies rather in Russell's utter unwillingness to grant Wittgenstein any epistemic authority.

As the above mentioned interpretations of the episode demonstrate, Wittgenstein could have been making an important philosophical point, but one that Russell, at least in part for reasons that the language he uses to describe the episode will reveal, was perhaps unable to see. Here are some of the relevant passages from Russell's account:

> An unknown German appeared, speaking very little English but refusing to speak German. He turned out to be a man who had learned engineering at Charlottenburg. (October 18, 1911)
>
> My German friend threatens to be an infliction . . . obstinate and perverse, but I think not stupid. (October 19, 1911)
>
> My German engineer very argumentative & tiresome. He wouldn't admit that it was certain that there was not a rhinoceros in the room. (November 1, 1911)
>
> My German engineer, I think, is a fool. He thinks nothing empirical is knowable—I asked him to admit that there was not a rhinoceros in the room, but he wouldn't. (November 2, 1911)

> [Wittgenstein] was refusing to admit the existence of anything except asserted propositions. (November 7, 1911)
>
> My German ex-engineer, as usual, maintained his thesis that there is nothing in the world except asserted propositions, but at last I told him it was too large a theme. (November 13, 1911)
>
> My ferocious German came and argued at me after my lecture. He is armour-plated against all assaults of reasoning. It is really rather a waste of time talking with him. (November 16, 1911)[36]

Many commentators agree that, at the time of the rhino episode, having been acquainted with Wittgenstein for merely two or three weeks and still to find out that he was Austrian rather than German, Russell "had . . . no great conviction of Wittgenstein's philosophical ability."[37]

The question I want to raise is the following: Was Russell's ridicule of Wittgenstein more than just a failure of attributing epistemic authority where it might have been due, or was it an epistemic injustice because of prejudice, prejudice stemming from the impression that Wittgenstein spoke very poor English and from his being not a philosopher but an engineer? I am interested in Russell's not taking Wittgenstein seriously as an epistemic authority inasmuch as the episode potentially poses a challenge to a recent argument about epistemic injustice offered by Miranda Fricker and as it will help us get a better grasp of what authority might be and what it is not.

Miranda Fricker on epistemic injustice

In her 2007 book on *Epistemic Injustice: Power & the Ethics of Knowing*, Miranda Fricker seeks to address a blind spot in Anglo-American epistemology, that is, "the lack of any theoretical framework conducive to revealing the ethical and political aspects of our epistemic conduct," in other words, of the "interdependencies of power, reason, and epistemic authority."[38] On the one side, Fricker is aware that there is "a need for hearers to use social stereotypes as heuristics in their spontaneous assessments of their interlocutor's credibility."[39] On the other side, "if the stereotype embodies a prejudice that works against the speaker, then two points follow: there is an epistemic dysfunction in the exchange—the hearer makes an unduly deflated judgment of the speaker's credibility, perhaps missing out on knowledge as a result; and the hearer does something ethically bad—the speaker is wrongfully undermined in her capacity as a knower."[40] Now, on which side does Russell fall? It seems obvious enough that, in the episode, some prejudice, stemming from Wittgenstein being a foreigner (Fricker mentions "ignorant outsiders" as a basic identity-prejudicial stereotype[41]), a non-English speaker, and an engineer rather than a philosopher, does play a role in Russell's assessment of Wittgenstein's capacity as a knower.

In Fricker's account, however, not just any prejudice constitutes an epistemic or testimonial injustice, and throughout her book she gives a series of distinctions to determine which ones do and what kinds of injustices there are.[42] For instance, she distinguishes between incidental and systematic testimonial injustices, both injustices, to be sure, but the latter more at the center of Fricker's "guiding interest in how epistemic injustice fits into the broader pattern of social justice."[43] She gives the example of the incidental prejudice "against a certain research method," which motivates peer reviewers of a journal to reject a submitted article. This is, in her view, incidental because the author is thus not made "vulnerable to any other kinds of injustice (legal, economic, political)."[44] Obviously, we do not need to imagine the example as taking place under a communist regime and pertaining to a "bourgeois" method, which would instantly turn it into an example of a systematic testimonial injustice. Such injustices are produced

> specifically by those prejudices that track the subject through different dimensions of social activity—economic, educational, professional, sexual, legal, political, religious, and so on. Being subject to a tracker prejudice renders one susceptible not only to testimonial injustice but to a gamut of different injustices, and so when such a prejudice generates a testimonial injustice, that injustice is systematically connected with other kinds of actual or potential injustice.[45]

Fricker adds to this the concept of social identity prejudice, but it is unclear whether it restricts in any way the realm of possible prejudice (is a nonsocial identity prejudice at all conceivable?) and whether it would be playing a lesser part in an incidental, non-tracker prejudice (using a certain research method certainly may be part of one's social identity).

One distinction that Fricker introduces only toward the end of her book deals with the wrong committed by testimonial injustice insofar as it "deprives the subject of a certain fundamental sort of respect" by turning it into an object, into a "source of information."[46] Leaning on the critical concept of sexual objectification and on the work of Martha Nussbaum, Fricker comes to highlight that not every "epistemic objectification" is ethically bad but that this can be decided on contextual grounds only, "the morally crucial [and Kantian] distinction" being the distinction between treating somebody as an object, while not denying that he or she is also a subject, and treating somebody as a mere object.[47] Again, and granting that Fricker introduces the distinction with a view specifically to Edward Craig's concept of the "good informant,"[48] I am not quite sure to what extent the distinction helps demarcate a testimonial injustice, for it seems that such injustice would not amount to treating somebody as a mere source of information, but rather not treating him or her as a source of information at all. Fricker herself seems to admit that the problem lies in there being something "about the context" that leads you to treat somebody as a "source of information," something that makes you deny "their epistemic subjectivity more generally,"[49] and which highlights prejudice rather than instrumentality. Be that as it may, with regard to my German rhinos, it seems difficult to argue that Russell treated Wittgenstein as "a mere object," a "source of information," for from the first encounter he does show interest in Wittgenstein, of whom he hopes "to see a lot"[50] and with regard to whose personal doubts whether to engage in philosophy Russell seriously strives to give some helpful advice.

A second and, I believe, more interesting, distinction that Fricker draws is between culpable and non-culpable testimonial injustice. In Fricker's view, a testimonial injustice is non-culpable if the perpetrator of the injustice has no access to the critical concepts and the critical consciousness that would be required to identify the injustice as an injustice. The example that she discusses concerns the novel *The Talented Mr. Ripley* and a testimonial injustice based on a gender prejudice on the part of a certain Herbert Greenleaf, to whom, on her analysis, "the critical concepts he needed were not historically available,"[51] and whom for that reason she considers to be in a sense epistemically and morally unlucky. By contrast, a testimonial injustice would be culpable if such critical concepts were available. With regard to my German rhinos, the question hence would seem to be whether, and to what extent, Russell had access to critical concepts that would have allowed him to be more virtuous in his epistemic conduct and more sensitive toward the prejudices at work in his encounter with Wittgenstein. Surely, if the concepts had been available at the time, Russell would have been in the privileged position to know about them, since he lived in a social environment characterized by very high "coverage-reliability," as contemporary epistemologists would perhaps put it.[52]

Fricker admits that the distinction is "surely fuzzy, and especially so across historical distance"[53] and goes on to engage in a reflection that is, I think, undermined by the Russell-Wittgenstein encounter and that also shows why it might be problematic to insert the concern of social justice into epistemic practices in the way that Fricker does. She begins by reconsidering the "moral conceptual resources that he [Mr. Greenleaf] *did* have available" (p. 103) and in view of these comes to find it "disappointing that he colludes with the gender ideology of the day quite so readily" (p. 104). This, however, does not lead to his being culpable, but to a "resentment of disappointment [on our side]—an attitude which is closely related to the resentment of blame, but falls short of it."[54] Distinguishing further between "routine discursive moves in a moral discourse and exceptional, more imaginative moves in which existing resources are used in an innovative way that stands as a progressive move in moral consciousness,"[55] Fricker concludes that "even Greenleaf *could* have judged exceptionally,"[56] which, in my view, amounts to saying that, to some extent at least, he did have access to the critical concepts required for more virtuous conduct.

In the background, there lurks a much larger issue, situated at a level at which Fricker seldom operates in her book, except when she briefly explores the idea of a "vegetarian future society"[57] that would in retrospect blame her for her habit of eating meat. The issue is not only who sets the terms of discourse, but also who is to decide, and how, what constitutes a case of epistemic injustice based on a negative stereotype; what to do with lingering negative identity prejudices that determine what is and what is not a prejudice; when somebody can be said to have tried just hard enough to judge exceptionally; and when we would have to admit that the critical concepts are now available (certainly some would claim today that they are available with regard to vegetarianism). Fricker's answer probably would be that this is all contextual. But, in my assessment, and I would add, regardless of the context, at some points in the book she clearly fails to live up to her own plea for a "distinctly *reflexive* critical social awareness,"[58] as certainly all of us do. In one passage, she (jokingly?) refers to "the honest second-hand car salesman" as "an exception to a reliable stereotype."[59] In another passage, and now entirely in earnest, she writes about her second guiding example, *To Kill a Mockingbird,* "that things would have gone differently at Tom Robinson's trial if the members of the jury had been black goes without saying."[60] If anything, in my view, this statement seems to be a straightforward prejudice about how a black jury would decide, without taking into account at least some counter-evidence of how, under certain circumstances, subjects may (they would not necessarily, but they might) enact the very prejudice held against them even more ferociously than their oppressors would, or they may come to hold that prejudice themselves.

The problem is also that Fricker's account would seem to reserve culpability for injustices that are pretty well established. Nobody, she says, can be blamed for a routine discursive move. What if those that she views as the more virtuous, exceptional discursive moves show no effect because they go against "the bounds of contemporary routine moral judgement,"[61] that is, against the ideology of the day? If I follow the majority, does that exculpate me? Fricker's account seems particularly tailored toward "achieving an appropriate moral response across historical and cultural distance," but it seems to me that it cannot function as a catalyzer of moral progress.

Epistemic authority and the ethics of dialogue and debate

Yet, does Fricker's discussion of epistemic (in-)justice really involve epistemic authority? She certainly uses precisely that expression every so often in her book. And, is the Russell-Wittgenstein episode really about authority after all? Perhaps it is, but it seems that this could be the case only if we were to stretch our imagination beyond Bocheński's, Kojève's, and Eschenburg's accounts.

Viewed through the prism of Bocheński's understanding of authority, the Russell-Wittgenstein episode appears in a different light. We must remember that Bocheński characterized authority as asymmetrical: if A is an authority for B in a certain domain, then B cannot be an authority for A in the same domain. It is safe to assume that Russell was a bearer of epistemic authority for Wittgenstein, both because of his belonging to the class of philosophers and because of Wittgenstein's inferences of personal experiences about Russell (having listened to Russell's lectures and turned to him for personal advice concerning his own philosophical prospects). To that extent, Wittgenstein seemed to have recognized Russell's greater competence. Yet, at the same time, Russell does not quite fit Bocheński's definition of an epistemic authority, for it seems that the proposition Russell presented to the young German engineer at the time was met with resistance, if not outright rejection, on the part of Wittgenstein. Wittgenstein was debating with Russell. Russell's "authoritative" status as a philosopher (and a most famous one) did not translate into the form of epistemic authority that makes the subject more likely to accept whatever the bearer of authority says regarding his or her domain of authority. The domain in question was certainly philosophy, although the issue seems to have been precisely about the specific nature of that domain, and Russell at least "was worried whether the two men were discussing anything at all."[62] Fricker's use of epistemic authority seems to leave out completely the constitutive feature of authority in Bocheński's account, namely, that authority is always restricted to a certain domain. Fricker focuses so much on the role of "social type" in dialogue, what Bocheński perhaps would refer to as "class," that epistemic authority is completely affirmed, impaired, or altogether negated in each given case on that basis alone and regardless of what domain is being discussed and how the social type relates to that domain.

Holding Kojève's account of authority against the Russell-Wittgenstein episode and against Fricker's discussion, I believe the most interesting point is the element of risk inherent in any exercise of authority and the possibility of a reaction or opposition coupled with the conscious and voluntary renunciation of the realization of that possibility. In Kojève's view, the realization would destroy the authority, but, again, it seems that Wittgenstein is all about reacting to and opposing Russell, while the latter's presumed status as epistemic authority is left untouched. There are several ways to try to solve this puzzle. It could be said that Wittgenstein's opposition shows that he does not really think of Russell as an epistemic authority at all, or only in what would be an erroneous understanding of authority. But it could equally be said that Wittgenstein does think of Russell as an epistemic authority, after all, and that his opposition is not really an opposition or "reaction" in Kojève's terms, that it does not even rattle Russell's authority, let alone destroy it. From this perspective, Kojève's account may come to be questioned, for it seems that perhaps not just any reaction is a reaction good enough to bear the authority-destroying consequences that Kojève attributes to it.

The issue, however, runs deeper. On the one hand, epistemic authority as conscious and voluntary renunciation of any and all opposition seems to preclude any dialogue, and certainly any debate. Dialogue and debate are all about reacting. On the other hand, epistemic authority as that which should be granted to any interlocutor understood in his or her capacity as a potential knower, seems to be a condition of any dialogue and debate that would approach the high demands of Fricker's virtue epistemology. There are two very different notions of epistemic authority at work here. Eschenburg's account of the early meaning of authority drives the point home, for authority as "helpful and ultimately quasi-commanding advice" seems to be at odds with Fricker's examples, which are not about advice at all or, conversely, are about helpful quasi-commanding advice, without it being clear whether it was sought in the first instance. A priori subordination to authority, while it is constitutive of the early meaning of *auctoritas*, in Fricker's account is part of the very problem she tries to address.

Fricker is right to foreground the role of social types, which in Bocheński's logic of authority are referred to simply as a variable called "classes" and represent one way of constituting authority, although without any critical discussion of how such class-based authority may be the result of power relations. For Bocheński, the recognition of such authority is based on reasons that are given by way of experiences with the class in question. But such experiences are certainly prefigured and configured by power relations, as much scholarship from within many philosophical quarters has amply shown. Stereotypes about "classes" may prevent some social types from ever becoming epistemic authorities, as described in the accounts of Bocheński, Kojève, and Eschenburg, as they are "simply not . . . asked for information in the first place."[63]

Fricker has a very instructive discussion about "the example of a prejudicial stereotype of epistemic authority that was operative in seventeenth-century England" and that concerns the "ascription to gentlemen of *perceptual competence*" across the board and to the effect that "being non-gentle and/or female was a negative marker [of authority]."[64]

Fricker's discussion of positive and negative markers of authority and their source in the unequal relations of power bears directly on the larger questions of social and political justice as well as on any attempt at reviving something like the sense of the early Roman Senate's *auctoritas*. At the end of her book, she admits that a redress of injustices at the structural level would take "more than virtuous individual conduct of any kind, it [would] take[] group political action for social change." She also expresses the hope that her discussion of the virtues of testimonial and hermeneutical justice may, nonetheless, prove helpful "at the level of the institutional" and if "placed more squarely in the political frame."[65] It is to this level that I now want to shift my discussion.

The authority of number

Three surely make a tiger: *Han Feizi*

I would like to begin this section with an anecdote, this time reported in a text titled *Han Feizi* 韓非子. I read it not so much with the intent of establishing what it meant originally, which would demand a much higher degree of textual and also intertextual engagement; rather, I am mainly interested in what the passage comes to mean on my reading of it. In other words, I am not relying on the authority of the *Han Feizi* for my argument. Here is the passage:

> 龐恭與太子質於邯鄲，謂魏王曰：「今一人言市有虎，王信之乎？」曰：「不信。」「二人言市有虎，王信之乎？」曰：「不信。」「三人言市有虎，王信之乎？」王曰：「寡人信之。」龐恭曰：「夫市之無虎也明矣，然而三人言而成虎。今邯鄲之去魏也遠於市， 議臣者過於三人，願王察之。」龐恭從邯鄲反，竟不得見。(內儲說上)

In W. K. Liao's translation:

> When Pang Gong together with the Crown Prince was going to Handan as hostage, he said to the King of Wei: 'Now, if someone says there in the market-place is a tiger, will Your Majesty believe it?' "No, I will not believe it," replied the King. "Then, if two men say there in the marketplace is a tiger, will Your Majesty believe it?" "No, I will not believe it," was another reply. "If three men say there in the market-place is a tiger, will Your Majesty believe it?" "I will believe it," affirmed the King finally. Thereupon Pang Gong said: "That there is no tiger in the market-place is clear enough, indeed. Nevertheless, because three men allege the presence of a tiger, the tiger comes into existence. Now that Handan is far more distant from the Wei State than the marketplace is from the court and those who criticize thy

> servant are more than three men, may Your Majesty deliberate over the mission of thy servant!" As expected, when Pang Gong returned from Handan, he could not secure an admission into the city.

There are two, perhaps three, different layers to the passage. The first layer concerns the issue of whether or not there is a tiger in the marketplace and boils down to the (paradoxical) central statement, which in Christoph Harbsmeier's translation reads: "It is perfectly clear that there is no tiger in the market, but when three maintain that there is one, that makes a tiger."[66] The second layer concerns the explicitly stated morale of the passage for which the issue of the tiger is simply invoked by way of analogy: the belief in the criticism launched in the Wei State against Pang Gong in far-away Handan being like the belief at the court in the presence of a tiger in the far-away marketplace. The judgment of a high-enough number of people makes the criticism true inasmuch as it makes a tiger, while it is perfectly clear, at least to Pang Gong, that the criticism is wrong. The third layer is revealed by the effect that the story about the tigers and the analogy has on the king of Wei, who, as in the case of the tiger, comes to believe what a high enough number of people think is true and who it must be assumed is behind the refusal to admit Pang Gong into the city upon his and the king's return from Handan. Pang Gong's plea that the king may deliberate about his mission reveals that the story about the tiger is not about a sort of Moore's paradox or about the distinction between "objective truth" and "a psychological notion of belief,"[67] but that it is an epistemological issue with a clear political message. On my reading, it is an instance of a deliberate intermingling of epistemic authority and strong deontic authority.

We find this kind of intermingling exemplified in other stories also, such as the famous one about the always-scheming and most brutal advisor Zhao Gao (赵高) testing his power against Qin Er Shi Huang Di (秦二世皇帝), the second Emperor of the Qin dynasty. According to the *Records of the Grand Historian* (*Shiji* 史記), Zhao Gao, in an attempt to find out whether he had enough support to rebel against the emperor, presented a deer to the emperor but called it a horse. When the emperor laughed, saying, "Is the chancellor perhaps mistaken, calling a deer a horse?," Zhao Gao asked the emperor to check with those around him, should he really not believe that it was a horse. Those around him gave different answers, but Zhao Gao punished those who called the deer a deer indeed and thus made himself respected among all. All officials were terrified of him thereafter. Epistemic authority here is instrumentalized in view of an attempt to test and increase strong deontic authority.[68]

It is the specific form of authority at the center of the story about the tiger in the marketplace that I find most interesting and that again brings into focus the issue of the authority of number. That the story is (also) about such authority is perhaps best corroborated by another passage in the *Han Feizi*:

> 言之為物也以多信，不然之物，十人云疑，百人然乎，千人不可解也。
>
> It is in the nature of words that they are taken to be trustworthy (*xin*) when many people advocate them. Take a thing that is not so. When ten people maintain it, one has one's doubts. When one hundred people maintain it, one thinks it is probably so (*ran*). When one thousand people maintain it, it is incontrovertible. [48, 6.6][69]

In light of this passage, the king of Wei in the tiger episode gave in to the opinion of three rather quickly, when clearly he still should have had doubts. How many it takes may depend on the case at hand, but the important claim is that at some number or another, the epistemic authority is often granted, and it may have consequences at the political level. This is most intriguing with regard to what Eschenburg had to say about the aspect of augmentation in the early meaning of *auctoritas* and with Kojève's discussion of the authority of the majority and the precarious relationship between its variants of authority of public opinion or hearsay and pejorative connotations such as the masses or the average person. It might also provide a further clue to examining Fricker's reliance on "the bounds of contemporary routine moral judgement."

Number as quantity and quality

There are different ways in which number might be involved in the augmentation that authority brings about, the one described in the *Han Feizi* being only one of them. This is well illustrated by a look at an example of an argument from authority. Consider the following statements:

1. Someone has said that Swiss chocolate is no longer produced in Switzerland.
2. Many have said that Swiss chocolate is no longer produced in Switzerland.
3. Ralph has said that Swiss chocolate is no longer produced in Switzerland.
4. The press officer of Chocosuisse, the Association of Swiss Chocolate Manufacturers, has said that Swiss chocolate is no longer produced in Switzerland.

While it is perfectly clear that Swiss chocolate is still produced in Switzerland, if somebody in a conversation, say, at a coffee shop in New York, utters the first statement, the speaker's claim to epistemic authority is augmented quantitatively by one (i.e., if the speaker also believes the statement). It is as if two people were telling you what this person tells you. If the speaker makes the second statement, the augmentation would still be quantitative, to be sure, but increasingly a qualitative element will be introduced. For instance, it might be thought that many are unlikely to err, which of course depends entirely on how you are disposed toward the thinking of the many—in the elitist judgment, no qualitative element would be added (as Friedrich von Schiller put it in his *Demetrius*: "Majority is folly; reason has always been with the few"). The argument from authority in this case—in line with Kojève's consideration of the authority of public opinion, hearsay, and gossip—is an appeal of sorts to popular opinion, which in its straightforward form ("the majority believes *p* [or does *x*]; therefore *p* is true [or *x* should be done]") has mostly been viewed as fallacious, but more recent accounts readily identify subtypes that would pass as a valid argument.[70] Fallacy or not, it is, in any case, often the most successful tool of persuasion. This way of involving number in the augmentation of authority is what the *Han Feizi* seems to put up for debate.

If, however, the New York café goer utters the third statement, although she would have certainly confused whatever Ralph had said (let us grant for the moment that the person is not making things up), you perhaps would be inclined to believe this person if you knew that I was from Switzerland and was generally considered to be a very trustworthy epistemic authority regarding Switzerland. If you did not know Ralph, the person could as well have said that "someone" has said that. . . . But if you did know him, I hope that the epistemic authority of that speaker would be increased qualitatively, as if many more people were saying what she is saying. If you think my authority in this domain to be at best questionable, then think of how many in philosophy cringe at somebody replying: "but Confucius himself said that" or "Immanuel Kant has said that": is that not as if a thousand people standing on the speaker's shoulders were shouting at you? Here, the augmentation of authority works quite differently from the discussion in the *Han Feizi*. The use of number is metaphorical ("as if") and not an appeal to popular opinion. The quality of the number might change in that it matters in some specific contexts whether "someone" or "Immanuel Kant" is invoked as having said something. It is not a higher number that carries (mistakenly or not) authority, but that one and the same number might be invested with different levels of authority. The equivalent in our example is the fourth statement, in which even more quality is added to quantity, since surely the representative of *Chocosuisse* is in the know, even though it is again just one person speaking.

It is difficult to describe the sense of augmentation that authority brings about, but it seems to me that understanding the quality of a number against its mere expression of a quantity might be helpful. In his *Sociology*, Georg Simmel discusses how groups are constituted by numbers in different ways, and considers the phenomenon in which numbers are used "to characterize a group, more particularly, a group of persons, within a larger totality" as "the Six" or "the Hundred," noting that:

> It is very remarkable how the most outstanding persons are called after the least characteristic feature, number, which is completely indifferent to all quality. The basis of this, it seems to me, lies in the fact that "six" (or any other such number) does not refer to six individuals and isolated elements but to their synthesis.[71]

The "synthesis" refers to a "particular differentiation" of the larger group, "by virtue of which six of its members are singled out and grow together into a leading unit."[72] It does not seem too far-fetched to suggest that "the Six" are invested with an authority, augmented in a way that just any group of six individuals is not. When, later in his text, Simmel comes to consider one of two ways in which authority may be formed, he seems to allude precisely to an augmentation in which the quantity a number expresses changes into a quality:

> A person of superior significance or strength may acquire, in his more immediate or remote milieu, an overwhelming weight of his opinions, a faith, or a confidence which have the character of objectivity. He thus enjoys a prerogative and an axiomatic trustworthiness in his decisions which excel, at least by a fraction, the value of mere subjective personality, which is always variable, relative, and subject to criticism. By acting "authoritatively," the quantity of his significance is transformed into a new quality; it assumes for his environment the physical state metaphorically speaking of objectivity.[73]

In an argument from authority, both ways of augmentation are in play, since there are at least two persons saying something (the equivalent of "someone has said that *p*"), and, to the extent that significance is ascribed to the invoked authority, it is not just "someone" that is being invoked but someone with a value beyond mere number and beyond the one of "subjective personality."

Extreme cases and the politics of the authority of number

It might be worthwhile to explore briefly some extreme cases in order to better understand what is at stake in the authority of number in terms of quantity and quality. Such an extreme case is the ascription of a maximum quality to a minimum quantity. The *Politeia*'s philosopher-king might be an example, but I would submit that the sage-king described in many ancient Chinese texts is an even better example of the extreme case: I will discuss one text, but there are many others that could serve the purpose. The *Guanzi* 管子 is a text put together at the famous Jixia Academy in the State of Qi sometime between the fourth and the end of the second century BCE; in the view of some commentators, it contains the earliest formulation of what was later called Daoism. Keep in mind that the title itself represents an argument from authority, relating the text to the famous minister Guan Zhong 管仲 of the much earlier Spring and Autumn period (eighth to fifth century BCE).[74]

The text describes what a sage, a *shengren* 聖人, should be like and how everything would succumb under the sage's all-pervasive virtuous power, *de* 德. The "authority" captured by that figure in Kojève's terms would be divine, since it bears no opposition.[75] The sage encounters no hostility (*bu yu ren hai, wei zhi sheng ren* 不遇人害，謂之聖人); nothing in the world can do the sage any harm (*wan wu bu hai* 萬物不害). The authority is not restricted to any one domain, but covers them all (making it no authority at all in Bocheński's view, a *Grenzbegriff* of authority at best); the world is in flux, it is pure *qi* 氣, everything is pervaded by *dao* 道, and the sage-king has perfected self-cultivation to the point that he can take all in, to become an organism without individuality. The sage is at the same time an epistemic, weak, and strong deontic authority. Such a figure is in no need of advisors. As in Kojève's account, the sage does not need to *do anything* to exert authority, and the text does elaborate on the notion of *wuwei* 無為, which seemingly means doing nothing, but also means much more than doing nothing. It is well captured in the following passage:

> 治心在於中，治言出於口，治事加於人，然則天下治矣。
> 一言得而天下服，一言定而天下聽，公之謂也。

> When the heart-mind is thus regulated at the center,
> The mouth emits well-polished words,
> Well-defined tasks are entrusted to others,
> And when this is so, the entire world is governed.
> A single word silences the entire world,
> Bidding the entire world to harken,
> Such is the [sage-king's] impartiality.

The sage-king is the highest expression of quality, and thus comes to have maximum authority over all others. The figure is also all-knowing, but there is something here that the *Guanzi* and other such texts remind us of that would be important to pursue in more detail. Similar to the corporeal aspects of the self-cultivated sage, emphasized and discussed throughout the text (the sage's flesh or skin, for instance, are described as full and radiant, *pi fu yu kuan* 皮膚裕寬), knowledge is also understood in an embodied manner. In some passages, mere learning is even ridiculed and the senses through which one knows are emphasized ("the people all want to know it, but there is none who seeks that through which one knows it"). This not only links back to Kojève's notion of the authoritative act and to Cicero's great Romans exercising authority with a mere wink, but it also suggests that Bocheński's logic of authority might, or should, be expanded beyond his two kinds of domains covering merely propositions and instructions or orders. There is an obvious corporeal dimension to authority that includes contingent positive markers of authority such as a deep voice, big stature, or a perfectly tailored suit—or the obligatory beard apparently sported by all serious Greek philosophers.[76] Of course, the same applies to negative markers, as highlighted in Fricker's discussion of stereotypes and epistemic injustice. The problem is that such (positive and negative) markers have to be decoded and understood, not least in terms of the domain over which the authority extends, and a failure to decode them might result in domain non-specificity (somebody with a deep voice or wearing a uniform is just *generally* knowledgeable) and verge on a *mistaken* ascription of absolute authority (Bocheński, Satz 3.7).

A figure such as the sage of the *Guanzi* perhaps represents the ideal of all personalist conceptions of political authority, and for that reason is worthy of theoretical reflection. Perhaps more practically important, however, is the other extreme case, that is, the attribution of a minimum quality to a maximum quantity. This is perhaps approximated by Rousseau's *volonté générale*, which still normatively lurks in the background of much of the discussion in contemporary political philosophy, but for which (given the problems already apparent in Rousseau and the points elegantly raised by Kojève) it is difficult to find an institutional translation, if minimum quality can at all furnish a basis for a desirable conception of *political* authority.

From the perspective of the authority of number, it appears that modern democracy has generated confusion, perpetuated by the discussions on political authority in contemporary political philosophy, which blurs the distinction between *auctoritas* and *potestas* and casts authority largely in terms of *potestas*. Instead of bringing power (*potestas*) to the many, to the *demos*, it is authority (*auctoritas*) that in modern democracies comes to rest in the hands of all (in terms of maximum quantity) and thus in nobody's hands (in terms of quality). Power (*potestas* and *potentia*), as the current crisis of modern democracy is often thought to showcase, has remained in the hands of the few who keep on operating behind closed doors and are driven by self-interest. Democratic authority might appear as nothing more than an Augustan rule in modern democratic disguise. In the context of politics, Hannah Arendt was then perhaps right to use the past tense for the title of her essay, "What was Authority?" and to claim that "authority has vanished from the modern world."[77] What has happened is the reverse of what was supposed to happen. Power should have been with the many, who would have been allowed to follow their self-interest, while authority should have remained under the influence of the few considered experienced or learned. Authority should be really about quality, not quantity. In other words, democratic sanction should be an exercise of the power invested in the people, but whatever receives such sanction should not have authority because of the mere quantitative act of sanctioning; rather, it should have authority because it boasts a particular quality even before it is sanctioned by an act of the majority, making the democratic sanction a "manifestation" of a prior recognition of authority, as Kojève put it. (Of course, a *democratic* authority possibly still originates with the people, for example, in the form of some initiative or some public deliberation, where there is ample room for expertise to be summoned and to be heard.) Kojève's ambiguous but skeptical stance against the authority of number might, indeed, in some important sense touch upon the Achilles' heel of democratic authority.

Conclusions

There have, of course, been attempts at institutionalizing authority as *auctoritas*, as officially licensed epistemic and weak deontic authority. Indeed, such institutions are firmly in place in modern democracies as well as in other forms of political governance, from case-specific consultation of academic and other expertise to regular meetings of expert councils and ethics commissions. These instruments are deliberately designed to factor epistemic and weak deontic authority (*auctoritas*) into strong deontic authority (*potestas*). The authority that is thus put into play, however, is quite different from the one exercised by a bearer of authority in a certain domain over a person who is subject to that authority. As in the case of the authority of qualitative number, the authority of institutions *qua* institutions serves as an augmentation with regard to some set of epistemic or deontic assertions, while the augmentation works in quite different ways from the personalist position that is paradigmatic in Bocheński, Kojève, and also in Eschenburg. The distinction is important, and it is from Eschenburg that we most clearly get a sense of how the institutionalization of authority often led in the past to a specific turn of events, unmercifully thrusting *auctoritas* into the force-wielding hands of *potestas*.

The destructive feature of institutional authority consists in its potential to make any personal authority irrelevant. Simmel, in his treatment of quantitative and qualitative number and of the "Six," captures this potential when he writes:

> It is exactly the characterless and impersonal nature of numerical designation which is characteristic here: more forcefully than any other less formal concept could do it, it indicates the fact that it refers not to individuals as persons but to a purely social structure.[78]
>
> The purely numerical concept implies the purely objective character of the formation, indifferent to any personal features the member may have, and only requires that he be one of the "Six": Really, there is perhaps no more effective way of expressing an individual's high social status, along with the complete irrelevance of whatever he may be as a person outside his group function.[79]

This, it might be said, depicts the state of affairs at the time of the successors of Emperor Augustus, as described by Eschenburg. But it also resonates with Bocheński's air-traffic controller, the only difference being that we would normally trust that the person holding such a function would have adequate qualifications. Authority is given on the basis of such trust. When necessary qualifications (or personal authority) are entirely lacking, an authoritative act might still be successful, but it seems likely that any further exercise of authority would present a substantial and ever-growing risk. This is when *potestas* historically has often supplanted *auctoritas*.

The instability of institutional authority devoid of personal authority is easy to understand in light of the mutual enforcement of authority (or augmentation) between a member and a group. Perelman and Olbrechts-Tyteca observe:

> If an academy sheds luster on its members, it is equally true that each of them contributes to the renown of the academy of which he is the representative.[80]

If this is true of luster and renown (or prestige), then it is also true of the more restricted concept of authority. Assuming a comprehensive understanding of the institution, it might be said that in almost all cases reported by Bocheński and Kojève, as well as Eschenburg, some sort of institution is at work. Personal authority can be distinguished from institutional authority, but it seldom comes, if at all (given the role of inferences from *experience* as justifying the attribution of authority), without institutional authority. I turn to somebody for advice because that person appears or even has proved rightly to represent something that has institutional backing of some sort (a teacher, a director, but also at the same time, "someone who knows," "someone with a scepter," or "someone representing tradition," etc.). The table with Kojève's types of authority is replete with examples.

This has serious implications for our understanding of authority, which is also the main conclusion of this chapter: an act of authority always comes, and is best understood as coming, with an *argument* from (institutional) authority, willful or not, on the side of the bearer, but having precisely that effect on the side of the subject. Bocheński and Kojève give too little importance to this insight. Eschenburg clearly sees the problem that such authority brings with it, but continues to take some sort of pure personal authority as paradigmatic of what authority is. If Bocheński and Kojève are right in insisting that, from a descriptive point of view, an authoritative act is always preceded by the voluntary renunciation to react against it, then Kojève with his emphasis on the perishability of authority leads the way to a normative understanding of authority.

Eschenburg directs our attention to the fact that *auctoritas* in the early Roman Republic was institutionalized in a combined system of "freedom to decide" and "obligation to consult." This combination ingeniously captures the fact that in the face of an institution of any kind, we might not always be willingly asking for advice, but it turns it into a positive and critical feature, since those in power are required to consult with those in authority and then are "free" to decide. Perhaps attempts at institutionalizing *auctoritas* would have to heed Kojève's point and design the institutions so as to as to have authority continuously tested, expose it to the risk of losing recognition, and, if abused, trigger a reaction strong enough to overturn it. The importance of detecting abuse, however, highlights the fact that a normative account of authority—in contrast with a descriptive account—would have to make room for questioning the authority, for arguing and debating with the authority (particularly to the extent that authority includes an *argument* from authority), much as Wittgenstein did with Russell, and would thereby not make any reaction good enough to destroy authority. Kojève's emphasis on authority being at risk would otherwise itself risk turning into a mere farce, at least on a normative view. How could authority ever be at risk without being questioned? Perhaps such an understanding of authority would also take care of Fricker's warranted concerns and be progressive at the same time.

Notes

1 See: Jean Goodwin, "Forms of Authority and the Real *Ad Verecundiam*," *Argumentation* 12 (1998), pp. 267–80.
Goodwin distinguishes a third form, which he takes from Locke's classic formulation of the *argumentum ad verecundiam* and which he calls "the authority of dignity." Goodwin foregrounds the different reactions in case an authority is not followed, that is, disobedience in the case of the authority of command and imprudence in the case of the authority of expertise. Showing that there is also impudence or shamelessness as a reaction against an authority of dignity, Goodwin argues for distinguishing this third form of authority. In contrast, I emphasize the element of *enforceability*, which is absent in the authority of expertise as much as in the authority of dignity (I find the latter to be a moral version of the former and treat them as one; Locke, in the relevant passage, explicitly mentions "Learning" and gives the example of the "learned doctor," which, Goodwin probably would agree, is not unlike what we mean by an expert). It might be due to Goodwin's focus on arguments from authority that he conceives only cases in which an authority "looks for the auditor to take what is stated as true and believe it" or "to take what is commanded and make it true" (pp. 268–69). This seems to unduly exclude cases in which an auditor actively asks for advice from an authority or cases in which an authority is not even aware that his or her words are taken as authoritative.

2 Richard E. Flathman, *The Practice of Political Authority* (Chicago: University of Chicago Press, 1980), p. 14.

3 Heidi M. Hurd, *Moral Combat* (Cambridge: Cambridge University Press, 1999), pp. 62–63.

4 Fabienne Peter, "Political Legitimacy," The Stanford Encyclopedia of Philosophy, Edward N. Zalta (ed.), http://plato.stanford.edu/archives/spr2014/entries/legitimacy/ (2010).

5 See, for some examples: J. A. Simmons, "Political Obligation and Authority," in *The Blackwell Guide to Social and Political Philosophy*, ed. Robert L. Simon (Malden: Blackwell Publishers, 2002), pp. 17–37. Simmons describes the "philosophical problem of political obligation and authority" in terms of "good citizens" and "a moral right to rule"; Thomas Christiano, "The Authority of Democracy," *The Journal of Political Philosophy* 11, no. 2 (2003), pp. 266–90, whose concern is an "authoritative rule maker" and "legislative authority," which he distinguishes from judicial, executive, and administrative authority; Thomas Christiano, "Authority," The Stanford Encyclopedia of Philosophy, Edward N. Zalta (ed.), http://plato.stanford.

edu/archives/spr2013/entries/authority/, last revised, 2012, who begins the entry on authority with the question: "When is political authority legitimate?"; Michael Huemer, *The Problem of Political Authority: An Examination of the Right to Coerce and the Duty to Obey* (Basingstoke: Palgrave Macmillan, 2012), the title of whose book says it all.

6 David M. Estlund, *Democratic Authority: A Philosophical Framework* (Princeton: Princeton University Press, 2008).

7 Certainly, there would be other angles from which to examine authority, such as psychological (Cléro), psychoanalytical-feminist (Benjamin), or even socio-psychoanalytical (Mendel) accounts, which discuss in more detail than other accounts why and how anybody would come to submit voluntarily to an authority. See Jean-Pierre Cléro, *Qu'est-ce que l'autorité?* (Paris: Librairie Philosophique J. Vrin, 2007); Jessica Benjamin, *The Bonds of Love: Psychoanalysis, Feminism, and the Problem of Domination* (New York: Pantheon Books, 1988); Gérard Mendel, *Une histoire de l'autorité: Permanences et variations* (Paris: La Découverte, 2002).

8 Joseph Maria Bocheński, *Was ist Autorität? Einführung in die Logik der Autorität* (Freiburg im Breisgau: Herder, 1974), pp. 19–20.

9 Ibid., pp. 60–62. For an extended argument on the related point that authority should not be conceived in opposition to autonomy, see: Richard Raatzsch, *Autorität und Autonomie* (Paderborn: Mentis, 2007).

10 Bocheński, *Was ist Autorität?*, p. 87.

11 Ibid., p. 90.

12 The objection is raised in the context of a more far-reaching dilemma attributed to Anacharsis of Scythia, but only the first part of the dilemma is of interest here: "Who is to be the judge of skill? Presumably, either the expert or the nonexpert. But it cannot be the nonexpert, for he does not know what constitutes skill (otherwise he would be an expert)." There is possibly some confusion since the nonexpert could well be an expert in knowing who is an expert on the skill. For the dilemma and the translation, see: Douglas Walton, *Appeal to Expert Opinion: Arguments from Authority* (University Park: The Pennsylvania State University Press, 1997), pp. xiii–xiv.

13 Alexandre Kojève, *La notion de l'autorité* (Paris: Gallimard, 2004), pp. 56–59. All translations are mine. A translation into English of Kojève' study, which appeared in its French original only in 2004, has recently been published: See: Alexandre Kojève, *The Notion of Authority*, trans. Hager Weslati (London: Verso, 2014).

14 Ibid., p. 63.

15 For an anthropological study focusing on the break-down of authority, see: Bruce Lincoln, *Authority: Construction and Corrosion* (Chicago: The University of Chicago Press, 1994).

16 Kojève, *La notion de l'autorité*, pp. 66–88.

17 A critique of Kojève's four types and of his take on authority more generally is Cléro, *Qu'est-ce que l'autorité?*, pp. 34–43.

18 Kojève, *La notion de l'autorité*, p. 51.

19 Ibid., p. 97.

20 Ibid., p. 103.

21 Ibid.

22 Ibid., p. 108.

23 Ibid., p. 110. Kojève also offers a metaphysical analysis of authority in terms of different temporalities (pp. 117–131), which is beyond the scope of this chapter, but I should like to mention that the authority of the judge turns out to be opposed to all

other types of authority, constituting a variant of the authority of Eternity, thwarting all attempts at temporalization, being itself outside of time, while manifesting itself in its relations with time. It is a classic view of Justice that Kojève describes and also subscribes to.

24 The Latin word *auctoritas* seems to have no direct equivalent in Ancient Greek, as Cassius Dio has already remarked (3, 4–5, 55), which prompted him to use the Latin word in his *Roman History*, otherwise written in Greek. See also: Rafael Domingo, "El binomio 'auctoritas-potestas' en el derecho romano y modern," *Persona y Derecho* 37 (1997), p. 184. Of course, saying that there is no direct equivalent is not saying that there are no words in Ancient Greek, let alone in Ancient Near Eastern or other early languages, that are readily and with good sense translated into English *authority*.

25 Cf. Georg Simmel, who discusses authority as a form of domination and an interaction and subtly distinguishes it from prestige, writes: "what is called 'authority' presupposes, in a much higher degree than is usually recognized, a freedom on the part of the person subjected to authority." See: Georg Simmel, *Sociology: Studies of the Forms of Societalization*, in *The Sociology of Georg Simmel*, ed. Kurt H. Wolff (Glencoe: The Free Press, 1950), p. 183.

26 Theodor Eschenburg, *Über Autorität* (Frankfurt am Main: Suhrkamp, 1965), pp. 10–11.

27 Ibid., p. 13.

28 Ibid., p. 25.

29 Hurd, *Moral Combat*, p. 64.

30 Christiano, "Authority."

31 Bertrand Russell, "Ludwig Wittgenstein," *Mind* 60 (1951), pp. 297–98. The reason for later talking about a hippopotamus instead of a rhinoceros is perhaps due to Wittgenstein's using the example of the hypothesis that there is a hippopotamus in the room in a lecture of the early 1930s. See Joseph F. McDonald, "Wittgenstein, and the Problem of the Rhinoceros," *The Southern Journal of Philosophy* 31, no. 1 (1993), p. 423, fn. 31.

32 Ray Monk, *Ludwig Wittgenstein: The Duty of Genius* (London: Penguin Books, 1991), p. 39.

33 Ibid., p. 40.

34 Brian McGuiness, *Wittgenstein: A Life* (Berkeley: The University of California Press, 1988), p. 91.

35 McDonald, "Wittgenstein, and the Problem of the Rhinoceros," p. 416.

36 Monk, *Ludwig Wittgenstein*, pp. 38–40.

37 Monk, *Ludwig Wittgenstein*, p. 40; see also: McDonald, "Wittgenstein, and the Problem of the Rhinoceros," p. 412.

38 Miranda Fricker, *Epistemic Injustice: Power & the Ethics of Knowing* (Oxford: Oxford University Press, 2007), pp. 2 and 4.

39 Ibid., pp. 16–17.

40 Ibid., p. 17.

41 Ibid., p. 116.

42 Fricker's definition of prejudice reads as follows: "Prejudices are judgements, which may have a positive or negative valence, and which display some (typically, epistemically culpable) resistance to counter-evidence owing to some affective investment on the part of the subject." (Ibid., p. 35)

43 Ibid., p. 27.

44 Ibid.

45 Ibid.

46 Ibid., p. 132.
47 Ibid., pp. 133–34.
48 Ibid., p. 129.
49 Ibid., p. 134.
50 Monk, *Ludwig Wittgenstein*, p. 39.
51 Fricker, *Epistemic Injustice*, p. 101.
52 See: Sandy Goldberg, *Relying on Others. An Essay in Epistemology* (Oxford: Oxford University Press, 2010).
53 Fricker, *Epistemic Injustice*, p. 103.
54 Ibid., p. 104.
55 Ibid.
56 Ibid., p. 105.
57 Ibid., p. 107.
58 Ibid., p. 91.
59 Ibid., p. 42.
60 Ibid., p. 91.
61 Ibid., p. 107.
62 McDonald, "Wittgenstein, and the Problem of the Rhinoceros," p. 412.
63 Fricker, *Epistemic Injustice*, p. 130.
64 Ibid., pp. 118–19.
65 Ibid., pp. 174 and 176–77.
66 Christoph Harbsmeier, *Language and Logic*, Part I, Vol. 7 of Joseph Needham, *Science and Civilization in China*, ed. Kenneth Robinson (Cambridge: Cambridge University Press, 1998), p. 246.
67 Ibid., p. 247.
68 See the comments in: Jean Levi (trans.), *Han-Fei-tse ou le Tao du Prince. La stratégie de la domination absolue* (Paris: Éditions du Seuil, 1999), pp. 29–31.
69 Harbsmeier, *Language and Logic*, p. 246.
70 For an extensive treatment, see: Douglas Walton, *Appeal to Popular Opinion* (University Park: The Pennsylvania State University Press, 1999), particularly pp. 91–92, 124–26, and 205–07. As proposed by Chaïm Perelman and Lucie Olbrechts-Tyteca, an appeal to popular opinion could rhetorically also serve the purpose of building "communion" with the addressed audience. See: Chaïm Perelman and Lucie Olbrechts-Tyteca, *The New Rhetoric: A Treatise on Argumentation* (Notre Dame: University of Notre Dame Press, 1971), pp. 51–57.
71 Simmel, *Sociology*, p. 107.
72 Ibid.
73 Ibid., p. 183.
74 Romain Graziani (trans.), *Écrits de Maître Guan: Les Quatre traités de l'Art de l'esprit* (Paris: Les Belles Lettres, 2011), p. xxvii.
75 For critical remarks that raise the possibility that the ruler is given the superhuman status of an "Almighty God" precisely in order to neutralize his power (and authority?), cf. Yuri Pines, *Envisioning Eternal Empire: Chinese Political Thought of the Warring States Era* (Honolulu: University of Hawaii Press, 2009), pp. 106–07.
76 The inclusion of "a perfectly tailored suit" obviously problematizes the corporeality of markers of authority, extending it to *things*. Indeed, the understanding of authority as a relation between two persons (Bocheński, Kojève) might diminish the importance of *things* as markers of authority that might be separable from persons (the authority of the constitution, etc.). Bruce Lincoln discusses cases of construction of authority

emphasizing the role of the scepter as an authorized and authorizing instrument in Homeric Greece; the body of an authorized and authorizing speaker in Sibylline practice in Rome; and the Old Norse Thing as an authorized and authorizing place. See: Lincoln, *Authority: Construction and Corrosion*, p. 112. Jean-Pierre Cléro proceeds from a definition of authority that takes *things* and *symbols* (including texts, images, laws, institutions) to be the great disseminators and bearers of authority. See: Cléro, *Qu'est-ce que l'autorité?*, pp. 8–10.

77 Hannah Arendt, "What is Authority?," in *Between Past and Future: Eight Exercises in Political Thought* (London: Penguin, 2006), p. 91.

78 Simmel, *Sociology*, p. 107.

79 Ibid., p. 108.

80 Perelman and Olbrechts-Tyteca, *The New Rhetoric*, p. 322.

References

Arendt, H. (2006), "What is Authority?," in: *Between Past and Future: Eight Exercises in Political Thought*, London: Penguin, pp. 91–141.

Benjamin, J. (1988), *The Bonds of Love: Psychoanalysis, Feminism, and the Problem of Domination*, New York: Pantheon Books.

Bocheński, J. M. (1974), *Was ist Autorität? Einführung in die Logik der Autorität*, Freiburg im Breisgau: Herder.

Christiano, T. (2003), "The Authority of Democracy," *The Journal of Political Philosophy*, 11 (2), pp. 266–90.

Christiano, T. (2012), "Authority, *The Stanford Encyclopedia of Philosophy*," Edward N. Zalta (ed.), http://plato.stanford.edu/archives/spr2013/entries/authority/.

Cléro, J.-P. (2007), *Qu'est-ce que l'autorité?* Paris: Librairie Philosophique J. Vrin.

Domingo, R. (1997), "El binomio 'auctoritas-potestas' en el derecho romano y modern," *Persona y Derecho*, 37, pp. 183–95.

Eschenburg, T. (1965), *Über Autorität*, Frankfurt am Main: Suhrkamp.

Estlund, D. M. (2008), *Democratic Authority: A Philosophical Framework*, Princeton: Princeton University Press.

Flathman, R. E. (1980), *The Practice of Political Authority*, Chicago: University of Chicago Press.

Fricker, M. (2007), *Epistemic Injustice: Power & the Ethics of Knowing*, Oxford: Oxford University Press.

Goldberg, S. (2010), *Relying on Others: An Essay in Epistemology*, Oxford: Oxford University Press.

Goodwin, J. (1998), "Forms of Authority and the Real *Ad Verecundiam*," *Argumentation*, 12, pp. 267–80.

Graziani, R., trans. (2011), *Écrits de Maître Guan: Les Quatre traités de l'Art de l'esprit*, Paris: Les Belles Lettres.

Harbsmeier, C. (1998), *Language and Logic*, Part I, Vol. 7 of Joseph Needham, *Science and Civilization in China*, edited by K. Robinson, Cambridge: Cambridge University Press.

Huemer, M. (2012), *The Problem of Political Authority: An Examination of the Right to Coerce and the Duty to Obey*, Basingstoke: Palgrave Macmillan.

Hurd, H. M. (1999), *Moral Combat*, Cambridge: Cambridge University Press.

Kojève, A. (2004), *La notion de l'autorité*, Paris: Gallimard.
Kojève, A. (2014), *The Notion of Authority*, translated by Hager Weslati, London: Verso.
Levi, J., trans. (1999), *Han-Fei-tse ou le Tao du Prince. La stratégie de la domination absolue*, Paris: Éditions du Seuil.
Liao, W. K., trans. (1959), *The Complete Works of Han Fei Tzu*, 2 vols, London: Arthur Probsthain.
Lincoln, B. (1994), *Authority: Construction and Corrosion*, Chicago: The University of Chicago Press.
McDonald, J. F. (1993), "Russell, Wittgenstein, and the Problem of the Rhinoceros," *The Southern Journal of Philosophy*, 31 (1), pp. 409–24.
McGuiness, B. (1988), *Wittgenstein: A Life*, Berkeley: The University of California Press.
Mendel, G. (2002), *Une histoire de l'autorité: Permanences et variations*, Paris: La Découverte.
Monk, R. (1991), *Ludwig Wittgenstein: The Duty of Genius*, London: Penguin Books.
Perelman, C. and Olbrechts-Tyteca, L. (1971), *The New Rhetoric: A Treatise on Argumentation*, Notre Dame: University of Notre Dame Press.
Peter, F. (2010), "Political Legitimacy," The Stanford Encyclopedia of Philosophy, Edward N. Zalta (ed.), http://plato.stanford.edu/archives/spr2014/entries/legitimacy/.
Pines, Y. (2009), *Envisioning Eternal Empire: Chinese Political Thought of the Warring States Era*, Honolulu: University of Hawaii Press.
Raatzsch, R. (2007), *Autorität und Autonomie*, Paderborn: Mentis.
Russell, B. (1951), "Ludwig Wittgenstein," *Mind*, 60, pp. 297–98.
Simmel, G. (1950), *The Sociology of Georg Simmel*, K. H. Wolff as editor and translator, Glencoe: The Free Press, 1950.
Simmons, A. J. (2002), "Political Obligation and Authority," in R. L. Simon (ed.), *The Blackwell Guide to Social and Political Philosophy*, Malden: Blackwell Publishers, pp. 17–37.
Walton, D. (1997), *Appeal to Expert Opinion: Arguments from Authority*, University Park: The Pennsylvania State University Press.
Walton, D. (1999), *Appeal to Popular Opinion*, University Park: The Pennsylvania State University Press.

8

To Justice with Love

Sari Nusseibeh

Love and justice: Close relatives?

Can it be reasonably argued that Love and Justice are relevantly—even genealogically—related to one another, and that the former must be seen as a necessary ingredient in any account of the latter? It shall be argued below that these two—in a primary sense—are inseparable. At first, it might not strike us that way. Quite the opposite, Justice and Love may seem to belong to two entirely different categories, the one being totally independent of the other. Indeed, they even stand at opposite extremes. One has only to think of such incidents as the aggrieved members of the clan in Philippine's Maguindanao province who are still waiting for the courts to issue convictions five years after the massacre of 58 of their members, standing last November in protest to commemorate the event and raising banners demanding Justice be done to see that it is feelings of vengeance and hatred that are closely associated with the meaning of Justice in peoples' minds, rather than Love. "No Justice, No Peace" is the platitude seen sketched, for example, on banners in Ferguson demanding the conviction of a police officer accused of killing a black youth. Rage, retribution, revenge, threats—but not love—underpin the call for Justice in such cases.

From the opposite end, one might also think of Justice as the right balance in nature, maintaining a cosmic order or harmony giving each part its due—just as in human relations within a polity such as that of Plato's Republic, each of its members is positioned to perform the function he or she is best fitted for. Love, in this picture, could be viewed (and has been so viewed) as what brings that *best* order together, whether as *first* or as *final* cause. Love here is seen as immanent, pervading the infinite causal structure of the world. As is Justice, though to see either, one's perspective must somehow transcend the infinitesimal parts of this structure and reach out to the infinite. Going even one step further, as in some mystical schools of thought such as that of Ibn Arabi (12th/13th century), Love, Justice, and God fuse into one another, as does, indeed, the entire cosmos: the things that are, the order they are in, and what explains their being in that order.

In between these two worldviews, the examples we normally come across seem to invite us to draw different conclusions. In typical situations of disagreement or conflict claims, where one party or both may feel shortchanged in a transaction between them, it is normal to feel that Justice should be turned to in order to settle the differences. Here, Love and Justice do not—ostensibly, at any rate—seem to have anything to do with one another. When a bloody and violent conflict between two different "rights-claimants"—like that between Israelis and Palestinians—begins to turn ugly and to have wider repercussions, finding *some* kind of solution between them becomes urgent. Not love or sympathy, whether between them or for them, prompts one party or the other to seek an end to the conflict. Rather, it is in spite of the deep feelings of enmity and hatred between them, as well as because of how these are reflected in their dealings with one another, on themselves and on others, that a solution is felt necessary. A solution, in this context, primarily comes to mean "a stable peace," and Justice becomes less urgent than such a peace.

When such a peace is sought, it is significantly not Love that is turned to for finding a solution, but practical *Reason.* While taking account of the emotions and beliefs involved in such conflicts, would-be mediators or peace-makers would turn to Reason and be guided by it, rather than turning to love. Indeed, any kind of sentiment is thought to be an obstacle for working out a rational solution. To complement this attitude, practiced negotiators would also train to set their eyes not on Justice as such, thinking this to be impracticable, but on *fairness*, or what might be considered a *relative* rather than an *absolute* Justice. Fairness comes to be viewed as the realistically practical alternative to Justice, and Reason as the method to rely on in the endeavor to reach it. In hard cases, where the conflict is judged to be irreducible to a fair deal, *any* solution that brings order back to peoples' lives can begin to make sense as an end in itself—even a cease-fire. Mediators (say, in the Israeli-Palestinian case) in such situations can be assumed not only to be dispassionately engaged in trying to reason out solutions, let alone to be motivated by love: they might even feel dislike for both parties or antipathy toward them, and may end up coming to the conclusion that *any* short or long-term solution that brings peace would be acceptable. An *end* to the fighting becomes an end in itself, regardless of fairness, let alone Justice. Indeed, order as such, whether instituted or restored, itself becomes a default end in itself.

The thinking process outlined above (faced with conflict or conflicting wants, to resort to Reason in search of a solution) is not alien to us. It is almost second nature. Closer to home, however, the dynamics involved are somewhat different, as is the frame: when two of our children begin to fight over a new toy or a piece of chocolate, our reasoned solution for their conflict is typically guided by our love for them. Furthermore, unless we are so overwhelmed by housework that we just wish them to be quiet in any way, our foremost concern would be to end the fight by teaching the children a lesson about fairness. We would wish to instill (or evoke) in them the sense or sentiment of *sharing* due between brother and sister. Order (Peace) and sharing (justice or fairness) enter hand in hand here. They are not viewed as being separable. In its turn, the principle of sharing, we remind them, is naturally akin to other sentiments and emotions they must have, such as love for one another, kindness, brotherliness—and therefore the readiness to compromise on one's wants for the sake of the other. While the thinking process involved (from wants to solution via Reason) is the same, the instinctual motor driving this process is different. Love is behind it, and Justice is its target.

One could conclude from the above account that Love and Justice are not necessarily or always separable from one another—a mediator may not be prompted by Love to find a Just solution for a conflict, but a parent may. But this may be thought to be more reason to consider them as belonging to entirely different categories. Love, it might also be said, is a personal affair. Justice, on the other hand, is the affair of the State, a system of rules defining an order of human conduct. Another manner of describing this difference is to say Love is subjective or private, whereas Justice is public. We may or may not be in love, or ever have experienced it, but we could, nonetheless, consider ourselves to be competent to discourse knowledgeably about Justice. After all, we take the subject of Justice to belong more to the domain of Reason, where discourse about it—like discourse about other "objective matters"—is assumed to be free of sentiment. "Lady Justice," paradigmatically, is fair only to the extent that it is blind to prejudice—this latter being a feeling, or sentiment, prompting us to favor one human being over another in a judgment concerning a conflict or dispute between them. Love, in contrast, in one of its most elementary forms, consists precisely in singling out or favoring one person over another, or, indeed, over the rest of the world. At the end of the day, Justice by its very definition needs to be institutionalized. Love defies any attempt at its institutionalization.

However, a cursory consideration of these two will immediately yield striking and underlying resemblances: although Love is what one *feels for* (e.g., someone), whereas Justice is what one feels *that* (it is done or undone), yet both, at bottom, are *felt*. By their nature, feelings are *immediate* experiences. Typically, one "finds oneself" feeling love, hunger, sadness—as well as (morally) pricked. Certainly, one does not feel love as one feels Justice; but one feels for *what* is just, or *that* something is unjust—the immediate instinct of this, or from this, being similar to the famous Socratic *daimon* (a self-reprobating instinct). This, in turn, becomes reflected in one's *gadfly* (an other-oriented act or expression). The latter may be expressed in an act, or a discourse, but it is significantly an instinct that lies behind it, which is immediately felt.

Although the feeling of or instinct for what is Just is different from Justice itself, it is *this* instinct, which prompts the sense of Justice, that surely cohabits the instinctual world with Love. It is in this sense that we can say that my feeling in love is like my feeling that such-and-such is Just or Unjust. Both are felt in one's guts. Both are immediate sentiments. Both are immediately experienced as psychological states in oneself. But clearly, one does not "feel" Justice as one feels love. From a higher perspective, however, Love and the moral instinct for Justice (that one *does* feel) can be seen to express themselves differently, the first being attached to (or objectified in) a particular person, or persons, while the second is attached to (or objectified in) a *rule* of conduct more specifically between human beings.

One may conclude from this that, in one essential sense, Love and Justice share a common origin, namely, their instinctual roots. True, our discourse about Justice may be carried out in rational terms, but ultimately it comes to reflect what we instinctively feel is right, and the beliefs we construct on the basis of that feeling. It consists in how we feel and believe human and social relations—even those closest to home—*ought* to be arranged. Thus, we feel justified in weighing in on what Justice is, or in engaging in a rational discourse about it, typically because of the beliefs we have come to hold, in each case prompted by our instinctive feeling for what is right and what is wrong—or, Socratically at least—for what is wrong. In an important sense, therefore, we are justified in reducing Justice (and similar notions, like Fairness) to instinct, or feeling.

Importantly, however, this instinct or sense we have does not have to do only with the need for order—for there to be rules of behavior that govern our social interactions, without which everything would go haywire. It is not, surely, the mere existence of order that answers to the sentiments or feelings we have in this regard. It is the existence of a particular kind of order, one that we *feel* is less wrong, or more right, or—if we have Justice in our eyes—as being "truer to form" or better than others. But even if it were just order, or quietude, that we are driven to seek, having reasoned this to be better for us, surely we must feel *a want* to bring this about, again akin instinctually to those other wants we may have, such as our want to fulfill a desire, or our want for our love to be requited. Our want for peace, or for Justice, is of the same kind. Justice or Peace are frozen exemplars, until we want them, just as Love is simply a word, until we feel it.

The claim here is not that the objects of the moral instinct referred to are standard, or uniform, among human beings. The moral instinct, however, surely is. What one person feels is unjust, another can regard neutrally, or can feel to be just. Likewise, how it feels to be in love for one person can be different from how another person feels the same emotion—let alone that different persons can be the objects of that emotion. Underlying those differences, however, is the sameness of the instinct, or feeling. That is why two persons can differ on what to consider beautiful or attractive, but not differ on the feeling each of them experiences that is aroused by someone they consider beautiful or attractive. Likewise, the "objectified" articulation of Justice, whether as theory, or as an actual state of human relationships, can and often does seem different for different people. The moral instinct informing these different articulations is the same, but unlike in the case of Love where the instinct is immediately attached to the person as an object, in this case the instinct's articulation of its "object" is typically intellectualized. After all, its object is a rule. Granted, the occasion may be related to one particular person, or more than one, but the judgment concerning it concerns a rule of conduct between them, or what is by definition a general judgment. That is why, at the end of the day, my judgment is public in nature, unlike my feelings of love, which are personal.

Concept and meaning

One does not typically encounter Love in contemporary accounts of Justice. Yet, Justice cannot be explained adequately without Love—and Love itself must be explained adequately to do the job. Before this, however, it is important to ask what the current accounts of Justice (e.g., particularism or statism versus universalism or cosmopolitanism) draw upon as foundations for their analysis. And how self-evident or *a priori* are the principles on which they are based? How can we understand a "fairness" theory of Justice, or a "law of the Peoples," or any one of two or more egalitarian accounts (e.g., luck or product-based), and thereby judge impartially between them? What is it that ultimately *justifies* one or another of the different approaches (or one or more moral positions) proposed? Are there self-evident "rational" principles (e.g., utilitarianism), or primary psychological instincts (e.g., egotism) that suffice to uphold one version or another of an account of Justice that we may wish to propound, or to believe in? And would invoking Love somehow undermine such "scientific" or "rational" accounts?

Understandably, the concepts of Justice, Freedom and Equality—along with other concepts thought to be somehow related—have occupied the larger part of the interest of philosophers throughout history. This interest has reflected itself, again understandably, in disagreements among philosophers over the very meanings of those concepts—if we allow ourselves to make this distinction between a concept and its meaning—and over how the concepts are or ought to be related with one another. Yet, since the debates continue, a consensus on what these concepts *mean* (and whether or not their underlying principles are self-justifying) has clearly not been reached yet. One way to simply bypass this conundrum would be to propose a positivist approach, that is, to construct a theory of Justice on the basis of definitions that are to be used as axioms in the theory. Here, while the expressions under review would remain the same, any disagreements over them could be reduced to a matter of definitions.

However, one does not get the impression that contending theories of Justice would be content with a positivist approach. More typically, embedded in the recognition that meanings may be different, there is the underlying assumption that the concept is the same, and that it is *this* concept that is the subject of the disagreement. The debate thus takes the form of an assertion by one party or another that the meaning *they* give to the concept—rather than that given to it by the interlocutor—is the one that truly represents the concept in question, or that represents a realistic account of *it*. Real arguments seem to be about providing the *right* meaning of the concept, or the right answer.

The question, "Could there be Justice in Israel irrespective of how matters stood for Palestinians?" rhetorical or otherwise, answered negatively or positively, is one that assumes that the same concept is the subject of discussion. (Here, *two* societies coexist under what is, in effect, *one* rule. But a similar question could also be asked about two separate societies, for example, the United States and Saudi Arabia, having "normal" transactions between them). While an answer may take the form of proposing that Justice can exist in one country (or society) independently of whether it exists in the other; or that, in any case, it has different meanings for different societies—so whether it (is argued it) may exist or not in one or both is a matter of what Justice means for those societies—the obvious *counter-argument* immediately questions this assumption, bringing the discussion back to whether or not different meanings given to the same concept (or signified by the same expression) are valid alternatives, or whether they are exclusively disjunctive, making out only one of them to be the right meaning.

In other words, a *relativistic* approach to viewing such matters as Justice, Equality, and Freedom (whether in the context of one society or more) falls short of being conclusive, while a *universalist* approach—given the widely different hypotheses proposed for a conclusive theory—still suffers from not yet having singled out one theory with a claim to a universal consensus. Likewise, we might question the justification for treating as an axiom a particular human right, or what to count as basic among these, not as we might impartially take note of it, but as to whether it is a realistic expression of what "we" might normally consider such a right. Here again, the underlying assumption in our approach is that an axiom is different from the real meaning of the concept in question; or that the entire theory built on this axiom does not correspond with what we might normally expect such a theory to reflect. That said, we might still disagree over the "real" meaning of such a concept, or over what a theory of it should look like. When this happens, the question once again arises: What are the ultimate principles underlying our different approaches? How are they to be justified?

Taking Freedom (Liberty) and Equality as examples, would we be justified in proposing that the first is *primary*, from which the second is to be derived—as a liberalist, or even a liberal egalitarian philosopher might propose? Or should we consider that Equality is primary, from which Freedom should be derived—as a Marxist egalitarian, drawing upon a dynamic theory of economic history, might propose? Or, rather, is it the case that the two are embedded in each other (as will be proposed in this account)? How do we go about settling this question in the first place, that is, determining a method for answering it?

Fear, politics, fairness

In Politics, meanings and interpretations of Justice directly impact peoples' lives—what it means within a particular group/population, or across different groups or populations. A particular theory that seems predominant in State practices (say, those in Israel or the United States) is one that is self-focusing: predicated on a select number of primary human passions, primarily fear for oneself (the *I*), but extended so as to apply to a self-identifying group (a *We*), it sets out a perimeter for itself wherein the self-security that the perimeter provides justifies the nature of the "rules" within—of regulation or prioritization between wants, whether of the individual herself or of the different individuals in the group—as well as "without"—determining the State's relations with the outside world.

Thucydides, whom Hobbes sufficiently admired to take it upon himself to translate the Athenian's major work, clearly sets out fear, besides self-interest and greed, as the primary driving force for human behavior. In this approach, fear, and more particularly *fear for oneself*, is immanent. A Hobbesian theory of Justice thereafter rests on establishing a state of peace (eradicating the causes of fear and managing the other passions of self-interest and greed) under the total control of a Ruler in whom the basic rights of individuals to defend themselves against others are collectively vested. Fear being the basic concern individuals have and their right to defend themselves against its causes being their basic need, a stable political system (order) ensuring their freedom from this fear automatically becomes the minimally sufficient system of government where Justice prevails. Political systems ensuring this freedom are (in this view) sufficient unto themselves, and self-vindicating as upholders of Justice within their borders.

Taking this line of thinking one step further, such a theory can be seen to underlie (or give justification to) the much larger picture of power-balances in international relations: Unless and until a world Government prevails in which all the powers of the different States can be vested, ensuring the freedom of fear of each from the other, the minimally preferred option that can be achieved is a power-balance under which each State seeks to fend for itself, but can at the same time ensure Justice (i.e., security) within its borders. In effect, this is the state of the world today: Saudi Arabia can boast of adhering to the value of Justice as much as Switzerland can, and Israel can boast of being a Just society irrespective of the Palestinians. It is not even necessary in this light to argue for cultural relativism to explain why Justice in Saudi Arabia includes rulings that discriminate against women; or why Justice in the United States implies abject poverty for sectors of its population or the absence of a national health service; or why Justice in Israel implies the disembowelment of Palestinians from their native land. Not in any way being derived from those other values or rights philosophers often come up with, such as equality, or those values now enshrined in the Charters of the United Nations, such as the right to education, all a State needs for claiming it upholds justice is a condition of controlled quietude among its populace, conditioned on a reasonable level of freedom from fear for itself—even if this is backed only by an oligarchic or authoritarian rule. (A judicial system of regulations and procedures for adjudicating in cases of conflicting claims among members of the populace can, of course, be flagged as proof of the existence of Justice, but *this* kind of Justice would clearly be different from that where the object of interest and discourse is the *whole* polity, within which adjudication is practiced).

That said, such a system of world order is generally found wanting. Rights- or political activists or philosophers (whether living in the "Western World" or outside of it) generally express their concerns that, whether in the context of political orders within (even) democratic systems of government or outside of them, a Hobbesian Justice is left to seem barren of moral—or even *enough* psychological—content. The Hobbesian psychological basis for constructing a theory of Justice is thought not to tell the entire story. So, discarding a Platonic approach that is thought as outdated and anyway as smacking of too much "metaphysics," political theorists have focused their efforts on finding ways to complement Hobbesian primary instincts (psychology) as a basis for developing theories of Justice with other equally basic (self-centered) instincts or needs, such as those having to do with the practical imperative for human cooperation (transactions). It is with Aristotle that this focus on what explains social interaction is first encountered, but further psychological insights to explain this felt need are sought, such as, for example, what is said to be the instinct for reciprocity. At the primary level, this instinct may be diagnosed (for the purposes of explaining Justice) first in terms of the "primitive" and ego-driven impulse to retrieve from the other that which has been snatched or taken away from one; or, as a minimum, to "get back at them" for having deprived one of a possession. The encounter with "the other" is thus portrayed—in line with the primary egotistic instinct of "fearing for oneself"—in *negative terms* as a matter of "an eye for an eye," or of a "restoration of a *status quo ante*."

This "encounter" paradigm presupposes (in the context of two or more individuals) unprovoked aggression—the ego-driven impulse of one person to snatch for oneself from another what one can, or what one feels the desire for. However, what starts out as a mutually aggressive paradigm is then supposed to introduce the foundations for a reciprocity notion—the determinant of the relationship with "the other." At this basic level, the notion of "Justice" is portrayed in purely restorative terms. It is a notion that prepares the groundwork for a more evolved *transactional* relationship with the other: if one person takes, the other takes back.

In time, and with experience and acculturation, the reciprocity principle evolves into a "give and receive" relationship, and even, much farther down the road, into a gift-making sentiment, with no returns expected or required. Finally, this initial (but primarily ego-driven drive) comes to be investigated by political theorists for the purposes of laying the foundations for a mature theory of Justice—whether a "liberalist" or an egalitarian one, and whether as confined to the perimeters of a single polity (statist) or as extended across different political contexts (universalist). An edifice of values comes to be constructed on the basis of how the first bricks are situated, accounting for those other notions that are normally associated with Justice (e.g., equality, freedom, basic human rights), which on the one hand are seen to be totally absent in a Hobbesian framework, but which on the other hand are "added bottom-up" in a calculating (or rational) way, rather than by being imported from some metaphysical space, such as that of Plato's Forms.

The "leap" from the psychological plane (ego-driven instincts) to the rational plane (an articulation of a "moral" theory of Justice) that would be required in this context is articulated in the form of an implicit consensus between members of the group—a kind of social contract, perhaps best explained through a thought-experiment, such as that of Rawls's *veil of ignorance*, where we can imagine persons extracted or disengaged from their current social positions coming together with a willingness to cooperate in order to agree on the best new arrangement between them.[1] Eventually, Rawls's interlocutors are not imagined to be "disembodied minds" simply trying to cut out a best deal for their individual selves: in order to make the arrangement to be worked out hold for future generations (as the best arrangement needs to), he finally (and significantly, as we shall later see) imagines them as "family representatives," or as individuals also having the best interest of their descendants in mind. The intergenerational projection envisioned here (from an "I" to a "We") is a rational extension of the "I" space, or of the first-person, moving from the singular to the plural, but remaining anchored in a reflexive mode of calculations. The virtual laboratory in which his interlocutors are engaged in negotiations is one in which each of those present seeks to work out a consensus over that package of goods which he or she believes suits his or her order of priority—a common *wants* (primary goods) list to serve as the ground-floor basis for a joint (re-engaged) life. Through this experiment, Rawls proposes to show how—even when we start off with egotistic individuals seeking to fulfill their wants—the condition of their being disposed to reason with one another for a final settlement between them will produce a common living arrangement that provides sufficient space for all, even accounting for their different "fortunes" (a circumstance to minimize the effects of which he formulates a special rule—see below).

As a best order of human relations given how human nature is perceived, Justice here is no longer defined merely in terms of the containment of internal aggressions (freedom from fear), but as an order providing for that space in human relations that allows for what are generally regarded as "democratic values," with lines being drawn (by some, if not all, "liberal theorists") across state borders to delineate what these values imply or oblige at the level of international relations (viz., the obligations and constraints on what are to be acceptable and unacceptable conditions in other countries with which the original country has dealings, and what the nature of those dealings should be like). In sum, what we have in these accounts, therefore, is (a) the discarding of the idealistic and metaphysical "baggage" of ancient theories of Justice, and (b) the attempt at preparing a more realistic, but primarily I-centered or "egotistic," account, by drawing either on the psychology and rationalism of human beings (liberal-libertarian theories), or on an in-built historical mechanism (Marxist) geared as *a final cause* toward Equality.

Communitarians

The so-called "communitarians"—who consider the building blocks of a civic order to be groups rather than individual units (sometimes clumsily called "unencumbered selves")—would downplay the significance of a "rationalist" contractarian approach as that proposed by Rawls, ultimately considering this to be neither historically meaningful nor conceptually relevant. Social groups are formed, and best preserved, being rooted in those "positive" sentiments and feelings known to bind people together in the first place—compassion, respect, tolerance, sympathy, love, and suchlike, to start with; and on the communal civic institutions that are established and in which the community members succeed in remaining bound to one another, such as the family, the church, the local clubs, the unions, and suchlike, in the second place. For the communitarians, even "a family representative" in the virtual laboratory would not do as an interlocutor—first, because the purpose for which the laboratory has been set up (the best arrangement for a group such as the family) is already vouched for in their account, the social unit with which one starts being a group rather than an individual; and second, because in this laboratory the family representative is proposed as somebody negotiating on the basis of Reason rather than Sentiment. It is Reason, in Rawls's account, that is the mechanism used to prune the ground structure of what are primarily individualist egotistic instincts, in order to create the best living arrangements possible. This account is different from that, say, of Hobbes, which is grounded in fear for oneself; or from that of other contractarian theorists (say, John Locke) who define egotistic wants in terms of specific "goods" (e.g., possessions or property). But the basic ground structure (a primary egotistic human nature) is the same, as is the pragmatic mechanism (Reason) needed for establishing suitable boundaries between individuals.

Communitarians view this egotistic basis for the construction of the best living arrangement as one-sided, and, therefore, as being misguided, since it totally ignores the fact that what binds people together in the first place, and what keeps them together, is the sentiment of affiliation of one kind or another, which is in due course translated as the values and civic institutions keeping that society intact. However, in spite of its well-advised attention to this other side of human nature—generally thought to be absent in a liberal account—the communitarian account has a basic shortcoming, which is its minimization of the role of the individual, even in the context of the area of sentiment. Being generally portrayed as a *group mode* of affection, its sentimental relationships begin to look more like *rules* governing these relationships (e.g., values), and more like separate community-centered values, than like general human instincts ultimately anchored in the individual herself (see below), and therefore reflecting a standard human account. In other words, here the danger in the account is that of its being too abstracted from the individual's instincts, and therefore from the individual's role in the construction of the "best arrangement." This in turn leads to the further question of how—out of the cauldron of instincts and emotions in individual human beings—the best cooperative arrangement in this account could finally emerge rather than any other. While the blatantly visible other side of human nature is highlighted, neither is the picture clear about how positive instincts and passions could be separated from negative instincts and passions to produce the best arrangement, nor is it clear what role positive instincts are supposed to play in that overall picture with respect to one another. If in Rawls Reason is chosen as the mechanism for determining the best order, it is not clear here how Sentiment is to play an analogous role.

But besides this visible shortcoming, there are many other reasons why a "rationalist" edifice built upon purely egotistic instincts is also found wanting, all boiling down to their being rooted in a conception of human nature that makes it out to be—in defiance of common sense—blatantly selfish: indeed, the selfish elements of human nature may describe much of the political world, but they by no means describe what people feel for each other.

Love is what binds: Ibn Khaldun

"The best possible arrangement for human relations" seems to define what Justice is, whether for the communitarian or for the liberal. Absent from both accounts (whether altogether or in practical terms) is the role Love plays in the picture. This is a crucial shortcoming, as Love is after all an essential part of human instincts, as is the instinct for Justice. To ignore it altogether would seem too arbitrary, while to subsume its distinctive and individualist role almost as part of a general rule describing human relations would seem too downplayed. While it may be a tall order to try to define or sift out Love's various meanings, it is nonetheless possible to isolate a particular meaning at this stage that seems very relevant to the discussion so far, as well as to the discussion that will follow on how, finally, the notions of Freedom (thought to be exclusively I-centered) and Equality (thought to be relational) could form a reasonable account of Justice. The particular meaning I wish to isolate can be initially formulated in answer to the simple question whether two individuals *find* themselves in love with one another *before* uniting as a couple and beginning to pursue a common interest (say in an arrangement of marriage), or whether they typically approach each other in a calculating way to determine a common interest as a prelude to falling in love and forming a union between them. Clearly, two real-life answers are possible. Unions can and do happen both ways. But if we were to dig deeper for a genealogical origin in order to determine whether utilitarian unions precede or succeed love bonds, we would surely find love as the instinct that brings them together in the first place, and it is love that determines afterward how strong or weak the bond between them is, while a common interest may determine—however weakly or strongly—a thin meaning of a working relationship between them. (Business relations are surely second-order to real human bonds.)

Can we find a psychological basis for drawing this conclusion? Many venues for doing this are obviously possible,[2] but in this regard I shall draw on a key insight by Ibn Khaldun (1332–1406), provided by his definition of his well-known concept of "*asabiyyah*," to introduce a method. This is sometimes translated as "compassion," or "affection," but this or any other cognate translation needs to be understood precisely in the terms he proposes as an explanation for it. It is that natural instinct of caring about the other, he tells us, common "from the beginning of time" to all human beings, which inclines us to defend *someone else* from danger. So powerful is this instinct that it makes us ready to place ourselves in the face of that danger on behalf or in lieu of that person, thus intercepting it, and preventing it from befalling the other. The "someone else" in this picture is—in the first place—a close blood relative, or a loved one (contrast, here, this impulsive filial instinct with Rawls's calculating "family representative" who is engaged in negotiations). Ibn Khaldun then extends its application to those who are physically farther and more distant relatives, a gradual replacement in one's perception beginning to happen here of those in whose physical surroundings one is, to those further away, for whom one's care instinct becomes a function of one's ability to *imagine* the union that binds them. This, already being an imaginative function, is subject to a gradual waning, until it dies out. When this happens, he tells us, the presumption of a union's existence becomes vacuous, or more theoretical than real, as the initial caring instinct "for the other" one needs to have for there to be a union in the first place would by then have totally disappeared.[3] With some modifications, "Imagined Communities" here would seem to fit Ibn Khaldun's conception of the civic association, and the role of *imagination* could form a basis for its further development (see below).

If—in view of his definition of it—one were to attempt to flesh out the deep meaning of "*asabiyyah*," one would need to interpret the special compassion or affection meant as the *love* a parent has for her child—in a sense, a love for another that exceeds even the love one has for oneself.[4] A problem faces us as we try to figure out how this basic instinct (which many parents presumably feel, paradigmatically, as they first hold their first newborn in their arms) can become translated into a wider context, as Ibn Khaldun wishes for it to do. Or indeed, how it could become translated into a universal feeling, as *sufi* writers portray it. In any case, Ibn Khaldun develops his theory on the rise and fall of States on the basis of this basic instinct—their growth, the power they possess, as well as their weakness and their downfall being in direct proportion to the strength or weakness of this basic instinct—or what one could nowadays perhaps describe as the communal identity.

It is not necessary for the purposes of this discussion to go into his elaborate theory concerning the evolution or lifetime of polities, (or his eventual elaboration of Justice as "fair" governance, especially in relation to the State's financial policies) except to point out that, while not discounting whatever other psychological or material requirements may be presented to explain the origination of a polity, these are in his theory posited as being posterior to and based upon this primal instinct of "*asabiyyah*." For example, the cooperation requirement for survival (e.g., the rational need for the distribution of tasks among the members of a group, fulfilling the self-interest of each of those members in the acquisition of food, or their coalition for the purposes of self-defense) *presupposes* an already existing *glue* holding those members to each other through "*asabiyyah.*" In an *original position*, Ibn Khaldun's basic "units" are (as they are also for the communitarian) already small groupings, paradigmatically family ones. However, unlike the communitarian, Ibn Khaldun seeks out and identifies one particular instinct found in the individual human being, around which a social group or community begins to coalesce. Without it, one is given to understand, human beings can, of course, interact with one another, but they do this in the absence of "a community." For this to come into being, even in a pre-civil state (i.e., among population groups living in the wilderness), a *glue* is required, which Ibn Khaldun identifies as "asabiyyah," its primary and deeper meaning being filial love. (Ibn Khaldun does not confine this "eternal and natural" instinct to human beings, and claims that it also exists in many other species).

Besides Love, and as a testing ground for it, what is particularly striking about Ibn Khaldun's primal "compassion" instinct is its rootedness, or expression, in fear—not that, *à la* Hobbes, which one person feels for oneself, thus explaining one's need for a social contract—but the fear one has for someone else. In Hobbes, fear for oneself is the reason for establishing a bond. In Ibn Khaldun, it is because the bond (love) already exists that fear for the other is felt or experienced. Fear of a danger or a threat is a testing ground because, in experiencing this fear of a threat, one's instincts could go in one way (to saving oneself) or in another (to saving someone else). The impulse to save another (paradigmatically, as Ibn Khadun wishes us to envision, the "other" being one's child or a loved one) is perhaps an expression of the purest form of love: wishing for the other even that which comes at the expense of one's own suffering. It is this love that one has for another that lies at the heart of what one can regard as the inception of a community. (As an aside, we can imagine that, in a pre-communal state, the mother is forced against her will to submit to a male aggressor's sexual assault, but also that only the love that will bind her to her newborn will explain the true genesis of community. It is *this* primal instinct that stands as the foundation glue for any kind of bond between persons.)

It is important to keep in mind here that Ibn Khaldun is not just recasting observations about human nature and family sentiments such as those Aristotle himself had highlighted in his treatment of the origination of a political association. Aristotle had recognized the role of such instincts, but had at the same time focused on individual self-interest as a foundation stone for those associations, evolving out of family groupings. For Ibn Khaldun, on the other hand, the basic glue binding a polity is this instinct, and it is significantly a glue in which "the other"—even though it is a specific other at its basis, a blood relative, the object of one's affection, or a loved one—counts at least as much as oneself, if not more.

In some current accounts on Justice where primal psychological roots are pried in search of how the family-related concept of equality—appropriately defined—could be "fitted into" the whole picture, it is suggested that one should look—beyond the first-order egotistic impulse—at what constitutes the foundation of the relation with the other. A subtle but important distinction is made here, making out this search to be a rational one for a derived or "*second-order*" question that could be of the form: How do I, in my pursuit of satisfying my egotistic wants, relate to the other (who happens to be around)? Further down the road, the answer to this question comes to determine how I come to see what equality with the other *must* (realistically) mean. But the very first steps down this "discovery" road—eventually to be described as a process of articulating a relational principle of reciprocity with the other—begins at the ground level of my instinctive pursuit of satisfying my egotistic needs through recognizing the value of the other for the satisfaction of these needs. This other-need may also evolve to become supported by the reflexive need one person has that the other should recognize one as a functional need for the satisfaction of *their* need. Still, the entire process remains self-centered. The principle of reciprocity that evolves from it (and, eventually, the standard for equality on which this is based) is a "second-level" criterion, coming into play only once the more fundamental or "ground level" criterion of self-identity—the individual's primary instinct for satisfying selfish wants (and, eventually, the primary roots for a standard of Liberty are grounded)—has been established. Being primarily driven by the satisfying of selfish wants, the individual discovers the need for both cooperation and recognition. Beginning with the notion "to take for oneself," moving onward to the notion "to retrieve or snatch back what is taken from one," it eventually evolves to the notion of "give and take." At the acculturated level of Reason (a rational standard for what the appropriate balance of "give and take" exchanges among members of a given society should look like), it becomes the basis for what can be considered a "realistic" account of equality, and a justified distribution of goods in society.

A theory of Justice taking its cue from this approach, in other words, proposes an order that accounts for what it claims to be the right distribution of goods among members of a chosen society (equality here becoming defined in terms admitting of the justifiability of distribution differences), and it may, indeed, propose how structural relations with other, less-endowed societies may be established. In like fashion, "International Justice" here may be so articulated as to rationally tolerate an international order in which—in practical terms—three-quarters of the world population live in poverty (or suffer from the deprivation of basic rights). It is not being claimed here that such a Theory would find such an order *desirable* (nor, indeed, would such a Theory find the absence of a decent level of living for its own members desirable): only that its interpretation of equality is made to fit its preferred interpretation of Justice, making blatant exclusions from a decent and dignified level of living of sectors of the population, or of the world, transitionally tolerable. However, as recently noted, a capitalist order (organically upholding such "liberal" theories of Justice) seems inherently geared toward exacerbating the gulf dividing the rich and the poor, even among its own populations.[5] In view of this, and of the liberalist's need for a justified level of toleration of difference, there is a clear need for one upholding such a Theory of Justice to revisit the principles on which it is based, and the corresponding level of toleration allowed for the gulf dividing the rich and the poor (and the "wants-endowed" from the "wants-deprived"), whether within or across societies and cultures.

Love or the restorative impulse?

Taken as a primary building block, Ibn Khaldun's principle of compassion, affection, or love preempts the construction of a theory of Justice in the fashion outlined above. If we leave aside for our present purposes the more complex issue of how this "glue" evolves sufficiently to sustain a political order (and how Ibn Khaldun himself construes Justice), we can try to construct a Theory of Justice on the basis of this principle, which, while not necessarily espousing blind egalitarianism, would still avoid the above-mentioned pitfalls of a "liberalist/capitalist" account. The point to start from is to acknowledge the instinct of defending against danger, but to tie this down to a primal affection for the other, of sufficient force as to wish to stand in the way of that danger, thereby "offering" to take the blow oneself. However one wishes to understand it (even, in a roundabout way, as an egotistic impulse to do with species—and therefore as self-survival— or as an expression of self-love in a projected form), it is primarily a "love instinct" based on which, directly or indirectly, altruistic behavior can be explained. This latter, being defined precisely in terms of affection, and reaching selfless concern for others, stands to be as important in explaining human (and some animal) behavior as what are normally highlighted as selfish instincts. While it does not receive the acknowledgment due to it for the role it plays in explaining behavior from many writers in this tradition, this altruistic instinct has recently been highlighted in some bio-ethical literature,[6] as well as in a recent and widely acclaimed work on history of science.[7] The challenge such studies, accounts, or proposals make us face is that of needing to return to the drawing board in order to re-think how to put the building-blocks of a Theory of Justice together, this time giving as much weight "at the ground-level" of "an original position" to altruistic as to selfish impulses—indeed, even more weight, going by "*asabiyyah*," to altruistic than to selfish instincts.

As already stated, while such a project would question some of the basic principles of both the liberal and communitarian approaches, it would nonetheless be of benefit and could build upon other basic elements in those approaches, in a sense seeking a more coherent overall picture. A particular principle to be questioned in an individualist approach is that of the primitive role of reciprocity—a concept that is itself rooted, as already noted, in the instincts of taking for oneself and the re-taking of what was snatched from one. These primitive instincts are articulated in terms of certain behaviors (such as "snatching back") and accompanying passions (such as revenge or vengeance, or the "restoring" something from the other deemed to be as worthy as what the other has taken from one)—all of which remain pertinent in more evolved human behavior—vengeance and suchlike passions clearly explaining much of this (unfortunate) human behavior. But it would seem to common sense to be stretching this line of thinking too far to propose that our (or a realistic) understanding of what Justice is resides precisely in (and remains pertinent to) this "lopsided" genealogical account for reciprocity. As Chakrabarti has amply shown, it does not even stand the test for being logically coherent.[8] Indeed, Chakrabarti's critique, which is also extended so as to reveal the negative implications of such a theory on world conflicts, illuminates for us once again that other side of human nature, namely, that deeply ingrained (Gandhian) culture of self-control allowing for accommodation—the kind that, even if *not* rooted in love for one's enemy (the other, guilty of usurping a good), is nonetheless a sufficient and commonsensical basis for toleration, and, therefore, for a state of peace (that aspired-for goal of human coexistence).

Chakrabarti's argument specifically aims to discredit the vengeance component (taking back) in the reciprocity argument for Justice. His dismissal of love as a factor, therefore—that I am not required to love my enemy in order for me to be able to formulate a state of peace between us—should not be read into more than for how it is introduced in that argument, namely, as not being the natural substitute for the sense of anger that can and ought to be contained instead of being given vent to through an act of vengeance. (As he shows, the very logic of restoring a *status quo ante* is incoherent.). However, while "loving" one's enemy raises the bar too high for there ever to be peace, recognizing that enemy as a fellow human being (allowing for toleration, or an admission of that enemy's own wants-space) is surely a prerequisite for making that peace with them.

Invoking "*asabiyyah*" again, this inclination for toleration, recognition, and a state of peace with the other must clearly reside in, or naturally complement, other primary instincts at the basic level, defined for our purposes as compassion, or the instinct for, and the act of, love. It is primarily the love with which one holds someone dear that instinctively makes one (physically) intercept a looming harm to the other, thereby endangering one's own life. It is not clear that such an instinct would be covered by the principle of reciprocity, as it has been explicated so far. (Would a mother impulsively covering her child from the blows of a soldier with her own body do so as a natural recognition of that child's own readiness to do the same for her in her old age?). To the contrary, it would seem more reasonable to suppose that the act is carried out impulsively, the sacrifice of oneself not even being given the time to be considered rationally, or in any other way. Or, if we insist on there being a deeply ingrained sense of reciprocity, it might well just be what is imprinted in one's psychology as what the natural or right thing to do for each other is among members of the group. But in this latter case, the generalization of this principle would make it out to be a primarily positive instinct rather than—as is often portrayed—a neutral principle to do with reacting, whether positively (in transactions) or negatively (in reaction to a slight of honor or a dispossession of a good). Indeed, if it were insisted that the "eye for an eye" is the root of the reciprocity instinct, there would be every reason to propose that this "compassion" instinct must then be rooted elsewhere in human psychology, with far more compelling "impulsion" power over human behavior than the revenge instinct—the former being directly impulsive and the latter often being more willful.

Introducing the compassion instinct into this kind of discourse is, of course, not new—as has already been intimated, communitarians base their approach on this kind of psycho-genealogical foundation. Altruism is not altogether absent in this kind of debate, but a liberalist approach seems to relegate it to a second-order level, as already noted. A communitarian approach, on the other hand, seems in effect to employ it in such a way that the individual's primary role in the formation of community becomes blurred. However, assuming that one's primary instincts are both self-centered and other-centered (thereby giving less weight to "*asabiyyah*" than Ibn Khaldun gives it, while not erasing it altogether from the initial logbook of human passions), it may then be possible to construct a theory of Justice (an account of the best arrangement for human relations) that stands on two feet simultaneously, rather than on one pillar only, later to be complemented with other factors that can accommodate with due constraints those other concepts normally related to Justice, foremost among them being equality. However, to do so would require drawing upon some of the observations made at the beginning of this chapter on the matter of definitions. Here I would seek support simply from the claim that the definitions I will be giving Justice, Equality, and Freedom in what follows approximate fairly well to a commonsensical view of these concepts. At the very least, they do not stray very far from other definitions, noting nonetheless that their articulation in what follows is more reasonable.

Freedom and equality on a par

The two primary—and, importantly, complementary—notions needed for constructing the proposed Theory of Justice are, not surprisingly, freedom and equality. These have been classically considered to lie on opposite sides of the same pole. Freedom is defined in terms of my own wants-space, while Equality is defined in terms of the balance between my own wants-space and that of others. Justice is typically portrayed in terms of striking the "right" balance between them. "Libertarianism" (highlighting freedom) and "luck egalitarianism" (highlighting equality) are traditionally viewed as representing extreme opposites.

"Striking the right balance" is clearly where the challenge lies. Generally speaking, one could start from two opposite points. One's departure point could be freedom—the wants-space of the individual, or the realization of self-serving wants. This is considered to be a *primary* instinct, covering a vast array of self-centered or egotistic wants, including, of course, first and foremost, the want for freedom from danger, or the want for life. As for the wants-space of others, its determination is then thought to be rationally workable as a second-order discourse, or a discourse that is derived from the discourse about Freedom. Typically, the thinking here is that one first explains adequately the freedom space for each individual, to be followed by an attempt to see how these different spaces *can be reconciled* with one another. However, this account is contested by proposing that the departure point should, instead, be the moral platitude that we are born equal. It is Equality here that is considered primary. Using this as our beacon, we can then work out a structure as a second-order discourse to determine the *appropriate limits* of the wants-spaces for each of us. If the first account invokes instinct as a primary departure point, the second invokes a universal moral value.

What is clear from the two accounts is that each of them, by proposing its preferred item as primary, in effect compromises the meaning of the other. Equality ceases being that if Freedom is given the first run (it gives way to the concept of reconciliation), while Freedom ceases being that if Equality is given the first run (it gives way to the concept of what is deemed appropriate). Justice on either account is reduced to being a system favoring one account over another, supported by a re-working of the definitions of the two "mutually exclusive concepts." However, we can free ourselves from this self-imposed conundrum if we take Freedom simply to mean the wants-space of one individual, and Equality to mean nothing more simple than that each individual has it, or that each is equal in having a wants-space of one's own. In other words, we need not consider Freedom as a function *of* wants, and Equality a function *between* wants: rather, as already said, it would make more sense to consider them both as functions of wants. Since Freedom is defined as a function of my own wants-space, Equality can simply be defined as the application of this function to each individual. This way, freedom and equality can be considered as being two sides of the same coin.

Viewing Freedom and Equality in this light retains for each of them its primary meaning. But we would still be left with the question of how then to incorporate Justice into the picture without compromising these meanings. It is suggested here that the fundamental flaw in the above account of Justice is to assume there to be a generic gulf between my wants and those of others. But we have already seen that even Justice is reducible to our wants. Its propelling impulse is an instinct that is just as natural as all of our other instincts. My list of wants, therefore, already allows for the want for justice for myself as well as for others. More generally and significantly, it is too thin a concept of wants to assume that what everyone wants as an initial position is only something for themselves, rather than what they may also want for others. Ibn Khaldun's "*asabiyyah*" makes it eminently feasible to claim that among the things I want at the most primary level are those (good) things I also want for others. We therefore have at our disposal in the list of my wants both my want that Justice be done and my want for the good of others. However, the latter—my want for those (good) things for the ones I love and care about—clearly comes first. At its most primitive level, Ibn Khaldun's compassion is rooted in the primal instinct of a parent to protect her child at her own expense. This is akin to her own instinct to protect herself, if alone, against a looming danger. At a more complex level, as we have already seen, it is also an extension of that same sentiment toward others, moderated by the imagination, as he tells us. Whether it could be built upon to extend further as to become a universal rule (whether between groups or among individuals) is something yet to be argued for (see below). For now, however, we could just accept as a general rule that included in my list of wants are those (good) things I want for others.

At the risk of some hair-splitting here, it should be added that by "the other" —that is, *all*—at this stage, we only mean "*any* (one) of the others" (even if "the others" only mean "some") rather than *each* of them. This rendering would first maintain the association of the felt affection by any one person for a specified individual or individuals as the initial meaning requires, rather than leaving it open as the one felt for each individual (regardless of the filial or similar relation that might hold between them), and it precludes the meaning from implying that what one wants for oneself is *ab initio* what one also wants for each person regardless of the relation (the mother would not want for her child exactly what she wants for herself). Although it is very likely that one's wants for oneself would far exceed one's wants for others, we would still be left with a space of overlapping wants: the (good) things I want for the other (still defined as lying within my own wants-space, or as expressing my freedom), and those very things wanted by the other (included in their wants-space, and being a function of their freedom). One item that would stand out in this context is my want for the other to be able to so develop themselves that they could acquire the (good) things I want for them. The list of the good things I want for them surely must include many other items that they want for themselves. A consensual space of wants can therefore be delineated. It stands to reason to view this consensual space of wants as being foundational for the delineation of a community's borders, and to understand our want that Justice be done as arising when one or more of the wants in this space are trampled on or abused. Justice therefore must surely consist—at least in part—in the satisfaction of those consensual wants. Equality, initially having been defined as what each person wants, here becomes "reified" by that consensual space of the good things that everyone wants.

Therefore, viewing freedom and equality as being on a par and already standing on the same platform helps us see a way to construct a model of Justice. We no longer need to build up a model for it so structured as to assume a "worthier" or more elementary status for freedom than for equality and, by so doing, to put constraints on how equality is to be defined. Also, in extrapolating a consensual space in the manner outlined we come to see freedoms in a positive light, and not only as self-serving spaces, the one needing to be offset by the other.

There is a strong tradition in political thought that gives more prominence to the concept of trade as a stabilizing force in and between communities than to sentiments like love or compassion. Common trading interests between parties are thought to be what bring about and guarantee (to the extent possible) peace between them. At its roots, this account also finds support in the emphasis, at the primary level, on the concept of reciprocity—that elemental psychological force or instinct that is thought to be what stands behind the formation of civic relations. Unlike a sentiment, like love or compassion, which is typically object-particularized, the principle of reciprocity is proposed as a general rule with universal applicability. Reciprocity, we recall, is defined as a mutuality function of how *any* two individuals may view, and interact with, one another. Ignoring for a moment its lexical ordering as what proceeds from and comes after an initial, but still unconsidered, basic ego impulse, it is the psychological mechanism through which—it is suggested—different egos become inclined to interact with one another. So, although the underlying presupposition of a social context may be the same for compassion and reciprocity, the difference between them as proposed is that whereas the reciprocity principle leaves the context abstract or undefined (it could be an exchange inclination between two total strangers), the compassion principle ties down that context historically, or confines it in *the first instance* to specified social units (family, friends, village, city, nation). For this reason, the compassion principle has been rightly viewed (in a negative light) as one that underwrites tribal, ethnic, or national chauvinisms. In this sense, it may be claimed that one cannot hope, on its basis as it stands, to be able to construct a *universalist* account of Justice. Indeed, arguably, it seems flagrantly to be a basis for group-specific (or culture-relative) accounts of values.

However, there is no evidence that suggests that a reciprocity instinct or inclination comes first. Indeed, it is more plausible to suggest that compassion comes first, reciprocity proceeding once a bond is established. A mother's selfless love for her child surely precedes any consideration she might have in her old age, when she feels in need of care, to be deserving of reciprocity from her offspring. Indeed, Ibn Khaldun's principle of compassion would seem—for the very criticism itself—to be a down-to-earth or realistic account of a community's genesis: it is a fact that closely knitted groups begin to form precisely on account of particularized (rather than abstract) sentiments. In contrast, reciprocity seems more likely to fit into the picture as a second-order or evolved disposition: it is within the context of an already existing communal structure (or between them) that individuals begin to engage transactionally with one another.

Secondly, however, the very claim to "universality" by the reciprocity principle is more theoretical than realistic. While it is proposed as a general rule (that for any two individuals, the one will incline toward a reciprocal relation with the other), it is not meant as what, in fact, inclines one individual to entering such a relation with another. In other words, the claim of the transactional instinct's so-called "abstractedness" from social context is, in reality, far-fetched: whatever universality it claims to have is surely based upon the specific context where its abstraction as a principle or rule is first made, and where, significantly, it is not made as an application of that rule.

Even so, it may be claimed, while its roots are object-particularized, it is, in fact—unlike compassion—generalizable as a rule, and better fitted therefore for a general theory on Justice. But as already indicated, doing away with reciprocity's lexical ordering in no way undermines our ability to rationally build up a project for Justice. Compassion (in its various deep meanings) could do just as well for building up such a project. But the difference in ordering has far-reaching implications: whether to look upon egotism or altruism as occupying a more basic natural place. Ibn Khaldun's "*asabiyyah*" being a primal psycho-anthropological account, one could easily see how, at an acculturated level, it could become generalized and develop into a universal value: though originating in a select environment for members in that group, it can and does by extension get carried over to other members of the human race (the compassion for the suffering of other groups—say, for a foreign population being devastated by a tsunami or a volcanic eruption or a nuclear disaster being felt *as if* it were like a devastation of a sector of one's own population—see below). In other words, it would not be logically incoherent to propose an articulation of "*asabiyyah*" (and love, more generally) as a principle of compassion ultimately applicable to the human race—or, therefore, to view egotism as well as altruism as each other's nemeses, with equal claims on human sentiments and behavior.[9] These two, then, could be proposed as the psychological foundations for the *two kinds of wants*—self-centered and other-centered, the former denoting egotistic wants and the latter, altruistic instincts.

At a first approximation, then, we can define freedom as that space needed for the fulfillment of one's wants, and equality as the mirror-reflection of this, or as the wants-space for *any* member of the same set. Equality being a function of a "wants-space" in this model, there is no need to seek an additional criterion—such as production or skill—to account for or to justify different distributions of social wealth: different "wants-spaces" already determine different amounts and kinds of "social goods" that different individuals seek to possess. A consensual space already determines a shared wants-space by all for all. But a "wants-space," by itself, does not justify the full possession of all the goods people want. It is a descriptive space and not a prescriptive one. While it is partly rooted in shared wants (the good things I want for myself, as well as those I want for others), it is also rooted in the egotistic instinct. At the primitive psychological level from where it originates, it will certainly cover—besides the want for life—greed, power, and general self-aggrandizement. But at an acculturated level, we can imagine how it could be turned into a range of wants having to do with self-betterment (or, to use Martha Nussbaum's terms, self-flourishing), or the self-realization of potential skills and talents, as well as with the conditions providing for economic security and well-being (Aristotle). But since this definition of the wants-space—for it to make sense—applies indiscriminately to any individual at all, thereby ensuring Equality, expressed tangibly in a consensual wants-space, then for two given different wants-spaces to fit well with one another, a default standard of harmony must be sought, and must, in fact, theoretically exist.

We could propose *as a first* approximation of such a standard of harmony, or Justice, that it be based, as a common platform, on the consensual space of wants. This can be stated as an *overlapping principle:* that there be a coincidence, across the board, of the want for those (good) things I want for others with those (good) things that they want for themselves. As already indicated, while "self-centered" wants must by virtue of the difference between individuals be quite different from one another—say, beyond certain common wants, like human security—"other-centered" wants of these individuals must overlap. One basic item here is my want for the other to be able to so develop themselves that they could get the (good) things I want for them to have, and which they themselves want. Taken together, these different common wants constitute a consensus. Being "extracted" from individual wants, such a consensus creates an obligation: that, being a member of the community, I come to be obliged to act in accordance with its consensus. However, given that, beyond those wants, different individuals must have more wants (good or otherwise), another principle would clearly need to be introduced as a complementary component to the guaranteeing of Justice. This additional component could be worked out from Rawls's *difference principle,* taking into account the different route just explained to reach it.

How the difference principle might work

The *overlapping principle* guarantees that I seek to help others to develop themselves. This calls for an active rather than a reactive role, obliging me as a member of a community to extend help to others. The *difference principle* must guarantee that I do nothing that might prevent their ability to so develop themselves, or that might harm them. A tentative rephrasing of a difference principle could be the following: any accumulation of goods in the wants-space of one that will prevent, directly or indirectly, the ability of the other to fulfill their ability to so develop that they could acquire the (good) things they want for themselves would constitute a violation of their freedom—this being the underlying pillar for the best order of human arrangement between them.

A clear example of such violation can be witnessed in the context of politics, say the current Israeli-Palestinian conflict: Israel's exploitation of a joint (Israeli-Palestinian) water aquifer in such a way as to prevent its use by Palestinians to develop their own economy and living styles; or its exploitation of the returns on religious tourism to the country's (joint) holy sites in such a way as to prevent the Palestinian tourism industry to develop itself; or its colonization (settlements) project on land conquered in the 1967 war in such a way as to preclude the Palestinian ability to exploit these territories for their own growth are all examples of infractions of the difference principle. All these are cases of the direct causing of harm to the other.

The above case could be likened to one in economic terms where two individuals, A and B, happen to find themselves sharing a joint bank account between them, but where each can draw out money from it singly. It is not (yet) determined which one of the two has rightful claim to more of what is in that account. In pursuit of her self-centered wants, A finds it necessary to draw out more from that account than B—without, *at first,* this making any difference to B's pursuit of her self-centered wants. At one point, however, any further withdrawals by A begin objectively to diminish from B's ability to realize her wants, whether in immediate or future terms. (We can imagine that A, though flourishing as a result of the withdrawals, does not feed back into that account any returns that may accrue from her activities). Clearly, in this case, A's activity begins to cause direct harm to B.

A and B need not be thought of as having a joint bank account in the same bank, but can now be viewed as being joint participants in the same national banking system. Once again, the difference principle should ensure that direct harm is not caused to B by A's activity. In what is presumed to be a consensual order of human arrangements in which A and B are members— which, by the way, is not the case in the above-stated political example—adjustment mechanisms such as an appropriate taxation system could be introduced to ensure that B's potential for self-flourishing is not caused harm.

However, as already stated,[10] one of the problems faced by free capitalist markets (like the United States) is the inevitably increasing gap between those few whose satisfiable wants-spaces continue to expand and those many whose wants-spaces, in relative terms, continue to shrink. Here, we cannot speak of *direct* harm being caused, but we could speak about *indirect* harm (Rawls's difference principle, while proposing to prevent this from happening, does not in view of Piketty's analysis guarantee this). How would it be possible to prevent this indirect harm? To address this, an adjustment taxation system geared toward equalizing incomes would constitute a violation of individual freedoms—or of what also goes under the name of the principle of "just-returns" (A's production of more units of output than B as a result of A's diligence or skills), while one adjusted simply toward establishing a welfare system might not by itself be sufficient.

Here, a different intervention can be contemplated, whose roots may go back to Aristotle, and which concerns the hoarding of unusable money. The "life of well-being" for Aristotle was one for which, beyond its basic living needs, there was no use for further money, unless such money was useful for further or tangible future needs. Aristotle warned against the hoarding of money through trade, or the accumulation of cash in excess of real goods. But the (justifiable) accumulation of wealth makes investment for the production of further goods possible, in theory thereby raising the bar for what may count as a life of well-being all round—still in line with Aristotle's stated target. Yet the latent danger remains when the financial-market begins to feed off itself, thereby creating an ever-increasing gulf between cash (paper and, thereafter, virtual money) and goods, and an ever-increasing risk of the sudden collapses of such gulfs (bubbles), as what was witnessed in the recent financial crises in the United States and Europe. When a party's financial returns begin to exceed their capacity to develop, or to invest toward increasing their capacity for self-development, thereby in effect becoming cycled into a financial depository whose function becomes that of simply hoarding more profits, inflating them indefinitely, and causing a major risk to the financial structure, then such an accumulation of wealth stands to harm (even though indirectly) the wants-space of others. In so delimiting their (want-space) freedom, such an accumulation would constitute an infraction of the overlapping principle around which a consensual wants-space constitutes a basis for the best order of human arrangements. Therefore, besides taxation as a means to prevent direct harm, an intervention should be made to prevent the indirect harm resulting from hoarding—one that can be done through recycling excess wealth back into the system (or into other systems, that is, into less-endowed economies, in implementation of a universal understanding of the consensual principle).

Justice, then, could be defined in terms of the enactment of the two principles (the overlapping ensuring positive help, and the difference ensuring prevention of harm), schematically ordered, with the one being the basis for the other.

Having drawn on economic and also political issues to explain the principles on which a definition of Justice is proposed, it is important to briefly address the question of when there are conflicts between two political systems, as in the Palestine-Israel example: in such a case, there is no consensual order to begin with. Classically, two approaches have been proposed to address such cases, trade and political agreement: trade (normalization) yields peace and order to what might have seemed like politically insolvable problems, and it is only by prior political agreement that trade can play a positive role. While examples from history could be brought forth to support either approach, it could be inferred from the line of argument so far (about reciprocity and compassion) that, in the view of this writer, without the two parties in conflict having effected a transformation in themselves (even via trade) such that each can look upon the other in terms of the overlapping principle, no lasting peace (as the best order of human arrangements) can be obtained between them.

Reversing Rawls

I have so far in the discussion "reduced" Ibn Khaldun's "*asabiyyah*" as a compassion instinct to the same level as that of egotism. But it can, arguably, be a more primary instinct. Thus, assuming such a (dual) model to be coherent, is it likely to be viewed as such or to win consensus (as a model) by rational individuals, *thinking from an original position*? This question is meant to address the cogent argument constructed by Rawls, in which reasonable but ego-centered interlocutors attempt to define the best arrangement between them. Rawls's choice of taking the individual (instead of a nebulous collective—as the communitarian might wish) as a "building-block" in his thought-experiment makes eminent sense: it is the individual after all who is the natural *primary substance*—to use a classical expression. However, what Rawls then assumes is that the individual's primary instinct is of a purely egotistic kind, defining a self-centered wants-space. Since, however, the individual is endowed with a reasoning capacity, it becomes necessary to negotiate the limits of this space with others. Simply put, he needs to reason with others in order to get what he wants for himself. The process guarantees a distribution of basic common goods, the possession of which by one is commensurate with their possession by each of the others. Built upon this, as a second phase or step, is the attempt to justify fair wealth differentials between them (the controversial part of Rawls's theory). But let us assume that what we begin with, instead, is an interlocutor whose nature is dual, that is, for whom self-love and other-love are equally potent impulses determining thought and behavior. In this case, Reason will not for him be divorced from Sentiment, as he is already disposed to take others (even potential loved ones), one way or another, into account, even before "negotiations" begin (Ibn Khaldun's fear presupposes bond, rather than causing it).

We assume a sudden intervention by God who tells us He wishes to transform the distribution of wealth and resources throughout the world, giving each of us a chance to participate in a polling process where we can state our chosen wishing lists (wants). He tells us that there will be an unlimited number of rounds in each of which we can choose only one item on our wishing lists. The item that gets the largest number of votes in any one round will be dispensed to all those who chose it—*if* it can be so distributed. All the existing resources and wealth, for example, *as one item*, cannot be so distributed among all. On the other hand, "being dispensed to all who chose it" clearly does not imply equal dispensation of that item (that item, e.g., the world's gold, can be distributed differentially among all who chose it). The votes will be cast in secret ballots, each individual mentally transmitting to God her preferred choice. Negotiations between individuals are permissible, but not required.

God's "intervention" immediately places each of us in a situation where, though able to reason singly for ourselves about what we really value, we need just as importantly to work out what all the others value. In addition, we need to work out, if we can, what order of priority these items have in people's minds (so that we can guess correctly which item to vote for in each round). Bearing in mind that only the item that gets the largest number of votes in any one round will be dispensed, a rational voter would need to set her priorities right: for a woman, choosing that Z, the man of her dreams, should become her spouse would have no chance of winning even after a billion rounds. Choosing "the man of my dreams" may become a viable winner, but only after a few million rounds (the more the commonly valued items are done away with, the more the chances that particularized items may finally be reached and dealt with). Some choices, such as "that I be wealthy" may certainly seem compelling and can be calculated to have a reasonable chance of success—if only in relative terms. However, one has to be sure of its order of priority among people's wants—whether it would be selected in the first round, or in some later round. Other *wants* may be subjected to a similar kind of reasoning (the want for life is already assured by God, who based his offer on the continued existence of living individuals). Indeed, going through Rawls's list of (ego-centered) "primary goods," our interlocutor would feel that although all of these are important and have a reasonable chance of success in one round or another, what everyone will first go for is what one thinks everyone else will first go for. Indeed, this reasoning will have to apply in most of the first rounds. In other words, though seeking to identify an item of highest priority for herself, our interlocutor will find she is compelled to identify—for the purpose of choosing an item that will win—one that she thinks is of the highest priority to everyone else.

We have assumed here that our interlocutor is primarily egotistic. However, given the unique opportunity God has given her, she might well think first of her loved ones rather than of herself. Her turn, she thinks, will surely come—given the open-ended rounds before her. Simply voting for the item "that *my* loved ones fare well in the new world" would not guarantee for *them* the wellness she wishes—even after some billions of rounds. Generalizing this to the item that "all loved ones should fare well" seems possible, but she cannot be sure that the majority of voters will go for it: can she be sure that they all, really, are as altruistic as she is? Besides, even if they were, they might easily come up with different formulations of wishing well for their loved ones.

Faced with all these calculations, our interlocutor will conclude that there is only one condition to be satisfied for a *first* item to be chosen above all else, however the voting proceeds afterward: that the item be so general—indeed, of the form of a rule rather than a specific "good"—that it will guarantee that neither her loved ones (nor she) would lose out on it, or on anything that might happen in the following rounds. She will figure out that even individuals who are primarily egotistically driven but who are thinking rationally would go for it: they are compelled to think of what the others want in order to identify an item to vote for first. They, too, then, will be driven by the same reasoning to identify a rule rather than a particular good, one that will guarantee that they will not be left out of anything others want for themselves. The condition, then, in both cases is the same. It can only be satisfied by the following choice: that I be on a par with everyone else, whatever is being parsed out.

Equality was earlier defined as a function of wants, rather than one between them. "Other-centered" wants were situated alongside "self-centered" wants, allowing us to delineate a consensual space of goods "reifying" the indispensable foundations for Justice. Here, again, it is "other-centered" dispositions and/or calculations that assume priority over—even for the sake of realizing—egotistical or "self-centered" wants. The rationalization of the choices in the manner expressed in the experiment reflects the psychological forces at work in human nature, namely, egotism and altruism. It may be objected that "the want for equality"—which is what equality in this light boils down to—is the opposite of altruism, it being essentially *purposive,* or an egotistic instinct. Likewise, the sentiments of love, compassion, mercifulness, comradeship, kindness, generosity, beneficence, friendship, and countless others belonging to the "same family" are often argued to be self-serving. In practical terms, this is a zero-sum distinction—the acts and behaviors reflecting those sentiments and feelings belonging to two classes that are objectively distinguishable. Indeed, it makes more sense to assume that the same person is instinctively impelled in one direction at any one point or in the other, than to assume that there are two mutually exclusive *kinds* of instincts. However, even were we to insist that they are of a kind, we could still view them as a *single account*: we can imagine the one instinct being "superpositioned" over the other, acting in parallel, or in alternation, much in the same way that, in quantum physics, we are told, qubits (i.e., quantum rather than the binary digital bits of 0 and 1) are found sometimes to be one and sometimes the other (setting scientists off on a trail to find how this phenomenon can be exploited for a better control of nature).

The above experiment, in effect, turns the Rawlsean structure for fairness upside down: the so-called "primary goods" are pushed back, while the subject of differential distribution is pushed upfront. We are required to think of what works for us living together before we begin to determine what works out for each of us living apart. A theory of fairness would then have to be based on starting out with a primal altruistic impulse that becomes self-regulated through a rationalization procedure in much the same way—but in the opposite direction—it was argued that the egotistic impulse is rationalized through self-regulation. I must accept what constitutes an acceptable living condition for others before I end up determining what constitutes an acceptable living condition for myself. Being a general principle, I would not see this as one that is applicable only to my own community, group, or state. To assume "each state to its own" is to assume that my structure for fairness is an expanded version of the *I* so as to cover a preferred *We*. In this converse perspective, on the other hand, only if I found it unacceptable for a child anywhere to die of starvation would it make sense for me to find it (morally) unacceptable for my own child to die of starvation. Only if I found the occupation of one people's land by another unacceptable would it make sense for me to claim that I find the Israeli occupation of Palestine (morally) unacceptable—that is, to constitute an injustice. Otherwise, my claims would have nothing to do with fairness, let alone Justice. They would simply be ego-centered claims, justifying the killing of an Israeli by a Palestinian, but not that of a Palestinian by an Israeli. A theory of Justice, to be one, has to be predicated on our common roots as human beings rather than on belonging to one tribe or another.

Love beyond borders

A major debate in the current literature is that which concerns particularism and universalism: whether a theory of Justice can only be limited by virtue of objective conditions to specific political structures—however, many of these we can imagine—or whether it can be reasonably formulated as to apply indiscriminately to humankind. In the above account, the argument was made in favor of universalism—that the theory has to be "pegged" to our understanding of ourselves as members of a human community. But both the Rawlsean and Khaldunian accounts are "particularist"—each defining specific perimeters for its envisaged political communities. In Rawls, the perimeters are those liberal democratic values held by modern western societies. Once established, they are commensurate with the "reasonable" articulation of the best order of human arrangements. In Ibn Khaldun, these have to do with what we might call "political economy" factors—what holds the political community together for a particular phase, after which it begins to disintegrate. One of the major factors determining its disintegration is the financial burden exacted from its members as taxation becomes excessive, its benefits beginning to serve the opulent lifestyles of the ruling class (rather than the welfare of the community), as well as to serve the increasingly militarized bases for that class's political authority. The "glue" holding the community together at the foundations—care and affection between its members—and which becomes institutionalized in a political authority, ceases to be properly represented by that authority, heralding its downfall. So, whether the beacon is that of Ibn Khaldun's prognosis of the cyclical life of authority, or that of its value-centered perimeter as prescribed by Rawls, the end-view we have is that of the "best order of human arrangements" being confined to borders of one kind or another.

Nothing in the two accounts prevents us from imagining a state of affairs in the world where such "best orders" can coexist contiguously with one another—even for a limited amount of time (to account for Ibn Khaldun's cyclical view). Theoretically, in other words, both accounts could be proposed as being universally applicable, in a discrete rather than continuous fashion. What remains a major distinguishing mark between the two accounts is that while Rawls's account—being pegged to values—seems to be culture-specific, Ibn Khaldun's account, though pegged to a cyclical view of history, seems a more basic human instinct that by nature permeates all such borders. It seems, therefore, to be a more likely candidate as a universal principle. If social mores and moral values may be different across societies, a basic emotion like love (in many of its manifestations) is constant. Wherever we may look (at whatever society or even animal group), it is this instinct that is the glue that underlies cohesion in groups. In *this* sense, it is, in effect, a universal principle. But the question is also raised—typically as a challenge for the role proposed for it—whether it is or can be conceived as a universal principle in another sense, or as a *single substance*, much like water or air, permeating humankind, or even the universe. Surely, it is argued, love is paradigmatically "object-particularized." On this basis, we cannot consider it an underlying principle for what holds everything together (A culture-based theory would not presume to have that reach in the first place).

These two ostensibly inconsistent *meanings* of love—love *for* mankind and love *of* another—are articulated and an approach for reconciling them for the practical purpose of social reform, or human development, has been proposed in a recent paper addressing contemporary feminist care-ethics and Indian philosophy.[11] Care-ethics is paradigmatically an ethics predicated on the particularized love mothers have for their children. An "Indian" ethic—presented in this case through the nineteenth-century anticolonial Hindu monk Vivekananda—is one that invokes *identity* and *difference*—a unity of existents underlying a manifold exterior. While not undermining the value each of these two ethics contributes to human reform, seeing them as exclusive of one another detracts from seeing the overall extensive power love has as an agent for that reform, an argument that is sensibly made.

However, the question still hangs whether any sense could be made of the "single substance" thesis—whether it is the same "substance" wherever it is found, and in whatever form. While seemingly entangled in Vivekananda's, as referred to above (and, as we shall presently see, *sufi*), concept of Monism, it is surely defensible independently of those traditions. As a basic instinct, it is as "single" as water is. The two sentences "Water gives life" and "Love provides order" are generically alike. Even self-love, as argued by H. Frankfurt, can be considered the purest form of love—purer, that is, in meaning what it does, than other-love. Also, love, like water or air, can be quantified: purer, less pure, more of, less of, particularized here, there, and so on—allowing one to imagine the different grades or degrees it is manifested in, whether in us for others, or among them (love, care, empathy, affection, sympathy, compassion, solidarity, kindness, concern, love of a person, love for humanity, etc.). While Ibn Khaldun defined an imagined line as a limit for its extension (those whom, though unrelated by blood to us, we can still identify with as members of our group), we can surely stretch this imagined line in our present day and age so as to cover humankind. Given, especially, the cognitive immediacy of world events today, we can and do *sympathize* with individuals and groups with whom we are never likely to form a single polity (and even with imaginary figures in plays, novels, movies, or operas).

The corollary (but arguably independent) and more controversial thesis in this context is that of the unicity of existents—the basic thesis here being that this *sui generis* love of which we all partake in different degrees (a love by all for, or of, all) is integrally bound up with the underlying fact that "the all" is in reality One, God being (in *sufi* versions) this One. Admittedly, this is a challenging thesis, and one that is difficult to articulate or to defend. A famous Muslim *sufi* called al-Hallaj (ninth–tenth century) was incarcerated for eleven years in Baghdad to make him renounce his declaration that he was one with God, and when he kept refusing to do so, the authorities took him to the scaffold to be hanged and beheaded, with his limbs cut and burned. If he wished to make a pilgrimage to God, he took to declaring, he did not have to go to Mecca, but could do it by looking deep into his own heart.

Love, as in selfless adoration of God, and in the burning desire to realize oneness with Him, is a theme that pervades *sufi* literature and poetry. But oneness with Him is also oneness with the other, so that self-love and other-love end up conflating into one, as the *sufi* master Ibn Arabi took to proclaiming.[12] For him love was immanent. *Sufi* "altruistic" practice (devoted to helping others in need) is understood as helping "oneself" (in the wider human sense). Our earlier distinction between Self and Other collapses: we need no longer define a space for ourselves before we can think of what space we are prepared to allow for others. So selfless and "otherful" do we become that suffering and death no longer matter. According to legend, al-Hallaj welcomed his own beheading with a smile on his face, declaring to his friends that the real *he* was elsewhere and everywhere.

As stated, love and oneness typically go together in the *sufi* tradition. Just as love is a single substance like air, so is that substance of Self, which underlies different physical forms. This Self is diffused but also layered, allowing us to experience different degrees of self-consciousness, and deluding us—in early stages—into believing in our uniqueness and underlying difference from others. Cognizing oneself *as* that Self is the labor of real love. The labor is that of devoting oneself to helping others and caring for them.

While one may not be fully persuaded by the full reach of the ideas just sketched, the two underlying themes of love and equal human worth are hard to ignore, providing us, as they do, with a far more plausible hypothesis than others for understanding what Justice really means: that human beings have the same worth, undifferentiated by contingencies, and that it is love that moves human beings to coalesce together, and on which, therefore, Reason has to build. Understanding this allows us (as we slowly begin to identify ourselves with the ever-widening human circles) to transcend contingent borders, and to identify with human beings with whom we do not share contingent identities. The rational imperative to do so is all too glaring, especially as we witness the bloody clashes of contingent identities in our long history, and as people incline to do injustices to one another simply on account of their belief that they have more worth just for being themselves. (This, however, should not dishearten us if we recall Gandhi's observation that—considered historically—people do far more good to each other than they do harm).

Aiming for a final cause

In his *Republic,* Plato at one point defended his Forms (importantly, Justice) by arguing that even if the ideal state cannot be achieved, its cognition can still inform us of what it is we should be seeking to bring about. In the beginning of this chapter, a distinction was made between a concept and the different meanings in which that concept is understood. Justice, it was proposed, is such a concept. The different attempts at articulating an acceptable meaning for it could be understood as seeking to disambiguate it, or to clear it of other closely related family concepts, which are also in need of disambiguation. The tendency seems misguided to brush that attempt off as a futile exercise in a world of different cultures, where Justice, Freedom, or Equality can be understood differently in each, and where, therefore, it is more "politically correct" or "liberally becoming" to view the discrimination against women or minorities, or authoritarian policies and even corruption of officials in foreign Governments as matters that are "cultural" and should therefore be recognized and dealt with as such. It is similarly misguided, in the opinion of this writer, to think it morally tolerable if economic development in one country is objectively being detrimental to the potential development of another—as when mineral resources in one country are excavated via special deals with its rulers to help develop another country, at the obvious cost of enablement of the source country. It is especially disquieting when one learns that a large sector of the population in the country in question lives under the poverty line: the principle of "cultural/moral" relativism' here "begs out." Whether it is culture-specific or religious beliefs, or the state of political development in any one country that supports infractions of Justice in any respect, human beings are a single species, their individual instincts for wants and compassion being the same, and they are as alike in their other physical constitutions. Keeping them in harmony for a healthy human condition should not seem to us to be different from maintaining good health in other respects. And if, in human history, *voodoo* magic was used instead of antibiotics to treat a bacterial infection, this should not call for more than the recognition that medical treatment has evolved over time, for the better. Likewise, whether in "Eastern" or "Western" cultures or political systems, the elements of a healthy "moral" human condition seem to be gradually evolving across cultures, although advances in this field may not at times be as dramatic as those in science. While we have not reached a universal application of that harmony principle yet, this need not discourage us from being guided by its beacon toward a better world.

Notes

1 John Rawls, *A Theory of Justice* (Cambridge, MA: Harvard University Press, 1971/1999). Rawls is rightly credited with having brought new life to a classic contractarian argument in current political theory debates, making his contribution in this field (from this work and others that followed on how to account for Justice in the context of other countries with different cultures and values) indispensable in those debates.

2 While altruism literature and that on the "prosociality instinct" in different cultures is abundant, it is worth noting the contemporary anthropological studies undertaken by Hinde. See Robert A. Hinde, *Individuals, Relationships and Culture* (Cambridge: Cambridge University Press, 1987). In this work, and others that followed, on communal and individual identity formations, the interaction between the individual and associative selves is highlighted. See, also, references to this kind of literature in an earlier paper of mine "Personal and National Identity: A Tale of Two Wills," in *Philosophical Perspectives on the Israeli-Palestinian Conflict*, ed. Tomas Kapitan (Armonk, NY and London: Sharpe, 1997). The reader will find, in the context of the discussion of the interplay between an egotistic and an associative identity, a complementary treatment of the subject in this chapter.

3 See Ibn Khaldun's *Muqaddimah* Bk.1, Ch. 2. Sec.8. F. Rosenthal's English translation can be accessed on the web asadullahali.files.wordpress.com/2012/10/ibn_khaldun-al_muqaddimah.pdf.

4 One of the conditions Harry Frankfurt lists for pure love of the other, see Harry Frankfurt, *The Reasons of Love* (Princeton and Oxford: Princeton, University Press, 2004), is the absence of self-interest and having the interest of the loved one as one's object.

5 Thomas Piketty, *Capital in the Twenty-First Century* (Cambridge, MA: Belknap Press, 2014).

6 See, for example, the report in the June 20, 2011 issue of *The Chronicle of Higher Education* on the debate over Patricia Churchland's claim reducing moral behavior to biological terms, citing specific neurochemicals as what determine instinctual bonds such as those between a mother and her child. In her book, *Braintrust: What Neuroscience Tells Us About Morality* (Princeton: Princeton University Press, 2011), she tries to show how these neurochemicals act as the platform for general altruistic behavior. In this respect, it is worth noting the growing appreciation in the related literature of the effect of the neurochemical *oxytocin*.

7 Oren Harman, *The Price Of Altruism: George Price and the Search for the Origins of Kindness* (London: The Bodley Head, 2010).

8 Arindam Chakrabarti, "A Critique of Pure Revenge," in *Passion, Death and Spirituality: The Philosophy of Robert C. Solomon*, ed. Kathleen Higgins and David Sherman (Dordrecht: Springer, 2012), pp. 37–53; see also Robert C. Solomon, "Chakrabarti's 'A Critique of Pure Revenge': A Response," in *Passion, Death and Spirituality, The Philosophy of Robert C. Solomon*, ed. K. Higgins and D. Sherman (Dordrecht: Springer), pp. 55–65.

9 I am grateful here to Ralph Weber who pointed out to me that the Confucian Mencius had declared that whoever would not feel the urge to rescue a baby from falling into a well was not human/e. Here the claim would be that the primal instinct of other-love and other-care, while initially applied to one's own child, "naturally" comes to apply to others. The question of the profusion of this sentiment—whether it has a universal

human reach or only a graded one—has apparently also been the subject of debate between Confucians and Mohists in that tradition.

10 Piketty, *Capital in the Twenty-First Century.*

11 Vrinda Dalmiya, "The Metaphysics of Ethical Love: Comparing Practical Vedanta and Feminist Ethics," *Sophia* 48 (2009), pp. 221–35.

12 In one of his poems in *Diwan,* he declares how, as dawn broke following a night of love-making with his bride, he awoke to find no one there but himself—as though it was himself he had been making love to. This theme—the ephemeral life of selves as they appear and disappear in different objects—reflects an underlying unity between them, revealed through love.

References

Chakrabarti, A. (2012), "A Critique of Pure Revenge," in Kathleen Higgins and David Sherman (eds), *Passion, Death and Spirituality: The Philosophy of Robert C. Solomon*, Dordrecht: Springer, pp. 37–53.

Churchland, P. (2011), *Braintrust: What Neuroscience Tells Us About Morality*, Princeton: Princeton University Press.

Dalmiya, V. (2009), "The Metaphysics of Ethical Love: Comparing Practical Vedanta and Feminist Ethics," *Sophia*, 48, pp. 221–35.

Frankfurt, H. (2004), *The Reasons of Love*, Princeton and Oxford: Princeton University Press.

Harman, O. (2010), *The Price Of Altruism: George Price and the Search for the Origins of Kindness*, London: The Bodley Head.

Hinde, R. A. (1987), *Individuals, Relationships and Culture*, Cambridge: Cambridge University Press.

Ibn Khaldun, *Muqaddimah*, www.asadullahali.files.wordpress.com/2012/10/ibn_khaldun-al_muqaddimah.pdf (accessed April 2, 2015).

Nusseibeh, S. (1997), "Personal and National Identity: A Tale of Two Wills," in Tomas Kapitan (ed.), *Philosophical Perspectives on the Israeli-Palestinian Conflict*, Armonk, NY and London: Sharpe.

Piketty, T. (2014), *Capital in the Twenty-First Century*, Cambridge, MA: Belknap Press.

Rawls, J. (1971/1999), *A Theory of Justice*, Cambridge, MA: Harvard University Press.

Solomon, R. C. (2012), "Chakrabarti's 'A Critique of Pure Revenge': A Response," in K. Higgins and D. Sherman (eds), *Passion, Death and Spirituality, The Philosophy of Robert C. Solomon*, Dordrecht: Springer, pp. 55–65.

9

Justice and Social Change

Sor-hoon Tan

Introduction: On comparisons

Compared to the vast literature on justice from Western philosophical perspectives, or comparative studies on virtue ethics or democracy, for example, there are as yet relatively few works on the topic of justice in comparative philosophy or Chinese philosophy. Among recent attempts is Ruiping Fan's use of the Rawlsian framework to "bring to light the intellectual legacy of Confucian views of justice in modern Western terms."[1] Based on the Confucian disagreements with elements in Rawls's theory, Fan argues that Rawls's political liberal conception of justice is inappropriate, even bound to fail, in East Asian societies "in which Confucianism is accepted as a major doctrine of social justice." Fan's faith in the endurance of Confucian moral teachings in the life of ordinary people in East Asia notwithstanding, there is no consensus even among East Asians themselves regarding how much of Confucian traditions have survived in their various societies, whether they should be preserved or revived, and in which forms. Not only is the "acceptance" of Confucianism less than unanimous, perhaps even insignificant in some cases, from a philosophical perspective, but treating Confucianism as a "doctrine of social justice" may also be too hasty and procrustean.

Yang Xiao takes seriously the worry that even to speak of "the concept of justice in Confucian ethics" is to do Confucianism an injustice by imposing an alien category that would distort its teachings. To do justice to the topic, Xiao begins with the question of what it is like to have a concept of justice, and argues that Confucianism has a concept of justice since the term "*yi*" (義) in early Confucian texts sometimes behaves like "just" in the sense of "treat like cases alike and treat different cases differently."[2] This meaning of justice, already present in Aristotle's understanding of "*dikaiosúné*," focuses on its formal or procedural dimension rather than its substantive meaning in social justice or distributive justice, although formal principles are relevant to the latter. For example, Aristotle's distributive principle of "proportional" equity implies treating like cases alike and different cases differently (1131a29–b16).[3] A comparison with Aristotle is tempting given the already existing comparisons between Ancient Greek and Ancient Chinese civilizations and interpretations of Confucian ethics as a form of virtue ethics. One could probably find evidence that, in its most general use such as Mencius' explication of the idea as "the human path" (6A11), "*yi*" sometimes behaves like "*dikaiosúnē*" in Aristotle's sense of "actual exercise of complete excellence" (1129b31); furthermore, the "meritocracy" that Confucian rule by the virtuous has been equated with (by Daniel Bell and Joseph Chan among others) resonates strongly with Aristotle's claim that "what is just in distribution must be according to merit in some sense" (1131a25).[4] But what would be the point of such a comparison, or any other comparison?

If one believes that a comparison should help one understand Confucianism (better), it might be argued that one would do better to choose for comparison a contemporary theory from one's familiar cultural context. However, if the contexts are too different, the comparison runs the serious risk of distorting what one is trying to understand by assimilating it to what is familiar to oneself. In that case, for a reader situated within the Western or Westernized modern context, Ancient Greek thought provides a context more familiar (because of its historical connection with the modern West) than Confucianism, but also less different from Confucianism (both being premodern) than contemporary Western philosophy, and, therefore, it reduces the risk of distortion in comparison. As a parallel to this, one could argue that some kind of contemporary Chinese philosophy, being contemporary to the modern West, could serve just as well for "reducing the distance," if it also has historical connection (which is debatable) to early Confucianism. In either case, one should not take for granted that contemporaneity or cultural continuity (especially under an over-broad description such as "Western") implies a greater similarity relevant to understanding. Beyond understanding better an alien culture or philosophy, one might be interested in cross-cultural philosophizing for the greater wealth of resources for solving problems that humans confront today. Looking around at the increasing disparities of income and wealth within and across national boundaries, in the wake of an international financial crisis in which those who have benefited the least from its causes seem to be suffering the worst of its effects, there is every reason to be interested in the question of justice, in asking what each member of a group (or of the whole species) owes to other members and to the group, and what the group owes to each member. It is an interest not simply in arriving at the best theory from an academic point of view, but in philosophical discussions that could go beyond interpreting the world to changing it for the better. In that case, it does not matter how far apart in distance and time the various cultures and traditions we include in our exploration are; instead, we should be more concerned about whether a comparative approach, and which one, is more likely to produce theories or views with greater pragmatic value in improving the status quo, even if philosophers continue to leave changing the world to others. The next two sections attempt to reconstruct a Confucian conception of social justice through a comparison of Confucian ethical ideas and views with Anglo-European theories of justice. This exercise will provide a study of how comparative purpose and strategy, as much as hermeneutic faithfulness, guide theorizing. The conclusion will explore the relation between the theoretical and interpretive choices made through comparison and the pragmatic potential of the comparative philosophical outcome.

To have or not to have . . .

I wish to return to Xiao's discussion of *yi* as a Confucian concept of justice, both because it is an excellent and thought-provoking essay, and because the choice of *yi* as part of the modern translation of "justice" as "*zheng-yi*" (正義) implies a perceived similarity between *yi* and justice. Huang Yushun (黄玉顺), a prominent Confucian scholar in China, also maintains that there is "correspondence" between "*yi*" in the early Confucian texts and "justice" in that one could understand the issues discussed with the use of *yi* in terms of modern concerns of justice, although the two are not always exactly the same in meaning. For Huang, *yi* includes "principles of justice" for constructing, judging, and reforming institutions and social norms, especially with regard to their function in regulating and resolving conflicts of interests.[5] According to Xiao, instead of universal application of rules or principles of justice, the practice of *yi* in the *Analects* and the *Mencius* does justice to the particular in treating alike cases that belong to the same kind and cases that belong to different kinds differently. Different understandings of which cases are alike, and how different kinds of cases should be treated, yield different conceptions under this concept of justice, which "can apply to actions, persons, etc. and not just to the basic structure of society." Xiao's discussion focuses on a group of uses of *yi* pertaining to having, taking and accepting things, which arguably are situations with distributive dimensions. However, a closer scrutiny of these cases reveals that it is not the distributive question that drives Mencius' discussions of whether it is *yi* to have, take, or accept things. There is no concern about whether those involved receive or deserve equal shares, or arguments over whether someone should have more or less of something, or something proportional to some kind of merit. Instead, the concern is overwhelmingly about the effect of actions on specific interpersonal relationships, actual or potential.[6]

A famous passage in the *Mencius* argues that *yi* is more valuable than life with the following example.

> Here is a basketful of rice and a bowlful of soup. Getting them will mean life; not getting them will mean death. When these are given with abuse, even a wayfarer would not accept them; when these are given after being trampled upon, even a beggar would not accept them. (*Mencius* 6A10)

Its concern is not distribution of benefits or burdens. Accepting food thus given is to allow others to treat one as little better, or perhaps even worse than animals, and no self-respecting person, certainly no exemplary person, should enter into such a relationship, which is totally inappropriate between persons. To have no scruple about how one takes or accepts things from others leads one into relationships that shame not just the person who ignores the standards of appropriate relations, but also those related to them, as we see in another story about a man from Qi, whose wife and concubine were shamed by his way of obtaining food and drink—begging for leftovers from sacrifices to the dead—a practice that rendered him an outcast. Instead of feasting in the company of "men of wealth and consequence," as he lied to his wife, in reality "not a single person in the city stopped to talk to him." (4B33)

Regardless of the value of the things involved, Confucian exemplary persons always consider whether having, taking, or accepting them would be in accordance with the rites, and thereby promote appropriate relations between themselves and others. Mencius' (2B3) explanation of his different responses to offers of gifts suggests that the criterion is whether a gift initiates or invokes an ethically appropriate relationship between the giver and the recipient. The same consideration applies to other transactions, such as economic support of rulers for visitors (5B6). Relational justifications are available for wages for employment with clear responsibilities and charity in specific circumstances, the absence of appropriate relational justifications in accepting things from the politically powerful and wealthy would place a recipient in the dubious position of "being bought" for unspecified purposes. The concern with relational appropriateness continues through discussions about the circumstances under which one should or should not "seek audience with the feudal lords" (3B7; 5B7), or answer summons from the politically powerful, and other issues of "social intercourse" including whether it should matter to a recipient that the source of a gift or financial support might not be ethical (3B10; 5B4).

Mencius explains the saying "too insistent a refusal constitutes a lack of respect" to mean that a gift is acceptable as long as "the superior makes friends with one in the correct way and treats one with due ceremony [*li* 禮]," regardless of whether the latter had come by the gift through means that are ethically appropriate (5B4).

> [Wan Zhang asks,] "Now the way feudal lords take from the people is no different from robbery. If a gentleman accepts gifts from them so long as the rites proper to social intercourse are duly observed, what is the justification?" [Mencius replies,] "Do you think that if a true King should arise would he line up all the feudal lords and punish them? Or do you think he would try reforming them first before resorting to punishment? (5B4)

If Mencius' point is that abandoning the appropriate relations with someone because he or she has wronged (that is, ignored the appropriate relationship with) a third party will not rectify the wrong, but, instead will add to it by increasing inappropriate relationships in the world, then the same must be applied to the case of the robber, unless there are grounds to claim that appropriate relationships with the latter, unlike with the feudal lords, is impossible even if they all observe "the rites proper to social intercourse." If Mencius implicitly assumes that reforming the feudal lords would bring more benefits for all than rejecting their friendship or punishing them, then explanation is needed as to why the same rationale does not apply to the robbers.

Without denying Wan Zhang's charge against the feudal lords, comparing them to a robber whom Mencius admitted one can "punish without first attempting to reform," Mencius' dismissal of the concern about the justification for accepting the feudal lords' gifts made possible by ill-gotten gains seems too hasty. If an exemplary person considers the relationship between himself and the people, then should he not, based on that, reject gifts from those whose wealth derives from treating the people unjustly? One might defend Mencius on the grounds that the relationship with the people is somewhat abstract because of the lack of actual social intercourse with specific individuals who were "wronged" by the feudal lords, compared to those with whom one already has established a relationship by appropriate social intercourse, which was the subject of the discussion. However, this defense would not avoid the comparison with the robber who "makes friends with one in the correct way and treats one with due ceremony." Moreover, it exposes serious limitations of too narrow a focus on actual particular relationships.

A better defense, not offered by Mencius, would be to "transfer" at least some or all of the gifts from such a source to those toward whom the giver has acted without *yi* in obtaining the wealth that made possible the gifts. This would give consideration to the appropriate relationship between the exemplary person and the people without undermining the appropriate relationship with the superior who has treated one ethically even if he has treated the people unethically. Moreover, it would rectify to some extent the social injustice of the situation. It is striking that Mencius who has been credited with founding the tradition of "government for the people" and advocated "benevolent government" should seem so unmoved by the patent injustice of this example of governments profiting wrongfully at the expense of the people. Other than inconsistency, perhaps arising from his eagerness to win arguments, it may be that he did not approach Wan Zhang's example as being about social justice.

A strong case can be made for understanding *yi* in the *Mencius* as norms of relational appropriateness rather than eliciting a theory of justice from the discussions of *yi* in that text. The term sometimes acts like the term "justice" only because issues of distributing burdens and benefits are relevant to human relationships, but these issues and possible solutions appear different when viewed from the perspective of a relational ethics that is more concerned with "how should we relate to one another?" instead of "who should get what and how much?" which is at the center of contemporary theories of justice. One perspective emphasizes our connectedness despite our separateness; the other highlights our separateness despite our connectedness.[7] Rather than subsuming *yi* in the focus on justice in contemporary ethical discourse, a comparison in which differences in dealing with what initially appear to be similar (distribution) problems suggest looking beyond justice *qua* distribution problems is illuminating and opens up different possibilities in dealing with the troubles of contemporary life. Confucian relational ethics would prefer to look beyond the question of justice in terms of the best distribution arrangement, but if we must reconstruct a Confucian conception of justice, at least for the time being, then we need to consider more than the concept of *yi*, as well as bear in mind that any Confucian conception of justice would be determined by the relational ethics rather than social relations being determined by a distributive justice-centered ethics. The next section will argue for a Confucian conception of justice based on meeting human needs in order for all to live the ethical lives envisioned in Confucian relational ethics.

Reconstructing confucian justice: From sufficiency to needs

Joseph Chan has reconstructed a Confucian perspective on social justice for contemporary discourse by asking a different question about the circumstances that give rise to the concerns of social justice. He argues that pre-Qin Chinese societies share with other societies characteristics that, according to contemporary theorists, give rise to circumstances of social justice; he then goes on to examine how Mencius and Xunzi responded to typical social justice "issues such as poverty, differentiation of social roles and functions, inequality of income and status, and the distributive role of government."[8] Chan's reconstructed Confucian perspective on social justice consists of the principles of sufficiency for all, priority for the badly off, and distribution of offices and emoluments according to merit and contribution. I shall argue that, rather than being viewed as three disparate principles, they can be integrated by modern Confucians into a needs-based conception of justice. Some might notice similarities between the principle of "priority to the badly off" and Rawls's difference principle, allowing for unequal distributions when such inequality benefits the worst off. However, the early Confucian worldview does not fit well with Rawls's egalitarian assumption that human beings are free and equal persons so that equality is a moral ideal, and unequal distributions are exceptions requiring justifications. Eschewing any comparison with Rawls, Chan points out that his reconstructed Confucian perspective closely resembles the "doctrine of sufficiency" developed recently by theorists challenging egalitarian theories of justice.[9]

Mencius would certainly agree with Harry Frankfurt that what matters morally is not how much you have—for example, as much as everyone else—but what you can do with whatever you have, whether it is enough for what is "fundamentally significant."[10] However, describing both their views as "doctrines of sufficiency" masks important differences in what they take to be fundamentally significant, and therefore their answers to "enough for what?" For Frankfurt, targeting mostly utilitarian calculus in contemporary economic egalitarianism, but retaining the vocabulary, "enough" means meeting a threshold standard whereby more money will not make one significantly less unhappy, or where the difficulties that account for one's unhappiness would not be alleviated by having more money.[11] In contrast, utilitarian happiness matters little to Mencius, for whom what is fundamentally significant is personal cultivation and living an ethical life as understood by the Confucians. If happiness matters at all, it is not as subjective contentment or satisfaction of desires, but takes the form of the "joy of Confucius and Yanhui" in the midst of great poverty.[12] Instead of the utilitarian aim of satisfying desires, Mencius considers too many desires an obstacle to personal cultivation (7B35). Liberal individualism, in contrast, sees human beings as creatures of desires and the unlimited increase of desires as both inevitable and good.[13] Classical liberalism, unlike the ethical liberalism of Mill, Green, and Hobhouse, does not discriminate between good and bad desires.[14] The distinction between desires that motivate ethical action and those that do not is critical for Mencius. Describing Mencius' views about distribution in terms of sufficiency is therefore not very illuminating, and may even be misleading if one thinks in terms of sufficient means to satisfy desires, whatever they may be.

William Meyer suggests, "To the extent that wants become the subject of judgment, evaluation, and purposeful change, we can begin to speak of needs."[15] Asking the critical question of "enough for what?" in the case of Confucius and Mencius directs one's attention to needs—what is enough to meet the needs of a Confucian ethical life.[16] A doctrine of need better fits Confucian views on social distribution. It encompasses the priority the early Confucians gave to the badly off, those who are not able to meet their own survival needs and lack family members who could help them.

> Old men without wives, old women without husbands, old people without children, young children without fathers—these four types of people are the most destitute and have no one to turn to for help. Whenever King Wen put benevolent measures into effect, he always gave them first consideration. (*Mencius* 1B5)

Xunzi also emphasizes first taking care of those with physical defects, so that "the deaf, blind, lame and halt, those who have been mutilated, and those who are stunted and dwarfed," "should be given official duties commensurate with their abilities and employment adequate to feed and clothe themselves so that all are included and not even one of them is overlooked."[17]

Mencius' benevolent government is one that strives first to ensure "that people always have sufficient food in good years and escape starvation in bad; only then does he drive them towards goodness" (1A7). A good government provides people with the means to meet survival needs and, beyond that, to cultivate themselves and live ethical lives embedded in appropriate interpersonal relationships.

Chan has described Confucianism as favoring "meritocracy" based on the third principle of Confucian social justice he identifies: the distribution of offices and emoluments (remuneration) according to merit and contribution. Confucius, Mencius, and Xunzi all stressed that those with virtue should rule, and this is meritocratic in a sense, distributing power according to merit in the form of virtue. However, it is not a principle of distributive *justice* in the sense of office or power being what is *due* to those with merit. The meritorious do not *deserve* office because of merit; political office is not a reward for merit.[18] Furthermore, unlike other items for social distribution subject to considerations of justice, the power of political office is not to become personal possession for personal benefit or enjoyment. Instead, early Confucians view political office in terms of responsibilities best discharged by those with virtue. Hence it is not fairness but functional effectiveness that matters. Confucian meritocratic appointments (*ju-xian-neng* 舉賢能) reflect the first half of the doctrine, "from each according to his ability, to each according to his needs." Though often identified as the Communist doctrine of justice,[19] it did not originate with Karl Marx, and was popular with social reformers such as Louis Blanc, who had used it more than a quarter of a century before Marx cited it in the *Critique of the Gotha Program*.[20]

Rather than advocating meritocracy in the form of rewarding contributions, the *Analects* and the *Mencius* provide evidence for prioritizing need over merit in determining how much to give to a person.

> When Zihua was on a mission to Qi, Master Ranyou asked to supply Zihua's mother with some grain. The Master said, "Give her a full measure of grain." Master Ranyou asked to give her more. The Master said, "Then give her a double measure." Master Ranyou gave her ten measures of grain.
>
> The Master said, "In traveling to Qi, Zihua was driving choice horses and wearing fine furs. I have heard it said, 'Exemplary persons help out the needy; they do not make the rich richer.'" (*Analects* 6.4)[21]

Confucius' disapproval is not over Ranyou giving more than what Zihua's or his mother's merit deserved, but over Ranyou giving more than what was needed because Zihua was already well off. For Confucius, those who are powerful and of high rank should be satisfied with what is available to those at the bottom of the social strata and not expect to be better off than them, however much the former's virtue and contribution to the community may exceed the latter's (*Analects* 12.9). Such remarks are relevant to reconstructing a Confucian view on social distribution and a Confucian conception of social justice.

While Mencius believed that the virtuous should be "honored," such honor should not be measured in material terms or conventional rewards usually found in the distributive policies of governments and the workings of market economies. At its most idealistic, Confucianism maintains that virtue is its own reward.[22] Some may argue that this is about different kinds of reward, not about the total rejection of rewards for virtues. However, what needs emphasizing is that human beings and institutions cannot offer the true reward for virtue. Humaneness is "the high honor bestowed by heaven" (*Mencius* 2A7). In Mencius' eyes, those who discard "honors bestowed by heaven"—humaneness, rightness, doing one's best and keeping one's words, and "unflagging delight in what is good"—in preference for rank or wealth, which are "honors bestowed by men" are "deluded to the extreme" and will eventually perish. "The point is that, being filled with moral virtue, one does not envy other people's enjoyment of fine food and, enjoying a fine and extensive reputation, one does not envy other people's fineries."[23] The only reward the virtuous should be concerned with is the opportunity to continue acting virtuously and thereby benefiting the world, including teaching others to be virtuous by example. One may reject this view as too idealistic, but what is worthy of note for the current discussion is its strong resistance against thinking of the relation between political office and virtue (merit) in terms of distributive justice—fair distribution of rewards, resources, or other items that can be distributed by human actions and institutions.

The *Xunzi* advocates matching (*cheng* 稱) the remuneration of appointed officers to the "differences between the noble and base, disparities between the privileges of age and youth, and the division of the wise from the stupid, the able from the incapable" (*Xunzi* 1:195), among other statements that could be construed as meritocratic. "In rewarding, one should not wish to confer more than what is warranted; in punishing, one should not wish to go to wrongful excess" (*Xunzi* 2:209). On one occasion, Xunzi cited Mo Zi's doctrine that "emoluments must match services to the state" (2:122). What Knoblock translates as "services to the state" (*yong* 用) could also be translated as "use"—and the later part of this passage indicates that what the remuneration should match is what people use to meet their needs.

> Employ the people so that they are certain to succeed in their assigned tasks; make certain that the profits from their assigned tasks are sufficient to provide a means of living for them. In all these cause income to match outgo in regard to clothing, food, and the hundred necessities of life so that with certainty the harvest surplus will be stored up at the proper season. (2:123)

Xunzi did not justify giving more to those in high positions in terms of their deserving more because of their greater merit or contributions. He made it clear that whatever is given to those occupying high positions is not to satisfy any desire for "reckless extravagance" but to provide what is necessary, that is needed, for them to effectively discharge the responsibilities of their positions, to contribute to the state and the people's well-being (2:122–26).

The argument that meritocracy provides incentive for people to serve the community finds some sympathy in Xunzi's criticism of Gongsun Nizi who praised the Duke of She's refusal of the reward for his service to the state (2:241–42). While being rewarded is not what motivates truly virtuous actions (acting out of virtue rather than merely acting according to virtue), given that people by nature have numerous materialistic desires, Xunzi considered it necessary for governments to "reward men with wealth and plenty and penalize them with reduction and deprivation" (3:48). It follows from Xunzi's view of bad human nature that moral achievements, merit, must be recognized and rewarded with what is desirable to most people so that others will emulate such behavior. The concern with functional effectiveness could extend beyond obtaining service to the state to encouraging virtuous conduct if, by repeating such acts frequently enough, the imitator could over time acquire the right attitudes and emotions so that desire for virtue rather than rewards becomes the motivation and the action in service to the state becomes truly virtuous. The discussion is not concerned with what the meritorious deserves as a matter of justice—Xunzi did not condemn the Duke of She because he refused the reward that his contribution deserved. It displays, instead, a concern with meeting the need of the state for certain kinds of service from its people if there is to be good government.

Needs versus desires

The pre-Qin Confucian texts do not use the common term (*xu* 需) in the Chinese language that usually translates as "need."[24] What is translated as "needy" in *Analects* 6.4, "*ji* 急," is more commonly translated as "urgent," matters demanding attention that merit priority.[25] A Confucian conception of justice focusing on needs is therefore a reconstruction that cannot be directly attributed to the early Confucians themselves. Applying their ideas today to refer to preventing starvation and providing sufficient food as concerned with meeting survival needs seems unproblematic. The above discussion's turn to needs is prompted by an assumed contrast between desires and needs, and between Confucian discrimination on ethical grounds and liberal impartiality toward desires. Some conceptions of liberal justice include needs by linking them to rights positively.[26] In the political discourse of existing liberal democracies, which are often welfare states, the concept of need is common and has a rhetorical force denied the concept of desire.[27] Though some may lament the neglect of needs in recent political philosophy,[28] there exist fairly extensive philosophical discussions of the concept of need and its moral and political relevance.

Most theories of need offer some clarification regarding the distinction and relation between the concept of need and the concept of desire (and/or related concepts, "want" being the most common choice). I may not desire an operation even though I need one; I desired chocolate cake at tea time but, not being hungry, I certainly did not need it. Inanimate objects can have needs but not desires: my computer needs repair but it cannot desire to be repaired. My desire for something depends on my belief about that which is desired, and may be specific to a particular description of it; my need for something depends on its characteristics independent of my beliefs and how it is described. Desires play a key role in explaining actions, needs only do so when they give rise to corresponding desires. The distinction is by no means obvious.[29] Though conceptually distinct, needs and desires are contingently but significantly related in complex ways that create difficulties in determining the presence and nature of either or both in many situations. Evolution ensures that most of the time we desire things that will meet our basic needs, such as thirst, hunger, desire for warmth; but even though one can have both a desire and a need for the same thing, a need could cause a desire, and vice versa, there is no mutual implication between them. Different theories distinguish needs from desires (or wants, which is broader than desire) in different ways.[30] In what follows, I shall focus on differences that are crucial to reconstructing a Confucian doctrine of needs as social justice.

Claims of need are often thought to have moral priority and imply obligations to meet them, whereas claims based on desires are always open to the question, "why should anyone give you what you want?" The moral force of needs claims is often associated with necessity. What one needs is necessary in some way, something one cannot do without.[31] In Alan White's analysis, the concept "indicates a relation, namely that of a certain kind of necessity, between one of a number of alternatives, which is said to be what is needed, and a situation which consists of a set of circumstances and an end-state."[32] For example, basic needs often refer to what are necessary for physical survival and minimal social functioning in a particular society. Even after necessity has been established, one can still challenge a need claim by asking if the end-state (what something is needed for) should be brought about. This renders the moral importance of meeting a need derivative from the importance of the end-state for which it is necessary.[33] It may be true that someone needs a good reference from me to get a job, but if I think that person is unqualified or unsuitable for the job, then I am under no obligation to provide that needed good reference. In contrast, unless I believe that life has no value, if not generally then in some particular circumstances, I will have to give moral weight to a claim for what is needed to sustain someone's life.[34]

Theories of need usually ground needs claims in end-states that they argue have objective moral validity or value, end-states such as avoiding harm variously defined, physical survival/health, decent standard of living, human functioning, agency/autonomy, or performance of certain important roles.[35] The objectivity of needs, if it could be established, means that it is possible for someone to know my needs better than myself. This is an important difference from desires, as we generally accept that a person is the best authority on her own desires.[36] This opens the gate to paternalism or worse that accounts for liberal antipathy to the concept of needs. Minogue compares it to the general will or the class consciousness of the proletariat, "oracular" devices ruling elites can use to replace the "confused, immoral, inconvenient, or otherwise defective" will of the inarticulate masses.[37] The obvious liberal solution is to insist that, insofar as the evaluative question "should it be brought about" can always be raised about any end-state that grounds a need, that end-state has validity only if chosen, that is desired by the person in need. Therefore, needs experts should be servants, "determining needs by reference to the wants of the individual client" instead of "masters, prescribing needs by reference to their own judgment of what their subjects ideally ought to want."[38]

It is undeniable that there is a dose of paternalism in Confucian political philosophy, but I believe that its paternalistic tendency need not result in authoritarianism but can be reconciled with the democratic ideal of freedom. This is not the place to take up such a reconciliation, which I have attempted previously.[39] Various contemporary solutions or safeguards against the paternalism problem have been offered by philosophers who wish to give needs an important role in politics.[40] A reconstructed Confucian doctrine of needs that aspires to be a conception of social justice for a democracy would need similar safeguards. The risks of paternalism notwithstanding, this needs approach is still appealing because of the Confucian reservation about emphasizing desires, its concern about the well-being of the less well off in society, and not least because it presents its ethical philosophy of personal cultivation and exemplary personhood as an objective ideal. Unlike liberal theories of justice following Rawls, in Confucianism its objective conception of the good life determines the right in what is just. The link between the two lies in what is necessary to live a good life from a Confucian perspective. Liberal principles of justice seek to solve distribution problems without taking a stance on the question of what is a good life for human beings to live, and the kind of society that facilitates the good life. While liberal conceptions of justice are also tools of social criticism, they offer a different kind of social critique from a reconstructed Confucian conception, which is part of the pursuit of a particular ethical-political ideal.

Basis of social criticism and scope of social change

In arguing for a Confucian conception of social justice, one might say that pre-Qin Confucians offered their own answers to problems similar to social justice problems confronted by other societies even if they understood those problems in some other terms. This approach brings Confucianism into current theoretical discussions about social justice by interpreting Confucian teachings in terms that contemporary theorists could easily comprehend. Even if this does not contribute unique Confucian answers to the key questions in theorizing about justice, such as the principles for deciding what is due to a person in a certain context, or the kind of rules and policies that should guide government actions or govern institutions with (re)distributive consequences, it can add its weight and varied insights from another long-standing cultural tradition to some particular theory among the many competing theories of justice. If human societies across different cultures and historical periods have confronted similar problems, then the different answers from different societies to each kind of problem could be edifying and helpful in solving the current version of that kind of problem. The hard task still remains in working out which answer (or a combination of answers) would best solve a specific current problem. Though eminently worthwhile, that is not the task of this chapter. Instead, I wish to first query the assumption about similarity of problems in this approach and conclude with some remarks about the different bases and pragmatic potential of social criticisms offered by different theoretical choices in reconstructing a Confucian conception of justice using comparative methods.

The similarity in problems is inevitably identified from a particular standpoint—the standpoint of the inquirer embedded in her particular historical and cultural context(s). That does not invalidate the above comparative approach, but it should caution us against dismissing the significance of the differences in descriptions of what we assume to be "similar problems" when those living in very different contexts do not discuss the problems they experienced using similar or equivalent vocabularies. We see a couple quarreling and it appears to us to be a "lovers' quarrel," which certainly is almost a universal phenomenon; but when those involved then talk about their "religious differences," instead, do we ignore that simply because they are lovers and they are quarreling even though *they* do not call it a "lovers' quarrel"? I want to argue that the presence of "circumstances of justice" giving us reason to assume that there are similar problems of social justice in societies vastly separated by space and time is not as significant as the different ways the problems are understood or diagnosed that result in different solutions. Circumstances of justice do not occur in an institutional vacuum; the social arrangements that already exist determine the form which problems of justice—contention over benefits and burdens—take and govern how people perceive those problems and their conceptions of justice. It is also possible that the problems arising from those circumstances need not be formulated as problems of justice, but as different kinds of social problems understood within different conceptual frameworks and solved with different conceptual tools. The above analysis of the meaning of *yi* in the *Mencius* shows that the choice between seeing it as a concept of justice or as a concept of relational appropriateness is an example of such a paradigm shift. I shall try to show with another comparison within the European tradition that such paradigm shifts open up vistas of more radical social criticisms and enhance comparative philosophy's capacity to bring about more significant social change insofar as the outcome challenges the *status quo* more than an approach that assumes the diagnoses of contemporary problems.

Aristotle, when applying his concept of distributive justice to the *polis*, recognized that, insofar as political justice is a constitutive means of the flourishing of the *polis* and there are different kinds of *poleis*, what is just in one *polis* could be unjust in another. "Similarly, the things which are just not by nature but by human enactment are not everywhere the same, since constitutions also are not the same, though there is but one which is everywhere by nature the best" (1135a3–5). Within this framework, the constitution, that is, the political structure of a society, determines for the most part the conception of justice. Does this mean that one could not criticize the arrangements in a *polis* as unjust except on the basis of its own political structure and its corresponding conception of justice? Aristotle avoids relativism by maintaining that political justice is not only legal, but also partly natural (1134b19). Although there are many constitutions, there is only "one which is by nature the best" (1135a5). This naturally best constitution provides Aristotle with a conception of political justice that can trump others. Based on Aristotle's understanding of political justice, there are two ways in which one could criticize a *polis* for being unjust: it could be unjust by its own standards because some transactions or institutions do not meet the demands of the conception of justice based on its own constitution; it also could be unjust because the entire *polis* does not meet the demands of the conception of justice based on the naturally best constitution. Even though we could describe both as criticisms in terms of justice, in the latter case, changing some social arrangements would not be enough, and nothing short of replacing the constitution with the naturally best constitution would do. We are talking about social change with a very different scope.

The earlier mention of the communist doctrine of justice notwithstanding, the role of the concept of justice, if any, in Marx's criticisms of capitalism is hotly debated by scholars of Marxism. The debate also raises the issue of the relation between justice and social change. For all their differences, there is a continuity between Aristotle's linking of justice with law (1134a29–32) and Marx's treatment of justice as a "juridical or legal (*rechtlich*)" concept.[41] This places justice in the role of a fundamental criterion for judging society in Aristotle's philosophy in which "man is by nature a political animal" (1253a3). In contrast, Marx treated political institutions as superstructural aspects of material productive activities to meet historically conditioned human needs; consequently, justice loses its primacy as a fundamental principle to evaluate social life. For Marx, conceptions of right and justice act as fundamental principles for judging actions or institutions only within a particular mode of production, since the political state, the regulative powers that sustain the legal and judicial system, operates within that prevailing productive mode.[42] An institution that is unjust in one mode of production may be just in another. The concept of justice may distinguish between just and unjust transactions in capitalism, but just transactions in such cases are simply those that correspond in a particular way to the capitalist productive mode. Reform of institutions on the basis of principles of justice cannot correct what is fundamentally wrong with capitalism. Any concept of justice, being meaningless outside its corresponding productive mode, cannot serve to criticize that entire mode of production.

According to Wood's interpretation, Marx denied that one can condemn capitalism as unjust by some postcapitalist concept of justice, since "any such standards would not be rationally applicable to capitalism at all, any such condemnations would be mistaken, confused, and without foundations."[43] Communism, when it materializes, will bring with it its own principles of justice; to apply those principles of justice before the time goes against Marx's historicist conception of society and social change. Unlike Aristotle, Marx did not have a teleology of the "naturally best" to provide a point of view to judge all other productive modes. Or did he? For those who interpret communism as both the descriptively inevitable historical outcome and the normatively justified productive mode that actualizes distinctive human capacities and satisfies human needs, it seems to provide such a viewpoint, whether it is teleological or not.[44] For our purpose, we need not take sides in the debate or get tangled in the details of contesting interpretations of Marxism. Suffice it to note that it is not the contest between principles of justice relative to different productive modes that is driving the radical criticism advocating revolutionary or systemic transformation of society. It is the contest between fundamental social ideals—constitutions for Aristotle and productive modes for Marx—in relation to their respective conceptions of human nature and society that is doing the work.

To the extent that each society historically adopts ways of distributing the benefits and burdens of association that suit its specific material and political conditions, as they must answer to specific forms of distributive problems that these conditions give rise to, attempts to reconstruct Confucian distributive principles from early Confucian texts for contemporary edification become problematic. What works in a set of conditions to produce certain consequences may not work in a different set of conditions or may work to produce totally different consequences. Unless a certain pattern of distribution is desirable in itself, which I do not think is the case for Confucianism, then we need to ask whether applying those principles we reconstruct from the texts (as Chan and I do) today would solve the distribution problems of contemporary societies consistent with the Confucian social ideal. If a reconstruction involves implicit or explicit comparison that yields principles resembling those in contemporary theories with very different cultural contexts, then we need to be cautious whether the reconstructed principles would still achieve the Confucian social and ethical vision or whether they would incline more toward replacing those ideals with contemporary ones. This is not an easy problem to tackle, as what appears to one as a necessary and desirable modification that can be justified on the grounds of making Confucianism relevant to contemporary life may appear to another as unacceptable distortion or total displacement. We also need to allow for the possibility that the early Confucians themselves, in taking for granted certain facts or norms (e.g., not questioning the political form that existed in their times), could be advocating distributive solutions that are self-defeating when viewed from the perspective of their more fundamental social and ethical ideals. Even if their views on distributive issues fit their ideals, both conceptually and in actual practice, acceptance of the Confucian perspective on justice is still contingent on sympathy with Confucian social and ethical ideals.

Assuming some similarity in circumstances, in apparently perennial problems faced by human beings living in different times and different cultures, may be a starting point for comparative philosophy. However, the comparative exercise must turn around and question that assumption as it proceeds, for greater pragmatic payoffs both in terms of possible solutions to the chosen problem being addressed and, more important, in terms of providing a more radical social critique that could transform contemporary life. The initial dissonance in my attempted comparison of *yi* with justice, and the debate about reconstruction of Confucian perspective on justice emphasizing sufficiency and meritocracy, aided by a fairly cursory study of the concept of justice in the philosophies of Aristotle and Marx, has prompted me to reflect on more radical differences in social ideals, and conceptions of social relations and human nature in those Western philosophies and in early Confucianism.

Liang Shuming points out that the Chinese society is based on relationships rather than individuals or groups.[45] Although there are terms for various collectives, such as *guo* and *jia* (usually translated as "state" and "family," respectively), early Confucian discourse focuses on relationships centered on the five basic relationships between ruler and minister/subject, father and son, husband and wife, elder brother and younger brother, and between friends (*Mencius* 3A4). All other human relationships are understood by analogy to these basic relationships. Within this context, it is not surprising that the concept of *yi*, as a key ethical notion, operates within particular human relationships, rather than in relation to the entire society. Society is a network of different kinds of relationships, each kind having its own ethical requirements of appropriate ways of behaving with one another. While early Chinese society also confronted the inevitable need to share benefits and burdens of association, and discussions of how to do so appear in early Confucian texts, I would argue that early Confucians did not develop principles of justice as a fundamental part of their ethics because they did not think of human beings as coming together in society solely or even primarily in order to cooperate so that they could all benefit and share the burdens. Dividing burdens and benefits is only one among many different considerations in how each person relates to others in a variety of relationships that constitute his or her social life. So "Who gets what?" did not become the central question of social life. While problems of justice are solved with effective application of principles of justice to the division of benefits and burdens, relational problems involving distributive issues need to adopt a more holistic approach in considering the overall consequences on the relationship of any particular distribution.

From the relational perspective, application of some just principle of distribution may not be the best solution to the problem involved—although as rules of thumb, such principles could be useful up to a point. While theories of justice need not subscribe to an atomistic conception of the individual anathema to Confucianism, with its inherently social conception of human beings, distributive justice is an individual-oriented idea and the act of distribution invariably emphasizes the separateness of those among whom something is being distributed.[46] *Yi*, on the other hand, is relation-oriented. The relational focus of Confucian ethics highlights human interdependence rather than the separation of individuals. Separateness and connectedness are both present in all human relationships, but they could be viewed very differently. Orientation toward justice is concerned about separateness despite connectedness, whereas Confucian *yi* orientation is concerned with connectedness despite separateness. Where competition for resources and other distribution problems have to be solved, Confucian relational ethics could provide answers, but not in terms of arrangements that assume the satisfaction of individuals' desires with fairness or equality of distribution to be of paramount importance. Rather, any proposed distribution arrangement must be assessed against the needs of the human participants in the social relationships at stake and the needs of those relationships.

Reconstructing Confucian perspectives on social justice, or interpreting *yi* so that it serves similar purposes as the concept of justice, is a useful exercise that makes available Confucian resources for solving contemporary problems concerning justice. However, it seems that if we take the dissonances in such exercises seriously, then we might tap into deeper differences that will provide more radically critical perspectives with which to interrogate contemporary experience. Rather than simply assuming the existence and importance of justice problems as matters of how to distribute benefits and burdens, asking whether there are other ways of understanding what is wrong or dissatisfying about certain kinds of experience, certain social arrangements and interactions, that give rise to justice concerns could lead to more fundamental critiques of contemporary societies and social relations.

Notes

1 See: Ruiping Fan, "Confucian and Rawlsian Views of Justice: A Comparison," *Journal of Chinese Philosophy* 24, no. 4 (1997), p. 427. For a more recent Confucian-Rawlsian comparison focusing on the sense of justice, see Erin Cline, *Confucius, Rawls, and the Sense of Justice*, Bronx, NY: Fordham University Press, 2012.

2 Yang Xiao, "Trying to Do Justice to the Concept of Justice in Confucian Ethics," *Journal of Chinese Philosophy* 24, no. 4 (1997), pp. 521–51.

3 Citations of Aristotle's works from Jonathan Barnes (ed.), *The Complete Works of Aristotle*, 2 vols (Princeton, NJ: Princeton University Press, 1984).

4 Citations of the *Mencius* from D. C. Lau (trans.), *Mencius* (Harmondsworth: Penguin, 1970).

5 Huang Yushun 黄玉顺, *Reconstruction of Chinese Theories of Justice* (Anhui People's Press, 2013).

6 Although contemporary Anglo-Saxon philosophical discussions of justice contrast strongly with this focus on relationality, Aristotle mentioned that "justice, alone of the excellences, is thought to be another's good, for it is related to others" (1130a3-4). Del Vecchio's historical study of the concept notes that justice concerns arise whenever people enter into relations of exchange or community that imply "the necessity for a measure and a limit for one or the other party." See Giorgio Del Vecchio, *Justice: An Historical and Philosophical Essay* (New York: The Philosophical Library, 1953), p. 92. Recently, Barden and Murphy have argued that justice rightly understood as about entitlement is communal and relational. See Garrett Barden and Timothy Murphy, *Law and Justice in Community* (Oxford: Oxford University Press, 2010), p. 461.

7 For a comprehensive study of *yi* in the *Mencius* and a more developed argument for understanding *yi* as norms of relational appropriateness instead of a concept of justice, and what this implies for distribution problems, see Sor-hoon Tan, "The Concept of Yi in the Mencius and the Problems of Distributive Justice," *Australasian Journal of Philosophy* 92, no. 3 (September 2014), pp. 489–505.

8 Joseph Chan, "Is there a Confucian Perspective on Social Justice?" in *Western Political Thought in Dialogue with Asia*, ed. Takashi Shogimen and Cary J. Nederman (Lanham: Lexington Books, 2009), p. 269 cites David Miller's formulation of those circumstances. See: David Miller, *Principles of Social Justice* (Cambridge, MA: Harvard University Press, 1999), p. 6. Cf. John Rawls, *A Theory of Justice* (Oxford: Oxford University Press, 1972), pp. 126–30. Huang, *Reconstruction of Chinese Theories of Justice*, also argues that all societies have circumstances that necessarily raise questions about justice, and therefore no society could be without the concept, whether or not there is an actual term that translates to "justice." See also Del Vecchio, *Justice*, p. 143.

9 Chan, "Is there a Confucian Perspective?", pp. 275–76.

10 Harry Frankfurt, "Equality as a Moral Ideal," *Ethics* 98, no. 1 (October 1987), p. 23.

11 Ibid., p. 38.

12 For a more detailed discussion about the relationship between desires and ethical life in the *Analects* and the *Mencius*, see S. Tan, "Materialistic Desires and Ethical Life in the Analects and the Mencius," in *Moral Cultivation and Confucian Character*, ed. Chenyang Li and Peimin Ni (Albany, NY: State University of New York Press, 2014).

13 C. B. Macpherson, "Needs and Wants: An Ontological or Historical Problem?" in *Human Needs and Politics*, ed. Ross. Fitzgerald (Sydney: Pergamon, 1977), pp. 29–30.
14 Ibid., p. 31.
15 William J. Meyer, "Democracy: Needs Over Wants," *Political Theory* 2, no. 2 (May 1974), p. 203; cf. a need can be seen as "a way of discriminating between conflicting desires," see: Kenneth R. Minogue, *The Liberal Mind* (London: Methuen, 1963), p. 107.
16 Frankfurt, "Equality as a Moral Ideal," p. 22, himself acknowledges that need is one among the many benefits that the doctrine of sufficiency could apply to; need is the focus of his argument that people's objection to economic disparities has less to do with desiring distributive equality than it has to do with satisfying what they perceive to be the more urgent needs of the worse off, see Ibid., pp. 34–37). On the salience of needs in distributive justice, see Norman Frohlich and Joe Oppenheimer's empirical experiment, which shows that under conditions of impartiality, rather than Harsanyi's maximizing of the average income, Rawls's principle of maximizing the income of the worst off, or maximizing an average with a range constraint (minimizing disparity between richest and poorest), a significant majority (78 percent) choose maximizing the average with a floor constraint. See Norman Frohlich and Joe Oppenheimer, *Choosing Justice: An Experimental Approach to Ethical Theory* (Berkeley and Los Angeles: University of California Press, 1992), pp. 35 and 59.
17 *Xunzi* 2:94. See also mention of special attention paid to the widowed, orphaned, and childless (Ibid., 162, 167). Text citations from the *Xunzi* henceforth give volume and page numbers.
18 Del Vecchio, *Justice*, p. 190, calls meritocratic distribution "rewarding justice."
19 Karl Marx, *Critique of Gotha Program*, in *Selected Works* by Karl Marx and Friedrich Engels, vol. 2 (Foreign Languages Publishing House, 1875/1962), p. 24.
20 Louis Blanc, *Organisation du Travail* (Paris: Administration de librairie,1841/1839); for more nineteenth-century historical references on this doctrine, see Del Vecchio, *Justice*, p. 147, n. 3. My intent is neither to model a Confucian conception of justice on the communist one nor to compare in any depth Marx's theory of needs and any reconstruction of Confucian views about needs. For this reason, the chapter will not get into debates about Marx's theory of needs, whether he has one, and problems with whatever theory (or theories) attributed to him. For a discussion of the topic, see Agnes Heller, *The Theory of Need in Marx* (New York: St Martin's Press, 1976); Patricia Springborg, "Karl Marx on Human Needs," in *Human Needs and Politics*, ed. Ross Fitzgerald (Sydney: Pergamon Press, 1977), pp. 157–73; Patricia Springborg, *The Problem of Human Needs and the Critique of Civilisation* (London: Allen & Unwin, 1981), chapter 6; Kate Soper, *On Human Needs: Open and Closed Theories in a Marxist Perspective* (Brighton: Harvester Press, 1981); David Braybrooke, "Two Conceptions of Needs in Marx's Writings," in *On the Track of Reason: Essays in Honor of Kai Nielsen*, ed. Rodger Beechler, David Copp and Bela Szabados (Boulder, CO: Westview Press, 1992), 119–33; Martin Hewitt, *Welfare and Human Nature: The Human Subject in Twentieth-Century Social Politics* (New York: St Martin's Press, 2000), chapter 6.
21 Translations from the *Analects*, see Roger T. Ames and Henry Rosemont, Jr., *The Analects of Confucius: A Philosophical Translation* (New York: Ballantine, 1998).
22 One can find evidence for this even in the *Xunzi* 2:74, "Accordingly, although the gentleman lacks rank, he is noble; although he lacks an emolument, he is wealthy . . . although he dwells in poverty, he flourishes."
23 *Mencius* 6A16, 6A17. See also *Analects* 4.5.
24 The term occurs as the fifth hexagram in the *Yijing*, which symbolizes "waiting." To need something is in one sense to wait for what is needed.

25 See also *Mencius* 3B3, 4B29, 7A46.

26 For an argument that one has a right to be enabled to meet one's basic needs, see David Copp, "The Right to an Adequate Standard of Living: Justice, Autonomy, and the Basic Needs," *Social Philosophy and Policy* 9 (1992), pp. 131–61; Kaufman argues that "claims about human needs imply corresponding claims about human rights," and sees Marxism and Liberalism converging. See: Arnold S. Kaufman, "Wants, Needs, and Liberalism," *Inquiry* 14 (1977), p. 194. For more discussions of the relation between needs and rights, see H. J. McCloskey, "Human Needs, Rights, and Political Values," *American Philosophical Quarterly* 13, no. 1 (January 1976), pp. 1–11; J. Galtung, *Human Rights in Another Key* (Cambridge: Polity Press, 1994); Alan Gewirth, *The Community of Rights* (Chicago: University of Chicago Press, 1996); Onora O'Neil, "Rights, Obligations, and Needs," in *Necessary Goods*, ed. Gilian Brock (Lanham: Rowman & Littlefield, 1998), pp. 95–112; Berma Klein Goldewijk and Bastiaan de Gaay Fortman, *Where Needs Meet Rights* (Geneva: WCC Publications, 1999); Bill Wringe, "Needs, Rights, and Collective Obligations," in *The Philosophy of Need*, ed. Soran Reader (Cambridge: Cambridge University Press, 2005), pp. 187–207. See also the reconciliation of needs with libertarian rights, Gillian Brock, "Is Redistribution to Help the Needy Unjust?," in *Necessary Goods*, ed. Gillian Brock (Lanham: Rowman & Littlefield, 1998), pp. 173–83.

27 David Braybrooke, *Meeting Needs* (Princeton: Princeton University Press, 1987), p. 7, argues that liberalism in practice has inevitably given much attention to needs, which are complementary to preferences emphasized by liberal economics. He offers his theory of need as an enhancement of a utilitarian approach to social policy, while Neumann tries to rescue utilitarianism from its deontological critics with a needs-based system as an alternative to a rights-based approach to justice. Michael Neumann, "Needs Not Rights," *Canadian Journal of Political Science* 22, no. 3 (September 1992), pp. 353–63. See also Minogue, *The Liberal Mind*, pp. 103–104; Ross Fitzgerald, "The Ambiguity and Rhetoric of 'Need,'" in *Human Needs and Politics*, ed. Ross Fitzgerald (Sydney: Pergamon, 1977), pp. 195–212.

28 David Wiggins, "Claims of Need," in *Needs, Values, Truth* (Oxford: Oxford University Press, 1998/1987), p. 2.

29 Some might argue that this distinction is salient only in the English language and may not be present, or at least not so clear, in other languages (Macpherson, "Needs and Wants", p. 27; Springborg, "Karl Marx on Human Needs", p. 158). According to Braybrooke, "Two Conceptions of Needs in Marx's Writings," in *Das Kapital* and other economic writings, "Bedürfnisse" in German, which the French "besoins" approximates better than "needs" in ordinary English, covers the ground that in English is covered by "needs" and "desires" together, so that Marx can be said to have both a restrictive conception of needs, approximating what people think of as basic needs, means of subsistence, or conditions of existence, that can be distinguished from desires and a generalized conception that includes desires.

30 The best analytic discussion of this topic is probably White's, the source of most of the differences cited in this paper. See Alan R. White, *Modal Thinking* (Oxford: Blackwell, 1975); Lawrence A. Hamilton, *The Political Philosophy of Needs* (Cambridge: Cambridge University Press, 2003), p. 61. Others maintain that "need" may sometimes mean "a comparatively strong drive, wish, or motive," see Paul W. Taylor, "'Need' Statements," *Analysis* 19, no. 5 (April 1959), p. 108. For a distinction from a social science perspective, see Don Slater, "Needs/Wants," in *Core Sociological Dichotomies*, ed. Chris Jenks (London: Sage, 1998), pp. 315–28.

31 This association of needs with necessity can be traced to Aristotle, whose conception of human flourishing presupposes the meeting of the basic needs of the community and its individual members, although the meeting of needs is ignoble in his ethical theory, see Soran Reader, "Aristotle on Necessities and Needs," in *The Philosophy of Need*, ed. Soran Reader (Cambridge: Cambridge University Press, 2005), pp. 113–35. See also a contrasting strand of ancient thought attributed to Socrates and Plato in some writings that run needs together with desires, Christopher Rowe, "Needs and Ethics in Ancient Philosophy," in *Philosophy of Need*, ed. Soran Reader (Cambridge: Cambridge University Press, 2005), pp. 99–112.

32 White, *Modal Thinking*, p. 105. This can include those theories of needs that relate needs to human nature or human essence. Although the needs may be caused/determined by human nature, what are needed are necessary *for* the end-state of maintaining or fulfilling human nature, or living the life defined/required by human nature.

33 Harry Frankfurt, "Necessity and Desire," in *Necessary Goods*, ed. Gillian Brock (Lanham, MD: Rowman & Littlefield, 1998), p. 20. This is a widely accepted view; cf. criticism of instrumental as well as purely normative approaches to needs, Hamilton, *The Political Philosophy of Needs*, pp. 47–62.

34 This does not mean I am personally obligated to meet such a need in every case. For some discussions of the complicated question of who is responsible, see Wringe, "Needs, Rights, and Collective Obligations"; John Baker, and Charles Jones, "Responsibility for Needs," in *Necessary Goods*, ed. Gillian Brock (Lanham, MD: Rowman & Littlefield, 1998), pp. 219–232. See also Flew's example of how saving someone's life does not give him what he needs, Anthony Flew, "Wants or Needs, Choices or Commands," in *Human Needs and Politics*, ed. Ross Fitzgerald (Sydney: Pergamon, 1977), p. 220.

35 Those grounding the moral priority of needs on avoidance of harm include Frankfurt, "Necessity and Desire", p. 23; Joel Feinberg, *Social Philosophy* (Englewood Cliffs, NJ: Prentice Hall, 1973), p. 111; and Wiggins, "Claims of Need", p. 14). Other end-states include physical survival/health and autonomy, see Len Doyal and Ian Gough, *A Theory of Human Need* (London: Macmillan, 1991), pp. 56–69; human functioning including agency, see Hamilton, *The Political Philosophy of Needs*; "performing the tasks assigned a given person under a combination of basic social roles, namely, the roles of parent, householder, worker and citizen," Braybrooke, *Meeting Needs*, p. 48; physical survival for biological needs, decent standard of living for basic needs, and "doing a particular job" for functional needs, see Stanley I. Benn and Richard S. Peters, *Social Principles and the Democratic State* (London: Allen & Unwin, 1959). Cf. Thomson argues, unconvincingly in my view, that there are fundamental needs with nonderivative, noncircumstantial, and inescapable moral importance. See Garrett Thomson, "Fundamental Needs," in *Philosophy of Need*, ed. Soran Reader (Cambridge: Cambridge University Press, 2005), pp. 175–86; Garrett Thomson, *Needs* (London: Routledge & Kegan Paul, 1987).

36 Unconscious desires can complicate matters, but even if we accept that they exist, some account of how they could be brought to consciousness is needed for the idea to have any impact on how we understand our mental lives and actions.

37 Minogue, *The Liberal Mind*.

38 Flew, "Wants or Needs, Choices or Commands", pp. 220–21; Goodin offers another liberal solution that subordinates needs to desires by denying the moral priority of the former, see Robert E. Goodin, "The Priority of Needs," *Philosophy and Phenomenological Research* 45, no. 4 (June 1985), pp. 615–25.

39 S. Tan, *Confucian Democracy: A Deweyan Reconstruction* (Albany, NY: State University of New York Press, 2003).
40 Two examples can be found in Meyer, "Democracy: Needs Over Wants" and Hamilton, *The Political Philosophy of Needs*, 167.
41 Allen W. Wood, "The Marxian Critique of Justice," in *Marx, Justice, and History*, ed. Marshall Cohen, Thomas Nagel and Thomas Scanlon (Princeton: Princeton University Press, 1980/1972), p. 5.
42 Ibid., p. 13.
43 Ibid.
44 See Husami's argument that "it is valid, on Marx's showing, for the proletariat and its spokesmen to criticize capitalist distribution using proletarian standards of justice." Ziyad I. Husami, "Marx on Distributive Justice," in *Marx, Justice, and History*, ed. Marshall Cohen, Thomas Nagel and Thomas Scanlon (Princeton: Princeton University Press, 1980/1972), p. 49.
45 Liang Shuming 梁漱溟, *Complete Works*, vol. 3 (Jinan, Shandong: People's Press, 1989), p. 94.
46 Chan, "Is there a Confucian Perspective on Social Justice?" p. 263, illustrates effectively why distributive justice is individual-oriented. Something may be distributed to different groups, but in such cases, each group is treated as an *individual* unit for the purpose of the distribution.

References

Ames, R. T. and Rosemont, H. Jr. (1998), *The Analects of Confucius: A Philosophical Translation*, New York: Ballantine, pp. 219–32.

Baker, J. and Jones, C. (1998), "Responsibility for Needs," in G. Brock (ed.), *Necessary Goods*, Lanham: Rowman & Littlefield, pp. 219–32.

Barden, G. and Murphy, T. (2010), *Law and Justice in Community*, Oxford: Oxford University Press.

Barnes, J., ed. (1984), *The Complete Works of Aristotle*, 2 vols, Princeton, NJ: Princeton University Press.

Benn, S. I. and Peters, R. S. (1959), *Social Principles and the Democratic State*, London: Allen & Unwin.

Blanc, L. (1841/1839), *Organisation du Travail*, Paris: Administration de librairie.

Braybrooke, D. (1987), *Meeting Needs*, Princeton: Princeton University Press.

Braybrooke, D. (1992), "Two Conceptions of Needs in Marx's Writings," in R. Beechler, D. Copp and B. Szabados (eds), *On the Track of Reason: Essays in Honor of Kai Nielsen*, Boulder, CO: Westview Press, pp. 119–33.

Brock, G. (1998), "Is Redistribution to Help the Needy Unjust?" in G. Brock (ed.), *Necessary Goods*, Lanham: Rowman & Littlefield, pp. 173–83.

Chan, J. (2009), "Is there a Confucian Perspective on Social Justice," in T. Shogimen and C. J. Nederman (eds), *Western Political Thought in Dialogue with Asia*, Lanham: Lexington Books, pp. 261–77.

Cline, E. (2012), *Confucius, Rawls, and the Sense of Justice*, Bronx, NY: Fordham University Press.

Copp, D. (1992), "The Right to an Adequate Standard of Living: Justice, Autonomy, and the Basic Needs," *Social Philosophy and Policy*, 9, pp. 161–231.

Del Vecchio, G. (1953), *Justice: An Historical and Philosophical Essay*, New York: The Philosphical Library.
Doyal, L. and Gough, I. (1991), *A Theory of Human Need*, London: Macmillan.
Fan, R. (1997), "Confucian and Rawlsian Views of Justice: A Comparison," *Journal of Chinese Philosophy*, 24 (4), pp. 427–56.
Feinberg, J. (1973), *Social Philosophy*, Englewood Cliffs, NJ: Prentice-Hall.
Fitzgerald, R. (1977), "The Ambiguity and Rhetoric of 'Need,'" in R. Fitzgerald (ed.), *Human Needs and Politics*, Sydney: Pergamon, pp. 195–212.
Flew, A. (1977), "Wants or Needs, Choices or Commands," in R. Fitzgerald (ed.), *Human Needs and Politics*, Sydney: Pergamon, pp. 213–28.
Frankfurt, H. (October 1987), "Equality as a Moral Ideal," *Ethics*, 98 (1), pp. 21–43.
Frankfurt, H. (1998), "Necessity and Desire," in G. Brock (ed.), *Necessary Goods*, Lanham: Rowman & Littlefield, pp. 19–31.
Frohlich, N. and Oppenheimer, J. (1992), *Choosing Justice: An Experimental Approach to Ethical Theory*, Berkeley and Los Angeles: University of California Press.
Galtung, J. (1994), *Human Rights in Another Key*, Cambridge: Polity Press.
Gewirth, A. (1996), *The Community of Rights*, Chicago: University of Chicago Press.
Goldewijk, B. K. and de Gaay Fortman, B. (1999), *Where Needs Meet Rights*, Geneva: WCC Publications.
Goodin, R. E. (June 1985), "The Priority of Needs," *Philosophy and Phenomenological Research*, 45 (4), pp. 615–25.
Hamilton, L. A. (2003), *The Political Philosophy of Needs*, Cambridge: Cambridge University Press.
Heller, A. (1976), *The Theory of Need in Marx*, New York: St Martin's Press.
Hewitt, M. (2000), *Welfare and Human Nature: The Human Subject in Twentieth-Century Social Politics*, New York: St Martin's Press.
Huang, Y. 黄玉顺 (2013), *Reconstruction of Chinese Theories of Justice*, Hefei, PRC: Anhui People's Press.
Husami, Z. I. (1980/1972), "Marx on Distributive Justice," in M. Cohen, T. Nagel and T. Scanlon (eds), *Marx, Justice, and History*, Princeton: Princeton University Press, pp. 42–79.
Kaufman, A. S. (1977), "Wants, Needs, and Liberalism," *Inquiry*, 14, pp. 191–206.
Knoblock, J. (1988), *Xunzi: A Translation and Study of the Complete Works*, vol. I. 3 vols, Stanford: Stanford University Press.
Knoblock, J. (1990), *Xunzi: A Translation and Study of the Complete Works*, vol. II. 3 vols, Stanford: Stanford University Press.
Knoblock, J. (1994), *Xunzi: A Translation and Study of the Complete Works*, vol. III. 3 vols, Stanford: Stanford University Press.
Lau, D. C., trans. (1970), *Mencius*, Harmondsworth: Penguin.
Liang, S. 梁漱冥 (1989), *Complete Works*, 8 vols, Jinan, Shandong: People's Press.
Macpherson, C. B. (1977), "Needs and Wants: An Ontological or Historical Problem," in R. Fitzgerald (ed.), *Human Needs and Politics*, Sydney: Pergamon, pp. 26–35.
Marx, K. (1875/1962), *Critique of Gotha Program*, vol. 2, in *Selected Works*, by Karl Marx and Friedrich Engels, Moscow: Foreign Languages Publishing House.
McCloskey, H. J. (January 1976), "Human Needs, Rights, and Political Values," *American Philosophical Quarterly*, 13 (1), pp. 1–11.
Meyer, W. J. (May 1974), "Democracy: Needs Over Wants," *Political Theory*, 2 (2), pp. 197–214.
Miller, D. (1999), *Principles of Social Justice*, Cambridge, MA: Harvard University Press.

Minogue, K. R. (1963), *The Liberal Mind*, London: Methuen.
Neumann, M. (September 1992), "Needs Not Rights," *Canadian Journal of Political Science*, 22 (3), pp. 353–63.
O'Neil, O. (1998), "Rights, Obligations, and Needs," in G. Brock (ed.), *Necessary Goods*, Lanham: Rowman & Littlefield, pp. 95–112.
Rawls, J. (1972), *A Theory of Justice*, Oxford: Oxford University Press.
Reader, S. (2005), "Aristotle on Necessities and Needs," in S. Reader (ed.), *The Philosophy of Need*, Cambridge: Cambridge University Press, pp. 113–35.
Rowe, C. (2005), "Needs and Ethics in Ancient Philosophy," in S. Reader (ed.), *The Philosophy of Need*, Cambridge: Cambridge University Press, pp. 99–112.
Slater, D. (1998), "Needs/Wants," in C. Jenks (ed.), *Core Sociological Dichotomies*, London: Sage, pp. 315–28.
Soper, K. (1981), *On Human Needs: Open and Closed Theories in a Marxist Perspective*, Brighton: Harvester Press.
Springborg, P. (1977), "Karl Marx on Human Needs," in R. Fitzgerald (ed.), *Human Needs and Politics*, Sydney: Pergamon, pp. 157–73.
Springborg, P. (1981), *The Problem of Human Needs and the Critique of Civilisation*, London: Allen & Unwin.
Tan, S. (2003), *Confucian Democracy: A Deweyan Reconstruction*, Albany, NY: State University of New York Press.
Tan, S. (2014), "Materialistic Desires and Ethical Life in the Analects and the Mencius," in C. Li and P. Ni (eds), *Moral Cultivation and Confucian Character*, Albany, NY: State University of New York Press, pp. 189–212.
Tan, S. (September, 2014), "The Concept of *Yi* in the *Mencius* and the Problems of Distributive Justice," *Australasian Journal of Philosophy*, 92 (3), pp. 489–505.
Taylor, P. W. (April 1959), "'Need' Statements," *Analysis*, 19 (5), pp. 106–11.
Thomson, G. (1987), *Needs*, London: Routledge & Kegan Paul.
Thomson, G. (2005), "Fundamental Needs," in S. Reader (ed.), *The Philosophy of Need*, Cambridge: Cambridge University Press, pp. 175–86.
White, A. R. (1975), *Modal Thinking*, Oxford: Blackwell.
Wiggins, D. (1998/1987), "Claims of Need," in *Needs, Values, Truth*, Oxford: Oxford University Press, pp. 1–57.
Wood, A. W. (1980/1972), "The Marxian Critique of Justice," in M. Cohen, T. Nagel, and T. Scanlon (eds), *Marx, Justice, and History*, Princeton: Princeton University Press, pp. 3–41.
Wringe, B. (2005), "Needs, Rights, and Collective Obligations," in S. Reader (ed.), *The Philosophy of Need*, Cambridge: Cambridge University Press, pp. 187–207.
Xiao, Y. (1997), "Trying To Do Justice To The Concept of Justice in Confucian Ethics," *Journal of Chinese Philosophy*, 24 (4), pp. 521–51.

Afterword/Afterwards

Arindam Chakrabarti and Ralph Weber

Der Gruß der Philosophen unter einander sollte sein: "Laß Dir Zeit!"
Ludwig Wittgenstein[1]

Borderless thinkers have to be slow travelers who keep leaving and coming back home even if they have multiple cultural or disciplinary homes. As intercontinental travel gets faster and faster, if intercontinental philosophy has to remain rigorous, serious, and deep, it has to get slower and slower. When Wittgenstein wrote in his diary "This is how philosophers should greet each other: 'Take your time!,'" it is likely that he was reacting to some unwelcome time-pressure to perform or deliver written work faster than he was happy to do as a professional but responsibly self-critical philosopher. Unfortunately, today philosophers without borders cannot afford to be philosophers without deadlines. Originally, we had planned a longer Epilogue charting out the road map for future comparative philosophy, which we had ambitiously wanted to call "*Beyond Compare*." But there was no more time to be taken. So, as "Prolegomena to Future Global Metaphysics," we are ending with some confessions, strategies, and visions from which future borderless thinkers can derive lessons and inspiration—or find hopefully fertile ground to disagree on.

Before we leave the subject of the undesirability of philosophy done in haste, let us formulate a dilemma that we feel about the job of writing, compiling, and editing genuinely original and creative philosophy. There are two very valuable pieces of moral advice found in classical Indian traditions. When thinking about knowledge and money (the word for money in Sanskrit, *artha*, incidentally, is also the word for "meaning," so it could easily be interpreted as "knowledge and meaning," which sounds much better), plan your work as if you will never die and never age. But when thinking of ethical duty and the task of becoming more virtuous, imagine that death is tugging at your hair and you have no time left. So, one should take one's time when thinking about philosophy and gathering (lucrative?) knowledge, but rush urgently when doing one's "dharma" or completing one's ethical tasks. The dilemma for the philosopher is that gathering knowledge of meaning *is* his "dharma." Should he take infinite time or should he feel a deadly urgency? What to do when sincere, authentic, creative philosophical thinking becomes our duty and we are bound by an ethic of knowledge advancement? Should we rush or should we take our time?

And the question of money-/meaning-making is not at all beside the point, particularly in endeavors of fusion philosophy. Philosophy of any kind, like the

Humanities in general, has a grim future in an increasingly aggressive "stupid-factory" (the name of an American early teens clothing brand allied to the company David & Goliath whose motto is "live stupid, die happy") of instant-gratification technologies. Comparative philosophy has the lowest status even inside the professional philosophy market. Some guaranteed readership and patronage exists *inside* the well-guarded factions of philosophy. Analytic Anglo-American, Continental Phenomenological, Asian (mostly East Asian), Indological, Religious/Spiritual Buddhist style, Literary/Culture Studies type, or Social Science Political Legal philosophies have their own large or small markets. But when your agenda is precisely to mix these styles, to compel each of these genres of philosophies to talk to the others, the resulting books and anthologies—however fascinating—would slip through the very communication gaps they are designed to bridge.

There is no dearth of enthusiastic talkers in the agora of multicultural philosophy. But they often talk past each other and do not listen to or learn anything from one another. Richard Rorty used to attend the two-week-long East-West Philosophers' Conference at the University of Hawaii for fifteen years quite regularly, listening to dozens of papers and interacting with hundreds of Asian comparative philosophers between 1989 and 2005. When asked if his philosophical outlook was influenced or changed by this exposure to the brightest scholars of Non-Western philosophy, Rorty would firmly reply in the negative. Given that philosophers are generally a garrulous lot, you can easily make them talk to one another, but you cannot make them "listen" to, let alone learn from, an alien style or tradition of philosophizing, unless they have the rare epistemic virtue of what Vrinda Dalmiya calls "relational humility."[2] We see this every day in the work done in the best comparative philosophy doctoral programs of the world (such as the one at the University of Hawaii at Manoa). Extremely collegial philosophers, if they are jointly supervising a dissertation that ambitiously adopts the fusion philosophy method—let us suppose on the topic of therapy of human existential suffering in Chinese, Indian, and Greek Philosophies—would encourage the project but would expect implicitly that the Chinese philosophy expert will read the Chinese bit, the Greek philosophy expert will read the Stoic philosophy part, and the Indian philosophy expert will confine his mentoring to the Indian discussions of freedom from suffering. This inescapable division of labor is jointly generated by a scholarly deference to the tradition one has not specialized in and—still too often—by a deep-rooted uncuriosity and a disinclination to spread oneself thin by learning new philosophical traditions (and if necessary, new ancient languages) "for alas one hasn't got an infinite life-time!" Although respect for other styles and traditions sounds incompatible with lack of interest in learning deeply about them, polite deference and uncuriosity usually go together. It is this atmosphere of superficial "comparativism" in what Daya Krishna called the "art of the conceptual" that "Beyond Compare"-styles of doing fusion philosophy are supposed to work against. Daya Krishna's own fond hope was that future comparative philosophers will be philosophers first and search outside their own times and traditions for new questions to raise, because the questions are intrinsically interesting to humanity in general: "Thus comparative philosophy has the chance to function as a mutual liberator of each philosophical tradition from the limitations imposed upon it by its own past, instead of being what it is at present, the imposition of the standards of one dominant culture upon all the others."[3]

Radically or conservatively, different futures always come from critiques of the present and a re-evaluation of the past. When Western philosophers will recognize that some of the most original ideas of modern or even ancient Western philosophy have come from interaction with the East, and when the postcolonial Asian or African philosophers will re-appropriate the riches they have inherited from their colonial "civilizers" by looking back at their pre-colonial pasts with fearlessly critical but decolonized minds, the future of fusion philosophy will be brighter.

Yet, one writes because one wants, needs, expects to be read, and publishers publish hoping to make some profit by selling even such an off-beat book. Whether we do it in a hurry or do it in a slow but not lazy, hardworking, textually meticulous manner, every dialogue, every collaborative work in hybrid styles of philosophy has had and will have an economics and politics. Future theoretical philosophy will theorize reflexively about that economics and politics also.

It is said that some time back in undatable antiquity a debating assembly of scholars was arranged by King Janaka of Videha (modern Bihar, India). A thousand cows with horns wrapped in gold were to be given as a reward to the wisest of all. Savants and wranglers from all over the country had gathered to take part in this Philosophical Olympics. Before the dialogue had even started, the young arrogant Yājñyavalkya got up and told his two helpers, "Please take these cows to my home." When the other brahmins raised a hue and cry at this outrageous appropriation, Yājñyavalkya explained, tongue in cheek, of course, "We salute the wisest knower of Brahman, we just crave those cows." After this ironic remark, for more than thirty sections of the Brhadaranyaka Upanishad, we get a deep metaphysical and phenomenological analysis of consciousness, desire, and the Self, which broke the path of nearly all future metaphysics in India, led by this same ironic philosopher (and whose pre-Socratic irony was no Greek influence).

Every dialogue also has a politics, a negotiation and competition for power, at least for persuasive rhetorical impact. And in every age, every science and every academic discipline, specialists working within well-defined and established borders do have a margin of power over the open-minded, self-doubting, eclectic, many-minded styles of thinking. Unlike in Western classical music where the conductor has over time assumed a status above the violinists, trumpeters, and flautists, in philosophy the first group calls the second group superficial, unrigorous, and confused, whereas the latter thinks of the former as prone to being culturally insular, methodologically single-minded, and collectively self-promoting. Between the two groups there runs a border that should, however, not be understood as a limit. Specialization is, of course, not at all a bad thing. Precisely because the specialist works within well-defined, established, and therefore unquestioned borders is it possible for him or her to bring the subject matter into a well-delimited and sharp focus—as if there were nothing else in the world. Yet, it is no coincidence that we fancy the bespectacled specialist behind shut doors in a room with all kinds of machines and laboratory appliances or locked away in the garret room with a pen and sheets of paper as the only material necessity for a focused and sharp mind. The imagery of shut doors leads us back to Simmel, for whom it portrayed "the human capacity over against nature" to "cut a portion out of the continuity and infinity of space and arrange [it] into a particular unity in accordance with a *single* meaning. A piece of space was thereby brought together and separated from the whole remaining world."[4]

The dangers that come with blinkered specialization are well known and many border-implying-words have been used to refer to it: "mainstream," "reification," "provincialism," etc. Some such dangers come to play themselves out quite naturally. In philosophy (as in other academic specializations), for instance, most of us come to know one's peers working on the same area or using the same style, and there is nothing unusual about us repeatedly meeting in conferences across the world almost the same bunch of people that read each other's work and perpetuate a highly specialized discussion. Reaching out beyond one's peer group and joining, say, an interdisciplinary event means leaving one's comfort zone and entering the insecure terrain of the inexpert. It is certainly a risky undertaking, and returning from such events with frustration is a common experience.

Of course, there remains the possibility and the aspiration of many a comparativist to become, perhaps with many years of preparatory scholarship and the intellectual humility to learn from his prospective audience, not just a widely read dilettante, but a specialist across borders. The task is daunting, but it should not be deemed impossible. We are already seeing in some younger scholars the assiduousness required to become a specialist in both Western formal logic and Indian or Buddhist logic, of learning German, French, Sanskrit, and Tibetan with equal seriousness, of trying to research consciousness from a neuro-scientific and phenomenological as well as Buddhist and Yoga points of view. There are quite a few who do seem to succeed. Still, the number of people ready to undertake this kind of proficiency in three or four or five disciplines and traditions dwindle as specialization gets rewarded—even as interdisciplinarity and multiculturalism are paid lip-service respect—and fusion thinking more often than not is not just ignored, it is implicitly punished. Michael Dummett predicted in one of his last published books *Nature and Future of Philosophy* that "The best point of contact between philosophers of divergent traditions surely lies in the philosophy of mind."[5] Signs of that global dialogue, across areas, styles, and traditions of philosophy, on the nature of embodied consciousness and theories of perception, conception, and emotions are already visible.

There will and should always remain many different ways of doing fusion philosophy. We would like to distinguish three, of which we find the first two ways quite desirable, though it is with the third that we would like to associate most strongly. The first way operates in close proximity to comparative philosophy in some of its current forms, but purposively and decidedly forgets about questions of sequence—which came first, which is the original—or questions of influence or direct refutation. Out to find exciting ideas wherever they come from, this way of fusion philosophy then sets out to juxtapose, compare, and contrast them, which, of course, involves the claim that the different ideas can somehow be related to the same subject matter. The result might be an argument that consists in an anticipation of an idea in one text and a sharp refutation of *it* (that much must be claimed) in another text, however distant the two texts may otherwise be in terms of time and space, their style or, indeed, their cultural or sociopolitical context.

The second way of doing fusion philosophy maintains a strong commitment to chronological sequence and historical contextualization amounting to a sort of global history of ideas. On the one hand, this simply means being more inclusive of various non-European textual traditions than many standard text books still are. It is amazing how many editors of new companions and handbooks believe that they are living up to the promise of more inclusion by including a chapter, say, on Chinese political thought, and three or four more of that kind, only to reserve the large bulk of the volume to a standard account from the Greeks to the moderns and include topical discussions of authority, justice, and so on, each without the slightest reference to "non-European" political thought. In any case, as much as more inclusion is desirable, it is certainly not sufficient. For one thing, there is a tendency of juxtaposing a fixed set of division between, for instance, European, Chinese, Japanese, Indian, and African histories of ideas, without departing in any significant manner from the terms of investigation that have defined the earlier exclusive study of the European history of ideas. More recent approaches methodologically reset the attention away from this and other sets of division, focusing on manifold interactions and crisscrossing paths under a great variety of labels and programs (from contact zones to transfers and entanglements). This is a very thriving field in historical studies and in some other disciplines, but it is probably fair to say that it has not yet found its equivalent in philosophical historiography.

The third way of fusion philosophy, the one we wish to introduce and promote, goes beyond the first two ways in the level of assimilation and intertextuality it demands. In the introduction, we have already characterized it as the next stage that the discipline of comparative philosophy has to enter. Here we simply remind the reader of its main tenets and develop what we have said earlier from a different angle. Fusion philosophy proceeds with an open eye toward philosophical ideas and thoughts wherever they can be met. It is the conscious attempt of filling one's mind in an almost terribly unsystematic manner with whatever one gets out of the study of different styles and traditions. Then, in a subsequent step, one forgets about one's sources. Instead of preserving, quoting and juxtaposing them, one picks up a concept, a line of reasoning or some, however, minor point arising out of years of imaginative rearrangement and cross-fertilization of the ideas retrieved from different cultures, periods, texts, and disciplines. Strategic oblivion of one's sources makes an unexpected osmosis of concepts possible. After that one can step back and wonder why no one ever thought of that before or, even better "overcome" (*aufheben*) also that synthesis with one's own criticism. To put it in terms not very fashionable these days, when something bordering on cultural relativism appears to be the default position, one asks oneself what the truth of the matter is. It is at this point where the person engaged in fusion philosophy is thrown back upon herself as her thinking might become truly borderless, which would presuppose a move "beyond compare."

The advantage of the third over the first and second ways of doing fusion philosophy lies in that it cannot possibly make its claims rest upon some authority attributed to the sources along the borders that comparative philosophy necessarily erects. The fusion philosopher of the third way cannot hide behind a sentence like "well, the Chinese think that . . ." She is expected to have assimilated the sources to an extent that would quite naturally prohibit such a move. Enriched by the sources, she could and perhaps should still acknowledge them, but without any appeal to an argument from authority. When making, say, Zhuangzi speak to Strawson about knowing other minds, the point cannot be which of them is right to say what he says, but simply what is the right thing to say, independent of who says it. What would come out would perhaps be less historical and less encyclopedic as a reference to this philosopher or that philosopher, but it would be something valuable, something in a twilight zone, surely something constructive, probably even something original (since one's conclusion can easily and quite naturally go beyond both Zhuangzi's and Strawson's views). The manner in which the results of such fusion philosophy would initially come to be sitting on a fence between different styles and traditions that eventually would be "forgotten" will certainly meet the resistance of specialists working within this or that side of the fence, who will find the sort of appropriation to be either illegitimate or irresponsible. The reproach would be that one is mixing up things, and quite rightly so—since the response of the fusion philosopher is, of course, "well, that's the whole point."

The fusion that fusion philosophy propagates should not be misunderstood as a syncretic inclusion of whatever thought one comes across. The fusion happens at the level of making viewpoints that some established borders might portray as unrelated, speak to each other. It is not to show that there is support, say, for the golden rule to be found in all traditions, but to say that *Analects* 15:23 and *Matthew* 7:12 are in some sense (that should be established as precisely as possible) discussing the same matter, then make them speak to each other, for example, asking what difference it makes that the *Analects* put it in negative form ("Do not do to others . . ."), and finally to argue that the most persuasive version of the golden rule resulting from all this is something that should be defended (or rejected) as a general rule. Fusion does not mean that everyone gets it right somehow. Fusion merely means relating two or more views under the horizon of some same problem or idea, while retaining the freedom of treating them as views to be rejected.

In fact, quite often, views on the same matter will appear to be diametrically opposed. And that is a good thing. For fusion philosophers of the third way, such tensions put the cherry on the cake. It is with them that the fusion philosopher finds the most rewarding terrain for formulating original and progressive philosophy. Tensions have to be indicated and upheld if they cannot be dissolved, or the opposing views have to be weighed against each other (i.e., compared), but this would lead to a deliberate appropriative decision by the fusion philosopher on what is the right view to hold. This would prevent the production of a shallow and flaky mishmash. Here, the work of the largely forgotten early German Enlightenment eclectics (e.g., Christian Thomasius and Arnold Wesenfeld) might be profitably drawn upon, as they sought to steer a course embracing the method of skepticism while upholding the goal of seeking truth. Like fusion philosophy of the third way, they foregrounded their own thinking capacity. Christian Thomasius emphasizes that in the end "one sees with one's own eyes rather than with the eyes of the others" (*ita suis potius oculis quam alienis videre*).[6] Such philosophical eclecticism, it has been said, "claims the right to choose freely from among the many possible viewpoints and thereby claims the always-to-be-renewed right towards an opinion of one's own"; looking at it the other way round, philosophical eclecticism is "critical of authority" but also "obliged to tradition."[7] According to Arnold Wesenfeld, the point is to combine freedom of thought with respect for the work and doctrines of others (*in respectu ad aliorum scripta et dogmata*), as he put it in his fourth *Dissertatio* on the use of elective philosophy.[8] Rejection of a view under scrutiny should hence not be decided on lightly. The affinity of philosophical eclecticism to our fusion approach is apparent in Gerardus Johannes Vossius's following statement, "How would it be in the future if we should be not Ionic philosophers, or Italians, Eleatics, Platonists, or Peripatetics, not Stoics, Epicureans, Skeptics, or any other such sects, but all of these?"[9]

In merely comparative settings, some sorts of failure seem in-built. As one learns about one's *comparanda*, even if one learns not only of differences (separations) but also of commonalities (connections), the entire comparative setting of a here and a there and of two (or more) *comparanda* tends to favor separation over connection. Comparative philosophy that is satisfied with the mere affirmation of differences and commonalities still crosses borders, it is true, but it leaves them perhaps largely intact. If this were enough for borderless thinking, how could one make sure that the mixture resulting from the comparison, that is, various relations between the *comparanda*, still deserved to count as philosophy? A comparative philosophy that is worthy of both its constitutive terms cannot be simply about comparison. Simply comparing philosophies, but not comparing them philosophically will not do. This is why fusion philosophy decidedly demands of the comparative philosopher not to be satisfied with the role of the comparatist. The comparative philosopher should aim beyond comparison at a philosophical argument (strictly or loosely understood) that can stand on its own, that is, it does not rely on the distinctness of the *comparanda*. The borders that any comparison necessarily erects should not be left intact as if untouched. Fusion means that the borders that separate are at least de-emphasized, perhaps even torn into tatters, but in any case transcended.

In a more limited sense, we can now argue that the first and second ways of doing fusion philosophy also do not leave borders intact. As laid out in the introduction, no comparison simply deepens the understanding of each *comparanda* taken on its own; whatever *comparanda* is looked at comes to appear also in the perspective of the others. In the end, that is what comparison is all about, that is, establishing relations that are said to pertain between two purportedly distinct *comparanda*. In any sort of more complex comparison, such as the ones comparative philosophy is often concerned about, it would seem highly unlikely that this mutual gaze at the *comparanda*, each in the light of the other, would not come to touch on the borders that one initially thought established their separateness. Sustained critical reflection on separateness should lead to connections. The simple question of the respects in which the *comparanda* are thought to be different helps point out connections that the very comparison must presuppose in order to function at all. The applicability of these respects, that is, of the *tertia comparationis*, is anticipated on the side of the comparer, but it is in no way guaranteed. If borders are initially drawn in view of what distinguishes *comparanda*, each in its presumed singularity, and if comparison changes the comparatist's understanding of the *comparanda*, then it seems that some erected borders would likely change, too, as they would become destabilized or undermined *by the comparison* itself. Of course, the modality here is possibility, not necessity, but the more complex a comparative setting, the more likely such border infringement would seem.

There are strategies that might help increase control of one's comparisons as best possible. One enabling condition of crossing borders of thinking is perceiving the borders in the first place. You probably should not like to and perhaps cannot really transcend borders that you do not see. Here, the analysis of the mechanism of comparison laid out in the introduction might be most useful, especially for making explicit one's commitments in terms of presupposed commonalities (and differences). Another enabling condition is detecting the politics of knowledge current in the world and the direction of conceptual grid versus terrain to be studied, and then reversing the direction. When we start asking questions like "Is Aristotelian Virtue ethics more centered on *ren* 仁 or on *li* 禮?," "Is Hume a Lokāyata Cārvāka style empiricist/skeptic?" or "Is he more a Dignāga-Dharmakīrti style phenomenalist?," then this reversal will take off. A third enabling condition would be to be vigilant and perpetually rethinking, asking questions such as the following:

- How much history of ideas will be necessary or sufficient for good fusion thinking?
- How much text-interpretation will be required?
- How much a-historical original conceptual creativity will be necessary?
- How much resemblance-discovery should be aimed for?
- How much contrast-discovery is essential?
- How to achieve a balance between giving rigorous clear arguments and being contemplatively authentic and phenomenologically descriptive?

As a matter of fact, the most reflexive question any fusion philosophy would do well to ponder concerns the units of comparison, that is, what has been fused. If fusion is the ultimate connecting act, then it is naturally prone and even set to gloss over the many separations that the connections have presupposed. The borders that fusion eventually de-emphasizes or shatters are, nonetheless, of the kind that have connected what was considered separate. The fusion is only a fusion because initially there was presupposed separateness. Indeed, fusion of horizons with an alien tradition will not only fray the edges of a blanketed tradition (such as "the Buddhist tradition"), but also create healthy fissions within the blanketed tradition, bringing in finer cracks and crevices and internal debates within what was seen from outside as a monolith.

Although we have been careful not to confine our unit of analysis to different cultures, but have spoken of various kinds of boundaries, including borders drawn between historical periods, languages, subdisciplines of philosophy such as metaphysics, epistemology, ethics, aesthetics, and political philosophy, and styles and traditions of philosophizing, we have sometimes used "philosophical traditions" as one, rather clumsy, umbrella term for all these *different* units of comparison. To end with, we should hence underline that crossing borders can be philosophically fruitful wherever a comfort zone has been established, and that can well be within one and the same (sub)discipline, one and the same culture, tradition, or (indeed) cultural tradition, one and the same historical period, one and the same language, one and the same style, etc. In principle, a German Frege scholar meeting with another German Frege scholar might turn out to be a border-crossing experience. But the likelihood increases if a German Frege scholar gets involved with a Feminist, a Marxist, a Thomist, a poet, or a Zhuangzi expert. It is a question of degree, to be sure, yet those who prefer "cultural traditions" over "philosophical traditions" and claim that they offer plenty of opportunities for initially presupposing borders are probably not wrong. Yet, that comparative philosophy today is almost automatically thought of as inter-, trans-, or cross-*cultural* reflects upon a state of affairs in politics and intellectual debate that marks a specific point in time that should be historically understood, critically questioned, and transcended—at least if fusion philosophy is right about the distinction between comparing philosophies and comparing philosophically. Only thus can the drawing on philosophical resources from across cultural traditions produce sound state-of-the-art progressive philosophy and open up a space for creative conceptual thinking outside all sorts of boxes.

All the contributors to this volume do not share any common vision of the future of comparative philosophy. Together they revel in their disagreements about their methods, motivations, and measures of success. Once the pernicious epithet "comparative" drops out, future unblinkered philosophers will welcome disagreements even with themselves. But all of them will need, and depend upon, an audience or interlocutor whose close-up as well as wide-angle view of good philosophy is not made hazy with smug uncuriosity, reverence, exoticism, or a cynical distrust in the very possibility of learning from each other.

As Spinoza, whose major work is called *Ethics*, realized, ethics is about improvement of self-understanding and conduct, becoming better. But hell breaks loose when we try to articulate what is that *good*, in terms of which we would call one life or person "better" than another. Now, improvement happens in the future. One cannot improve the past. And if what you are improving or improving upon is the present, because improvement takes time, the end result of betterment cannot be in the present. You look at the present, find it somehow unsatisfactory, and set yourselves targets for making it better in the times to come. The drive to doing it better in the future gets its impetus from the revulsion one feels in the present.

When, in a chapter of his latest book *Time Treks*, entitled "The Future of Futurelessness," the Indian public intellectual Ashis Nandy observes that, "all imaginations of the future, however bizarre and far removed from life, cannot but be (terribly immediate and practical) comments on the present," he is alerting us to the simple metaphysical truth that the future never arrives.[10] It is, by definition, yet to come. Elsewhere, in a paper called "Bearing Witness to the Future," he argues "that the future is mainly a state of awareness."[11] Awareness of what? Of course, of the present. A dissident, radically grumbling, self-cursing critique of the present takes the form of a utopia. Rabindranath Tagore, whom Nandy claims to be among his company of Utopians, especially during the last decades of his life, carps against his own present times, in classic essays like "*sabhyatār samkaṭ*" (Crisis of Civilization) and in a series of songs and poems where he wishes to get out of this here, this now, and dreams of how cultures will read his poem a hundred years from now.[12]

Will the future be better? Will it be an improvement on the present? Being an awareness of the shoddy, self-delusive, violent, unfair, unjust, culture-stifling present, the future is hoped to be better. A better-than-now is what is called a future. But how so? It is here that Nandy insists on a plurality of alternative utopias, an opulence of options unconstrained by any scientific exit-polls or market-trend analyses. Although this insistence on nonexclusive alternatives of hope is very un-Kantian, Nandy's well-known critique of "development" could be compared with Kant's deep suspicion of predicted "improvement" or "progress" of European civilization, especially when Advancement of Reason meant colonial expansion. Immanuel Kant concluded his last—somewhat senile—book, *Conflict of Faculties*, with the following prophetic joke on improvements:

> A doctor who consoled his patients from one day to the next with hopes of a speedy convalescence, pledging to one that his pulse beat better, to another an improvement in his stool, to a third an improvement regarding his perspiration, received a visit from his friend. "How is your illness, my friend?" was the doctor's first question. "How should it be? *I am dying of improvement pure and simple*." I can blame no one when considering the ills of the state, he begins to despair of the health of humanity and its progress towards the better.[13]

Yet, Kant was not a garden variety of apocalyptic pessimist. After answering the two questions of pure reason, for asking which he is famous, "What can I know?" and "What ought I to do?" Kant raises the futuristic question "What may I hope?" (*Canon of Pure Reason,* in the last part of the First Critique). Hope, technically defined as a moral—rather than epistemic—certitude, is constitutive of human dignity.

In the face of crisis—personal, moral, cultural, social, or global—when acting ethically becomes incredibly hard and most certainly unrewarding or positively disadvantageous, Kant's argument for non-epistemic moral faith or hope goes as follows:

1. The state of the world is currently known to be such that there is little likelihood that we can live morally and still flourish.
2. But we ought to perform our moral duties, unconditionally, and it must therefore be possible to do so (if we believe that "ought" implies "can")
3. Since that *requires* that the state of the world should eventually change for the better, we must hope that things will get better; for, otherwise, doing what one should do would mean not living well enough to do anything, which is inconsistent. (A practical motivational *reductio ad absurdum*)
4. Therefore, even though there is no empirical or scientific evidence that things will get better, we must act as if they will and believe that the world is ultimately aiming at the highest good where virtue and happiness will be united, and communities will stop killing each other.

Having died a hundred years before the start of that century which Ashis Nandy calls one hundred years of physical, intellectual, and cultural mass violence, Kant had seen enough ravages of war in Europe to have opened his utopian treatise about the future of mankind by confessing that he borrowed the title "Perpetual Peace" from a Dutch shopkeeper's sign on which a graveyard was painted. Will permanent peace, then, come only in the graveyard of civilizations?

In the *Anthropology* he emphatically asserts that all pre-sentiment or alleged prevision of the future is a chimera,[14] and elsewhere he writes:

> Is the human race as a whole to be loved: or is it something that one is to view with distaste, wishing it all the best . . . but not really expecting it, so that we can turn our attention away from it, though with feelings of regret?[15]

Our dream is that future fusion philosophy will shed its local epithets, even the epithet "comparative." All good philosophy should be unapologetically, and, eventually, unselfconsciously, comparative and culturally hybrid. But this is a utopia, or in Kantian terms, perhaps a regulative ideal of reason. Richard Rorty once said that he would be disappointed if Indians had epistemology or Chinese had ethics in the sense of Aristotle, Kant, or Mill. This shows that before Rorty leaves his home tradition he has already decided to encounter something surprisingly unlike what he already has plenty of in the European traditions. If he finds more of "rationalism" and "empiricism" in China or India, he would be disappointed and bored! Jacques Derrida might have aimed at making a similar point when insisting, during a lecturing tour throughout China, that there was in the past no philosophy but only thought in China. This was far from derisive or dismissive of China. Derrida reserved the label of philosophy for singular, but deficient, Western philosophy and, capsizing the established colonial taxonomy, exalted *thought* to something above and beyond philosophy.[16] Rorty's and Derrida's points might make sense, at least initially and at first glance. But besides reifying philosophically asymmetric borders between "Aristotle, Kant, or Mill" on the one hand and "[all?] the Indians" and "the Chinese," on the other, between "Western philosophy" and "Chinese thought" into constituting limits, they also commit another variant of the fallacy of mistaking the *comparandum* for a possible *tertium comparationis* (A for F in our symbolic representation). They are not criticizing a distorted comparison for overfamiliarity of one *comparandum*. But they too believe that a comparative statement drawing on a singularity as *tertium comparationis* might make sense. There would be no point to their statements if they did not hold that belief. From this point of view, Rorty was wrong to frame the issue in terms of surprise, because pitting the singularity of one context against the comparative inquiry into another context could not possibly result in the sort of counterfactual surprise that his statement pretends is a real possibility.

We must strive toward a better understanding of comparison, naked and clothed, in order to be able to transcend the borders that comparative philosophy constantly erects by the very act of comparison and to reach the sort of fusion philosophy that rightly claims to be first-rate philosophy. For this end, we need to understand comparative inquiries within their political subtexts. As Gayatri Spivak reminds us:

> Comparison in extremis is a political gesture when response . . . is denied. . . . Speaking of the people to whom human rights were denied millennially in India, he [Rabindranath Tagore] writes. . . . "You (addressing his unfortunate country) will then be equal to all of them in the ashes of death," thus predicting the death of a nation. The only thing that will make me equal to you, because you deny response, is a shared death. . . . Perhaps it may be said that our lesson of learning equivalence, practicing equivalence, indexing a small epistemic change or shift,

may come to facilitate a world where comparison in extremis will no longer be required.[17]

Once we have climbed up to the level playing field of global combative cooperative critical creative philosophy from the fetid wells of centuries of unacknowledged epistemic inequalities (from the dark depths of the Enlightenment, one could say), we can, it is hoped, throw away the ladder of comparison. We can then do just philosophy in both the senses.

Notes

1 L. Wittgenstein, *Culture and Value* (Chicago: University of Chicago Press, 1980), p. 80.
2 V. Dalmiya, "From Good Knowers to Just Knowers in the Mahabharata: Towards a Comparative Virtue Epistemology," in *Philosophical Traditions*, Royal Institute of Philosophy Supplements, #74, ed. A. O'Hear (Cambridge: Cambridge University Press, 2014), pp. 195–220.
3 D. Krishna, "Comparative Philosophy: What It Is and What It Ought to Be," in *Interpreting Across Boundaries: New Essays in Comparative Philosophy*, ed. G. J. Larson and E. Deutsch (Princeton: Princeton University Press, 1988), p. 83.
4 D. Frisby and M. Featherstone (eds), *Simmel on Culture* (London: Sage Publications, 1997), p. 172.
5 M. Dummett, *Nature and Future of Philosophy* (New York: Columbia University Press, 2001), p. 150.
6 C. Thomasius, *Introductio ad philosophiam aulicam*, Ausgewählte Werke: Band 1 (Hildesheim: Georg Olms Verlag, 1993), Ch. 1, §90.
7 W. Schneiders, "Vernünftiger Zweifel und wahre Eklektik: Zur Entstehung des modernen Kritikbegriffes," *Studia Leibnitiana* 17, no. 2 (1985), pp. 151–52.
8 A. Wesenfeld, *Dissertationis Philosophicae Quatuor Materiae Selectioris de Philosophia Sectoria et Electiva*, Diss IV (Frankfurt: 1694), §1, p. 3.
9 "*Quam sisequamur, futurum, ut non Ionici simus, vel Italici, vel Eleatici; non Platonici, vel Peripatetici; non Stoïci, vel Epicurei; non Sceptici, vel cujuscunque alterius sectae; sed haec omnia.*" Gerardus Johannes Vossius, *De Philosophia et Philosophorum Sectis*, Libri II (Hagæ, Comitis: Adrianus Vlacq, 1658), caput xxi, §16, p. 117.
10 A. Nandy, *Time Treks: The Uncertain Future of Old and New Despotisms* (Delhi: Oxford University Press, 2008).
11 A. Nandy, "Bearing Witness to the Future," *Futures* 28, no. 6/7 (1996), p. 637.
12 R. Tagore, *Crisis in Civilization* (Calcutta: Visva-bharati, 1950).
13 I. Kant, "The Conflict of the Faculties," in *Religion and Rational Theology*, ed. Immanuel Kant and Allen W. Wood (Cambridge: Cambridge University Press, 1996), p. 308.
14 I. Kant, *Anthropology from a Pragmatic Point of View*, trans. M. J. McGregor (The Hague: Martinus Nijhoff, 1974), p. 187.
15 I. Kant, "On the Common Saying: This May Be True in Theory but It Does Not Apply in Practice" (1793), in *Perpetual Peace, and Other Essays on Politics, History, and Morals*, ed. Immanuel Kant and Ted Humphrey (Indianapolis: Hackett Publishing, 1983), p. 85.

16 See: J. Derrida, *Delida Zhongguo jiangyanlu* 德里达中国讲演录, ed. Du Xiaozhen and Zhang Ning (Beijing: Central Compilation and Translation Press, 2002); N. Zhang, "Jacques Derrida's First Visit to China: A Summary of His Lectures and Seminars," *Dao: A Journal of Comparative Philosophy* 2, no. 1 (2002), pp. 141–62.

17 G. C. Spivak, "Rethinking Comparativism," in *An Aesthetic Education in the Era of Globalization* (Cambridge, MA: Harvard University Press, 2012), p. 475.

References

Dalmiya, V. (2014), "From Good Knowers to Just Knowers in the Mahabharata: Towards a Comparative Virtue Epistemology," in A. O'Hear (ed.), *Philosophical Traditions*, Royal Institute of Philosophy Supplements, #74, Cambridge: Cambridge University Press.

Derrida, J. (2002), *Delida Zhongguo jiangyanlu* 德里达中国讲演录, edited by X. Du and N. Zhang, Beijing: Central Compilation and Translation Press.

Dummett, M. (2001), *Nature and Future of Philosophy*, New York: Columbia University Press.

Frisby, D. and Featherstone, M. eds, (1997), *Simmel on Culture*, London: Sage Publications.

Kant, I. (1974), *Anthropology from a Pragmatic Point of View*, translated by M. J. McGregor, The Hague: Martinus Nijhoff.

Kant, I. (1983), "On the Common Saying: This May Be True in Theory but It Does Not Apply in Practice" (1793), in *Perpetual Peace, and Other Essays on Politics, History, and Morals*, ed. Ted Humphrey, Indianapolis: Hackett Publishing, pp. 61–92.

Kant, I. (1996), "The Conflict of the Faculties," in *Religion and Rational Theology*, ed. Allen W. Wood, Cambridge: Cambridge University Press, pp. 233–327.

Krishna, D. (1988), "Comparative Philosophy: What It Is and What It Ought to Be," in G. J. Larson and E. Deutsch (eds), *Interpreting Across Boundaries: New Essays in Comparative Philosophy*, Princeton: Princeton University Press, pp. 58–69.

Nandy, A. (1996), "Bearing Witness to the Future," *Futures* 28, no. 6/7 (1996), pp. 636–39.

Nandy, A. (2008), *Time Treks: The Uncertain Future of Old and New Despotisms*, Delhi: Oxford University Press.

Schneiders, W. (1985), "Vernünftiger Zweifel und wahre Eklektik: Zur Entstehung des modernen Kritikbegriffes," *Studia Leibnitiana* 17, no. 2 (1985), pp. 143–61.

Spivak, G. C. (2012), "Rethinking Comparativism," in *An Aesthetic Education in the Era of Globalization*, Cambridge, MA: Harvard University Press, pp. 467–83.

Tagore, R. (1950), *Crisis in Civilization*, Calcutta: Visva-bharati.

Thomasius, C. (1993), *Introductio ad philosophiam aulicam*, Ausgewählte Werke: Band 1, Hildesheim: Georg Olms Verlag.

Vossius, G. J. (1658), *De Philosophia et Philosophorum Sectis*, Libri II, Hagæ, Comitis: Adrianus Vlacq.

Wesenfeld, A. (1694), *Dissertationis Philosophicae Quatuor Materiae Selectioris de Philosophia Sectoria et Electiva*, Diss IV, Frankfurt.

Wittgenstein, L. (1980), *Culture and Value*, Chicago: University of Chicago Press.

Zhang, N. (2002), "Jacques Derrida's First Visit to China: A Summary of His Lectures and Seminars," *Dao: A Journal of Comparative Philosophy* 2, no. 1 (2002), pp. 141–62.

Index

Lightning Source UK Ltd.
Milton Keynes UK
UKOW01f0039181017
311179UK00004B/147/P